Markéta Hajská

The Stojka family
Spatial mobility and territorial anchoredness of Lovara Vlax Roms in the former Czechoslovakia

UNIVERZITA KARLOVA
NAKLADATELSTVÍ KAROLINUM 2024

KAROLINUM PRESS is a publishing department of Charles University
Ovocný trh 560/5, 116 36 Prague 1, Czech Republic
www.karolinum.cz

© Markéta Hajská, 2024
Translation © Valerie Talacková, 2024
Photography © author's private collections; Milan Vrba (p. 278, fig. 6, 7), 2024
Copyediting by Gwendolyn Hubka Albert
Set and printed in the Czech Republic by Karolinum Press
Layout by Jan Šerých
First edition

A catalogue record for this book is available from the National Library
of the Czech Republic.

Research for this book was financed by Grant no. 19-26638X,
"Genocide, Postwar Migration and Social Mobility: Entangled Experiences
of Roma and Jews", funded by the Czech Science Foundation.

ISBN 978-80-246-5917-6
ISBN 978-80-246-5918-3 (pdf)

The original manuscript was reviewed
by Pavel Baloun (Faculty of Humanities, Charles University, Prague)
and Martin Fotta (Institute of Ethnology, Czech Academy of Sciences).

Contents

Acknowledgements	7

0. Introduction, methodology and theoretical basis — 11
0.1 The aim and subject of this book — 11
0.2 Vlax Roms and Lovara: Who are they? — 15
0.3 Methodology — 24
0.4 Theoretical base — 43

Part 1: Before the creation of Czechoslovakia — 53
1.1 Lovara on the territory of present-day Slovakia — 53
1.2 Lovara in the Czech lands before the creation of Czechoslovakia — 55
1.3 The roots of the Stojka family from Trenčianska Teplá — 60

Part 2: The Interwar Period — 71
2.1 Lovara territorial anchoring and spatial mobility in Slovakia — 71
2.1 The Stojkas of Trenčianska Teplá in the interwar period — 95
2.2 The transformation of the spatial mobility of the Lovara
    in the Czech lands after the creation of Czechoslovakia — 119

Part 3: The eve of war — 143
3.1 Increased Romani mobility in the Protectorate — 143
3.2 Change of citizenship as a reason for leaving the Protectorate — 148
3.3 Returning to Slovakia from the point of view of Lovara witnesses — 149

Part 4: The Second World War — 157
4.1 Roms during the Second World War on the territory
    of the Slovak State (1939–1945) — 157
4.2 The situation of the Lovara on territory occupied by Hungary — 169
4.3 The Second World War in Trenčianska Teplá — 174
4.4 The end of the wartime chapter — 191

Part 5: The postwar period   195
5.1 The forced departure of Roms from Trenčianska Teplá in 1947   195
5.2 The postwar trajectories of Štefan Stojka, Sr.   219
5.3 The trajectories of the late Zaga Stojková's descendants   227

**Part 6: The implementation of the law on the permanent
settlement of travelling persons and its impact**   245
6.1 The drafting of Act no. 74/1958 at the central level   245
6.2 The preparation of the register in Louny   251
6.3 The listing of persons in the register   260

Part 7: Conclusions   279
7.1 The interdisciplinary approach, combination of methods,
    broad spectrum of sources and other innovative aspects   280
7.2 Conclusions for individual historical periods   282
7.3 The position of Roms in society: The paternalism of the state,
    anti-gypsy policies and the agency of Roms   290

Appendix (photos)

Bibliography and sources   293
List of abbreviations   302
Genealogical diagram   303
Index   304

Acknowledgements

This book is the result of my work on the project "Genocide, Postwar Migration and Social Mobility: Entangled Experiences of Roma and Jews" (grant number 19–26638X), funded by the Czech Science Foundation, on which I worked from 2019 to 2023.

First and foremost, I would like to thank all the witnesses who were kind enough to share their memories with me, without whose willingness and openness this work could never have happened. Above all, I would like to thank Berci Stojka from Louny, the grandson of Anna Lakatošová and the great-grandson of Zaga Stojková. It was he who led me in his narrative to the unique Stojka family, which forms the subject of this book.

I would also like to thank all the colleagues and friends with whom I consulted my conclusions and approaches and who advised me on how to take my research further, above all those who made valuable comments on my draft text, namely: Kateřina Čapková, László Csősz, Jan Grill, Dana Ema Hrušková, Jan Ort, Iveta Kokyová, Pavel Kubaník, Michaela Lônčiková, and Milada Závodská. Thank you to Zuzana Bodnárová for help with translations from Hungarian and to Eva Zdařilová for help with translations from German. Thank you to Zuzana Ramajzlová and the non-profit Člověk v tísni, o.p.s. [People in Need] for making available the testimonies of those seeking compensation for the period of the Second World War. Thank you also to employees of the state archives, the regional archives and the district archives, above all Jana Kuprová of the Louny archives and Soňa Michalcová of the state archive in Trenčín, as well as their other colleagues who willingly advised me and helped me select archival materials which might contain information on the family at the centre of my interest or on other Lovara, as well as on the implementation of measures targeting "travelling gypsies".

I would like to express special thanks to Jan Červenka, Helena Sadílková and Lada Viková for their advice, support, comments and critical read-throughs of key passages, which enriched and advanced my perspective in many ways. Additional heartfelt thanks are due to Lada Viková for sharing her finds in local and regional archives, including concrete reports on "travelling gypsies", among which were crucial records pertaining to members of the family who form the subject of my work. I would like to thank Milan Vrba, the owner of a private photo archive from the Trenčín district, and Pavol Pytlík, photo collector for the municipality of Trenčianska Teplá, for providing valuable historical photographs of the Stojka family, which enriched my book. Thank you also to reviewers Martin Fotta and Pavel Baloun for extremely painstaking, thought-provoking comments, made for the purposes of the publication of the work by Karolinum. Last but not least, I would like to thank my daughter Tamara for her patience with me while I was writing this book.

Klocová	Jana	5		/
Klocová	Božena	1	/	.
Ružba	Jan	20	.	/
Klocová	Marie	1	/	.
Kloc	Jan	20	.	/
Lakatošová	Anna	24	/	.
Stojka	Filo	7	/	.
Lakatoš	Vidlem	5	/	.
Lakatoš	Josef	2	.	/
Lakatošová	Antonie	43	.	/
Stojková	Zaga	17	.	/
Stojková	Barbora	7	/	.
Stojka	Josef	8	/	.
Stojka	Kubus	8	/	.
Stojková	Grofojka	60	/	.
Lakatoš	Pavel	46	.	/
Lakatošová	Marie	20	/	.
Lakatoš	Juraj	12	/	.
Lakatoš	Ludvík	21	/	.
Lakatoš	Martin	17	/	.
Lakatoš	Antonin			

Dohromady: 9 žen, mezi tím

List of "gypsy vagabonds" stopped by the police station in Mnichovice, Říčany district, in 1931.

0. Introduction, methodology and theoretical basis

0.1 The aim and subject of this book

This book reconstructs the stories of the Lovara community and their legal, economic and social ties to the territory of the Czech lands and Slovakia from the end of the 19th century to the end of the 1960s. My primary focus is the mobility and trajectories of a family with the surname Stojka, reconstructed from archival records, respondent testimonies and other sources. Using a diachronic perspective, I trace the stories of descendants of the Stojka family who, in the final decades of the 19th century, were granted the right of domicile in the western Slovak municipality of Trenčianska Teplá, a family who gradually grew in each following generation through new descendants, their partners, and those couples' children. The family I follow represents a part of the Lovara community that lived and still lives on the territory of the former Czechoslovakia. I follow their lives until their forced sedentarisation in the towns of Žatec and Louny in the late 1950s and through the following decade, when they were listed by the state in the register of "travelling" and "semi-travelling" persons.

I try to connect this historical study of an extended Lovara family over several generations with a description of the approaches taken by state policy towards "gypsies" and specifically towards "travelling gypsies". Above all, I look at the impacts of those measures on Romani spatial mobility and the (im)possibility of their becoming settled in certain localities. This unavoidably requires the inclusion of measures and policies imposed by the state on other persons falling into the same category across a highly varied spectrum of political regimes and changing socio-economic conditions. Against the background of these trajectories, pieced together from a combination of various archival records and family member testimonies, I focus on selected aspects and on the continuity of such policies towards Roms, or, to use the terminology of the time, towards "gypsies", "travelling gypsies" or "gypsy vagabonds" in Czechoslovakia. These include measures which were in force under the Austro-Hungarian monarchy, the First Republic Act "on wandering gypsies" (no. 117/1927, Coll.) and finally, the introduction of the Act "on the permanent settlement of travelling persons" (no. 74/1958, Coll.) and its impacts. I also follow the way in which these groups were conceived of in the discourse of the various periods outlined above.

It was more or less by chance that I came across the Stojka family toward the end of my research[1] focusing on the impact of a law banning itinerancy (no. 74/1958) on the situation of Lovara families. My initial studies in the local administration archives which contained records on their situation at the end of the 1950s, as well as the testimonies of family members who remembered those events, suggested that these were Roms who, during the period preceding the itinerancy ban, were not anchored to any particular place, nor did they have any permanent place to which they were in the habit of returning. The picture that arose from my initial data was that in the mid-1950s they still lived "on the road" in horse-drawn wagons. From my previous research I had considered such a lack of ties to be fairly rare during the period in question. I noted that during the Second World War in Slovakia, a number of Vlax Roms had been forced to stop "travelling" and to live in the municipalities where they were officially domiciled. A number of other Lovara communities had houses in Slovak communities or places where they wintered, dating from the interwar period or even earlier. It was, therefore, a challenge to find out what the previous trajectories of the family had been and why these Roms were "travelling" around the Czech lands in the 1950s.

As I discovered during my research, the extent and the means of such spatial mobility changed over the decades in various branches of the Stojka family. Various circumstances caused the extent and the means of their territorial ties and socioeconomic strategies to be modified. As a result, the Stojka family who was perceived as "travelling" by Czech local administrations and security services during the postwar period had, in previous decades, been anchored in the municipality of Trenčianska

---

1   My research, entitled *Forced settlement of "travelling Gypsies" in Czechoslovakia (1959) and the Vlach Roma*, took place at the Faculty of Arts, Charles University in 2018 and was supported by Bader Philanthropies, Inc.

Teplá in western Slovakia, some of its members continuously so over a period of several decades.

My book is grounded in an analysis of extremely extensive archival material from both the local and the central Czech and Slovak archives, as well as from newspapers of the period and, to no small extent, my own interviews with respondents and the testimonies of those who remember the period. Both its choice of subject and the corpus of its source materials make this an innovative, interdisciplinary work that fundamentally enriches both the hitherto historically-oriented research in Romani history and the specialist writing on Roms from the perspective of social and cultural anthropology, sociology and Romani Studies. My book also contributes new insight into "Romani itinerancy" and the life of the Lovara community on the territory of the former Czechoslovakia.

Organization of the chapters and their structure

This book is organized by historical periods: Before the creation of the Czechoslovak Republic, the interwar period (i.e., the First Czechoslovak Republic), the eve of the Second World War (approximately the Second Czechoslovak Republic), the Second World War proper, the immediate postwar period, and the period after the register of "travelling gypsies" was introduced under Act no. 74/1958, Coll. I have done so despite the fact that for the Lovara themselves, the divisions between these periods were not always notable milestones. On the basis of my experience with my respondents, I know that many of them see their pasts as something more or less continuous, without the divisions into various stages imposed from above. Some periods of history, such as the First World War, I deliberately leave out of my historical timeline, since there are not enough detailed data or eyewitness testimonies extant to provide us with sufficient information about the lives of the family members during that period.

Two lines of information run through the book and form the basis for its division into chapters. One line consists of events in the Stojka family members' lives over the course of the period in question. The second line focuses on the impacts of state approaches and policies toward these and other Vlax Roms. Through the latter, I try to focus on the ways in which the legislative measures and orders issued during these periods affected the Lovara families who were seen by the state as falling into the category of "travelling gypsies". I also focus on how these families faced and coped with the measures of the period. I then tried to tie the families' strategies to how the implementation of such measures were perceived by the Lovara themselves, understandably just during the historical periods for which I was able to access testimonies. In the course of fulfilling this aim, I created several further microstudies of Lovara families whose perspectives on these situations I also provide. I managed to trace some of their movements and fortunes continuously over several time periods (for example, the families anchored in Topoľčany; in Pastuchov in the Hlohovec district; in Dolná Seč in the Levice district; or in Tekovské Lužiny in the Levice district). This created a relatively vivid mosaic of the lifeways of the Lovara community in the former Czechoslovakia during the periods in question. Moreover, many of these families were in contact with the Stojka family during some of the historical periods under review.

As far as each historical period is concerned, I draw a complete distinction between the situations of these Roms in the two main parts of Czechoslovakia. I am aware that the situation in the Czech lands differed considerably from that in Slovakia. Even during the interwar period when the two parts of the republic were connected by the same laws (1918–1938), the same state administration and the same security forces, the differences in the historical developments of each part of Czechoslovakia meant that "travelling gypsies" had a different social status and met with different attitudes from municipalities and the local population in each part, all of which influenced their life strategies. An exception in this book is the period of the Second World War, when I just look at events in Slovakia at that time, for the reason that no Lovara families remained in the Protectorate of Bohemia and Moravia. In the postwar period, by contrast, I focus mainly on the situation in the Czech lands, where the Stojka family moved. During this final period, the limited scope of this book means I am unfortunately able to focus just marginally on the Lovara situation in Slovakia. On the basis of my research findings, however, I can state that the way in which the register of "travelling" and "semi-travelling" persons was drawn up differed considerably in Slovakia from the way it was implemented in the Czech lands. In certain localities in Slovakia there was much greater benevolence towards persons categorised as "travelling".

0.2 Vlax Roms and Lovara: Who are they?

The term *Vlax Roms* covers a number of emically-defined Romani subgroups living in many countries of Europe today. In Central and Western Europe, most Vlax Roms define themselves as belonging to the Lovara and Kalderash / Kalderar subgroups. Vlax Roms live not just in many European countries, but also in North and South America and Central Asia (above all in the countries of the former Soviet Union). Vlax Roms tend to be generally defined by researchers on the basis of language (which, on the territory of the former Czechoslovakia, is a North Vlax dialect of Romani);[2] culture (a specific system of norms and customs, with an emphasis on isolation and the preservation of traditions);[3] and their specific historical development, something I shall look at more closely below.

Among researchers in Romani Studies, the adjective "Vlax" refers to Roms whose origin is derived from Wallachia, an historical principality of Romania. As is generally known, the term is widespread internationally, above all in linguistics, where it denotes a speaker of Vlax Romani, now the most widespread Romani dialect in the world as the result of Romani emigration from Wallachia and Moldova in various phases over the centuries.[4] Linguists agree that the Vlax Romani language can be divided into a northern and a southern group of dialects. According to Tcherenkov and Laederich, the northern Vlax dialects form a relatively unified group that may be divided according to the traditional livelihoods of the various Romani communities – horse traders (Lovara, Patrinara, Churara), clothes sellers (Dirzara) basket makers (Churara) and so on.[5] Elšík and Beníšek have described northern Vlax Romani as a relatively coherent group in which the main divisions are between the dialects of the Lovara – formerly horse traders – and groups related to them, and the Kalderash (Kelderasha, Kelderara etc., which means

---

2   For example, Viktor Elšík, "Interdialect contact of Czech (and Slovak) Romani varieties", *International Journal of the Sociology of Language* 162 (January 2003): 47; or Viktor Elšík and Michael Beníšek, "Romani dialectology", in: *The Palgrave Handbook of Romani Language and Linguistics*, ed. by Yaron Matras and Anton Tenser (London: Palgrave Macmillan, 2020), 389–427.

3   E.g. Margita Lakatošová, "Některé zvyklosti olašských Romů", *Romano džaniben*, vol. 1, no. 3 (Autumn 1994): 2–13; Peter Stojka and Rastislav Pivoň, *Náš život. Amaro trajo* (Bratislava: Sd studio, 2003); Ivana Šusterová, *Život olašských žien* (Bratislava: Veda, 2015).

4   Elšík and Beníšek, "Romani dialectology", 405.

5   Lev Tcherenkov and Stéphane Laederich, *The Rroma. Otherwise known as Gypsies, Gitanos, Tsiganes, Tigani, Çingene, Zigeuner, Bohemiens, Travellers, Fahrende, etc.* (Basel: Schwabe, 2004): 412.

"copper beaters" or "copper engravers", from the Romanian *căldăraş* or *căldărar*) and the communities related to them.[6]

Lovara on the territory of the former Czechoslovakia

I focus herein on Vlax Roms living on the territory of the former Czechoslovakia. They may be classified on the basis of language and their formerly dominant way of life as belonging to the Lovara group. This label is originally a professionym for horse dealers (from the Hungarian *ló* = horse). It is estimated that of the total number of 440,000 Roms living in Slovakia today[7] approximately 5–15% belong to the Vlax Romani group.[8] Today, most live in the strip of land bounded by Bratislava and Senec to the southwest, and by Topoľčany and Zlaté Moravce to the northwest (covering the districts of Šaľa, Galanta, Nové Zámky, Nitra, Komárno and Levice) and bounded to the southeast by the more geographically isolated communities in the district towns of Lučenec and Rimavská Sobota.[9] It may be assumed that the percentage of Lovara in particular, as well as their geographical localisation in the above-mentioned districts, was similar even more than a century ago, when Czechoslovakia was created, and seemingly also at the time when the story herein starts to unfold.

---

6   Elšík and Beníšek, "Romani dialectology", 405.

7   Úrad splnomocnenca vlády SR pre rómske komunity (ÚSVRK), Atlas rómskych komunít 2019. Available at: https://www.minv.sk/?atlas-romskych-komunit.

8   The exact number of Lovara in Slovakia is not known. There are not even many approximate estimates, and those that exist tend to be cited in the literature over and over again without the actual state of the population being reliably ascertained. In this book I use Nina Pavelčíková's estimates in *Českoslovenští Romové v letech 1938–1945* (Brno: Masarykova univerzita, 2004) and Milena Hübschmannová's in *Roma: Subethnic groups: Index of appellations* (Graz: Rombase, 2003), which are also used by most authors who give numbers of Lovara in Slovakia and the Czech lands

9   In addition to the above-mentioned Lovara, we find a group of Lovara that differs slightly in culture and language in eastern Slovakia in the districts of Prešov, Sabinov and Košice. This group of Lovara, numbering several hundred persons in Slovakia, uses the appelation Vlašika Rom to refer to itself (Markéta Hajská, "Ame sam vlašika haj vorbinas vlašika!", *Romano džaniben*, vol. 19, no. 2 (Winter 2012): 35–53; Markéta Hajská, "Gažikanes vaj romanes?" in: *Čierno-biele svety. Rómovia v majoritnej spoločnosti na Slovensku*, ed. Podolinská and Hrustič, 347–373 (Bratislava: Veda, Ústav etnológie SAV, 2015); Markéta Hajská, "'Polokočovníci'. Migrační trajektorie olašských Romů na Prešovsku od poloviny 19. století do současnosti", *Romano džaniben* vol. 23, no. 2 (Winter 2016): 7–37. At present, as seems to have also been the case historically, these Roms from eastern Slovakia have not maintained significant contacts with the Lovara from the south and southwest of Slovakia, with the exception of families from the southwest who took part in horse fairs in Košice or in other easterly directions.

There are several theories regarding the initial Lovara arrival on the territory of present-day Slovakia. According to some researchers, Vlax Roms started to leave Moldova and Wallachia in connection with the end of serfdom or slavery and to travel to other European countries, where they might not have arrived until the second half of the 19th century.[10] Among Czech and Slovak authors, this circumstance is explicitly related to the Vlax Roms' arrival on the territory of the former Czechoslovakia.[11]

Other researchers, however, have concluded that Vlax Roms left the territory of Moldova and Wallachia before the end of slavery there. Angus Fraser cast doubt on the idea that Vlax Roms remained in slavery until the mid-19th century and pointed out that many traditional cultural elements and the form of social structure and kinship relations preserved by these Roms are not compatible with time spent in slavery.[12] Fraser connected the Vlax Roms' ethnogenesis with the areas of Transylvania inhabited by the Romanian population, not the historical principalities of Wallachia and Moldavia.[13] The linguist Yaron Matras also inclines towards the idea that the Lovara dialect was formed on the territory of Transylvania, under the influence of contact with the Hungarian-speaking population.[14] Some linguists provide proof that the Wallachian dialects of Romani gradually spread from their core area, in other words, Wallachia and Moldavia.[15] Viktor Elšík states that although it is often thought these dialects' dispersal outside of today's Romania occurred in the second half of the nineteenth century after the abolition of Gypsy slavery/serfdom in Wallachia and Moldavia, it is likely that the Lovara

---

10 E.g. Ian Hancock, *The Pariah Syndrome: An Account of Gypsy Slavery and Persecution* (Ann Arbor, Mich.: Karoma, 1987), 37; Ian Hancock, *Země utrpení*, trans. Karolína Ryvolová and Helena Sadílková (Praha: Signeta, 2001): 51–52; Jan Kochanovski, *Gypsy Studies, part 1* (New Delhi: International Academy of Gypsy Culture, 1963), 86; Jean-Pierre Liegeois, *Gypsies: An Illustrated history* (London: Al Saqi, 1986), 45; Jean-Pierre Liegeois, *Roma in Europe* (Strasbourg: Council of Europe, 2007), 45; Rüdiger Vossen, *Zigeuner* (Frankfurt: Ullstein, 1983), 58.

11 E.g. Milena Hübschmannová, *Šaj pes dovakeras. Můžeme se domluvit* (Olomouc: Univerzita Palackého, 2002), 21; Nina Pavelčíková, "Příchod olašských Romů na Ostravsko v padesátých letech 20. století", *Romano džaniben*, vol. 16, no. 1 (Summer 2009): 37; Šusterová, *Život olašskych žien*, 45.

12 Angus Fraser, "The Rom migrations", *Journal of the Gypsy Lore Society*, no. 2 (1992): 39.

13 Ibid.

14 E.g. Yaron Matras, *Romani: A linguistic introduction* (Cambridge: Cambridge, 2002), 8.

15 Norbert Boretzky, *Die Vlach-Dialekte des Romani. Strukturen, Sprachgeschichte, Verwandtschaftsverhältnisse, Dialektkarten*. Wiesbaden: Harrassowitz, 2003; Yaron Matras, "Mapping the Romani dialects of Romania", *Romani Studies*, vol. 23, no. 2 (2013): 199–243, doi: 10.3828/rs.2013.11; Viktor Elšík, Petr Wagner and Margita Wagnerová, *Olašská romština. Vlašské dialekty*. (online). Praha: FF UK, 2005. Available at: http://ulug.ff.cuni.cz/lingvistika/elsik/Elsik_2005_HO_Vlax.pdf.

and related groups actually originated in Transylvania, so they might have arrived in Slovakia decades earlier.[16]

Elena Marushiakova and Veselin Popov state that some Roms also left Wallachia and Moldavia much earlier than the 19th century. They say that in the 16th and 17th centuries, the ancestors of today's Vlax Roms were already reaching areas of Poland and Ukraine, for example, or the Ottoman Empire's borders.[17] They believe that while the end of slavery was an important factor in the migration of Vlax Roms from Wallachia and Moldavia, it did not mark the start of, nor was it the main reason for, their migration to other parts of Europe.[18] Marushiakova and Popov also put forward proof that the ancestors of today's Vlax Roms, the Laesi, had a special status during slavery in Wallachia and Moldavia, connected with the exercise of itinerant professions. These allowed them to move freely around the estates, to a certain extent, requiring only payment of a tax on their earnings to the lords, and they were also allowed to cross state borders.[19]

Another researcher to posit an earlier date for the Vlax Roms' arrival in the area of present-day Slovakia is Zbyněk Andrš, who cites, for example, Vlax Roms having been recorded on the territory of present-day Slovakia from the 18th century (or even earlier).[20] Slovak ethnologist and Romani studies specialist Arne Mann also states that occurrences of the surname Stojka may be found on the territory of present-day Slovakia in the 18th century: he provides records from the area of Gemer and Košice for the period 1730–1760.[21] My own previous research into registry office records for eastern Slovakia confirmed the presence of Lovara in that area prior to the years 1855 to 1856,[22] in other words before the end of

---

16 Elšík, "Interdialect contact", 47.

17 Elena Marushiakova and Veselin Popov, *Gypsies in the Ottoman Empire: A Contribution to the History of the Balkans* (Hertfordshire: Univ. of Hertfordshire Press, 2001), 50.

18 Elena Marushiakova and Veselin Popov, "Segmentation vs. consolidation: The example of four Gypsy groups in CIS", *Romani Studies*, vol. 14, no. 2 (2004): 169–170.

19 Marushiakova and Popov, "Segmentation vs. consolidation", 167–168; Elena Marushiakova and Veselin Popov, "The Gypsy Court in Eastern Europe", *Romani Studies*, vol. 17, no. 1 (2007): 75–76; Angus Fraser, *Cikáni*, trans. Marta Miklušáková (Praha: NLN, 1998), 54.

20 Zbyněk Andrš, "Our God is Gold: Vlashika Rom at a Crossroads?" *Ethnologia Actualis*, vol. 16, no. 2 (December 2016): 70.

21 Arne Mann, "Historický proces formovania rómskych priezvísk na Slovensku", in: *Milý Bore... profesoru Ctiborovi Nečasovi k jeho sedmdesátým narozeninám věnují přátelé, kolegové a žáci*, Brno: HÚ AV ČR, 274–275.

22 I found records of the presence of the predecessors to today's Lovara on the territory of eastern Slovakia in the registry books from Kráľovský Chlmec (1825), from Veľká Ida (1843), Ruskov (1844), Spišská kapitula (1856) and probably also from Belža in 1808 (Hajská, "'Polokočovní-

slavery in Moldavia and Wallachia. At the beginning of the historical overview below, I shall address the question of whether it is possible to find confirmation that Lovara were present in other areas of modern-day Slovakia at an earlier date as well.

Lovara / Vlax Roms – choice of a suitable appellation

From the very beginning of my work, I tried to find a solution to two fundamental challenges: how to define the category of Lovara / Vlax Roms and whom to include in it (see the chapter on theoretical underpinnings), and what term for them I would use in this book. I am aware that use of the more precise and exact appellation "Lovara" (Romani pl. *Lovára*; sg. *Lovári*) is not particularly widespread on the territory of the former Czechoslovakia, either among academics or the Lovara themselves. The general term *Vlax Roms* is the one commonly used in academic discourse in both Czech and Slovak. The term is used with various nuances in both ethnographical and historical works on the Lovara.[23]

However, the problem with using the label *Vlax Roms* is that this term is a hypernym covering various subgroups. According to Hübschmannová, this umbrella term has, on the territory of the former Czechoslovakia, lost its hypernymic function and become a label identifying only

---

ci'"). The earliest record I have discovered is from 1747 and is of a child with the surname Stojka with a note saying *Zingari*. This shows that a family with the surname Stojka was present in the mid-18th century in Košice (Ibid., 15).

23 Eg. Emília Čajánková, "Život a kultura rožkovianských Cigánov", *Slovenský národopis*, vol. 2, no. 1–2 (1954): 149–175 and 285–306; Emília Horváthová, *Cigáni na Slovensku. Historicko-etnografický náčrt* (Bratislava: Vydavateľstvo Slovenskej akademie vied, 1964); Jelena Marušiaková, "Rodinný život valašských Cigánov na Slovensku a jeho vývinové tendencie". *Slovenský národopis*, vol. 34, no. 4 (1986): 604–634; Lakatošová, "Niektoré zvyklosti", 2–13; Davidová, *Romano drom*; Nina Pavelčíková, "Příchod olašských Romů na Ostravsko v padesátých letech 20. století (ve světle dobových zpráv)", *Romano džaniben*, vol. 16, no. 1 (Summer 2009), 37–66; Stojka and Pivoň, *Náš život*; Šusterová, *Život olašskych žien*; Andrš, "Our God"). While Čajánková – Horváthová and, in her earlier work in Slovakia, also Elena Marushiaková mainly used the term *valašští Romové*, Davidová alternated the Czech *olašští Romové* with the Romani equivalent *Vlachicka Roma* (which is an exoethnonym among speakers of north-central Romani, in other words, non-Vlax Roms, for Vlax Roms). Pivoň and Stojka (Stojka and Pivoň, *Náš život*) are following the same line of thought. Also, Zbyněk Andrš (Andrš, "Our God") used the Romani ethnonym *Vlašika Rom*, which I use only in connection with Lovara living in the east of Slovakia, the only ones who use this term naturally and on a daily basis to refer to themselves. On the differences in the use of the adjective *olašský, valašský* and *vlašícký*, see Igor Kutlík-Garudo, "Olaskí, valasskí alebo vlašickí Rómovia?" *Romano džaniben*, vol. 4, no. 1 (Spring 1997): 35–38.

the traditionally-itinerant horse traders who, elsewhere in the world, are known as the Lovara.[24] The reason for this is that in recent decades, no other groups of Vlax Roms have lived on the territory of the former Slovakia, and so the appellation has become a synonym for the Lovara. Nevertheless, I consider it more precise to use the term Lovara in an international context, since in many countries this is just one group in the Vlax Rom category. It is for this reason that I have decided to use the term, although its use among Lovara in the successor states to the former Czechoslovakia is infrequent.

Limited use of this term in the region by the Lovara themselves has also been confirmed by other researchers.[25] According to an earlier work by Viktor Elšík, this professionym was either largely abandoned by Vlax Roms on the territory of the former Czechoslovakia or probably was never used.[26] Nevertheless, on the basis of my own research, I have reached the opinion that the appellation has in recent years once again become more widespread among Vlax Roms. This may be a result of the influence of contacts with Vlax Roms from other countries who are more likely to stress the difference between various Vlax subgroups, but it may also result from the influence of the Internet and social media networks, where the label is spreading.

For the above-mentioned reasons, in the work that follows I use both terms alternately (Lovara and Vlax Roms) as a synonym. However, where the hypernymic function of the term Vlax Roms needs to be nuanced, I of course differentiate and leave the term *Vlax Roms* in its superior position compared to the term *Lovara*, who, in the wider world, are just one of the subgroups.

The appellation of the Lovara from their perspective

So far I have focused mainly on this appellation as it is used in research, but we also need to look at the terms that Roms themselves use. Lovara from the south and southwest of Slovakia refer to themselves using an

---

24 Milena Hübschmannová, *Roma: Sub ethnic groups: Index of appellations* (Graz: Rombase, 2003), 2.

25 Hübschmannová, *Roma: Sub ethnic groups*, 1; Elena Marushiakova and Veselin Popov, "The Gypsy Court in Eastern Europe", *Romani Studies*, vol. 17, no. 1 (2007): 68; Jan Červenka, "'Cikán, Gypsy & Rom' – dynamika pojmenovávání Romů v různých diskurzech", *Čierno-biele svety. Rómovia v majoritnej spoločnosti na Slovensku*, ed. Podolinská, Tatiana and Hrustič, Tomáš (Bratislava: Veda, Ústav etnológie SAV, 2015), 327–8.

26 Elšík, "Interdialect contact", 47.

ethnonym, most often *amare Rom* ("our Roms"), *čače Rom* ("real Roms") or also *Romane Rom* (literally translated "Romani Roms"). They also use an exoethnonym from the majority languages, *Olaskíva/Olašskíva Rom* (the ending *-íva* being an ending typical of adjectival borrowings). To be precise, of course, the term that the Lovara most often use to refer to themselves is simply the word *Rom* (sg., pl. *Rom*), which is a denotation that all Lovara living in the south and southwest of Slovakia use to refer to themselves. They do not include those Roms whom they do not consider Vlax Roms in the term *Rom* at all, but refer to them using the concept *Rumungri* (pl., sg. *Rumungro*). This is an exoethnonym that the Lovara use to refer to all non-Vlax Roms in general, in other words, Roms from surrounding groups. The original meaning of the word *Rumungro* comes from *Rom Ungro,* or "Hungarian Rom". This name was later extended by the Vlax Roms to include all the settled Roms in the Czech Republic and surrounding lands, and according to the context may have a pejorative meaning. For this reason, when referring to Slovak or Hungarian Roms who are not Vlax Roms (or Lovara), I prefer to use the academic term *non-Vlax Roms* rather than the not entirely neutral *Rumungri*.

It is also common among the Lovara to identify individuals using the group name of a concrete "family" group, referred to by the term *kranga* ("branch"), such as the Bougešti, Jovanešti, Loulešti, Ferkošti, Júcovára, Kurkešti and so on. The name of a particular *kranga* is usually derived from the Romani nickname of the group's common ancestor (e.g. Bougo, Jovan, Loulo, Ferko, Júco, Kurko). As the genealogical memory of the family groups weakens, *kranga* are divided into new sub-groups and are renamed according to significant common ancestors who are accessible to the collective memory.[27] Given that after analysing my respondents' testimonies I was able to ascertain their membership of a certain *kranga* in just some cases, I will not use that category further in this book.

From my respondents' perspective, the use of sub-ethnic categorisation is (and always has been) clear and simple: The idea that one belonged to a group of Roms was based on a common origin and relations, sometimes labelled a blood tie, and on an objectively-existing, specific culture that clearly differentiates the Lovara from other Roms on the basis of signs they perceive as objectively definable (e.g. a common language, cultural manifestations such as a way of dressing, or economic strategies).[28] During the interviews my respondents fully self-identified

---

27 Markéta Hajská, *"Hranice jazyka jakožto hranice etnické identity. Vztah užívaní jazyka a etnické kategorizace u olašských Romů na východním Slovensku"* (PhD diss., Charles University, 2020), 30.

28 Ibid., 58–60.

with the Lovara category without necessarily using this label. They included their forebears – parents, grandparents and other members of the extended family whom they always considered to be members of the same (sub-ethnic) group – in the category Lovara as well. They also included other families and family groups under this label whom they did not consider their relatives.

Roms, "gypsies" and "gypsy vagabonds"

In this book, I use the ethnically-defined word *Roms*, referring either equally to all Roms or as an umbrella term[29] that also includes the Lovara. However, the term "Rom, Roms" was fundamentally absent from all the period sources with which I worked.[30] All Czechoslovak legislation and the entire state administration, whether during the interwar First Republic, in wartime, or postwar, exclusively used the term "gypsy, gypsies" (Cz. *cikán, cikáni*). Later on, above all during the postwar period, specific terms such as "citizens of gypsy origin" or "the gypsy question" can be found, while in the interwar and wartime period it was also common to find the negative term "gypsy nuisance". To refer to groups which were observed to be geographically mobile, the archival materials across the decades which I study here use terms such as "travelling gypsies", "gypsy vagabonds" and "gypsy travellers". The term "Gypsies" (*Cikáni*) is a traditional label for the Romani minority in the Czech environment used by the majority population. Its most commonly-used form, written in the archival materials of the period with a small "c", reflects the way in which these people were perceived as a social class of the majority population. They were not regarded as a nation in their own right founded on their membership of an ethnic group and use of a common language.[31]

---

29 The definition of the term Rom/roms are looked at in detail by Jan Červenka (Červenka, "'Cikán, Gypsy & Rom'"). Unlike the Lovara themselves, however, in line with most researchers, I include under this heading non-Vlax Roms living on this territory, with the exception of Sinti, for whom I use, separately, their own term (in Czech, *Sinto/Sinti/Sintové*).

30 The term Rom or Roms first started to be publicly used in the Czechoslovak context in the 1960s, above all in connection with the activity of the Svaz Cikánů-Romů (Union of Gypsies/ Roms), the first officially-permitted Romani organisation in Czechoslovakia, functioning between 1969 and 1973. After falling into disuse in the following two decades it was not until the 1990s that it started to be used abundantly (Červenka, "'Cikán, Gypsy & Rom'", 335). However, the documents that I use date from before this time and do not reflect the label Roms in any way.

31 Tomáš Zapletal, "Přístup totalitního státu a jeho bezpečnostních složek k Romské menšině v Československu (1945–1989)", *Sborník Archivu bezpečnostních složek* 10, Praha: Archiv bezpečnostních složek 2012: 14.

Equivalents of the terms "Gypsy/Gypsies" were also used to refer to Roms in many other countries. Ilsen About and Anna Abakunova have pointed out that the process of defining who is to be considered a "Gypsy" has always been connected with the labelling of persons as Roms and Sinti by the authorities. Since this process has undergone considerable change over time, it is not at all clear, they say, whether the persons so labelled actually shared a common ethnic identity. According to these authors, despite the growth in the historiography of the identification and categorisation of persons in the 20th century, it is still necessary to pay due attention to the identification methods and everyday practices of the Romani and Sinti populations themselves.[32]

The appellation "Gypsies", in various historical contexts, served to denote considerably heterogenous groups which, according to the connotations of the period, may also have included travelling tradesmen, actors and showmen, pedlars and other people with a travelling lifestyle who were not ethnic Roms and were mostly lumped together under the Czech term *světští*.[33] This broad definition of the term "gypsies" is found above all in the First Republic Act no. 117/1927, Coll., "on wandering gypsies", which defined "wandering gypsies" on the basis of their lifestyle as "gypsies who wander from place to place and other vagabonds who avoid work and live a gypsy lifestyle, even if for part of the year – above all in winter – they have a permanent dwelling place in either case".[34] The law used a dual definition of the target group: "wandering gypsies" and "other vagabonds", and was related to an unspecified "gypsiness", based on the idea of "innate nomadism" which was perceived as a typical characteristic of the "Gypsies".[35]

The term "gypsies" (*cikáni*) which I came across in the state archives is an external categorisation that does not in any way reflect the internal di-

---

32 Ilsen About and Anna Abakunova, *The Genocide and Persecution of Roma and Sinti. Bibliography and Historiographical Review* (International Holocaust Remembrance Alliance, 2016), 12.

33 Hanka Tlamsová, *Lexikon světem jdoucích* (Brno: Nakladatelství PhDr. Josef Sperát, 2020).

34 Act no. 117/1927 of 14 July 1927, "on wandering gypsies", section 1.

35 Pavel Baloun, *"'Cikáni, metla venkova!' Tvorba a uplatňování proticikánských opatření v meziválečném Československu, za druhé republiky a v počáteční fázi Protektorátu Čechy a Morava (1918–1941)."* (PhD diss., Charles University, 2020), 46. Pavel Baloun has performed a detailed analysis of the anti-gypsy measures of the time, not just in the area of criminology and police prevention, but also in the broader debate on the "Gypsy question." He focused on the rationalisation of the period category "Gypsiness" connected with the entrenched assumption of criminologists that "Gypsies" represented a specific group of criminals (Ibid., 56). They were often labelled the "scourge of the countryside" and in the context of this term were considered permanently suspicious people who had to be regularly controlled and subjected to police raids (Ibid., 59–65).

vision of Roms into individual groups. A similar conclusion was reached by historian Celia Donert, who found the label "Gypsies" was used in interwar Czechoslovakia to refer to a wide range of groups. The term could, she says, relate to German-speaking Sinti, settled Moravian Roms, Slovak- and Hungarian-speaking Roms or peripatetic Vlax Roms.[36]

Following the example of other authors,[37] I have decided to use the term "gypsies" and its equivalents given above, as well as other period labels, only in scare quotes. I retain the form of writing them with a small initial letter that can be found in the documents. My main reason for doing this is an attempt to maintain the categories of the period and its specific discourse, including the language used. I am aware that if I were to use the word "Rom" where the period documents use "gypsy", I would be guilty of considerable imprecision, since the two categories do not overlap and have different connotations.

0.3 Methodology

This book is the result of an interdisciplinary approach, combining above all ethnographic, socioanthropological and historical methods. In terms of sources, it is based on a combination of archival research and interviews with witnesses. At some times, in particular when reconstructing events from the period preceding the Second World War, I was forced to rely exclusively on state archives. When researching the period from the Second World War onwards, I was able to add testimonies as a significant source from Roms in the Stojka family researched here, as well as from other Lovara families and other witness testimonies. I tried to combine these with other sources. I use different types of sources for various periods, diversified with regard to whether they are from Slovakia or the Czech lands.

---

36 Celia Donert, *The Rights of the Roma: The Struggle for Citizenship in Postwar Czechoslovakia* (Cambridge: Cambridge University Press, 2017), 19.

37 For example, Pavel Baloun, *"Metla našeho venkova!" Kriminalizace Romů od první republiky až po prvotní fázi protektorátu (1918–1941)* (Praha: FHS UK – Scriptorium, 2022); Victoria Shmidt and Bernadette Nadya Jaworsky, *Historicizing Roma in Central Europe: between critical whiteness and epistemic injustice* (London and New York: Routledge, Taylor & Francis Group, 2021); Dušan Slačka, "Usazení kočovníků nebo řešení „cikánské otázky"? Kočovníci na Hodonínsku a provádění opatření podle zákona č. 74/1958 Sb." *Bulletin Muzea Romské kultury,* 23 (2014): 57–70; Matěj Spurný, *Nejsou jako my. Česká společnost a menšiny v pohraničí (1945–1960)* (Praha: Antikomplex, 2011); Zapletal, "Přístup totalitního státu".

Reflexivity and the course of the research

The beginnings of my research into the Lovara family with the surname Stojka date to December 2018, when I visited Berci Stojka (*1949 in Louny) to record, as part of an earlier research project of mine, his memories of forced sedentarisation and the implementation of the law banning itinerancy. The name Berci is of course a nickname (*romano ánav*, literally, Romani name). During a visit of several hours, he provided me with a highly detailed testimony touching not just on the events connected with the settling of his family in the old brickworks in Louny in the second half of the 1950s, but also on specific information regarding his family and the routes along which they travelled before coming to Louny. The amount of detailed information that emerged from the interview compelled me to set out for the state archives in Louny, where I acquainted myself with the archives of the District National Committee (*Okresní národní výbor – ONV*, the socialist-era state administration at the district level) concerning the "gypsy" population register and the list of travelling persons in both the Louny district and the former Žatec district. On that first visit to the Louny archives, I discovered a considerable amount of information that matched very precisely what Berci Stojka had told me. However, the angle from which these facts were being interpreted by the documentary record differed diametrically from his. Among the persons included on the list made on the basis of Act no. 74/1958 I identified, from the names and nicknames given to me, Berci's grandmother Anna Stojková, née Lakatošová, with the Romani nickname Čaja, as well as his uncles with the Romani names Bobko and Janino, his great-uncle Jouško (Anna's brother-in-law) and other members of the family about whom Berci Stojka had told me. With this basic information (i.e., names, places they stayed, birthdates and birthplaces), I began intensive research in regional archives in the Czech Republic and later also in Slovakia, where I tried to find any possible record of the sojourn or movement of the Stojka family from the interwar to the postwar period. Still, for all that Berci's memories of his childhood and youth were detailed and vivid, his knowledge of his family's life before they came to Bohemia from Slovakia after the Second World War was fairly patchy. He said that his family had "travelled", that they had never been settled anywhere and that they had come "from Slovakia", but in our first interview he was unable to remember the precise place or region. It thus became all the more of a challenge for me to ascertain where his family came from and around which area(s) they had moved before the postwar period.

Since my main specialty is social and cultural anthropology, I decided from the beginning to create a genealogical map on the basis of Berci Stojka's information and data from various archives. I continued to add to this map and revise it on the basis of information from the archives of the register, police reports, and other official documents containing information on family relationships and other personal information. As a result, I managed to reconstruct a family tree of the Stojka family containing over a hundred persons and going back to the second half of the 19th century. This became an important research tool that helped me identify records of family members across the Czech and Slovak archives, and also helped me to reconstruct their spatial trajectories during various historical periods. I also noticed how these trajectories changed over the decades and how they differed from each other in a relatively significant way, as the branches of the family gradually changed and became distinct.

While transferring information to the genealogical diagram, I noticed that a single municipality came up again and again in the personal data and other information on the Stojka family members' birthplace and domicile from the interwar period: Trenčianska Teplá in the Ilava district, later Trenčín district, in western Slovakia. I gradually began to entertain the hypothesis that this was a municipality in which the family I was following may have had, in a certain sense, *roots*. To verify this hypothesis, I set out for the state archives in Trenčín, where I discovered that the Stojka family had been largely based in the municipality of Trenčianska Teplá since the end of the 19th century. Archival materials in the Trenčianska Teplá District Notary Office then showed the country-wide movements and sojourns of people domiciled in Trenčianska Teplá.

At the same time, I tried to find other accessible sources with which I might be able to supplement these often very brief archival records. Of key importance to me was the search for witnesses in Trenčianska Teplá, the municipality to which my research had taken me. However, it was difficult to find Roms there from the family in question, which prevented active engagement of respondents. Most who would have remembered the period with which I deal in this book were no longer alive when I was writing it. I was unable to locate contact details for the descendants of Štefan Stojka, Sr.'s branch. No locals today knew where the family had moved after his death.

A further highly significant complication was the public hygiene and social distancing measures in place during 2020 and 2021 in connection with the Covid-19 pandemic, in other words, during a key period of my research. These restrictions meant I was unable to work in person more intensively with witnesses, since they were elderly people whom my visits could have endangered.

Where relevant, however, I have tried to make use in this book of other Lovara testimonies, which fundamentally enrich the one-sided, biased view provided by the archival materials. In the case of Trenčianska Teplá, there were also non-Romani witnesses who remembered when the Stojkas lived in the municipality. I give great weight to all these narratives and consider them an absolutely fundamental source.

My interviews with these research participants, undertaken more or less after 2009, were conducted in their native languages, so in the case of the Roms, in the Lovara dialect of Vlax Romani. Having a very good knowledge of this dialect helped considerably to open the door for me to my interlocutors, who did not hesitate to state their positions and describe all the events as well as they could remember them.

Integrating the memories of Roms into research into Romani history

Oral history is an extremely popular research method in contemporary history and is an historiographical method I have used here for qualitative research. The method is also used in various fields of the social sciences and humanities, by interdisciplinary researchers, and by those on the border between "academic" and "lay" work.[38] An undoubted benefit of oral history is that it offers a new view of all sorts of individuals who negotiate and create their situations and then give accounts of them. When working with memories, it is possible to focus on the various elements which intermingle in the process of memory construction, such as reflections on the narrator's community, its history, its central events, its organisation and composition, as well as the social forces at work in and around it. Other factors are psychological, the ways in which individuals come to terms with what they and their family members have experienced, and last but not least, there are cultural features, "memory techniques", and the current situation of the community in question and its needs.[39] Although this is a dynamic, open method of research that

---

38 Miroslav Vaněk and Pavel Mücke, *Třetí strana trojúhelníku: teorie a praxe orální historie* (Praha: Karolinum, 2015), 16–17.

39 Katalin Katz, "Story, history and memory: a case study of the Roma at the Komarom camp in Hungary," *The Roma, a Minority in Europe. Historical, Polical and Social Perspectives*, ed. Stauber, Roni and Vago Raphael, 69–87 (Budapest: Central European University Press, 2007).

at present includes a number of methodological approaches and paradigms, it is nevertheless important to regard oral history as a discipline with a relatively clearly definable research methodology that has rules for the process of conducting and recording a research interview, including its preparation, subsequent processing and analysis. This is systematic work that does not include randomly recording respondents or the use of other recordings that do not involve an expertly-led, structured dialogue between questioner and respondent.[40]

In the Czech environment, the recording of Romani witnesses and the subsequent intensive work with such testimonies is something that by now has a long tradition.[41] Although the use of testimonies is often viewed as oral history research, not all researchers subscribe to this method, not all make direct use of it, and not all specify in detail the research methods they have used. It may happen, therefore, that in the general consciousness, oral history may be perceived to involve kinds of testimony which do not meet the definitions and methodological

---

40 Vaněk and Mücke, *Třetí strana,* 15.

41 Milena Hübschmannová, the founder of the field of Romani Studies in Czechoslovakia, devoted herself intensively to collecting Romani testimonies, above all concerning the interwar and wartime periods. Her publications in book form include *"Po židoch cigáni."* (Milena Hübschmannová, (ed). *"Po židoch cigáni." Svědectví Romů ze Slovenska 1939–1945.* Vol. I., *(1939–srpen 1944)* (Prague: Triáda, 2005), where the method of oral history is explicitly mentioned. She also published a number of other Romani testimonies in the journal *Romano džaniben* etc. Other researchers carried on her methods, focusing above all on the events of the Second World War and postwar developments, including the postwar migration of Roms from Slovakia to the Czech lands. They include Jana Kramářová, (ed.), *(Ne)boli: vzpomínky Romů na válku a život po válce* (Praha: Člověk v tísni, 2005); Kateřina Sidiropulu Janků, *Nikdy jsem nebyl podceňovanej. Ze slovenských osad do českých měst za prací. Poválečné vzpomínky* (Brno: Masarykova univerzita, 2015); and Eva Zdařilová, "Faktory ovlivňující narativ na příkladu životních příběhů několika romských pamětníků války", *Romano džaniben,* vol. 13, no. 2 (Winter 2013): 13–36. The historian Ctibor Nečas also recorded the memories of Moravian and Bohemian Roms in his work *Českoslovenští Romové v letech 1938–1945* (Brno: Masarykova univerzita, 1994). Another pioneering work in this direction is the extensive commentated trilogy *Česká cikánská rapsodie* by historian Jan Tesař, based on the memories of the Romani partisan Josef Serinek, taken down by the author in 1963–1964 and as Josef Serinek and Jan Tesař, *Česká cikánská rapsodie.* Vol. I.–III. (Praha: Triáda, 2016). In recent years there have been publications based on a combination of oral history methods and archival research (Sadílková, Helena, Slačka, Dušan and Závodská, Milada. *Aby bylo i s námi počítáno. Společensko-politická angažovanost Romů a snahy o založení romské organizace v poválečném Československu* (Brno: Muzeum romské kultury, 2018) or Lada Viková, *"Dlouhá cesta za důstojným postavením: Příspěvek aplikované etiky k výzkumu holokaustu Romů osmdesát let od událostí"* (PhD diss., Charles University, 2020). My own research activity and its outcomes were conceived in the same direction (Hajská, "Polokočovníci", "Forced settlement"; "'We had to run away': The Lovára's departure from the Protectorate of Bohemia and Moravia to Slovakia in 1939", *Romani Studies,* vol. 32, no. 1 (2022)), where I extended this method to research into the following decades.

requirements of the discipline as outlined above. This methodological limitation also concerns the present work in which, for purposes of further analysis, I use interviews which were recorded in keeping with oral history methods[42] and other ethnographic narratives, biographical narratives and testimonies which did not arise in absolute compliance with the methodology of oral history. I therefore try in my analysis to approach the testimonies in a diversified way, reflecting on their limitations while giving the context in which the various interviews and testimonies arose. Although I openly subscribe to oral history as a discipline, in the case of some oral sources it is more precise to speak of using ethnographic narratives or just testimonies.[43]

The oral history method also has its disadvantages. These include the fact that memory is selective, that events are forgotten, and that imprecise connections are created between certain circumstances. This gives rise to questions regarding the subjective nature of this method and its validity. It also opens the question of how complex it can be to understand certain events, as well as the question of the limitations of retrospection, when those remembering may judge certain past events in the light of subsequent developments.[44] The most problematic issue in my work with witnesses was that they would sometimes be imprecise with regard to the date when the events described took place. This happened because in the families in question, the tracking of time might have had a different character and been of marginal importance.

The involvement of Roms in research into Romani history

I also try to build on attempts to involve Roms as actors in the research into Romani history. This is something very much present in the current field of Romani studies and aims to involve the Roms themselves in the creation of publications. I agree with Paola Trevisan that the history of Romani groups in Europe should not be limited to the analysis of antigypsyism, anti-Romani policies, and anti-Romani feeling, but should

---

42 Vaněk and Mücke, *Třetí strana,* 148–202.
43 In this category I include mainly the testimonies in the database of the applicants for compensation for genocide during the Second World War kept by the nonprofit organisation Člověk v tísni, o.p.s. and the testimonies which form part of applications for certificates of eligibility under Act no. 255/1946, Coll. kept in the VÚA-VHA archive in Prague (f. Sbírka osobních spisů žadatelů o vydání osvědčení podle zákona č. 255/1946 Sb.).
44 Vaněk and Mücke, *Třetí strana,* 27–28.

instead put forward new research questions capable of reintegrating Sinti and Roms into the history of Europe and vice versa.[45] Current historiography accentuates the need to write Romani history with the involvement of Romani actors and to integrate various stories into historiographical context. This could broaden the scope of attention of researchers who have focused heretofore on antigypsyism and the relations of various state actors toward "gypsies".[46]

I therefore try to provide space to those Roms who have had personal experience of harsh surveillance by state bodies and who were also labelled the "most problematic" members of the group officially referred to as "persons of gypsy origin", namely, the "travelling gypsies". As such, they were subjected to (and continually had to come to terms with) institutional and structural racism from state bodies on the basis of their ethnic difference. During various periods, this was perceived by the surrounding society either in terms of Romani racial and social difference, or in terms of the independent Romani way of life and professional orientation.

Archival research

My research is largely based on my findings in various archives in the former Czechoslovakia. As far as central-level archives are concerned, my work is based on my research in the National Archives in Prague, especially those collections relating to municipal police headquarters in general, the Interior Ministry and its old registers, the provincial headquarters of municipal police forces, Police Directorate II, Interior Ministry II – additions, the Central Committee of the Communist Party of Czechoslovakia's Ideological Division, and the Provincial Office in Prague. At the regional and local levels, my research took place in the regional branches of the state archives (above all in Litoměřice and Hradec Králové) and last but not least in the district branches of the state archives in Benešov, Beroun, Frýdek Místek, Kolín, Litoměřice, Lo-

---

45 Paola Trevisan, "Austrian 'Gypsies' in the Italian archives. Historical ethnography on multiple border crossings at the beginning of the twentieth century". *Focaal—Journal of Global and Historical Anthropology* 87 (2020): 61–74.

46 Baloun quotes the founding declaration of the Prague Forum for Romani Histories of the Institute for Contemporary History of the Czech Academy of Sciences: http://www.romanihistories.usd.cas.cz/cs/wp-content/uploads/Prague_Forum_česky-1.pdf (Baloun, *"Metla našeho venkova"*, 23).

vosice, Louny, Mělník, Mladá Boleslav, Olomouc, Nymburk (Lysá nad Labem office), Prague – East, Prague – West (Zdiby – Přemyšlení office) and Teplice. I also made use of the archival materials in the Provincial Archive in Opava (Olomouc office) and the City of Brno Archive. My colleague Lada Viková was willing to share her archival findings with me concerning the Stojka family from the local archives in Blansko, Jindřichův Hradec and Pelhřimov, as well as from the National Archives in Prague, and with her permission I will cite several of those archival materials. In terms of my archival research in Slovakia, I drew above all on the collections in the state archives in Trenčín, and additionally on my findings in the Nitra state archives (Levice branch), Nové Zámky, Topoľčany and Trnava.

A very important source of information regarding family ties that is able to confirm the presence of the Lovara at a certain time and place even during historically more remote periods is the study and analysis of local registers of births, marriages and deaths.[47] I used this method when performing research for my study *"Polokočovníci"* (2016), and researcher Lada Viková also used this resource.[48] Viková pointed to the problem of mistakes made by those transcribing Romani names and surnames, as well as to the incompleteness of the recorded details in such registers.[49] Despite these shortcomings, what was fundamentally important was that the digitalisation of the registry office data allowed me to search in the parish registers for a large part of Slovakia. Entering typical Lovara surnames, I was able to search for information on the forebears of to-day's Lovara in certain municipalities.

Searching the records of "travelling gypsies"

In my research in the regional and district archives, I focused on various sources such as registers of births, marriages and deaths, other kinds of registers in document or book form, municipal police station records,

---

47 For the territory of today's Slovakia there is a web page, FamilySearch, where the individual digitalised registers are uploaded in aggregate, covering a time span usually of several centuries, with the most recent registers ending in approximately 1900, for some towns and villages several years earlier. The digitalised registers have also been copied into a central database, so people may be searched for according to their date and place of birth, name and surname, the type of event registered (baptism, funeral, wedding), or the names of their parents.

48 Viková, *"Dlouhá cesta"*.

49 Ibid., 66–67.

reports from municipal authorities and, for the postwar period, the files of regional and district administrations, as well as other documents concerned with the movements of "travelling gypsies" somehow. I looked for key documents containing official procedures and orders relating to this category, as well as lists of such persons and any other reports regarding their movements on the territory of specific municipalities and districts. I am aware that sources from the state authorities at various levels provide a one-sided view of "gypsies", formed from records of clashes between the state system and the Roms, and that there is therefore a need to approach such sources as biased and to continually reflect on the bias in the available materials. The historian Michal Schuster points out that the use of written materials from majority-population officials involves a number of limitations, above all the limited, one-sided views of such officials at the regional or central levels.[50] It was these officials who contributed to the implementation, recording and passing of various measures regarding "gypsies" and those specifically aimed at "travelling gypsies". Without thorough study and contextualisation of these documents, including a reflection on the historical processes of how people who were viewed at the time as being on the fringes of society were treated, only limited use can be made of them. There is also a need, with period sources, to be aware of the continual formation of the stereotypical "travelling gypsy", "gypsy vagabond" or just plain "gypsy", of whom a "tendency to itinerancy" is considered a self-evident feature. This perception of "gypsies" finds its way into documents, decrees and orders, not just in the interwar and postwar periods, but also during socialism, even though the ideology of that time had officially disavowed racial discrimination.

Differentiation among kinds of "travelling gypsies" in state records

When conducting research in the Italian archives, researcher Paola Trevisan posed a question related to the identification of Roms that is also key for my study: How can we analyse the persistence of Romani families across historical periods? She believes that "we need to research what traces were left in the archives by people who were identified by the state institutions as 'gypsies' and how these records may be interpreted from

---

50   Michal Schuster, "Jinak bychom tady nebyli." Příběh rodiny Dychovy z obce Hrušky (okr. Břeclav), *Romano džaniben*, vol. 27, no. 2 (Winter 2020): 9.

an ethnographical perspective".[51] The question occurs as to whether, or how, state institutions differentiated between groups of "travelling gypsies" and on what they based such differentiation. In the Czech lands, the Lovara may be identified in the state records from the period of the First Republic until the end of the 1950s in a category that is, in most cases, described as "travelling gypsies /gypsy vagabonds". A rare exception consists of some local records in the area of southern Slovakia, where the note "Vlax gypsy", or its Hungarian equivalent "oláh gypsy" (*oláh cigány*),[52] appears sporadically as early as the interwar period in some records. This term appears repeatedly as information on the profession of the person in question. I did not come across this term in the Bohemian or Moravian archives for this period at all.

The "gypsies" mentioned in the state records are sometimes differentiated according to their profession or livelihood. With a certain amount of caution, it is possible to find Lovara under the profession of horse trader, but horse trading was something in which Bohemian and Moravian Roms and Sinti also engaged. Moreover, the testimonies show that some Lovara families earned their living in other ways which also required mobility, such as by cleaning kettles, sharpening knives, metalworking or collecting feathers or rags. It is difficult to differentiate these families from other Roms.

Some state institutions' records differentiated between "gypsies" according to their places of origin – the region or state from which they came. Lovara families, it may be assumed with great probability, fall into the category labelled "gypsy (travelling) hordes from Slovakia", but it cannot be ruled out that this term may have also been used to describe, for example, Sinti whose domicile was in Slovakia.

The only reasonably reliable method of establishing that certain archival records concern Lovara is to focus just on archival materials containing specific surnames found only with Lovara (see below). I only compared records of this kind with information on families or localities available from my long-term research into this subject. However, the problem with my method, identifying Lovara families on the basis of

---

51 Trevisan, *Austrian "Gypsies"*, 61–62.
52 Found during the interwar period (ŠA Nitra/ Levice, f. ONÚ Dolná Seč – Trestné listy 1908–1938: repeated occurrence), during the Second World War (ŠA Nitra/ Levice, f. Hlavnoslúžnovský úrad v Leviciach z let 1938–1944: repeated occurrence), and also during the communist period (ŠA Nitra/ Nové Zámky, f. ONV Nové Zámky, i. č. Vn. 17, k. 238, zpráva Rady MNV v Tvrdošovcích (8. 8. 1955), č. j. 1420/1955 mentions 36 Oláh Roms living in brick houses in the municipality).

surname, is the fact that Romani surnames in the state archives tend to be fairly rare, which gives us a limited amount of archival material with which to work. Municipal police reports often concerned the movements and arrivals of specific individuals and police checks of them. The only person whose name was given in such reports was the "leader of the horde", in whose name an itinerancy document was drawn up. The number of group members was often given at the end, but the individual members were listed only exceptionally. A typical report contained the name, birthdate and birthplace, the number of the leader's "gypsy" identification card or itinerancy document, the size of the "horde", the place where the police checked them, and either a description of the alleged offence committed or a statement that the group was "without fault".

The difficulty in identifying the Lovara in archival sources has also been dealt with by historian Rastislav Černý. In his study on the Lovara, involving migration trajectories in the Místek district during the interwar period, he worked with records which had categories defined as "hordes of Gypsies" or "vagabond Gypsies from Slovakia".[53] Černý believes records pertaining to Lovara may be distinguished from records pertaining to Slovak (non-Vlax) Roms according to their method of mobility: While Lovara tended to move about in groups with horses and wagons, Slovak non-Vlax Roms frequently came on foot in small groups, and often just frequented areas in the vicinity of the border.[54] I believe an exception may have been the Sinti families who, like the Lovara, moved about in horse-drawn wagons and over a wider area that went beyond the border area.

Searching across the archives for records on the movements and stays of specific families

As part of my archival research, I specifically focused across the various localities on the movements and stays of people from the Stojka family, using the genealogical diagram described above. I also followed other individuals and families with the surname Stojka, as well as other surnames typical of Lovara (Sztojka, Rafael, Kudrik, Banda, Lakatoš, Daniš, Bihari/Bihary, in combination with Lakatos/Lakatoš) who might be expected to belong to the Lovara category on the basis of their described

---

53   Rostislav Černý, "Lovárové v době první republiky – na příkladu okresu Místek." *Romano džaniben*, vol. 19, no. 1 (Summer 2012): 11.

54   Ibid., 11.

lifestyle or place of origin, who were often jointly recorded with other families of Lovara.

Searching the archival records by surname was something that I had also done for the earlier period in the digitalised registers of births, marriages and deaths. In particular, I analysed records relating to the above-mentioned surnames where the registers included a note confirming these were "gypsies", "gypsy vagabonds", "vagabonds" or even "Wallachians".[55]

This method is one of the few ways of finding information on Roms from certain families, or even just the places where they stayed or moved about. However, it involves various difficulties, above all the fact that this type of search is fairly demanding. The archives differ considerably in the extent to which collections of this type have been preserved, and so it is far from assured that a researcher will be able to find archival material across the Czech and Slovak archives containing, for example, First Republic municipal police orders on the stays of "gypsy hordes" for a particular district. Although I did manage to find such collections, only some archival materials contained the names and personal data of "travelling gypsies" with which it was possible to work further.

Still, finding records pertaining to the Stojka family was even more complicated. In this regard, it was a great advantage that some of the first names in the family were highly unique. The first name "Zaga", borne by the oldest woman who was the leading personage in a main branch of the Stojka family, is extremely rare. It is a first name that is found only very sporadically in both the Czech and Slovak environments[56] and hardly appeared at all during the period in question, although it was sometimes possible to find it in Croatia, Serbia or Moldova.[57] Hungarian researcher Rudolf Horváth gives the name Zaga as an example of an old-fashioned Romani female nickname,[58] so it is probable that this nickname (*romano*

---

55 This was a note written in Hungarian indicating that a particular person was a *vándorló cigány* or *kóborgó cigány* (i.e., a "gypsy vagabond") or an *oláh cigány* ("Vlax Gypsy", with the original meaning of "Romanian Gypsy" [Bodnárová 2009: 9]); in registers written in Latin, the notes state the person was a *zingarius peregrinus, zingos peregrinos, zingarius vagabundus, zingara sub tentorio* (sleeping in a tent), etc., or relating their identity to Wallachia: *zingarus valachicus*, feminine *zingari valachici*.

56 The online source *Slovenské krstné mená začínajúce na Žága* (web-stranka.sk) lists this name (spelt Zága) among Slovak names, but other sources do not mention it.

57 According to online sources, this was a very rare name even in Croatia (https://actacroatica .com/en/name/Zaga) and also in Serbia and Moldova (https://mondonomo.ai/forename /Zaga).

58 Rudolf Horváth, *A magyarországi kóbor czigányok nyelvtana Czigány-Magyar Szótár* (Szeged: Primaware Kiadó, 2014), 43.

ánav, literally Romani name) was extant among the Slovak Lovara previously. However, I did not manage to find, in the former Czechoslovakia, a record of any other person with the full name Zaga Stojková. It is this fact that helped me to identify the data on this person as unique.

Likewise, the name of Zaga's son, Filo Stojka, was unique. The name Filo may be considered a familiar form of the common first name Filip, but officially-recorded shortened forms of names were at that time extremely rare – and yet the Filo Stojka whom I was interested in was recorded across the former Czechoslovakia as Filo and not Filip, although it was common practice for the Czech authorities and police to record the Czech equivalents of Slovak names (so Juraj was recorded as Jiří, Peter as Petr, Pavol as Pavel, etc.).

The first name of Zaga's daughter Kuluš, also found in some records as Kuluše or Kuluša, was also extremely rare, and from what I could find did not appear anywhere else in the former Czechoslovakia. Once again, it was clearly an officially-recorded *romano ánav*. This was also the case with the nickname of Zaga's daughter Grófa, although in her case the name is now once again widespread among the Lovara. In the latter case, however, I came across several occurrences of this *románo ánav* officially recorded as a first name in the form Grófa, Grófka or Grófojka.

These rare first names made it easy to find information on their bearers and to identify them with the family being researched herein. It was also possible to identify other people who had much more frequent or extremely common names and travelled across Czechoslovakia with the holders of the above-mentioned rare names. These included Filo Stojka's wife Anna Lakatošová, married surname Stojková, his sister Barbora Stojková, married surname Horvátová, and his brothers-in-law Juraj and Antonín Horvát.

Impediments to and difficulties with the method of searching for Lovara on the basis of surname

The situation was entirely different when it came to looking for records on another branch of the family represented by Štefan Stojka, Senior (*1891), his son Ján (*1905) or his grandsons, also named Štefan Stojka, and other members of the family who had very common names. I could not use data on persons named Ján or Štefan Stojka without further personal data to verify their identities because these names were also found at the same time in a number of other Lovara families and it would have been easy to confuse them. I was able to work with data on a person named Ján or Štefan Stojka only if further personal data, such as the date and place of birth or the name of the partner and children, were also given. At the same time, it is important to remember that when communicating among themselves, the Lovara exclusively used their Romani nicknames, which were rarely recorded in majority-society, official records, and if they were, then frequently with spelling mistakes mangling the Romani words. For example, the nickname of Ján Rafael, recorded as *Gulgo*,[59] was probably in fact *Guglo* ("sweet"), and the nickname recorded for Anna Lakatošová, *Jedra*,[60] was clearly meant to be *Sedra*, which is still a very common nickname used by Lovara women. Their official names were of only limited significance to Roms, and they themselves used them only in contact with officials and security forces. The personal identity of Roms was created in their own community of family ties and by using special names (nicknames). Their officially-registered first names and surnames had little significance for the Roms in question and would sometimes be changed over the course of their lifetimes.[61] These *romane ánava* gave Roms the ability to confuse their identities, to make them unclear, an providing them with opportunity for escape, concealment and defence, and not just against non-Roma persecution, but also in the sense of magical protection.[62] Since official names were not used by the Roms with each other, it frequently happened that more than one child in a family was given the same official first name. This fact is, of course, extremely confusing for the researcher. Although I was aware that this situation could occur, I nevertheless found that when creating the genealogical map, there was a discrepancy in the data concerning the son of Ján Stojka (*1905), named Štefan, for whom various archival materials gave birth dates of 1919, 1923 and 1933. Although I asked myself whether there might not be more than one son named Štefan in this nuclear family, I thought it improbable. That the name really did occur repeatedly among these siblings was first confirmed to me by Báno Bihary, the grandson of Štefan Stojka (*1919) and the great-great-grandson of Štefan Stojka, Sr. (*1891):

---

59 SOkA Pelhřimov, f. OU Kamenice n. L, i. č. 1008, k. 510. Hlášení Okresnímu úřadu v Kamenici, Stanice Horní Cerekev č. 17 (1. 8. 1934).

60 Ibid.

61 Eva Thurner, "Bez státní příslušnosti (téměř) až do konce života. Zvláštní úpravy práva na získání státního občanství pro „Romy" („Cikány")" *Romano džaniben*, vol. 16, no. 1 (Summer 2009): 67–68.

62 Hübschmannová, *Šaj pes dovakeras*, 63–65.

My great-grandmother had seven children – four daughters and three sons. The sons were all called Štefan. The eldest was born in 1919, that was my grandfather and they called him Turko. Then there was another, born in 1923, and then another, about 10 years younger. He died two years ago in Prague.[63]

The difference and apparent lack of connection between the Romani nicknames and the official names of Roms understandably complicates historical analysis and the creation of a genealogical diagram, above all when information from respondents is being linked to archival records. Witnesses frequently cannot remember the official names of their Romani relatives and friends beyond their closest relations. They just remember the Romani nicknames, which feature only sporadically and imprecisely in official records. Data on individual persons may thus be linked only after careful consideration of all the information and continual comparison with the genealogical diagram, an essential working tool.

Another variable that complicates the historical analysis of documents and the ascribing of data to individuals or families is the fact that some Roms who moved across various localities would occasionally use false names. This is something that the historian Pavel Baloun came across in his research, finding that the police, when arresting "gypsies", would continually complain about the use of false names by these persons to mask their identity. Baloun interpreted the use of false names by Roms as creating a certain manoeuvring space in order to avoid persecution by local authorities.[64] Some Romani witnesses confirmed that giving bogus names was common practice among their Romani forebears, for example the Lovara Mária Lakatošová (*1951)[65] or, in detail, Tony Lagryn from a Sinti family in an interview for *Romano džaniben*.[66]

As an example of the considerable administrative confusion surrounding a certain person, connected with such deliberate mystification and the giving of various names, I shall use Grófa Stojková from the Stojka family researched here, the youngest daughter of Zaga Stojková. Various personal details appear in official records pertaining to Grófa from childhood onwards, and this continued until she obtained her first

---

63 Personal recording with "Báno" Bihary (1958) recorded by Pavel Kubaník on 3. 10. 2008 in Roudnice nad Labem, Czech Republic.

64 Baloun, *"Metla našeho venkova"*, 50.

65 Personal recording by the author with Mária Lakatošová (1951), recorded in Pečky on 24. 4. 2018.

66 Jana Horváthová, "Rozhovor s Tony Lagrynem: Já už dneska se nedívám, kdo co jí, ale kdo jakej je, to mě život naučil. Životní příběh Tonyho Lagryna," *Romano džaniben*, vol. 20, no. 1 (Summer 2012): 105–139.

identity card in 1959 after the registration of "travelling persons" under Act no. 74/1958 by the local administration (MNV) in Louny. On that occasion she was ascribed a birthdate of March 1924 and her birthplace was given as Louny, where she had definitely not been born.[67] In the official records, Grófa first appears under the name Grófojka (a Romani diminutive of the name Grófa) on a list of "gypsies" camping in Mnichovice, then part of Říčany district, in the year 1931. Next to her name the age of eight years was listed, corresponding to a birthdate in 1923.[68] During the war, in 1942, Grófa was recorded in Trenčianska Teplá with her date of birth and birthplace given as 1923, Veľké Topoľčany. In the postwar period she suddenly appears in official records under the name Zaga Fatona/Fatonová, which was a combination of her mother's first name and the (clearly mangled) surname of her father.[69] The authorities' confusion regarding Grófa Stojková's identity is also shown by a record from the district administration (ONV) in Litovel dating from July 1953 that deals intensively with the identity of a person who used, alternately, the name Grófa Stojková, Pinka Stojková, Helena Kudriková and Helena Lakatošová, née Stojková. The authorities finally declared her correct name to be the last one stated, Helena Lakatošová, and her correct date of birth to be May 1927.[70] However, going by the names of this person's children, which correspond exactly to other data, this was in fact Grófa Stojková. The name Grófa Stojková also appears on the register in Louny from January 1959, where her date of birth is given as July 1923 and her birthplace as Trenčianska Teplá. However, the birth date of March 1924 that was decided on by the authorities and inscribed in her identity card in 1959 in Louny is definitely not correct, because it

---

67 The practice of the local administrations in the period after the register was, however, to give people whose birthplace was unclear an officially-designated birthplace, so that the place of birth would be the same as the place of registering. The same practice is described in his application for a certificate under law 255/1946 by J. R., born in January 1943 in southern Slovakia, who was officially designated as having been born in Nová Paka, in the Jičín district of eastern Bohemia, which was also the place that he was registered in 1959. Source VÚA-VHA Praha, f. Sbírka osobních spisů žadatelů o vydání osvědčení podle zákona č. 255/1946 Sb., personal file of applicant J. R. (1943).

68 SOkA Přemyšlení. OU Říčany, i. č. 427, ev. č. 246 – Výkaz cikánů potulných přistižených v roce 1931 četnickou stanicí v Mnichovicích.

69 The right spelling was Facuna. ŠA Trenčín, f. ObNÚ Trenč. Teplá, i. č. 99, k. 23 – Evidencia cigáňov 1942.

70 The record states that the supply of names meant that she could not be found by the security bodies all over the state. ZA v Opavě – pobočka Olomouc, f. KNV Olomouc, Národnostní politika sign. 608, i. č. 1745, k. 1029, 1951–1958. (Here fol. 649 – Úprava poměrů osob cikánského původu – zpráva za 1. pololetí 1953, zn. III-215–30/6–1953/kr. (1. 7. 1953).

is just a week before the birthdate of her brother Josef (Jouško), who in fact was a year younger than her.

Anonymisation and research ethics

My study includes research into various periods of history for which there are different limitations on the use of personal data. From the perspective of research ethics, it is a challenge that the research focus falls into the fields of both historical research and social science (above all, social anthropology and ethnology). It was necessary, therefore, right from the initial phase of analysing the data and writing this book to balance the different approaches taken by historians and social scientists toward anonymising names and the personal data not just of respondents, but of the people whose names I had identified mostly from archival research. In Romani studies, in the field of social and cultural anthropology, it is customary to anonymise names and localities in view of the potential consequences for respondents arising from interpretations of the research findings. From the historical research perspective, however, anonymisation is a more complicated step that prevents the further verifying of sources, mainly archival ones.[71] A further aspect of historical research is its emphasis on enabling scholars to build on previously researched and published data that they expand further through their own exploration. I thus have an obligation not just to previous researchers, but to contemporary and future ones, as well as to the descendants of the families who worked with me,[72] who will potentially have an interest in the lives of their predecessors. On the other hand, from the social sciences research perspective, a certain degree of anonymisation is essential in working with living respondents, since such research publishes sensitive personal data, including data on their ethnic identity and other sensitive matters which could have an unfavourable impact on these living persons.

I therefore decided on a compromise that balances the approaches of both academic disciplines. In the historical research, I give entire, non-anonymised names (i.e., the whole first names and surnames, plus nicknames, if I know them) of people who are already dead. Since personal data is legally protected for 100 years from birth,[73] this chiefly

---

71   Baloun, *"Metla našeho venkova"*, 40.

72   Viková, *"Dlouhá cesta"*, 54.

73   Tlamsová, *Lexikon*, 11.

concerns those who were born over 100 years ago, i.e., persons born up until the middle of the 1920s. In the case of people born more recently who were active from approximately the postwar period, I decided to use – with the exception of people from whom I have personal consent to do otherwise – just their Romani nicknames, if I have them, or the initial of the first name accompanied by the surname (e.g., R. Stojková). This is because to use both initials (e.g., R. S.) would make no sense in the case of the Stojka family, as it is obvious that the final initial S. is a shortening of the surname Stojka/Stojková. The Romani name (nickname), on the other hand, is almost unknown to outsiders, and thus guarantees a level of anonymity for the outer world while providing "full data", allowing rapid identification, for members of the narrator's family or of the local Vlax community. Moreover, Romani names (*romane ánava*) are not unique and are repeated with a frequency similar to the repetition of common first names, and so they also guarantee anonymity for the persons described somewhat. I also use the Romani nicknames of living persons only with their full agreement.

In this way I anonymise the names of my respondents who are connected to the Stojka family and with whom I recorded more extensive memories. I give the full names of other Lovara respondents with whom I recorded memories during previous research projects, if they gave me signed consent to the publishing of their names. Some video interviews which I recorded or took part in recording as the questioner have already been published on the website Romea.cz as "The Memory of the Roma"[74] or on the YouTube channel "Vlach Roma Testimony",[75] and these interviewees had given their written consent to such publication. In the case of interviews where I did not secure such consent, I use just their initials.

An exception is the use of a collection for which there are other norms established by its owner concerning the publishing of personal data. In these cases, I proceeded in accordance with the rules established by the owner of the collection. A case in point is the database of personal testimonies of those who in 2001 and 2002 applied for compensation for genocide during the Second World War, which are stored in the archive of the nonprofit organisation Člověk v tísni o.p.s. [People in Need] in the Czech Republic. This is a unique source containing intimate, emotionally-charged, highly sensitive testimonies which need to be handled with great caution. On the basis of an agreement with the organisation's staff,

---

74   Online link: www.pametromu.cz.
75   Full online link: https://www.youtube.com/@vlachromatestimony9781.

I chose to follow the path of thorough anonymisation, using just initials and the year of birth. I also avoid citing the sensitive, intimate parts of these testimonies. Instead, I focus just on describing and reflecting on the sociopolitical context of the events in the municipalities where each Lovara family was domiciled.

To these sources that gives I add one more source of an archival nature: The files on those applying to be issued certificates of participation in the Resistance (as per Act no. 255/1946),[76] which are kept in the Military Central Archives in Prague. I make use of these applicants' statements regarding the events they lived through in the Second World War, focusing on testimonies where they describe themselves as Roms, sometimes as "travelling" Roms, or directly as Vlax Roms (Cz. *olašští Romové*). Given the sensitivity and specific nature of the data, in the case of this source I also thoroughly anonymise the witnesses' personal data, again using just the initials of the witness and maintaining the same ethical approach as in the cases described above.

In addition, I make use in my work of some rather complicated archival sources toward which a specific approach has to be maintained for ethical reasons. One example is the register from the archives of the District Notary Office in Trenčianska Teplá entitled *Evidencia trestaných osob obce Trenčianska Teplá 1933–1949* [Register of convicts from the municipality of Trenčianska Teplá, 1933–1949], which contain all the offences perpetrated by persons domiciled in that municipality that were committed on Czechoslovak territory. I am aware that the use of this source is considerably problematic, since it includes persons from the Stojka family who were found by the courts to have committed various offences, and that by citing from it I may contribute to the stereotyping and criminalisation of (Vlax) Roms. I nevertheless decided to use the source to a limited extent, since I believe it is one of the few sources that

---

76 It was the Romani studies specialists Milada Závodská and Lada Viková who first drew attention to the applications for a certificate under Act no. 255/1946 as a potential archive source for the history of the Roms (Lada Viková and Milada Závodská, "Dokumentace genocidy Romů za 2. světové války v Československu – nálezová zpráva: diskontinuita a kontinuita odhalování historie Romů po roce 1946". *Romano džaniben*, vol. 23, no. 2 (2016): 107–124). I found this a highly valuable source for research in the field of Lovara history. During my research in 2018–2022, I put together a set of 70 applications from people who came from Lovara families. They contained material supporting their application for a certificate that they had been the victims of racial persecution during the war. Just one application was assessed positively, that of a Romani woman from the Topolčany district. The other 69 were rejected. The set also included four applications by people from the family I am following here. I make use of their personal testimonies in the text and quote considerably from them in the chapter on the Second World War.

shows systematically where the Roms became visible to the state authorities. The source is also unique in showing Romani spatial trajectories and the ways in which they were registered at that time by the authorities. It is thus valuable for the localisation of the Stojka family and capturing their ties to the municipality of Trenčianska Teplá.

Other sources that require a sensitive approach are the media articles of the time. I searched for these more as complementary sources of information, using the digital library of the Moravian Provincial Library, above all the Department of Digitalised Newspapers and Periodicals, as well as the digital library in Bratislava. I am aware that media articles focusing on "gypsies" during the period in question are a specific, relatively complicated source involving elements of sensationalism and orientalism. They are also a mirror of the contemporary moral panic in which gypsies are described as the "scourges of the countryside" who are supposedly a "permanent evil", and the "gypsy question" is described as a problem that needs to be solved.[77] For this reason, I use newspaper articles as a source only to a limited extent for dating and localising Lovara families, and I approach the information contained in them critically.

0.4 Theoretical base

Identification of the categories of Lovara in the archival files

In the chapter devoted to methodology, I looked at the possibilities of researching historical records on the mobility and sedentarisation of the Lovara and outlined the limits of this approach.

In recent years, similar issues have been dealt with by a number of researchers in Romani history. As Henriete Asséo found, in the research of Romani history it is often assumed that Roms are internally homogenous and that they are also "other" in terms of European society.[78] On the basis of my long-term research, I consider the internal integrity of the Romani communities living on the territory I study as questionable – indeed, problematic. From the viewpoint of the Roms themselves first and foremost, there were considerable differences and hierarchies between and among these groups. In the various sub-ethnic groups distinguished

---

77 Baloun, *"Cikáni, metla venkova"*, 22.
78 Henriette Asséo, "La Gypsyness une culture de compromis entre l'Art et l'éclectisme savant", in: *Bohémiens und Marginalität/Bohémiens et Marginalité,* ed. by Sidonia Bauer and Pascale Auraix-Jonchière (Berlin: Franck & Timme, 2019).

by these actors, their diversified historical development and socioeconomic strategies can be observed, as well as their linguistic, dialect and cultural differences. Adèle Sutre discusses the various forms of mobility which need to be observed not just as the result of various social and economic activities, but also as an actual modality of anthropological function, displayed in various forms.[79] A more detailed investigation of various Romani families living on the territory in question of the former Czechoslovakia shows that it was this anthropological function that varied from case to case.

I am aware that the state archive records use the external categorisation of "gypsies" in a certain way and that I have to deal with this somehow when working with such material. As a result, I approach the category of Lovara (or Vlax Roms) in an analytical way, and I consider it to be an internal category based chiefly on the perspective of such actors. I try not to generalise or essentialise these ethnic categories, which is sometimes difficult not to do. Still, I am well aware of the fact that these groups' boundaries are socially constructed and that there is a need to avoid possible groupism.[80] I therefore use these group categories in this book chiefly because they are part of how my Romani witnesses identify their social space.

I am also aware that I may be committing various forms of epistemic violence, above all because I am interpreting historical records pertaining to specific families as data on the Lovara.[81] However, I believe that my very reflection on these ethical and methodological dilemmas, in combination with my long-term, in-depth knowledge of the subject, may help to overcome these limits. From this position, I try to use the given category in a certain context while considering how these people were perceived and classified by the state authorities at various levels and what influence this classification had on the course of historical events during the period in question.

---

79 Adèle Sutre, "'They give a history of wandering over the world'. A Romani clan's transnational movement in the early 20th century", *Quaderni Storici*, vol. 49, no. 2 (2014): 472.

80 Rogers Brubaker, "Ethnicity without groups". *European Journal of Sociology/Archives européennes de sociologie*, vol. 43, no. 2 (2002): 163–189 or Rogers Brubaker, "*Neither Individualism nor 'Groupism' A Reply to Craig Calhoun.*" *Ethnicities*, vol. 3, no. 4 (2003): 553–557.

81 Markéta Hajská, "Forced settlement of Vlach Roma in Žatec and Louny in the late 1950's", *Slovensky národopis*, vol. 68, no. 4 (2020): 56–57.

Rethinking the "settled" – "travelling" dichotomy

During my work with various period materials, as well as with the literature focusing on Romani history, I repeatedly came across the widespread use of terms labelling the mobility of Roms as "travelling" versus "settled". The description "travelling" (*kočující*) is used entirely automatically to describe the historical situation of the Lovara in the space of the former Czechoslovakia and influences the understanding of their history. Their itinerancy in the period preceding their forced settlement tends to be stressed as a distinctive characteristic of the group, one that rules out their being "settled" in a locality or region.

Generally speaking, this division of Roms into "settled" and "travelling" is literally inscribed in a whole number of documents and in the way Roms are thought about. In the former Czechoslovakia, a contrast tends to be drawn between "settled" Roms, typically represented by what are known as Slovak Roms, and "travelling" Roms, who are supposed to be most typically represented by Vlax Roms, plus further "travelling" groups. These attributes are often used automatically, without an attempt by the authors to explain more closely or redefine the concepts and also without critical reflection on how this division is connected with historical reality or with specific findings concerning the Romani communities in question.[82] This division was used consistently as early as the pan-Hungarian register of "gypsies" from the year 1893, in which they were classified as "settled", "temporarily settled" and "travelling" ("nomadic").[83] Of the 36,000 Roms on the territory of what is now present-day Slovakia, the register recorded, according to Horváthová, 2,000 "temporarily settled" and 600 "travelling" Roms.[84] Similar divisions of Roms according to the degree of "itinerancy" and "sedentariness" can also be found in the work of several researchers who write about Roms, not just Czech and Slovak researchers,[85] but also researchers in other

---

82 Hajská, "'Polokočovníci'," 9–11.
83 Horváthová, *Cigáni na Slovensku,* 137–138.
84 Ibid., 137–138. Other authors draw attention to the higher estimates of Hungarian authors compared to the data published by E. Horváthová, such as Roman Džambazovič, "Rómovia v Uhorsku koncom 19. storočia (Výsledky Súpisu Rómov z roku 1893)", *Sociológia,* vol. 33, no. 5 (2001): 491–506 and Anna Jurová, "Niektoré aspekty súpisu kočujúcich a polokočujúcich osôb v roku 1959". *Romano džaniben,* vol. 16, no. 1 (Summer 2009): 29. The overall number of Roms in Hungary was estimated by the register at 280,000, with the largest number (160,000) on the territory of Transylvania (Ibid., 30).
85 Čajánková, *Život a kultura*; Davidová, *Bez kolíb*; Davidová, *Romano drom*; Eva Davidová, *Poválečný život a osudy Romů v letech 1945–1989*, Černobílý život, ed. By Z. Jařabová 67–78.

countries.[86] I sometimes find the term "nomads" in this context, which can be seen as even more burdened by orientalism. In Czechoslovak legislation, the division of Roms into "settled", "semi-travelling" and "travelling" was established in connection with the drafting of the 1958 law on the permanent settlement of "travelling persons". The division into the three categories mentioned above also took hold in the period after the register was established, a time when officially nobody could be a "travelling" Rom any more. These terms should be perceived as burdened considerably by their previous usage and the political goals[87] they served, and for this reason their use is problematic. I shall therefore use them further in this work just when directly citing or referencing period materials, and if I use them outside of direct citations, I shall always put them in quotation marks in order to express my distance from them.

The need to redefine the established dichotomy "travelling/settled" was formulated by social anthropologist Martin Fotta in his study of the spatial strategies of the Brazilian Calon, in which he highlights several critical points concerning these categories. He says the dichotomy simplifies the relationship between the past (which is thought of as "travelling") and the present by reducing the past to an idealised, neutral point of comparison. This dichotomy is founded on discontinuous observations of the external displays of spatiality (living in a wagon or caravan vs. living in a house), despite the fact that there is ample historical evidence for a high degree of porousness between "itinerancy" and "sedentariness" such that this dichotomy can no longer be maintained.[88] In his study, Fotta traced the relationship of Roms toward place, time and the method of inhabiting a space, and also toward mobility. These

---

(Praha: Gallery, 2000); Horváthová, *Cigáni na Slovensku*; Jana Horváthová, *Kapitoly z dějin Romů* (Praha: Člověk v tísni, 2002); Anna Tkáčová, "Rómovia v období od vlády Marie Terézie po vznik I. ČSR", *Čačipen pal o Roma. A Global Report on Roma in Slovakia,* ed. Michal Vašečka (Bratislava: Inštitút pre veřejné otázky, 2003); Šusterová, *Život olašských žien*, etc.

86 Marushiakova and Popov, "Segmentation vs. consolidation"; Will Guy, "The Czech lands and Slovakia: Another false dawn?", *Between Past and Future: The Roma of Central and Eastern Europe,* ed. Will Guy (Hatfield: University of Hertfordshire Press, 2001); Jean-Pierre Liégeois, *Roma in Europe* (Strasbourg: Council of Europe, 2007) and a number of others.

87 An explanation of these concepts is provided by Sus, who authored a quasi-expert justification for the law on the permanent settlement of "travelling persons" and implementing an assimilatory policy towards Roms (Jaroslav Sus, *Cikánská otázka v ČSSR* (Praha: Státní nakladatelství politické literatury, 1961): 18–19, as well as, for example, Josef Nováček, *Cikáni včera, dnes a zítra* (Praha: Socialistická akademie, 1968) and Karel Kára (ed.), *Ke společenské problematice Cikánů v ČSSR* (Praha: Ústav pro filosofii a sociologie ČSAV, 1975).

88 Martin Fotta, "'On ne peut plus parcourir le monde comme avant': au-delà de la dichotomie nomadisme/sédentarité." Brésil(s). *Sciences humaines et sociales*, no. 2 (2012): 13–14.

constants, he believes, are also significantly complemented by the social dimension, created by interaction with other Roms (in Fotta's case the Calons), relationships with people and the complex demands of kinship relations, which each give rise to various causes for mobility, be that a sudden change of place or remaining in a certain place.[89]

I believe Fotta's conclusions may be very usefully applied to describe the situation of the Lovara in the former Czechoslovakia. On the basis of my own research, I entirely agree with the suggested incorporation of social relationships as a dimension in research into spatial mobility. However, the problem of historical studies is that there is often no access to the actors' own explanations of the above-mentioned dimension of their social interactions, which may have had a fundamental influence on all possible modes of their mobility (or decisions to remain in one place) which I describe in this book. The state records contain just brief statements which reveal nothing, recording external displays of mobility only and their dates and localisations, whether short-term (in the case of camping, staying overnight and living in a wagon or caravan) or long-term (in the sense of living in a house or other dwelling place).

In the rest of this book, especially in the chapter devoted to the interwar period, I propose not to make a division between displays of "itinerancy" and "sedentariness", but to describe and analyse modes of spatial mobility on the one hand and links to a specific place or region on the other. Territorial ties are something which I perceive as a specific form of spatial belonging, meaning the place from which the Lovara would set out on their trading journeys and to which they returned. If the family was also domiciled in that municipality, then under certain circumstances its members could even be returned there against their will by state bodies.

Place as a category in creating the complex identity of Roms in connection with their situation in the social hierarchy is a current subject of anthropological research. The anthropologist Aspasia Theodosiou, who performed research in Greek border areas, has looked at the connections between the category of place and the identity of the Roms and reached the conclusion that belonging to a certain place was of key importance for the self-identification of local Roms. Roms from the area she researched said they belonged to the villages in which they settled after the border was created because earlier they had moved around

---

89 Ibid., 26–27.

and traded in the area around those villages.[90] Ethnographic research concerning Roms who lived for generations in the Slovak countryside shows varying ways in which the category of place is connected with a certain social status and how it plays a part not just in understanding the position of Roms in local socioeconomic hierarchies, but also in the structuring of relationships between the Roms themselves.[91] It was from this category in the past that all individuals drew their identity in local societies, which had a fundamental influence on their belonging and overall on the position of Roms in local socioeconomic hierarchies, above all in rural environments.

However, the question of belonging to a place is much more complicated in the case of those Roms who in the historical and ethnographic literature are standardly perceived as "travelling". When it comes to the Roms seen as "travelling" the patterns of their local socioeconomic networks may follow, to a certain extent, patterns similar to the Roms seen as "settled". Despite the received notion of the Lovara as typical representatives of "travelling" Roms who are seen as having no spatial ties, when researching their history it is possible to find examples of long-term spatial links to specific locations, as well as their belonging to certain places. It is a challenge to focus on how the Lovara themselves related to the spaces through which they moved, how they described their spatial mobility, and what reason they gave for it.

My first research investigating the question of Lovara territorial ties in connection with their concurrent ongoing territorial mobility concerned a group that had settled in eastern Slovakia in the second half of the 19th century in a village that I call "Borovany".[92] In 1918, seven Roms bought some land there outside the municipality on which, over the next few years, a Romani settlement developed. By the time of the Second World War it had several dozen wooden houses and a few hundred in-

---

90 Aspasia Theodosiou, 'Be-longing' in a 'doubly occupied place': The Parakalamos Gypsy musicians case. *Romani Studies*, vol. 14, no. 1 (December 2004): 25–58.

91 Jan Ort, "Romové jako místní obyvatelé? Přináležení, cikánství a politika prostoru ve vesnici na východním Slovensku." *Sociologický časopis / Czech Sociological Review*, vol. 57, no. 5 (2021): 3–4.

92 In the case of the municipality that I call Borovany, I am giving an anonymised name, unlike the other real names. The decision to use the made-up name "Borovany" was made because previous works with a socioanthropological and sociolinguistic orientation contained sensitive information on the members of this community. In order to maintain continuity, I also used the anonymised name of this municipality in other work, including this book, where I just mention this municipality briefly. I am aware of the limitations that come from the use of anonymisation in historical texts, but I do so in order to protect my respondents, who wished to remain anonymous.

habitants.[93] In its day it was probably the largest Lovara community in Slovakia to be territorially connected to a concrete municipality. During my attempt to reconstruct, on the basis of witness statements and archival findings, the spatial trajectories of the "Borovany" Roms, I reached the conclusion that their spatial mobility was various in its forms and geographical scope depending on a family's social status. While some families created and maintained longer circuits of travel in the interwar period, crossing the borders of Czechoslovakia and the internal border between the Czech lands and Slovakia, other families moved in medium circuits around neighbouring districts, while those lowest on the social scale only maintained short circuits in their immediate vicinity. These routes could change gradually over time, depending on the circumstances. At the same time, until the borders were closed in 1939, "Borovany" was an important (and probably also a regular) stopping place on the routes of other Vlax Roms from Poland, Ukraine, Russia, Romania and Hungary. They headed that way clearly – although not solely – for marriage exchanges, and their arrivals strengthened the image of the intensive mobility of the "Borovany" Lovara in the eyes of the surrounding community.[94] I thus proposed various concurrently-appearing forms of itineration accompanied by a process of gradual or repeated sedentarisation in the municipality.

In my current research, I have tried to build on these previous conclusions while ascertaining whether they are also relevant for the culturally and historically different Lovara living in the south and southwest of Slovakia. My previous research forced me to include among my essential research questions the investigation of the ways in which spatial mobility is described from the actors' perspectives, from the perspective of the Roms who themselves spent their lives or parts of their lives "on the road".

---

93 It is possible to gain just a rough idea of Romani numbers in "Borovany" in the pre-war period on the basis of witnesses' fragmentary memories, complemented by genealogical maps. According to Josef Kolářik-Fintický's First Republic-era photographs, the local Romani settlement at that time consisted of approximately 20–30 houses, and I estimate there could have been 200–300 Roms there. On a list of the "gypsy" numbers from 1942 sent to the regional office in Prešov, a total of 176 Roms was listed for this village (ŠA Prešov, bad. Nižná Šebastová, ŠŽŽ – prezidiálne r. 1944, k. 2846, krab. 78, č. j. 3844/42 z 8. 9. 1942 – výkaz o počtu cikánů). It is highly likely that in the interwar period the number of Lovara Roms there was even higher since, as I discovered, some of them did not return to the village after the start of the war (for more see Hajská, "'Polokočovníci'").

94 Ibid., 33.

Approaches and policies regulating the mobility of Roms

A negative phenomenon that encumbers the idea of the "travelling" past of the Roms is their "nomadisation", in other words, the idea that all Roms share a common "travelling" past. This notion persisted until recently and is viewed as an essential characteristic of all Romani groups without exception. Roms are often considered to be travelling people without roots who do not belong to Europe or any nation-states there because of their supposed homeland in India and their alleged characteristic of being a "people without history".[95] Even in countries where Roms have been settled for years, Roms were – indeed, still are – generally perceived as the descendants of former "nomads".[96] From the historical point of view, however, most Eastern and Central European Roms have lived settled lives since the 18th century or even earlier. This is true of today's Slovakia, where Romani families can be shown to have lived in particular municipalities in the 17th century and maybe even earlier. Although the number of Roms without spatial ties was in fact small, they were long stigmatised because of their allegedly hard-to-govern mobility, repeatedly becoming the subject of state attempts to regulate their travelling and sedentarise them.[97] As this book demonstrates below, across historical periods there are two types of policy being carried out simultaneously: Attempts by local self-governments to ensure that Roms move out of their localities as soon as possible and to prevent them from settling there, versus the state's policy of trying to limit or stop Romani mobility, with these policies often at odds with each other.

Nevertheless, the mobility of some Romani families or whole communities should be regarded as a historical fact. Movement over a certain area was essential in order to carry out various professions and also involved other specific anthropological functions. For this reason, I made

---

95 Hugo van Baar, "The Perpetual Mobile Machine of Forced Mobility: Europe's Roma and the Institutionalization of Rootlessness", *The Irregularization of Migration in Contemporary Europe: Deportation, Detention, Drowning*. Ed. Yolande Jansen, Joost de Bloois, and Robin Celikates, (London / New York: Rowman & Littlefield, 2015), 4.

96 Can Yıldız, Nicholas De Genova. "Un/Free mobility: Roma migrants in the European Union". *Social Identities*, vol. 24, no. 4 (2017): 425–441; Hugo van Baar, "Europe's Romaphobia: problematization, securitization, nomadization". *Environment and Planning D: Society and Space*, vol. 29, no. 2 (2011): 203–212; van Baar, "The Perpetual Mobile Machine"; Will Guy, "Ways of looking at Roma: the case of Czechoslovakia", *Gypsies: A Book of Interdisciplinary Readings*, Ed. Diane Tong (New York: Garland, 1998).

97 Tara Zahra, "Condemned to Rootlessness and Unable to Budge": Roma, Migration Panics, and Internment in the Habsburg Empire, *American Historical Review*, vol. 122, no. 3 (2017): 2.

it my goal to ascertain in what ways some of those who had lived on the road in the past reflected on and explained their spatial mobility. These were Lovara from the area of the former Czechoslovakia, from families who had earned their living through horse trading, cleaning kettles, sharpening knives, "travelling" blacksmithery and other activities officially labelled at the time as "travelling professions".

In addition to the "nomadisation" of Roms, in various countries and at various times in history there have also been continual, restrictive measures against "nomadism" and "the travelling way of life",[98] such as various kinds of deportation, expulsion, being moved on and other forms of forced mobility, as well as arrests, raids, ethnic profiling and surveillance.[99] Consistent testimonies regarding all these forms of repression are given by Lovara witnesses from the area of the former Czechoslovakia. They encountered fingerprinting and the need to register with state authorities; continual ejection and expulsion, especially during the First Republic; displacement and limitations on their mobility during the Second World War in Slovakia; constant police raids during which their movable property was taken from them (gold and silver jewellery was confiscated); and attempts to limit their mobility by seizing their means of transport (horses and carts), especially in the postwar period. Roms have been perceived by politicians and journalists in the framework of the antisocial behaviour discourse with a direct link from their alleged "nomadism" and their ethnicity to crime and antisocial behaviour.[100] This is also true of the former Czechoslovakia, where there was the generally widespread idea that Roms have in their "blood" an irrepressible tendency towards itinerancy that is closely connected with asocial behaviour and poses a security threat.[101]

---

98 Peter Kabachnik and Andrew Ryder, "Nomadism and New Labour: constraining Gypsy and Traveller mobilities in Britain", in: *Romani mobilities in Europe: Multidisciplinary perspectives.* University of Oxford: Conference Proceedings (2010): 110–125.

99 Hugo van Baar, "The Perpetual Mobile Machine"; Giovanni Picker, "Nomads' land? Political cultures and nationalist stances vis-à-vis Roma in Italy", in: *Multi-disciplinary perspectives on Romany Studies*, ed. Michael Stewart and Marton Rovid (Budapest: Central European University Press, 2010): 71–86.

100 Colin Clark and Becky Taylor, "Is Nomadism the Problem? The Social Construction of Gypsies and Travellers as Perpetrators of Anti-Social Behaviour in Britain", in: *Anti-Social Behaviour in Britain: Victorian and Contemporary Perspectives*, ed. Sarah Pickard (Basingstoke: Palgrave Macmillan, 2014): 166–178.

101 Věra Sokolová, *Cultural Politics of Ethnicity: Discourses on Roma in Communist Czechoslovakia* (Stuttgart: Ibidem-Verlag, 2020), 80.

Old postcard of Trenčianska Teplá showing villagers in traditional local costumes, before 1918.

Part 1:
Before the creation of Czechoslovakia

1.1 Lovara on the territory of present-day Slovakia

Before I start to look at the life stories of the Stojka family, regionally connected with the area of western Slovakia, I consider it important to briefly examine the general situation of the Lovara on the territory of present-day Slovakia during the period in question.

In the introductory chapter, I indicated that it is highly likely that Lovara families were moving around the space of the present-day Slovakia before the mid-19th century, some of them definitely already in the 18th century, and it is not impossible that they were there even earlier.[102] The area was part of Upper Hungary. Roms were allowed to move throughout the entire territory of Hungary, not just in the districts now part of present-day Slovakia. When thinking about their spatial mobility, we need to forget about the borders between the current states, which they often crossed.

Nevertheless, even during this earlier period, it is possible to speak of ties between some Lovara families and certain territories. The baptism records of some families with the surname Stojka show that these families

---

102 I found these records most often in municipalities in what are today the modern-day districts of south and southwest Slovakia, such as Galanta, Levice, Pezinok, Komárno and Nové Zámky. The oldest of them come from approximately the mid-18th century, while I found a greater number of records from the early 19th century. For example, a registry entry from the municipality of Ipeľský Sokolec (earlier Sakáloš) in today's Levice district shows the baptism of Barbora Stojková on 12 January 1757, born to Joannes Stojka and Clara (surname illegible: Batani). The record contains the repeated note *Zingari vatanti* (i.e. "Gypsy vagabonds"). Three days later in the same village there was another baptism of a Romani child, this time a girl, Theresie, to a mother named Catharina Stojka. In her case, too, there is a note saying *Zingari vatanti*.

repeatedly, at intervals of several years, had their children christened in a certain municipality. Since at that time baptism took place just a few days after birth, a practice that is confirmed by the records of particular events I have found, that means these children were born in these specific municipalities. The repeated birth of children from one family in one locality indicates that these families were anchored in these municipalities. One example is a couple named Gorgius Stojka and Barbara Györi, who had five of their children, born between 1791 and 1801, baptised in the municipality of Kálna nad Hronom, Levice district (Andrea in 1791,[103] Francisca in 1793,[104] Joseph in 1795,[105] Theresia in 1797[106] and Georgius in 1801[107]). It is likely that the family spent time in the municipality, repeatedly returned to it or lived there. However, other records show that families with the surname Stojka gradually christened their children in various municipalities. These archival traces are testimony to their spatial mobility. For example, in the case of a record from Číčov, Komárno district from 1797 referring to the son of Rebeka Stojka and Joannes Rafael being baptised with the name Carolus Florianus Rafael, there is a note after their names saying *Zing.Per.* ("travelling gypsies").[108]

In the case of some municipalities, I managed to connect their registry records with other documents found in the Slovak archives to create a more comprehensive sample testifying to the continuous territorial link between a Lovara family and a particular municipality. That their generationally-remote ancestors had been present in a municipality was in some cases also stated by Romani witnesses from that locality.

An example of such a municipality where it may be assumed that the ancestors of today's Lovara were present before the mid-19th century is Tekovské Lužany in the Levice district (the Hungarian name of the municipality, used at the time, was *Nagysalló*). Here, in 1791, Mária Rafael

---

103 Slovakia Church and Synagogue Books, 1592–1935, *FamilySearch* (https://www.familysearch.org/ark:/61903/1:1:QVNH-W76R), [cit. 18. 5. 2022]; microfilm number not given.

104 Ibid. (https://www.familysearch.org/ark:/61903/1:1:QVNH-WF5G), [cit. 28. 6. 2022]; microfilm number not given.

105 Ibid. (https://www.familysearch.org/ark:/61903/1:1:QVNH-W7LP), [cit. 18. 5. 2022]; microfilm number not given

106 Ibid. (https://www.familysearch.org/ark:/61903/1:1:QVNH-4SMK), [cit. 18. 5. 2022]; microfilm number not given

107 Ibid. (https://www.familysearch.org/ark:/61903/1:1:QVNH-W5G1), [cit. 28. 6. 2022]; microfilm number not given.

108 Ibid. (https://www.familysearch.org/ark:/61903/1:1:QVNH-63PN), [cit. 18. 5. 2022]; microfilm number not given.

(parents Josephus Rafael and Rosa Lakatos, with the note *Zingari vagi*.)[109] was baptised. I also found the surname Rafael in the municipal registers with the baptism of Teresie Rafael in 1777, but with no further notes. Over the course of the 18th and 19th centuries, several children with the typical Lovara surnames Rafael or Banda were also baptised here.

Although there are records proving the ancestors of the present-day Lovara were present on the territory of present-day Slovakia before the years 1855–1856, in the second half of the 19th century there is a sharp increase in the number of records in the register books connected with the above-mentioned surnames, which may indicate the arrival of more such families into Upper Hungary. Still, although some records indicate that these families were geographically anchored in certain municipalities, others show indirectly that the Romani families were just travelling through the municipalities in question. At this time there is also an increase in records with notes stating that these are "travelling" or indeed "Wallachian" Roms. For example, the record in the registry book for Dojč in the Senice district concerning the baptism of Martin Stojka on 9 December 1856[110] describes the family as "migrating": "[This] descendant [was born] when migrating gypsies were passing through with a tent."[111] Martinius Stojka was in fact born in a house in the above-named municipality – "under house no. 13" – (*sub tero domus 13*), so the note is clearly meant to explain that the family did not belong to the house and did not have ties to the municipality. They were being provided with shelter during the birth, but otherwise clearly slept in a tent.

1.2 Lovara in the Czech lands before the creation of Czechoslovakia

As on the territory of present-day Slovakia, the Lovara moved around the Czech lands before the creation of Czechoslovakia. However, for the most part these were different Lovara families who belonged to the Cisleithanian part of the Austro-Hungarian Empire and came to the Czech lands from other parts of Cisleithania. Roms belonging to the area of

---

109 Ibid. (https://www.familysearch.org/ark:/61903/1:1:QVNX-37TS), [cit. 28. 6. 2022]; microfilm number not given.

110 Father Josephus Stojka, mother Catharina Lakatoš. Ibid. (https://www.familysearch.org/ark:/61903/1:1:V1HG-TG3), [cit. 28. 6. 2022]. FHL microfilm 1,479,038.

111 Latin: "Occasione transennae tormae/turmae Migrantium Zingaror in tentorio progenitus". Ibid.

present-day Slovakia and other parts of what was then Hungary, which at the time was also part of Transleithania, made their way to the Czech lands only to a limited extent. The division of the monarchy into two relatively autonomous parts after the Austro-Hungarian Compromise of 1867 made itself felt significantly in the two parts' attitudes towards Roms. In Cisleithania the treatment of "gypsies" by the state and security forces at that time was underpinned legally by the decree on "the abatement of the gypsy nuisance" issued by the Cisleithanian Interior Ministry on 14 September 1888, which summed up the existing measures concerning vagrancy, begging, coercive workhouses and other measures against "gypsies".[112] The decree also allowed measures to be taken against what were called "foreign gypsies", a term that included "gypsies" from the other part of the monarchy. As "bothersome foreigners", they were to be "completely prevented from entering Cisleithania" and not allowed to become domiciled there.[113] The fact that this decree was still valid during the first few years of independent Czechoslovakia may well account for the conclusions of my own archival research in the Bohemian and Moravian archives, which shows that until approximately the mid-1920s, the Lovara came to the Czech lands from Slovakia only exceptionally, despite the fact that legally speaking they were no longer "foreign gypsies", although it seems the state authorities still had a tendency to view them as such. Even after the creation of the new southern Czechoslovak border with Austria, the trend continued for Lovara to come from areas belonging to the former geographical area of Cisleithania.

However, let us now go back several decades to the period preceding the creation of Czechoslovakia. No historian has yet looked at the question of to what period the coming of Lovara to the Czech lands can be dated. Only from the end of the 19th century on was I able to find sporadic records in regional archives and in digitalised sources[114] testifying to the presence of individual Lovara families on this territory, and in the first decades of the 20th century such records are also few and far between. It is not impossible, however, that individual members or whole families

---

112 Ctibor Nečas, *Romové na Moravě a ve Slezsku (1740–1945)* (Brno: Matice moravská, 2005), 49–50.

113 Baloun, *"Metla našeho venkova"*, 49.

114 These are chiefly digitalised media reports and printed materials. Registers of births, marriages and deaths in which persons living on the territory of Bohemia and Moravia during that period might be looked up by surname were not available online when this book was being written, nor did I manage to find any such registers in the state archives in the Czech Republic.

from this group may have been moving around the territory of Bohemia and Moravia much earlier.

One of the sources – however problematic and insufficiently objective – providing information on the presence of Lovara on the territory of the Czech lands is the digitalised media reports from the Czech lands. The periodical *Národní politika* devoted itself repeatedly to "hordes of vagabond gypsies" with the surname Stojka in the 1890s and their movements around a strip of land stretching from Lower Austria, including Vienna, to the territory of South Bohemia. In December 1898, *Národní politika* mentions the case of Anna Stojková, known as Perala, and her husband, Josef Horváth, providing a highly exoticising description of their group:

> Thirteen adults and as many children formed a horde that was headed by a swarthy, hairy chap named Jan Stojka. The wagons had barely come to a halt when seven women left the hurriedly-pitched "camp" and set off into the town in search of plunder.'[115] The family was apparently arrested several times for vagrancy, was moved on, was said to have repeatedly escaped during these incidents on the territory of what is today Austria and, among other things, was said to have committed criminal offences in the South Bohemian town of Písek, which is interesting with regard to the Lovara presence in the Czech lands.[116]

I managed to find more detailed information on the presence, pre-Czechoslovakia, of the Lovara in the Bohemian capital, Prague. One example is a residency document preserved in the Prague police headquarters' collection of residency documents (*konskripce*) from 1850–1914, issued to a person named František Stojka. According to the document, Stojka was a horse dealer who was born in 1873 in Vienna and registered in December 1913 at house no. 48 in the Prague district of Královské Vinohrady together with his wife and six children.[117] It is worth noting that this address, close to the present-day Vinohrady Hospital, was not a flat as might be expected in a residential area, but a farmstead with the name Horní Stromka. Established in the 18th century on the foundations of a yard from the 16th century, by the 19th century its buildings housed a sugar refinery and classic agricultural facilities such as cowsheds, barns and storehouses, which were said to be already falling into disrepair at

---

115 [author n.a.] "Pro loupežnou vraždu." *Moravská orlice*, vol. 36, no. 287 (18. 12. 1898), 5.
116 Ibid.
117 NA, f. Policejní ředitelství I, konskripce, b. 566, image 223.

the time. [118] The buildings at Horní Stromka could have provided space for stabling horses and keeping a wagon, and it is not out of the realm of possibility that they could also have housed the family described (see Fig. 1).

According to a newspaper report published in 1917 in the paper *Národní listy*,[119] another Romani family lived in the same building at approximately the same time, apparently (according to their surname) also Lovara. The article begins with these words:

> A few years ago the gypsy Jan Schubert[120] settled with his family at Stromky in Královské Vinohrady. He[…] stressed that he was a well-preserved and very wealthy horse dealer. […] Not long ago this gypsy moved to Balabenka in Libeň, where he provided refuge mostly to Hungarian gypsies until the police caught up with him and raided the whole nest.[121]

The report goes on to describe the unscrupulous ways in which Schubert was said to deal in horses. Above all, however, it carries news of an accusation made by the "gypsy" Karel Horwáth from Vienna who accused Schubert of murdering his brother-in-law, Josef Kolumbár, several years earlier. The paper reports that it subsequently came to light that the accused was in fact called Matěj Stojka and also came from Vienna. Stojka, alias Schubert, was taken into custody, the paper says, and the scandal also appeared repeatedly in other periodicals. According to an item in the periodical *Večer* on 15 March 1917[122] the man in question was 52 and was said to have resided in Prague for nine years, at that time in house no. 88 in Balabenka. However, according to another report published in the daily *Venkov* on 21 March 1917,[123] it turned out that Stojka/

---

118 There was a farm of a similar type not far away, known as Dolní Stromka. The buildings were demolished after the Second World War. Odbor památkové péče, památkový fond. Usedlosti na území hlavního města Prahy – informace a fotografie z knihy Pražské usedlosti (URM).

119 [author n.a.] "Tajemství cikánské rodiny Schubertů v Libni." *Národní listy*, vol. 57, no. 73 (16. 3. 1917), 4.

120 I am aware that the surname Schubert (in its Czech form, Šubrt) is not a name typical of Czech Roms (see Jana Horváthová. "Meziválečné zastavení mezi Romy v českých zemích (aneb tušení souvislostí)". *Romano džaniben*, vol. 12, no. 1: 65). As we will see shortly, however, it was very probably a false surname, used by this Austrian Lovara to ensure that he blended in with his surroundings more.

121 [author n.a.] "Tajemství cikánské rodiny Schubertů v Libni." *Národní listy*, vol. 57, no. 73 (16. 3. 1917), 4.

122 [author n.a.] "Po devíti letech zatčen pro zločin zabití." *Večer*, vol. 4, no. 61 (15. 3. 1917), 6.

123 [author n.a.] "K zatčení cikána Josefa Schuberta (Křivě nařčen.)" *Venkov: orgán České strany agrární*, vol. 12, no. 67 (21. 3. 1917), 7.

Schubert had made a false accusation against Karel Horwáth out of a desire for personal revenge, since the allegedly murdered brother-in-law Josef Kolumbár turned up in person in front of the examining judge and provided proof that he was alive and well. The authorities continued to hold Stojka/Schubert in custody, however, so that they could ascertain his true identity.[124]

These media reports, written in the sensationalist style typical of the time, point to several interesting facts. Above all, they locate Schubert/Stojka's family at the address at Stromky. This seems to have been the same farmstead of Horní Stromka, or maybe the neighbouring building, Dolní Stromka, which was similar in character. Both Stojka families earned their livings by horse trading and came from Vienna. Both seem to have resided in Prague long-term. The first family had a residence document and the second had been accommodated in Prague for almost nine years in 1917. The second family were in contact with other Lovara from Vienna, on the basis of information regarding contact with Roms stated as having the surname Horwáth (sometimes written as Horváth or Horvát) and Kolumbár (Kolombár, Kolompár), which in both cases are surnames that appear frequently among not just Austrian Lovara, but also among the Lovara in Upper Hungary at the time. This family also illegally provided accommodation to "Hungarian gypsies", which gave the police a reason to take action. The question remains as to who these Hungarian Roms might have been. Personally, I think they could have been Lovara from the area of present-day Slovakia or from elsewhere in the Hungarian monarchy (probably from present-day Hungary) who were residing – probably illegally, given the Interior Ministry decree of 1888 then in force – on the territory of the Czech lands, in other words, Cisleithenia.

Another case of a horse dealer with the surname Stojka is described in the weekly *Čech: politický týdeník katolický* in July 1917. The report describes the case of an alleged horse theft by the "30-year-old gypsy and knife-sharpener" Petr Stojka of Münchendorf, who had previously long been resident in Vienna and the districts of Lower Austria. According to police, after the theft he hid in the Prague suburb of Vysočany, where he was apprehended.[125] The same weekly repeatedly carried news of other horse traders with the surname Stojka who were originally from Austria and who were said to have sold horses in the Czech lands which had been

---

124 Ibid.
125 [author n.a.] "Ukradl dva páry koní." *Čech: politický týdeník katolický*, vol. 42, no. 190, (14. 7. 1917), 8.

acquired in Austria (in 1917[126] and 1924[127]). Although these were isolated cases, they indicate that the above-named persons with the surname Stojka were horse traders and came to the Czech lands from areas now part of Austria, in other words, over the (future) southern Czech border. There were also more sporadic arrivals via the eastern, Moravian-Slovak border who seem to have been (as follows from the cases cited and from the validity of the 1888 decree) illegal residents hiding from the law.

1.3 The roots of the Stojka family from Trenčianska Teplá

Having provided the necessary historical background, in this chapter I will finally begin to introduce the Stojka family which forms the main focus of this book. As in the case of many other Lovara families living in southwest Slovakia, in the case of this Stojka family it is possible to find a specific municipality of which we could say in lay terms that these Roms have their *roots* there. This municipality is Trenčianska Teplá, now in the district of Trenčín, but during the pre-war period initially belonging to the Ilava district. My witnesses also derive their origins from this municipality and identify it as the place from which their grandparents or great-grandparents came. We can differentiate according to the place of origin between, for example, the Stojkas of Topoľčany or the Stojkas of Trenčianska Teplá.

How far back must we go to determine these local roots, though? How long did our own ancestors have to live in a certain place in order for us to be able to declare that we have "roots" somewhere? These are the questions that surface when we try to find the "roots" of the Stojka family. When exactly the family came to Trenčianska Teplá is not known. We also do not know whether the oldest generation of Roms, about whom I managed to find the oldest records, came there as part of their economic activities and whether Teplá was at first just one of the places they stopped over, or whether they formed more permanent ties in the municipality and regularly returned there. What I can say with certainty is that they managed to acquire the right of domicile in Trenčianska Teplá, apparently in the last decades of the 19th century. This was later passed on to their children and to further generations of their descendants. The question of domicile is one I will look at later in the chapter

---

126 [author n.a.] "Obviněn z vraždy." *Čech: politický týdeník katolický*, vol. 42, no. 73 (16. 3. 1917), 7.

127 [author n.a.] "Krádež koní." *Čech: politický týdeník katolický*, vol. 49, no. 53 (23. 2. 1924), 6.

covering the interwar period. At this point I shall merely indicate that this circumstance became crucial for their returns to the municipality and their remaining there.

The municipality is a fairly populous one, numbering several thousand inhabitants.[128] It lies on the main route leading from Trenčín to Dubnice nad Váhom, Ilava and Považská Bystrica. The road also branches off here in the direction of the spa town Trenčianske Teplice. Both these routes were significant roads even in the 19th century and both had railways along them, although in the case of the Trenčianske Teplice spa it was just a narrow-gauge train for visitors.

The oldest record of a stay by the Stojka family in Trenčianska Teplá that I have managed to find is from 1875, when Mária Stojková, daughter of Peter and Agnesa Stojka, was born here. Although I do not know from where Peter and Agnesa Stojka came to Trenčianska Teplá, or where they themselves were born, or whether they stayed in the municipality, they may be considered the founding couple of the community I am following. This is because also two of their children were later born in Trenčianska Teplá: Zaga (1887) and Štefan (1891).[129] In the official records kept by the local notary's office, as well as in other official records, all three listed the municipality of Trenčianska Teplá not just as their place of birth, but also as their place of domicile. The interwar records include requests from Štefan Stojka or his son Ján Stojka for the issuing of domicile documents, which were then issued. The right of domicile here was also held by their children's children, with the exception of Zaga's children, who were domiciled in the smaller neighbouring municipality of Dobrá. That is where Zaga's partner, the children's father, was born. I shall look at these circumstances in more detail below.

I was unable to find any other records on the Stojka family from the end of the 19th century other than the birthdates and names of their parents. I thus do not know what the parents of these three siblings,

---

128 In 1900 the municipality had a total of 1,846 inhabitants and by 1910 already 2,294 (Jozef Karlík. *Trenčianská Teplá*. Zvolen: Slovakiaprint, 1990: 50). According to census reports, in 1930 it had 3,446 inhabitants and 420 house numbers, in 1940, 3,560 inhabitants and 836 dwelling places (ŠA Trenčín, f. ObNU Trenč. Teplá, ev. č. 4311/36a, Sčítanie ľudu 1936 a ev. č. 6692/940 Sčítanie ľudu 1940). In the post-war period the number of inhabitants continued to grow.

129 The parish register record from Trenčianska Teplá for the baptism of Štefan Stojka on 11 February 1891 lists just his mother under the name Catharina Stojka with the note *Zingara vagabunda*. Other records in the municipal archives give the name of his mother as Agnesa Stojka and his father as Peter Stojka. Slovakia Church and Synagogue Books, 1592–1935, *FamilySearch* (https://familysearch.org/ark:/61903/1:1:V1C3–5RT), [cit. 18. 7. 2020]; FHL microfilm 2,428,024.

Agnesa and Peter Stojka did for a living, nor do I know how large their family was at that time. It may be assumed that they had other children[130] and that other relatives also lived with them. On the basis of the assumption that professions are passed down through the generations from father to son, it may be conjectured that they were horse traders, carrying on a profession that was the Lovara's traditional livelihood and was later the profession of the descendants of this couple in the male line, i.e., Štefan Stojka and his oldest son Ján, as well as his sister Zaga's oldest son, named Filo.

Mária Stojková (*1875)

As I have just indicated, I have the least information on the eldest sister of these three siblings, named Mária. I shall therefore deal with her only in passing. In 1899, she gave birth in Trenčianska Teplá to a daughter, Karolína, whose father was not officially recorded. There are no more records on the births of further children to her or on her relationship with a partner, although this does not rule out those possibilities. According to the records in the municipal register, Mária had the Romani nickname Maryša, a typical diminutive of the name Mária. The officials list her in the records as a "travelling gypsy", with notes also appearing of the type: "gypsy without employment", "vagabond", "beggar and vagabond", "gypsy beggar".[131] Indeed, it was for begging and vagrancy that she was arrested several times in the Trenčín district, with the district of Ilava listed once too, and sentenced to one to three days in jail, and it was for this reason that she was also listed in the book of criminal offences committed by those domiciled in the municipality. In these records her name, date of birth and domicile in Trenčianska Teplá is always given, and her residence is mostly also given as in Trenčianska Teplá, although sometimes there is a record stating: residence *unstable*. Mária was also included on the list of "Gypsies" present in the municipality in 1939 and again in 1942, when she was listed as living together with the family of her younger sister, Zaga. Since I unfortunately have no more information on her in later periods, I will not concern myself with her separately.

---

130 Amateur photographer Pavol Pytlík form Trenčianska Teplá, who photographed Štefan Stojka's funeral several decades later, said Štefan's younger brother attended the funeral. However, I have not found any information about this person in the archives.

131 ŠA Trenčín, f. ObNÚ Trenč. Teplá, ev. č. 77, k. 19 – Evidencia trestaných občianov obce Trenčianska Teplá 1933–1949.

Unlike Mária, her siblings Zaga and Štefan had numerous offspring who were recorded and, from the authorities' perspective, they each became the head of their branch of the family. These large family units functioned to the end of their lives and will be present with us for a large part of this book.

Štefan Stojka, Sr. (*1891)

I shall now take the liberty of jumping forward through time and starting with a description of Štefan Stojka, Sr.'s appearance from the postwar period as portrayed by the Slovak journalist Kalný. The description is also quite certainly valid for the interwar period in particular, as becomes apparent from his story:

> A portly figure, a barrel stomach, a full beard that would not shame a retired Hungarian policeman, roguishly mocking eyes and thick black stubble evenly spread over his face. He always wore red or brown boots and leather riding breeches, but he was best known for his greasy black-brown-blue broad-brimmed hat, on which a piece of boarskin swung irregularly. On his waistcoat he wore a long, thick, heavy gold chain that was more suited to tying up horses than to holding a watch. And the essential wallet, stuffed full of five-hundred and thousand crown bills, was another identifying characteristic. This was Štefan Stojka, horse merchant.[132]

Of all the Roms, Štefan Stojka, Sr. is without a doubt the person about whom the most detailed and numerous archival records exist, as well as the person who has the closest ties to Trenčianska Teplá. He was born in Trenčianska Teplá in 1891, and there are records of him in the archives throughout all the subsequent decades, right up until 1968, when he died aged 77 and was buried there. Štefan's life is considerably bound up with the municipality, although his spatial mobility during some stages of his life spread in varying degrees over other districts near and far.

From the records in various registers, including those of births, marriages and deaths, Štefan was a horse dealer, and remained one until the end of the 1950s. From the information available it is clear that, com-

---

132 Slavo Kalný, *Cigánsky plač a smiech* (Bratislava: Osveta, 1960): 59. Below I will devote myself in detail to this journalistic source, which describes the life of Štefan Stojka in a sensationalist way. I believe the source does capture Štefan's likeness from the period of the First Republic, when he amassed considerable property (q.v. the thick gold chain and wallet full of money).

pared to other Roms, he enjoyed a special status in the eyes of local non-Roms. Although I cannot today define his social status precisely from the viewpoint of the Romani community, the records made by the local administration over the course of several decades reflect his higher social status compared to other Roms from the viewpoint of the non-Romani community. From various records it can be seen that he was relatively well off, and that as such he was, to a certain extent, respected by the local non-Romani authorities who later, during the Second World War, nominated him for the position of *vajda* (chief), a title by which he was referred to by both Roms and Neroms in the following decades.

In the records connected with him there is never any doubt cast on the fact that he is domiciled in Trenčianska Teplá. While in the case of some Roms the registers state in the column for employment things such as "vagabond" or "gypsy vagabond", Štefan is always listed as a horse dealer or merchant. As I shall show in detail in the following chapters, it was also he who later, in the 1930s, was the first and only Rom to buy a house in the municipality.

Štefan's family life is also interesting. He became a father at the young age of 14, in 1905, when his first-born son Ján Stojka was born. Ján later continued in the family business of horse trading. Like his father, at 14 Ján Stojka also had a son, who received the name Štefan. Štefan Stojka, Senior thus became a grandfather at the age of 28. He then had at least five more children with several partners in succession (he seems to have been twice widowed). His youngest son, who like his first-born son was named Ján, was born in 1953 and was thus two generations younger than his half-brother of the same name. I shall deal with these facts in even greater detail later.

During the first two decades of the 20th century there are relatively few records on Štefan Stojka, Sr. The mother of his first-born Ján is recorded in some places as Mária, elsewhere as Agnes Stojka (the name of the father is always the same). The mother of Iboja, born in 1919, was Karolína, née Lakatošová. She was born in 1902 and was thus just three years older than Štefan's son Ján. It is not clear whether Štefan split up from his first wife or if he was widowed. It is possible that had more children during the time in question who do not figure in the records of the local notary's office. His children mentioned above were born in Trenčianska Teplá and were domiciled there.

To what extent Štefan's family lived in the municipality on a more permanent or regular basis is not clear. I do not even know the place where the family may have dwelt or spent the winters. However, it is clear that during this period they at least used to return there on a regular basis.

Zaga Stojková (*1887)

I also have fairly detailed information from this period on Štefan Stojka Sr.'s older sister, named Zaga Stojková. Although she was born into the Lovara Stojka family, domiciled in Trenčianska Teplá, according to all the records she lived together with a man called Ján Facona,[133] with whom she had at least six children. However, she never married him and thus kept her maiden name of Stojková all her life. Judging by his surname, birthplace and residency, Ján Facona was a non-Vlax Rom (*Rumungro,* or Slovak Rom) from the village of Dobrá near Trenčianska Teplá, about a kilometre away.[134] A Romani family with the surname Facona had been established for generations there,[135] earning a living as day labourers.[136]

From the records of the district notary's office in Trenčianska Teplá it can be seen that at a later period, the Faconas of Dobrá earned their living by trading untanned hides, for which they had a trade licence.[137] In the 1930s, the Facona family lived permanently on the edge of Dobrá in a Romani settlement "in gypsy huts"[138] (see Fig. 2). It may be assumed that they lived similarly during the preceding period. From the Lovara perspective, the fact that Zaga lived with a *Rumungro* may have influenced her lower status including in the eyes of her brother Štefan Stojka

---

133 There is an interesting, gradual switch in the documents from the name Facona to Fatona, which is also a name that some of Zaga's children used to identify themselves – such as in *Súpis Cigánov* (the Gypsy Register) from 1942 compiled by the ONÚ (ŠA Trenčín, f. ObNÚ Trenčianska Teplá, Evidencia cigáňov 1942, ev. č. 99, k. 23, no č. j.).

134 Dobrá was only officially part of Trenčianska Teplá from 1971. Until then it was a separate municipality, although situated nearby. I have not managed to find the birthdate of Ján Facona.

135 In the baptism books we find several birth records for children with the surname Facona from the second half of the 19th century where it is stated that they were "Gypsies" (*Zingara*) living in Dobrá. For example, for the child of Josef Facona, born in 1865, the address is given as Dobrá 26, but in other records only as "Dobrá", with no house number. Slovakia Church and Synagogue Books, 1592–1935, FamilySearch (https://www.familysearch.org/ark:/61903/1:1:V1C3-RQ1), [cit. 18. 5. 2022]; FHL microfilm 2,428,023.

136 ŠA Trenčín, f. ObNÚ Trenčianska Teplá, Evidencia obchodníkov a remeselníkov 1901–1913, kn. 52, f. 167. According to the records from the 1930s onwards the Faconas from Dobrá earned their living by trading raw hides.

137 ŠA Trenčín, f. ObNÚ Trenčianska Teplá, Administratíva, k. 30, Evidencia obchodníkov a remeselníkov v obciach notárstva Trenčianska Teplá 1927–1942.

138 ŠA Trenčín, f. ObNÚ Trenčianska Teplá, Sčítanie ľudu z roku 1930, ev. č. 6009/30. There are four families listed with the surname Facona.

Sr. and his nuclear family. I base this statement on my long-term research into the environment of the Lovara in the Czech lands and Slovakia, during which they have declared repeatedly and clearly that intra-ethnic marriages with non-Vlax Roms were essentially inadmissible for them.[139] The same findings have been made by other researchers.[140] Marriage with a *Rumungro* brought "great shame" to the family in question and could lead to the ultimate punishment, exclusion from the community.[141]

Zaga seems to have lived for the first two decades of the 20th century with her partner, Ján Facona, in the small village of Dobrá near Trenčianska Teplá. It is here that their children appear to have been born, and it is here that official records of the time have them and their children down as domiciled. Here, however, it is necessary to point out that the official records regarding a person with the name of Zaga Stojková gave her domicile alternately as Trenčianska Teplá and Dobrá. Dobrá was even given as Zaga's birthplace in some records, although in others her place of birth was given as Trenčianska Teplá. It is, however, certain that her partner, Ján Facona, was born in Dobrá and that their three eldest children were also born here: Filo (*1907), Minka (*1911) and Barbora (*1914). According to some records[142] their daughter Kuluš was also born here (*1920). Other records locate the birth of Kuluš in Trenčianska Teplá,[143] where her younger siblings were apparently also born (Grófa, seemingly in 1923, and the youngest, Josef, in 1924).

I have not managed to find any records testifying to the spatial mobility of Zaga's nuclear family from this period. It is therefore unclear how the family earned a living during this period, whether its income came entirely from Ján Facona's labour, or whether Zaga too had a share in ensuring their income.

---

139 E.g., Hajská, *"Hranice jazyka"*, 205.
140 Marušiakova, "Rodinný život valašských", Stojka and Pivoň, *Náš život. Amaro trajo.*
141 Personal recording of J. B. (*1934) by the author, made on 12 August 2020 in České Budějovice.
142 For example, ŠA Trenčín, f. ObNÚ Trenč. Teplá, ev. č. 77, k. 19 – Evidencia trestaných občianov obce Trenčinska Teplá 1933–1949.
143 Data given e.g. in the register for February 1959, kept in the SOkA Louny: ONV II Louny, vnitř. 608, k. 332.

◀ Teplická street in Trenčianska Teplá with the single-track pleasure railway. At the end of the street on the left, underneath the stone quarry that can be seen in the background, is where Štefan Stojka had a house built in the interwar period.

Part 2: The Interwar Period

2.1 Lovara territorial anchoring and spatial mobility in Slovakia

Lovara living on the territory of the former Czechoslovakia are often described as "traditionally travelling" people who were not "settled" until the year 1959.[144] The image of Lovara as "nomads" who were not territorially anchored in any way is abundantly reinforced by various media stories. However, this concept is reductionist and imprecise. In this chapter, which focuses on the Stojka family situation in the interwar period, I will continue my search for an answer to the question of the extent to which it is possible to speak of the Lovara living in Slovakia during this period as an example of territorial anchoring at odds with the above-described stereotypical image of them as "travelling".

At this juncture I will turn to the situation of the various Romani families living in the south and the west of Slovakia. I will put forward several case studies concerning various Lovara family histories, people who were territorially connected with specific municipalities or with a certain historical region. Detailed records from the individual municipalities allow us to better investigate the degree and form of territorial anchoring of various Lovara families. Using selected examples, I will try to show the various types of their spatial mobility and point to the need to work in a more nuanced way with the idea of the place to which they belonged. The debate that follows in this chapter will further develop the

---

144 E.g., Davidová, *Cesty Romů*, 96; Nina Pavelčíková, *Romové v českých zemích 1945–1989*. Praha: Úřad dokumentace a vyšetřování zločinů komunismu, 2004.

facts stated above regarding spatial movement and territorial anchoring in the earlier period.

Spatial mobility from the perspective of the actors

People often think that all Vlax Roms used to be travelling. But that's not the case. Even before the war anybody who could, acquired a house. After the war, the only people who were still travelling were the poor people trying to get away from the police who didn't want them anywhere.[145]

This testimony of Viktor Salinas, a Lovara witness born in Dolná Seč, Levice district, contains the witness's subjective opinion that the Lovara who were still "travelling" on the territory of the south and southwest of Slovakia during the interwar period were by then a minority. This statement, which is fully at odds with the ideas of historians and Romani studies scholars regarding the itinerancy of this group during the period in question, forced me to focus on investigating the hypothesis that the Lovara during this period were territorially anchored in certain municipalities. Salinas's statement may be affected by the fact that he himself came from a community in which Roms had built dwellings on the edge of the municipality even before Czechoslovakia declared independence. The situation was similar in other municipalities in Levice district, where a number of Lovara families had created more permanent ties to the region during that time. However, things may have been different in other regions of Slovakia.

In this chapter I shall work with the perspective of Lovara families or communities as captured in the testimonies of witnesses who were small children at the time or who were descendants of these families and shared a narrative regarding "travelling" that had been created in the families and handed down through the generations. Over the course of more than 20 years (2001–2023) I recorded, for various purposes, biographical interviews touching in various ways on the spatial mobility and territorial ties of my respondents' families. As a complement to this, I will once again make use of state records kept in the Slovak archives, which contain various registers from the municipalities in which Lovara families were domiciled.

---

145 Personal recording of Viktor Salinas (*1941) by the author, made on 7 August 2016 in Postoloprty, Czech Republic.

The forms and functions of their mobility differed from family to family, as did their spatial trajectories and the intensity of their life "on the road". These families have various kinds of territorial ties. Their livelihood strategies differed from family to family, which is something I will review at the end of this section. The social status of each family and the wealth that was generated which allowed some Lovara horizontal mobility in the conditions of the Slovak countryside were both related to the variables of their livelihood strategies, mobility and territorial ties. I shall present below examples of municipalities in which the territorial anchoring of Lovara families took place to a certain degree. In the second part of this section, I will look at the Stojka family, with its territorial anchoring in Trenčianska Teplá, building on the findings I have formulated generally on the situation of the Lovara during the period in question.

Domicile

Movement and dwelling is not a constant expression of culture, but is enabled and influenced by non-Romani jurisdiction and territorial divisions.[146] These factors have a significant influence on the limits of and opportunities for Romani mobility. One of the key things to substantiate when tracing the territorial ties of Romani families is where they were domiciled. This was an official relationship, but its actual substance varied from case to case. The right of domicile (or place of domicile) was understood at that time as a legal relationship between an individual and a particular municipality. It did not require actual presence in the municipality in which the person in question was domiciled.[147] The acquisition of domicile was governed by Act no. XVIII of 1871, "on municipalities", by paragraph 6 of Hungarian legal article V/1876, by legal article L/1879, and definitively by Act no. XXII of 1886, "on municipalities". Domicile could be gained automatically through birth, and in the case of women, through marriage, by being accepted into the municipality, by settling there (in the Hungarian part, a stay of three months at least was

---

146 Leonardo Piasere, "Les slovensko roma: entre sédentarité et nomadisme". *Nomadic Peoples*, vol. 21/22 (December 1986): 37–50.

147 Anna Jurová, "Domovské právo vo vzťahu k Rómom v predmníchovskej ČSR", in: *Historický vývoj súkromého práva v Európe: zborník príspevkov z medzinárodnej vedeckej konferencie konanej v dňoch 27.–28. mája 2011 na Právnickej fakulte UPJŠ v Košiciach*, ed. Erik Štenpien (Košice: Právnická fakulta UPJŠ, 2011), 121–144.

required to be domiciled) or through forced inscription.[148] Act no. XXII of 1886, "on municipalities", contained the principle that each citizen of Hungary had to be domiciled in a municipality. It also confirmed the right to social support from municipal assets in the event that somebody became impoverished in his or her municipality of domicile.[149] It is for this reason that municipalities tried to prevent the acceptance of people who were perceived as a burden into the municipality. They attempted to prevent it in various ways, above all by denying domicile to migrants.[150] The problem of failure to grant domicile was of fundamental concern to Roms,[151] but in my archival research I have not managed to discover a single documented case where the failure to grant domicile to a Lovara family was directly mentioned. It was also not mentioned by witnesses, although it must have happened.

It is clear that all the Lovara, as citizens of the state, would have had to be domiciled in a municipality, and the domicile was then, for the most part, passed on to their children. In the chapter on the Second World War, I will show that domicile had a fundamental impact on the situation of Lovara families, when such Roms were suddenly "returned" to the municipalities where they were actually domiciled.

My research in the south and southwest of Slovakia has shown that although the Lovara models of official anchoring and actual anchoring in space varied, the official place of domicile often played a significant role in them. At the same time, it was a variable that said a considerable amount about the situation of a particular family or community in relation to a certain municipality. I shall look at various examples of the way in which spatial mobility was implemented, as described by Lovara narrators, and in these examples I shall focus on the forms in which such domicile was realised.

---

148 Jurová, "Domovské právo", David Scheffel, "Belonging and domesticated ethnicity in Veľký Šariš, Slovakia". *Romani Studies*, vol. 25, no. 2 (2015): 115–149.

149 Gabriela Dudeková, "Právo alebo milosrdenstvo? Domovská príslušnosť ako základný princip sociálnej starostlivosti v Uhorsku", *Sondy do slovenských dejín v dlhom 19. storočí*, ed. Dušan Kováč et al. (Bratislava: Historický ústav SAV, 2013), 203.

150 Ibid., 203; Scheffel, "Belonging", 122–124.

151 Jurová, "Domovské právo".

The "unanchored" as "regionally-anchored"

On the basis of the testimonies of other witnesses, we may have the impression that some families were not territorially anchored during this period in any way, which means that they did not return regularly to a particular municipality, but were permanently "on the road". An example of such a family is described by a witness from Nitra with the Romani nickname "Mala" (*1936).[152] She said that from the interwar period until the 1950s, her family were permanently on the road over an area corresponding approximately to the Nitra district. Her father and other Roms earned a living by making unfired bricks from clay and straw. They moved around the villages where there was an interest in their services. They would camp with their wagons in places close to water, where they then made unfired bricks in moulds, dried them, and sold them. According to this witness, they would stay in one place for a maximum of several months, sometimes less. She recalled that they did not always have a canvas or a tent available to stretch over their temporary wooden dwellings, often making simple roofs from maize stalks covered with straw. The whole family lived in great poverty, she said, without any property at all. However, her testimonies show that they owned the above-mentioned wagons and horses.

The case described by "Mala" represents an absence of territorial ties to a specific municipality. However, the routes that the Roms from her family travelled are connected with the district of Nitra or its close vicinity. Their mobility could thus be described as moving about in search of work to perform locally in the short term. The manufacture of unfired bricks is a profession considered to be a traditional livelihood of the Roms known as "Slovak" Roms. The testimonies show that families of Lovara started to devote themselves to this trade on the basis of demand from local residents, since it was presumed that as "gypsies" they knew how to make such bricks. The same type of work is also described by a witness from a Lovara family with the nickname "Gagarin" whose grandfather is said to have made unfired bricks on the basis of demand from local non-Roms after he settled in the municipality of Trdošovce, Nové Zámky district. However, it seems that this type of work was not totally commonplace among Lovara in the period in question.

---

152 Personal recording by the author with the witness "Mala" (*1936), made on 1 May 2015 in the Orechovo district of Nitra, Slovakia.

The family of Mrs. R. B. (1921) also lived without ties to a particular municipality, earning their livelihood by making copper kettles and tinning. She says the family lived a "travelling life" and "never lived anywhere, they were always on the road".[153] Another witness, "Villo" (1945), states that his family never settled anywhere before the war.

> My dad travelled, he had horses, they didn't have their own houses back then. If the mayor was nice, he would let the Roms camp for several days in the village, but in other places they would drive them away. Back then, Roms used to travel until they were old. They said that if you didn't have horses and a wagon, you weren't even a [Vlax] Rom. That was their life: Horse, wagon and off they'd go to see their family. They'd travel all over the place. In time, the Roms tried to build houses in the villages where they did the best. Some of them managed that.[154]

These two testimonies are a good contribution to the debate on the emic understanding of "travelling" or "being settled." Both witnesses focus on emphasising the lack of belonging to a concrete municipality, which once again does not rule out ties to a certain territory and cultivating a range of customers for their goods and services who clearly lived in various municipalities in the region to which the families cyclically returned. From these statements, it can be seen that the idea of "living/ residing" implies "living in a house", which is considered a feature of being "settled", all the more so because the meaning of the Romani verb *(te) bešel* covers both the meanings *live* and *sit*. The opposite of *living/ residing somewhere* is seen by the narrators as *"travelling"*, which is connected with not owning property and with spatial mobility, and which took place with the aid of horses and wagons. For this reason, when describing their territorial movement in Romani, Lovara witnesses most often use the developed verbal form *te phírel le grastenca, le vurdonenca* (literally: to travel with horses, with wagons). In addition, the witnesses used the loan word *te kočoválij* (from the Czech word *kočovat*, to travel, lead a travelling lifestyle) or another Romani phrase, *te phírel gava* (literally: to travel around villages).

The witness "Villo" Stojka, who was born in 1945 and therefore remembers travelling with wagons as a small child in the postwar era,

---

153 VÚA-VHA Praha, f. Collection of personal files of applicants for certificates under law no. 255/1946 Sb., personal file of applicant R. B. (*1921).

154 Personal recording by the author of the witness named "Villo" (*1945), made on 31 May 2015 in Cabaj Čápor, Nitra district, Slovakia.

spoke of "travelling" with a certain pathos and nostalgia. However, he immediately undermined this impression with the pragmatic statement that the Roms themselves tried to bring an end to this lifeway. According to "Villo" Stojka, the Roms from the period in question tried to acquire houses but were not allowed to by the leadership of the municipality (and further states that they were not allowed to by the local residents, either). I assume this happened not just as a result of the ever-present anti-gypsyism among non-Roms, but also due to their lack of functional relationships with the local residents and the leadership of the municipality.

Another respondent who stated that his family had not been territorially anchored was G. R: (*1936), who said: "We had our Romani camp, which was called Jovanešti. I come from Vlax Roms, and we never had a proper place of permanent residence. We moved around the area of the Lesser Carpathians, Vištuk, Modrá, Pezinok."[155] As can be noticed, in this testimony the witness does not define his home through localization, but defines it socially: He calls his family his home, or rather his family group (the *kranga*, see introduction), called the Jovanešti – not a specific municipality or place. For him, home was connected with the "camp," in other words, living in the form of "camping", which took place in certain localities. The framework once again shows the territorial tie his family had to a certain geographically-defined region. We also came across this definition of "travelling" as a social affair in "Villo"'s testimony, who stressed as an important aspect of spatial mobility "going to see the family", in other words, the strengthening of social ties between Roms across space.

An example of a family which was not anchored to a particular municipality but which was connected with a certain region (on the boundaries of Nitra and Nové Zámky) is in the testimony of a Romani woman with the nickname "Ďivoj" (*1946). She says the family was very poor and the mother earned her living by telling fortunes from cards and begging. "They slept in wagons or shacks made out of tents and wagons. They never lived anywhere permanently, they travelled around villages such as Velký Cetín, Vinodol, Nesvady, Hurbanovo, around Nové Zámky."[156]

Among the Roms who remembered the interwar period or who were capable of reproducing the narratives of their parents and grandparents regarding life during that time, some talked about a "travelling life"

---

155 VÚA-VHA Praha, f. Sbírka osobních spisů žadatelů o vydání osvědčení podle zákona č. 255/1946 Sb., personal file of applicant G. R. (*1936).

156 Personal recording by the author of the witness named "Ďivoj" (*1946), made on 31 May 2015 in Cabaj-Čápor, Nitra district, Slovakia.

without the creation of ties to a particular municipality, but they were distinctly in the minority. However, even in their cases it is possible to discern a connection with the particular region around which they moved, although this area might have changed over time.

This lack of territorial anchoring and intensive spatial mobility has also left its traces in archival documents, most frequently apparent when different places of birth are given for the children of one family, indicating that each child was born in a different municipality. This is often accompanied by an official description of their place of domicile as "impermanent" or "unascertained". Intensive spatial mobility may be assumed where various places of birth are given for the children and where these places differ from the details of the municipality where the individual family members were domiciled. Domicile was automatically given to children by the authorities, at least through one of the parents. In this case, it is open to question whether the family (or one of the parents and his parents, and so on) had been connected with the municipality in question in the past or not. As I shall go on to describe in more detail, there is a need to reduce the somewhat evolutionistically-inclined assumption that Lovara families moved along a scale of historical development from "travelling" to "settled". A stay in a certain municipality could be ended and a family might move elsewhere for all sorts of reasons. Likewise, a newly-arrived "settling" family did not need to have had a "travelling" past, as there is a tendency to believe.

Territorial anchoring: Lovara families owning a house in a particular municipality

Some degree of territorial anchoring can be assumed where registers contain persons with typical Lovara surnames and next to them domiciles that coincide with the birthplaces of most of their family members. Above all, this applies where such details correspond to the recorded place of their actual residence or stay. Sometimes these may have been municipalities where the Roms were registered and to which they had to return periodically for administrative reasons. It is more likely, however, that they could have been places where the Roms in question repeatedly camped or stayed for a longer length of time. As I describe below, this territorial anchoring could also acquire an even firmer character.

The registered domicile in archival sources of an official nature is fortunately not the only indication available when researching territorial anchoring. Property ownership or the fact of living in a house with a number is another indication. Finding this type of record shows clearly that Lovara, as the inhabitants of these houses, "lived" in the properties and were thus connected with certain municipalities both territorially and officially in the event that they were also domiciled in the municipality. This factor is one that I consider to have been so far utterly ignored by historians and ethnographers in connection with the Lovara community in particular. During my research, I managed to collect information on a number of municipalities and Lovara families who were owners of such properties in the period under study. I shall show below, albeit on the basis of limited sources which are fairly different from each other, that despite the prevailing ideas regarding the non-settled nature of the Lovara, there are a number of municipalities where their territorial anchoredness had a tangible form, although the character and the types of their dwellings varied.

An example already mentioned of a municipality where Roms managed to acquire their own place to live during this period, and probably also earlier, is Dolná Seč in the Levice district. According to the testimony of witness Viktor Salinas (*1941), Lovara settled there on land close to the river Hron in the second half of the 19th century, and until the Second World War they earned their living not just through horse trading, but also by helping their non-Romani neighbours with work in the fields, primarily.[157] Viktor Salinas said:

> It was sometime in the 1860s or the 1870s that those three Roms, three brothers came to Dolná Seč, and they still live there today, in the same place. Roms from Dolná Seč used to travel with horses and wagons. That was how they earned their living, until the war. There were no other possibilities, they were forced to just buy and sell horses. No one would give them a job, there was nothing for them to live off, and yet they still lived in the same place in the settlement in Dolná Seč. The Romani women used to walk into the village and beg the farmers' wives for food.[158]

According to Salinas, one of the three brothers[159] who came to Dolná Seč was his great-grandfather Karoly Lakatoš, whose Romani nickname

---

157 Markéta Hajská, "'O trajo si t'al pestrívo / Život musí být pestrý.' Vyprávění Viktora Salinase", *Romano džaniben*, vol. 27, no. 2 (Winter 2020): 141.

158 Ibid.

159 The other two brothers were Hego and Júca. Hego later went to Levice, where he started a family, and Júca to Topoľčany, where he founded the famous family called the Júcovára after him.

was Ďuri. On the basis of an analysis of documents from the Dolná Seč notary's office in the Levice branch of the state archives in Nitra, I found that Karoly Lakatoš was born in 1854 and really did live for most of his life in Dolná Seč.[160] He still lived there during the Second World War, dying shortly after it ended. He was the father of more than 10 children over three decades, from the 1880s to the 1910s. Many of his children were born in Dolná Seč and some of them lived there as adults as well.[161] According to Salinas, before the Second War these Roms lived for many years in houses on the site of the current Romani settlement. This is confirmed by my archival findings.

According to the 1930 census, among the permanent inhabitants of the village were the family of Ján Rafael (*1887), a horse dealer and owner of house no. 130, his spouse Mária Rafaelová (*1890) and a further seven family members. One of them had next to his name the note: agricultural labourer.[162] Another house, with no number and described in a note as a lean-to shed, was permanently inhabited by Rudolf Rafael (*1892), who had two occupations: horse dealer and agricultural labourer. He lived there with his partner Mária (*1897) and their seven children.[163]

In the collections of the police chief's office[164] in Levice from 1938–1944[165] there is a record relating to a dispute over domicile in the municipality concerning János Lakatoš (Romani nickname Rudi)[166] stating that he lived in a Romani settlement (in Hungarian, *cigánytelep*) in Dolná Seč,[167] which is also confirmed in other documents by non-Romani witnesses who knew him and his father well.[168] Nine of Rudi's children

---

160 ŠA Nitra/ Levice, f. ONÚ Dolná Seč.

161 For example, Jozef Banda (Joško), Ján Rafael and Salinas' grandfather Karoly Lakatos (Čuri), officially also registered as János Lakatos, born in 1895 ŠA Nitra/ Levice, f. ONÚ Dolná Seč– Trestné listy 1908–1938 and ŠA Levice, f. Hlavnoslúžnovský úrad v Levicích, spis. zn. 2777/1943.

162 Slovenský národný archív, Sčítáni lidu 1930, obec Dolná Seč, č. hárku 001, č. škatule 0444, identifikátor urn:nbn:sk:cair-ko1b478, availible: https://slovakiana.sk/scitacie-harky.

163 Ibid., č. hárku 002, č. škatule 0444, identifikátor urn:nbn:sk:cair-ko1b47b.

164 The office was created on the basis of the district office after Levice (Léva) was occupied by Hungarian troops on 10 November 1938 and functioned until 20 December1944, when the Red Army liberated the town of Levice (Léva). Source: ŠA in Nitra, Archív Levice, f. Hlavnoslúžnovský úrad v Leviciach, available online: Föszolgabíroi hivatal Léva [cit. 14. 7. 2023].

165 ŠA Nitra/ Levice, f. Hlavnoslúžnovský úrad v Leviciach, 1938–1944, spis. zn. 2777/1943.

166 This was the brother of Salinas' grandfather Čuri (Károly/ János Lakatoš), son of Károl Lakatoš (Ďuri), born 1854. János Lakatoš (Rudi), born 1884 in Žemliary, states that his father is still living in Dolná Seč and that he is 85.

167 ŠA Nitra/ Levice, f. Hlavnoslúžnovský úrad v Levicích z let 1938–1944, spis. zn. 2777/1943, unmarked document entitled *Nyilatkozat* (declaration) of 23. 12. 1942.

168 Ibid.

were born in the 1920s and 1930s in Dolná Seč,[169] where the family appears to have lived and which served as the base for its economic activities in the surrounding area. In the criminal records from the Dolná Seč authorities concerning the period 1908 to 1938, which contains records of several dozen people from Dolná Seč, it is possible to identify around 18 people who, on the basis of surnames and other notes (e.g. occupation: "gypsy") may be presumed to be Lovara. Fifteen of them listed Dolná Seč as their place of birth (from 1884 to 1924), 13 had it as their domicile, and 10 listed it as their current place of residence. In two cases, different places of residence were noted for their repeated appearances in the register, or there was a note stating "residence unstable", while with the other eight, their place of permanent residence was always listed as Dolná Seč. In the occupation column, most of them had "gypsy vagabond", while three even had their profession described as "Vlax gypsy". Three men and one woman have "labourer" listed as their employment, while another has "agricultural worker"[170], which again indicates that Roms had permanent residence in the municipality in the prewar period. The last-mentioned performed activities locally. From the testimonies of witnesses and other records it is clear that the Lovara community there was relatively large. The information on the domiciles, occupations and residences of the above-mentioned 18 people captured in this specific police source therefore illustrates the means and the frequency of the local Romani anchoredness there, both on the official level and in terms of the time they actually spent in Dolná Seč, insofar as such sources can provide us with this kind of information.

Another municipality where, according to witnesses and archival records, Lovara lived in their own houses in the interwar period was Tekovské Lužany, also in the Levice district. According to witness Josef Molnár (*1945),[171] Lovara had lived in their own houses, which stood in the Romani settlement, long before the Second World War. Josef Molnár said:

I don't know when the Roms built their houses there, but it was a long time ago. My grandfather had a house and a stable next door. That was where my grandmother lived, my father's mother. They had houses, but they weren't

---

169 Ibid., document with case no. 1121/1941, of 3. 12. 1941, p. 3.
170 This is the above-mentioned great-grandfather of Viktor Salinas, Károl Lakatoš (Ďuri), born in 1854. Ibid.
171 Personal recording of Josef Molnár (1945) by the author, made on 19 January 2019 in Hořice, Czech Republic.

well off, they slept on straw. They didn't have furniture or anything. During that time they traded horses and went round the markets. My grandfather was the *vajda* back then. If a woman went past his house without a scarf, she had to pay a fine, otherwise he himself would personally shave her head.[172]

This mention of Romani women going past his grandfather's house, a story handed down in the family, may be considered "tangible" proof of the actual residency of Lovara in Tekovské Lužany. This is also confirmed by (sporadic) archival finds. In the file of the police chief's office in Levice for 1938–1944 the case is recorded in detail of Simon Rafael, born in 1892 in Tekovské Lužany and domiciled there, who from 1939 to 1941 sent protests to various authorities that his horses had been taken away from him. Rafael repeatedly called for their return, arguing that he was a disabled veteran of the First World War, that he needed his horses for transport and that he had a house in Tekovské Lužany, where he had also had a stable built for his horses. All this information was confirmed as true by the War Committee in a document issued to the district War Board in Levice in 1939.[173]

The house as wintering place: A combination of spatial mobility and territorial anchoredness

A slightly different example of house ownership is the large family with the surname Stojka who owned a house at number 11 Práznovská Street in Topoľčany, according to official records and the testimonies of witnesses. Although the witness statements do not indicate when precisely the family acquired the house, several descendants of the family independently corroborated each others' claims that it was definitely before the war. The head of the household and my respondents' grandfather, named Michal Stojka (* in 1863, according to archival records), had several children, and they and their families used the house on a seasonal basis. His grandson, Štefan Stojka (*1932) said:

---

172 Ibid. Molnár was describing a traditional way of punishing Lovara women for breaking the rules of ritual purity and for acts considered as shameful. Such behaviour was formerly deemed to include the non-wearing of headscarves by Lovara women.

173 ŠA Nitra/ Levice, f. Hlavnoslúžnovský úrad v Leviciach z let 1938–1944, file no. 6318/1942. Also in a file entitled A levai járási hadigo ndozo bizottságátol, č. j. 6/1939. Tärgy: Rafael Simon nagysallói.

We had this huge house, the whole Romani family lived there. Some people were still travelling, they mostly traded horses. We had a house. My parents settled down and tried to live a civilised life. They bought the house with the money from a horse, but even though we had a house, we still travelled in the summer. It was not like [how we had travelled] before – summer, winter, all year round. Not us, not any more. We only went travelling in summer, in the winter we went home. My father Jozef lived there with my mother Helena. They had 13 children. My uncle Ondrej Stojka lived with them too.[174]

This testimony contains various generally-held judgments, stated in a matter-of-fact way, in which the witness distances himself in a certain way from travelling, although he himself experienced it. The connection between being a "travelling" person and an "uncivilised" one reflects the discourse he faced as a "travelling gypsy" in the postwar period with the need to register as such under Act no. 74/1958, a discourse he must have come across in his life repeatedly. He also points to the higher social status of his family, which acquired its own house at a time when other (Vlax) Roms were still "travelling", expressing distance from those who did not buy a home. An interesting detail is that the house is said to have been bought with money from selling horses. This again shows that horse trading could be a way of easily earning money, which other Roms managed to earn with great difficulty in those days, although the idea that the sale of *one horse* would enable the purchase of a house is clearly an exaggeration. Nevertheless, this information is valuable, especially if we compare it with the fairly limited, almost negligible possibility for Slovak (non-Vlax) Roms, who during this period were frequently limited to receiving payment in kind, to buy a house. Vain attempts by Roms to acquire houses are often described as the result of non-Romani un-willingness to let Roms live "amongst them". The territorial and also the social boundary between Roms and non-Roms tends to be described as impermeable. Although we do not know the details of the sale described or similar transactions, it is likely that financial wealth was, under certain circumstances, able to break through this boundary.

The narrator's brother František Stojka (*1940), when asked whether his family had travelled before the war, replied: "It wasn't quite like that. They all went to the fairs, but even before the war they had houses and they'd trade. So even though we travelled, we still had houses to which

---

174 Personal recording of Štefan Stojka (*1932) by the author, made on 22 March 2002 in Ostrava. Czech Republic.

we returned."[175] The testimony of František Stojka shows the already-outlined combination of spatial mobility and territorial anchoredness, in other words, the fact that owning a house did not rule out "travelling" carried out for the purpose of horse trading.

A cousin of both men (Štefan, *1940) confirmed what František Stojka said and enlarged upon the idea of the house as a point to which the family would return: "We travelled when I was little. We travelled, but at the same time we had a house. It was like our base from which we'd set out and to which we used to return. My dad dealt in horses."[176] The cousin of these three witnesses, Mrs. G .S. (*1939), also the granddaughter of Michal Stojka, said: "The family home in Topoľčany was where my grandfather lived, Mr. Stojka. The family travelled throughout Slovakia, but they'd always go back to my grandfather's house after a time, mostly for the period from autumn to spring."[177] From her description it can be seen that the house may have been used by (at least some) families as a wintering place, in other words, a house to which the family returned for the winter period, described by witnesses as a period very unsuited to moving around with wagons.

The generation of my respondents' fathers, Michal Stojka's sons, were all born in Topoľčany (Josef in 1884, Pavol in 1887, Ladislav in 1888, Ondrej in 1898, Anton in 1903). According to the registry records, their father was born there in 1863[178] and still lived there during the Second World War. Topoľčany was also listed as the birthplace for the vast majority of Michal's grandchildren, born in the interwar period. The registry of gypsy identity documents held by the Topoľčany district authorities[179] confirms that Michal and all his sons earned their living as horse traders during the second half of the 1920s and the entire 1930s. For five sons in one family to become horse traders is relatively rare. As they were all engaged in the same profession, the brothers and their father would have had to compete against each other. Such a situation was possible if they branched out and widened their territories to include various districts of

---

175 Personal recording of František Stojka (*1940) by the author, made on 29 March 2002 in Ostrava, Czech Republic.

176 Personal recording of Štefan Stojka (*1940) by the author, made on 16 April 2002 in Ostrava, Czech Republic.

177 VÚA-VHA Praha, f. Sbírka osobních spisů žadatelů o vydání osvědčení podle zákona č. 255/1946 Sb.

178 Parents' names František Stojka and Terezia Lakatošová. Note in register: *Zingarus Valachicus.* Slovakia Church and Synagogue Books, 1592–1935, FamilySearch (https://www.familysearch .org/ark:/61903/1:1:QVNX-4T3D)), [cit. 18. 6. 2023]; microfilm number not given.

179 ŠA Nitra/ Topoľčany, f. OÚ Topoľčany, k. 25a – kn. Evidencia cigánskych legitimácií.

the former Czechoslovakia, with a clear orientation towards the Czech lands, in the 1930s. The fact that all the sons managed to maintain their profession points to the family's high social status, which is also indicated by witnesses and described in the press of the period.[180] They all regularly returned to Topoľčany and some family members stayed there regularly. They were all domiciled there.

The official records also repeatedly mention the address of "11 Práznovská" in Topoľčany during the Second World War.[181] All the family members who were registered there had to return there after the ban on itinerancy and live there together. According to the official register, in 1942 a total of 44 people lived at that address,[182] including women and children. A further record from the same year even adds a further seven adults.[183] The question arises of how large this house had to be if, according to witnesses, it was used during normal times by various branches of the extended family just as a wintering place or temporary staging post and managed to hold more than 50 people in 1942. It is not impossible, however, that some family members may have lived in their wagons on land attached to the house. This underlines my conclusions that spatial mobility and anchoredness could be combined and could complement each other. Within a single family, for example, the less well-off members might camp on land belonging to a richer relative. I shall show a similar model when it comes to the situation during the war in Trenčianska Teplá.

---

180 In the periodical *Neues Tagblatt für Schlesien und Nordmähren* an article was published on page 6 of the 2 June 1937 edition entitled "Unsuccessful election of gypsy king in Opava", describing the election of a new gypsy king to replace the deceased king of Polish origin, Michal Kwiek. One candidate for the post was Anton Stojka, a son of Michal Stojka from Topoľčany. The article states that: "Stojka is a respected man. He is the leader of the Topoľčany district and has 2,000 Slovak gypsy families subject to him. From his position he is authorised to pass judgments, and he has to defend the interests of his clan. He is helped in his dealings by an assistant whom he has at his disposal." According to the description, Anton Stojka was a Romani judge who took part in Romani court cases. ([autor] -fchil. "Mißglückte Zigeuner Königswahl in Troppau." *Neues Tagblatt für Schlesien und Nordmähren*, vol. 4, no. 128 (2. 6. 1937), 6.).
181 According to the testimonies of all the above-cited witnesses, the house was destroyed during the war by German soldiers.
182 ŠA Nitra/ Topoľčany, f. OÚ Topoľčany, Žandárská stanica Topoľčany, ref. 4408/42 – Odvod asociálních osôb – príprava (10. 9. 1942, part of the appendix Seznam asociálnych živlov a cigáňov.
183 Ibid., ref. 15.607/1942. Dodatočný odvod osob z asociálneho živlu pre pracovný útvar v Dubnici nad Váhom.

Roms also owned houses in neighbouring municipalities. The narrative of Helena Danišová (*1940) shows that her family owned a house in the municipality of Solčany:

> I was born in the municipality of Solčany in the Topoľčany district. We had a house there. The whole of my mother's family lived there, her parents, brother, sisters. Just Vlax Roms, there were no *Rumungros* there. Our settlement was at the very beginning of the village. Before the war we didn't travel and we didn't even have horses. That was after the war.[184]

The address of their house, number 245 Solčany, was listed next to their parents' names in the official registry during the war.[185] The witness's emphasis on the position of the Romani settlement points to a further important aspect that needs to be taken into account when studying the territorial links between Romani families and a certain municipality, and that is the spatial location of their settlement or houses within the municipality. A location "at the beginning of the village" or in the centre of the village for the most part testified to the good or acceptable situation of Roms in the municipality. Important information, such as whether someone bought the house, built it himself, or had it built is not always available, but can sometimes be found in witness narratives – as was the case above with the testimonies of Roms originally from Topoľčany.

Another place where the Lovara lived in houses in the interwar period was nearby Chynorany, Topoľčany district. According to a register of the "gypsies" living in the municipality in 1924, 29 Roms lived there, of whom 16 can be identified by their surnames as being Lovara. The head of the Lovara family was Ján Lakatoš, "horse merchant", born in 1871 in Chynorany and living with his wife Erža, born in 1870 also in Chynorany, and their eight children and six "unlawful children". They all had the right of domicile in Chynorany.[186] According to the witness M. S. (*1945), granddaughter of Ján Lakatoš and Erža Lakatošová, the Roms had their own houses in the municipality even before the war.[187] This is

---

184 Personal recording of Helena Danišová (*1940) by the author, made on 29 March 2002 in Ostrava, Czech Republic.

185 ŠA Nitra/ Topoľčany, f. OÚ Topoľčany, ref. 15.607/1942. Dodatočný odvod osob z asociálneho živlu pre pracovný útvar v Dubnici nad Váhom.

186 ŠA Nitra/ Topoľčany, f. ONÚ Chynorany, šk. 9, zn. 1924. Zoznam cigánov nachodiacich sa v obci Chynorany.

187 VÚA-VHA Praha. Sbírka osobních spisů žadatelů o vydání osvědčení podle zákona č. 255/1946 Sb., personal file of applicant M. S. (*1945).

confirmed by a report issued by the notary in Topoľčany in August 1939 concerning the revision of domicile for "all gypsies", according to which the M. S.'s father, born in Chynorany in 1912 and also domiciled there, was an inhabitant of house no. 326 and was employed as a "labourer".[188] The territorial mobility outlined in the case of the Topoľčany Stojkas can also be observed in other places where Roms spent the winter. However, such mobility could take various forms. A typical example of a place to which the Lovara regularly returned is described by witness J. P. (*1939) from the municipality of Madunice, Trnava district:

> We lived in Madunice in a Romani settlement about 300 metres from the village, about six families of us. We would just spend the winter in Madunice, we were registered as resident there, and we had a little house there. Summer was the time for travelling and horse-dealing.[189]

A different type of wintering place was the site in Hrnčiarovce, Trnava district, clearly connected with the relatively less intensive presence of Romani families in that municipality. Witness M. B. (*1932) wrote in her statement: "Hrnčiarovce was where we spent the winter. We were among the travelling Roms. My family earned its living from sharpening knives and scissors. We would travel to places where there was a demand for that service."[190] From what she goes on to describe, however, it was not a permanent building, but "a place by the river where we set up our wagons and that's where we lived".[191] A similar experience is confirmed by another witness from the same locality, I. L. (*1942), who says that before the war her family lived in wagons: "We travelled, just before the war we lived in wagons on a site by the village of Hrnčiarovce in Trnava district. We were one big family, five brothers, 20 wagons, maybe 200 to 300 people."[192] Many of their family members were domiciled in Hrnčiarovce, which was why they had to return there at the start of the war.

---

188 Report for OÚ Topoľčany, submitted 30 August 1939 with ref. 5922. Kept as part of the documentation/personal file of the applicant in VÚA-VHA Praha. Sbírka osobních spisů žadatelů o vydání osvědčení podle zákona č. 255/1946 Sb., personal file of applicant M. S. (*1945).

189 J. P., (*1939) recorded 18 September 2002 in Holešov by Jana Kramářová, Archives of Člověk v tísni, o.p.s.

190 VÚA-VHA Praha. Sbírka osobních spisů žadatelů o vydání osvědčení podle zákona č. 255/1946 Sb., personal file of applicant M. B. (*1932).

191 M. B., female (*1932) recorded 4 June 2001 in Prague, Czech Republic by Jakub Krčík. Archive of Člověk v tísni, o.p.s.

192 I. L., female (*1942) in Hrnčiarovce, Trnava district, Slovakia, recorded by Milena Alinčová in Sadská on 11 September 2002. Archive of Člověk v tísni, o.p.s.

The territorial bond with a particular municipality could take all kinds of forms. The list of Lovara who, according to official evidence and testimonies, were anchored in a particular municipality in Slovakia does not, of course, end with these few cases.

It is definitely worth mentioning the municipality of Voderady in the Trnava district where, according to the official register of "gypsies" from 1932, there were 31 Lovara[193] with the surname Rafael, Stojka or Horvát. With the exception of partners who had married into the family, all of the Roms on the list were born in Voderady (between 1896 and 1928). All adults, with the exception of a few housewives, listed their occupations as "worker" (*robotník*). That they were actually resident in the municipality was confirmed by the notary's office in 1933 and 1934, while in 1936 another 10 people with the surname Rafael were added to the list.[194] The fact that all the adult Lovara apparently earned their livelihoods as "workers" contradicts the generally-received idea that Roms from this sub-ethnic group traditionally avoid physical labour.[195] That this was a stereotype is confirmed by the above-mentioned examples showing Roms as brickmakers, metalsmiths, agricultural workers, day labourers and other manual labour professions. The horse-trading families did not perform physical work and ranked highest among the Lovara in terms of status and material wealth, and it is this aspect that differentiated them from families with a lower social status. However, not every horse trader managed to earn a living selling horses, and some less successful ones turned to complementary livelihoods.

A resident of Dolný Hričov, Žilina district[196], witness V. S. (*1939), describes a family of Lovara homeowners there before the Second World War, as does witness M. L. (born 1940) from the municipality of Veľké Lovce, Šurany district[197] and witness J. B. (*1934) from the municipality of Mýtne Ludany, Levice district, where he says his family owned a house

---

193 For more on the Romani settlement in Voderady in the early 1960s and the local Lovara community, see Kutlík – Garudo 1999: 18.

194 ŠA Nitra/ Trnava, ObNÚ Voderady, kn. 27 – Evidencia cigáňov

195 Nina Pavelčíková. "Vztah Romů k práci – konfrontace stereotypů s historickými doklady". *Český lid* 102, no. 3 (2015): 308.

196 VÚA-VHA Sbírka osobních spisů žadatelů o vydání osvědčení podle zákona č. 255/1946 Sb., personal file of applicant V. S. (*1939).

197 "Before the war we lived in a settlement near the municipality of Veľké Lovce, about 500 metres from the village. We had a little house made of unfired bricks, one room." (Ibid). Roms settling in Veľké Lovce after the First World War are also described by witness Peter Lakatoš, whose grandfather, a blacksmith, settled there together with his sons. Personal recording with Peter Lakatoš (*1956) by the author, made on 30 March 2018 in Tvrdošovce, Slovakia.

"right in the village, among the *gadjos* [non-Roma]".[198] Another official record from the Chief of Police's office describes three wooden houses belonging to Roms with the surname Rafael and Banda in Marušová, Levice district being burnt down in 1938 and the subsequent expulsion of these Roms from the village. The Roms were said to have lived permanently in the houses until that time.[199]

Of course, the question remains open as to what the houses the Lovara owned at that time looked like. I believe we should envisage them as being similar to the houses that the so-called Slovak Roms owned and lived in at that time in Slovakia. It cannot be excluded that some of them were wooden buildings and dwellings of an improvised nature, sometimes referred to pejoratively by the authorities as "gypsy shacks" and by the witnesses themselves as "huts". If the house was made of brick or stone, that fact was duly stressed by the witnesses. It should be noticed, however, that some houses owned by Lovara had officially-issued and registered house numbers, which were not usually allotted to non-standard buildings (shacks, hovels etc.). A house number indicates that the dwelling-place was of a permanent nature and its owner's financial situation reasonably secure. In some places, however, the relevant building and registration laws and decrees may have been circumvented, and so these cases of dwelling-places must be judged individually.

Influence of livelihood on spatial mobility

The profession in which a particular family was engaged had a fundamental influence on the form of its spatial mobility. It was often also one of the main reasons why families either moved territorially or remained in a certain place.

In the register of Roms undertaken in 1925 in the Slovak regions, a total of 60,315 "settled" Roms and 1,877 "travelling" Roms were listed. These were understood by Nečas to be Vlax Roms.[200] He said the above-mentioned register contained information on 63 horse dealers,

---

198 VÚA-VHA Praha, f. Sbírka osobních spisů žadatelů o vydání osvědčení podle zákona č. 255/1946 Sb., personal file of applicant J. B. (*1934).

199 The houses were said to have been destroyed by local residents who wanted to drive the Roms out of the village by so doing. ŠA Nitra/ Levice, f. Hlavnoslúžnovsky úrad v Levicích z let 1938–1944, složka 5744/1944, č. j. 3004/42 – Ráfael Antal és János továbbá Banda Miklos cigányok tartózkodása of 20. November 1942.

200 Ctibor Nečas, "Slovenští Romové v letech 1938–1945". *Sborník prací Filosofické fakulty brněnské univerzity* C 51 (Brno: Masarykova univerzita, 2004).

of whom 46.3% were in the Košice Region and 24.6% in the Bratislava Region. Nečas considered this number to be well under the actual figure and speculated that the actual number of Roms was incomparably higher and the area over which they were spread was much larger .[201] Horse dealing, according to Nečas, "brought considerable wealth, and some of those who engaged in it were among the wealthy and, at the same time, highly conservative elements of the Romani ethnic groups".[202] Horse dealers' high status is also reflected upon by witnesses, who describe them mostly as rich, influential figures with great authority among the Roms, although their wealth and status could fluctuate in some instances. Dealing required extensive spatial mobility and regular attendance not just at the different horse markets, but also other local events where people offered and sought horses. As I shall show below, this also did not exclude the family of the horse dealer being territorially anchored in a particular municipality –in fact, the opposite seems to have been the case. It was the horse dealers who managed to put together the necessary finances to enable them to buy houses in the Slovak countryside.

Many witnesses from Lovara families said that their fathers and grandfathers in Slovakia had earned their livings through horse trading before the Second World War. However, that profession, which was prestigious (and not just among the Roms), usually provided a livelihood for the father of a family and his eldest adult son. Only with difficulty could several brothers at the same time earn a living from the profession. The exception, it seems, was the above-described Stojka family from Topoľčany, who dealt with the competition among them by members choosing different sales circuits. In other families, however, many breadwinners in nuclear families had to find additional sources of income so as not to compete with their relatives who were also horse traders, especially if they wanted to continue to live in the same area. From this it follows that the diversification of professions may be considered another factor in creating spatial ties. Transferring to a new profession could be tied to a limitation of spatial mobility, a switch to a more locally-oriented mobility, or it could require one's spatial mobility to extend to more distant areas.

A transfer to locally-oriented activity is described by Salinas in the case of his great-grandfather Ďuri in Dolná Seč, who reoriented towards metalwork and drill production. The grandfather of witness Petr Lakatoš

---

201 Ibid., 157.
202 Ibid.

(*1956) had earned his living in the same way. After building a house in Veľké Lovce after the First World War, he had started smithing with his own anvil, and an addition to that sharpened scythes, scissors and knives for local non-Roms and made drills.[203]

Likewise, the grandfather of Tibor Bihári, who had the Romani nickname Bakro, worked as a blade sharpener in Tvrdošovce. The fact that he knew how to sharpen knives, sickles, scythes and files and to make wooden tool handles for local farmers helped him gain permission from the local non-Roms to settle on the edge of Tvrdošovce between the wars and build a house of unfired brick.[204] As I mentioned above, on the basis of demand from local non-Roms his family later reoriented towards the production of unfired bricks. Sharpening knives and scissors was also mentioned by witness M. B., domiciled in Hrnčiarovce. For her family, engaging in this trade was a reason to move about even more.[205] I. L., born during the war, also in Hrnčiarovce, said that before the war her relatives "travelled around and sharpened knives, mended umbrellas, made wood drills or, in season, worked on farmers' fields cutting beetroot. My grandfather made kettles, they made tubs and troughs out of wood, he could make them from a single tree trunk."[206] The Lovara domiciled in Madunice near Trnava, according to witness J. P., engaged in a seasonal combination of the above-mentioned professions: "My father was a blacksmith, he made drills and chains, but just in the winter. Otherwise he traded horses. During the season he would also work for a farmer."[207] The metalworking activities of "former travellers" from Madunice are also described by Rostislav Pivoň in his study. He says some of them specialised in making drills and also produced nails, hooks and other things.[208] A family with the surname Bihari/Bihary or Kudrik, domiciled either in Pastuchov or the nearby district town of Hlohovec, earned their living exclusively by tinning and making copper kettles and leading

---

203 Personal recording of Peter Lakatoš (*1956) by the author, made on 30 March 2018 in Tvrdošovce, Slovakia.

204 Markéta Hajská, "Gagarin". *Romano džaniben*, vol. 24, no. 2 (Winter 2017): 33.

205 VÚA-VHA Praha, f. Sbírka osobních spisů žadatelů o vydání osvědčení podle zákona č. 255/1946 Sb., personal file no. 337578/02.

206 I. L., female, (*1942) recorded by Milena Alinčová in Sadská, Czech Republic on 11 September 2002. Archives of Člověk v tisni, o.p.s.

207 Ibid.

208 Rastislav Pivoň, "Zákon č. 74/1958 Zb. a jeho výkon v niektorých obciach trnavského regiónu (aj s ohľadom na práce iných bádateľov)". *Studia Ethnologica Pragensia*, no. 1 (2021): 80.

"a travelling life", as a witness decided to characterise her family's way of life.[209] Another descendant of the same family (J. B.) stated:

> My grandfather was a kettle-maker. We used to travel around with him and help him. The whole of our family made kettles: bakers' troughs, confectioners' kettles, kitchen cauldrons, ladles. We'd travel around with 15 wagons in a row, and they were huge wagons, carriages pulled by horses. We children would travel all warm under the feather quilts and outside it would be cold. We'd travel like that for maybe 20 kilometres. Then we'd stop near a wood, they'd make a fire, and then they'd pitch the big tent made out of tarpaulins.[210]

J. B.'s grandfather, his grandfather's siblings, and the generation of their children were, he says, all born in Pastuchov. After a while the families left the municipality and continued to engage in the kettle-making profession itinerantly, but their work had required territorial movement even when they had been living in the municipality. As can be seen from a reconstruction of the Biháry family's movements, during the interwar period they managed to perform their trade over a wide geographical area, and in the 1930s they travelled mostly around the Czech lands. The story of the Bihárys from Pastuchov also shows that the perception of the "sedentarisation" process as a linear, gradual development moving from (earlier) "travelling" to (later) "settling down" is problematic and oversimplified. In the grandparents' generation, the family was much more territorially connected with the municipality of their domicile than were their descendants one or two generations later, who no longer had any ties to the municipality at all.[211] The intensive renewal of their spatial mobility and the family's departure from the municipality may have been caused not just by various outside influences, but also by intra-group or inter-group disputes, by reactions to various situations in their lives, or by a shift to another type of livelihood.

The witness narratives also show that with the exception of horse trading, which could bring in a decent amount of money, Roms in the Slovak countryside at that time often received remuneration for their

---

209 Witness R. B. (*1921). VÚA-VHA Praha, f. Sbírka osobních spisů žadatelů o vydání osvědčení podle zákona č. 255/1946 Sb.

210 Witness J. B. (*1934) recorded by Markéta Hajská on 15 February 2002 in České Budějovice, Czech Republc. Archives of Člověk v tisni, o.p.s.

211 I shall look at this circumstance in more detail in the chapter 4 "The Second World War".

services or craft products in kind[212] and frequently had trouble providing for their families.

I have not yet looked at the gender aspect of the traditional livelihoods, but it is certain that women were also involved in providing for their families. Among the livelihoods in which some Vlax Romani women were engaged, regardless of their family's social status, were palm reading or divination from cards. A number of women tried to obtain food through providing small services or simply by begging for it from non-Romani women. As Tibor Bihari from the municipality of Tvrdošovce said: "My grandfather sharpened all sorts of things for *gadjos*, but there wasn't enough work for him to provide for us all, so my grandmother used to go and ask for food." He said she would go on foot round the surrounding villages, ranging over dozens of kilometres, and ask for food from the farmers' wives whom she knew personally. Several witnesses said their mothers and grandmothers engaged in similar activity. After forming good relationships locally, some Romani women would go in search of food and clothing from farmers' wives, helping them out regularly with various kinds of work, as Viktor Salinas described.

For families in the lowest social position, living on the edge of poverty, the main income was such begging, which was fairly difficult to distinguish from the "asking for food" described by the witnesses. It was often complemented by poultry theft, which could be practised when moving around, but clearly did not take place in municipalities where Roms had functional, solidary relationships with local non-Roms. As the witness nicknamed "Mala" (*1936) said, whose itinerant family lived in great poverty:

> My grandmother didn't even have shoes. Her clothes were made of old sacks sewn together. Back then they would also make footrags for their feet out of sacks. Often there was no food. I'll be honest, if my mother hadn't stolen a hen there would have been nothing to eat.[213]

Similarly, the witness "Ďivoj"(*1946) remembered her mother's stories from the interwar period: "Before the war they were very poor, they had nothing to wear. My mother said she would beg or tell fortunes

---

212 Milena Hübschmannová, "Rozhovor s Terou Fabiánovou". *Romano džaniben*, vol. 7, no. 1–2 (Spring/Summer 2000): 32–38.

213 Personal recording by the author of the witness named "Mala" (*1936), made on 1 May 2015 in Orechovo, Nitra district, Slovakia.

from cards, sometimes she'd steal a hen."[214] Helena Davišová of Soľčany described how her father – her only parent and the family breadwinner – would regularly help out a farmer: "My dad used to help a farmer. He'd muck out stables, for example."[215] It was this manual work that enabled him to provide for his nine children and meant a permanent source of income tied to the municipality in question; she said that was the reason the family did not travel at all in the interwar period. This case may also be explained by the generally precarious situation in which such a large family found itself when it needed to provide for all its members and these were unable to find work. Being reliant on local sources of livelihood was the main reason why this Lovara remained in a municipality.

It is striking just how much the above-described models of subsistence are entirely in keeping with the means of livelihood and remuneration in kind described by Milena Hübschmannová, for example, in the case of Slovak and Hungarian non-Vlax Roms.[216] Here it should be stressed that although some professions are often held to be typical of certain sub-ethnic Romani groups,[217] the testimonies and other information I have gathered show that in the case of the above-mentioned Lovara families, a number of trades and other livelihoods were practised which in the Romani studies literature are described in connection with other Romani groups, not with Lovara. A case in point is the manufacture and cleaning of kettles, which Nečas connected with the Kalderash Roms, "outright travellers, who came to Slovakia clearly from the southeast, from which they also brought their name from the Romanian word *căldare*, which means kettle."[218] The Biháry family described above, however, speaks a Lovara dialect typical of southwest Slovakia, so the connection with the traditional livelihood of the Kalderash is clearly just coincidental. Another example considered typical of another Romani group is the manufacture of troughs, said to be produced by the traditional makers of wooden items, the Beash, originally from Romania.[219] Other professions described by witnesses such as metalwork, knife polishing, or the above-mentioned manufacture of unfired bricks are considered typical of

---

214 Personal recording by the author of the witness named "Ďivoj" (*1946), made on 31 May 2015 in Cabaj-Čápor, Nitra district, Slovakia.

215 Personal recording by the author of the witness named Helena Danišová (*1940), made on 29 March 2002 in Ostrava, Czech Republic.

216 Milena Hübschmannová, "Vztahy mezi Romy a Židy na východním Slovensku před druhou světovou válkou". *Romano džaniben*, vol. 7, no. 1–2 (Spring/Summer 2000): 17–18.

217 For example Ctibor Nečas, *Českoslovenští Romové*.

218 Ibid., 155.

219 Ibid., 156.

Slovak, non-Vlax Roms, but as I show here, some Lovara families earned their living in such ways for years.

In the examples described above, it is possible to see that where Lovara families had created ties with a certain municipality, they made visible attempts to acquire dwelling-places there. Some of these Romani families could have lived in such houses, whether bought, self-built or illegally erected and improvised, while devoting themselves to professions that either did or did not require movement. In practice, what was most common among Lovara families on Slovak territory was a combination of living in houses while pursuing professions requiring spatial mobility. The most frequent such profession was horse trading, already mentioned several times, which involved either short journeys into the surrounding area with regular returns "home", or more time-consuming journeys to geographically more distant destinations which sometimes took place on a seasonal basis. In such a case, the journey back to a certain municipality would have occurred in the cold season, when it was not suitable to be on the road. In practice, there were all sorts of ways to combine and blend these different kinds of mobility with remaining in a certain territory.

2.1 The Stojkas of Trenčianska Teplá in the interwar period

The 1920s: Mobility on the territory of western Slovakia

Let us now return to the Stojka family's territorial ties to the municipality of Trenčianska Teplá. The official records show that in the 1920s, the extended Stojka family lived in western Slovakia, moving around the district of Trenčín and occasionally the adjacent districts as well.[220] At that time, however, it was already possible to discern differences in the spatial mobility of Štefan Stojka, Sr.'s nuclear family and the nuclear family of his sister Zaga, so I shall look at their trajectories separately.

The family of Zaga Stojková

At the beginning of the 1920s, Zaga Stojková probably lived together with her partner Ján Facona and their children in the municipality of

---

220 I base this statement on the birthplaces and birthdates of the family members, on archival records, mostly from the ŠA in Trenčín, and on articles in the press of the time.

Dobrá. As I have mentioned above, this municipality immediately neighbouring Trenčianska Teplá had already been settled for generations by a family of Slovak (non-Vlax) Roms with the surname Facona. This is also where Zaga and Ján's three eldest children were born. We may speculate whether Zaga and her children lived together with her partner Ján Facona's parents in one of the three houses that the authorities labelled "gypsy shacks" (see Fig. 2), or whether she resided in the municipality in a different way. There are no documents from the beginning of the 1920s showing the spatial mobility of Zaga's family.

Zaga's partner Ján Facona is a slightly unclear figure about whom there are only fragmentary official records, which end in the mid-1920s with the birth of their youngest children, Grófa (*1923) and Josef, nicknamed Jouško (*1924). After they were born, Zaga Stojková does not seem to have had any more children, probably because when her youngest son was born she was already 37. How old Ján Facona was when Josef was born is not known from official records, since I have not been able to find Ján's date of birth anywhere. From the mid-1920s, the name of Ján Facona no longer occurs in connection with Zaga Stojková's family, and so I may surmise that he was no longer living with Zaga and their children. It is not impossible that by this time he had already died. I have not been able to find any detailed information regarding his death.

In the 1920s, Zaga's eldest son Filo (*1907) starts to become a notable figure. In official records from the First Republic era he is labelled a "horse trader", revealing that this branch of the family was in that business. At the beginning of the 1920s, Filo took a wife, Anna Lakatošová, whose Romani nickname was Čaja and who was born in Veľké Ostratice in the district called Partizánske today.

In subsequent years, their family seems to have gradually become more oriented towards the neighbouring, considerably larger municipality of Trenčianska Teplá. This is where Anna's daughter Grófa was born, seemingly in the spring of 1923, followed in 1924 by a son, grandson of Zaga, named Vilém Stojka, with the Romani nickname Janino. Next to the record of his birth in the register there is a note stating *"born in a tent below Dubovec"*[221], indicating that the family was at that time camping or living in a tent beneath the hill called Dubovec at the edge of the village. Filo Stojka was 17 when his son was born, and so it is likely that Filo's

---

221 Data imparted by employees of the registry office at Trenčianska Teplá. Dubovec is a wooded hill that divides Trenčianska Teplá from neighbouring Nová Dubnica. The mother initially told the authorities her name was Mária Kudriková, but later amended this to her real name, Anna Lakatošová.

nuclear family was living at that time together with the family of Filo's mother Zaga and his younger siblings. From the places of birth of other children, Zaga's youngest son Jouško (1924, Trenčín) and Zaga's next grandson, Filo and Anna's son with the nickname Bobko (1926, Sereď) it is clear that Zaga Stojková's branch of the family was mobile in the 1920s in the district of Trenčín and its surroundings but does not seem to have exceeded the area of western Slovakia. The family engaged in horse trading. Zaga and other women in her family were caught and arrested for "begging and vagrancy" several times, which indicates that this was a frequent complementary source of making a living. It was consistently punished by the authorities at that time and in many cases resulted in short prison sentences, mostly of one day or a maximum of several days.

The family of Štefan Stojka, Sr.

I have managed to learn somewhat more from the records of the 1920s about Zaga's brother Štefan Stojka (*1891) and his descendants. Given that from this decade on there were several other men named Štefan Stojka who were part of the family, I refer to the eldest Štefan, the founder of this family line, as Štefan Stojka, Sr. The birthdates and birthplaces of his family members show that Štefan Stojka Sr.'s three grandsons, the sons of his son Ján, were born in Trenčianská Teplá in 1919, 1923 and 1933, and were also named Štefan, and that Štefan Stojka, Sr. himself had another son, born in 1929, who was also named Štefan. They were all domiciled in the municipality. According to the *Evidencie vydaných domovských listov* (Register of domicile certificates issued), Štefan Stojka, Sr. applied twice, once in 1924 and once in 1927, for a domicile certificate in Trenčianska Teplá (in both cases the application states: "for reason of identity").[222]

In the April 1924 nationwide register of "gypsies" domiciled in municipalities in Slovakia, published in part by Nečas, the number of Roms in Trenčianska Teplá is given as eight and in Dobrá, 11.[223] However, Roms who were domiciled in the municipality but who were not present during the census were evidently not on the list, so the information on the size of

---

222 ŠA Trenčín, f. ObNÚ Trenčinska Teplá, k. 62 – Evidencia vydaných domovských listov obce Tr. Teplej a Dobrej od roku 1924–1939.

223 This is very probably the Facona family, who lived there in several houses with numbers described in the 1930 census as "gypsy huts". ŠA Trenčín, f. ObNÚ Trenčianska Teplá, Sčítanie ľudu z roku 1930, ev. č. 6009/30. Ctibor Nečas, "Materiál o Rómech na Slovensku z roku 1924". *Historická demografie*, vol. 22, no. 1 (1998): 177–178.

the Romani community in Trenčianska Teplá is clearly incomplete. Lists of names from the same period show that there were no other Romani families living directly in the municipality except for the Stojkas, so the number of eight Roms ought to correspond to the number of people on the list from this family.

From the official records, however, it is impossible to pinpoint to what extent Štefan Stojka, Sr. and his relatives were territorially connected to Trenčianska Teplá. It may be asked – and this is a question which I also dealt with in the case of Zaga Stojková – to what extent his family had a relatively permanent base here and whether they set out from here to do business (above all, horse trading) in the surrounding area, or whether, on the contrary, they spent most of their time travelling these routes and only returned sporadically to Trenčianska Teplá. If they did reside there reasonably permanently, did they live in a wagon or tent, or did they already have an improvised dwelling or wintering place to which they returned?

I cannot answer these questions with certainty for the period of the 1920s. A detailed search of the Trenčín archives and the local chronicle yielded no results. It is interesting that in the archival files for the municipality, all the official records relating to Štefan Stojka, Sr. in that decade and the following one list his place of residence (or actual residence) as Trenčianska Teplá, but with no specific address or house number as the other residents have. This indicates that Štefan Stojka, Sr. and his family did not live in a house with an officially registered number, but were just registered as belonging to the municipality, with their domicile there.

Still, the records relating to Štefan Stojka, Sr. in this and other decades in the collection of the notary's office in Trenčianska Teplá are more complete and consistent than are the records of other Roms from his family. They always list his full birthdate and it is always the same, just as the names of his parents are always the same, and his profession is "horse merchant". It is clear that the officials knew Štefan. This was not the case with other Roms, including his partner and children, whose dates and places of birth, first names and surnames vary across the records.

Štefan Stojka, Sr. and his eldest son Ján (*1905) earned their livings as horse traders, travelling with horses and a wagon around the municipalities of the nearby area. A unique picture of their life is given in an article published by the newspaper *Lidové noviny* in July 1924, describing their alleged conflict with the "gypsy blacksmith" Herák in Veľké Bierovce, a municipality in the Trenčín district about 25 kilometres from Trenčianska Teplá. The dispute is said to have arisen over a silver chain with a horse's head. In the article, Štefan Stojka is presented as a "gypsy merchant who was selling and buying horses here, [...] a gypsy duke, wealthy, who does not speak to every gypsy", but who because of the desired jewellery[224] "lowered himself and went to Herák to ask him to sell him the chain."[225] The value of this article as testimony is unfortunately reduced because of its sensationalist tone,[226] but it indicates the high social status and socioeconomic position of Štefan Stojka, Sr. (*merchant, duke, wealthy*) compared to Herák, whose position could not have been too low, however, since he was a blacksmith who had his own house and a maid, which was certainly not common at that time among the group known as Slovak Roms. In addition, the report indicates that an added factor in the dispute was the distance between the two groups of Roms. These may be recognised as the Slovak Roms, represented by Herák and his wife, and the Lovara, represented by Stojka father and son.

The 1930s: A change of spatial trajectories

While in the 1920s both Stojka siblings and their families had been territorially connected to a similar degree with the municipality of Trenčianska Teplá, and while their spatial trajectories clearly did not differ much either, being limited to the wider region of Western Slovakia at the most, in the 1930s there was a divergence between the spatial mobility of Zaga's family and her brother Štefan's. Once again, I shall reconstruct the spatial mobility of the family's two branches separately. First I shall look at the trajectories of Štefan Stojka, Sr., which in this decade were more connected not just to the area of western Slovakia, but also to the municipality of Trenčianska Teplá. I shall then describe my findings

---

224 Jewellery like this is still thought of by Lovara in the Czech lands and Slovakia as a status symbol, especially among high-status Roms (Angluno Rom, Krísako Rom, atd.), see also Markéta Hajská, "The presentation of social status on a social network: The role of Facebook among the Vlax Romani community of Eastern-Slovak origin in Leicester, UK". *Romani Studies*, vol. 29, no. 2 (2019): 135.

225 [author] -el. "Cikáni Stojkové (Porota v Trenčíně)." *Lidové noviny*, vol. 32, no. 331 (3. 7. 1924), 6.

226 It is interesting that *Lidové noviny* – which might be described as one of the most serious dailies in Czechoslovakia in the period in question and of key importance to analysing the political situation in the Czech lands – when writing about Slovakia or Sub-Carpathian Ukraine, would often write in a prejudiced and sensationalist manner about the local inhabitants and ethnic minorities. The historian Kateřina Čapková has drawn my attention in this context to stories written in a similar tone about Hasidic Jews and other minorities from the sub-Carpathian region.

concerning the mobility of Zaga Stojková and her children, which became more and more oriented towards the Czech lands.

Trajectories of the family of Štefan Stojka, Sr. in the 1930s

As shown by archival records, in the 1930s Štefan Stojka, Sr. and his family moved around the area of Western Slovakia. According to the available archival sources, their spatial mobility chiefly covered the Trenčín district and the nearby areas. The great majority of records localise Štefan Stojka, Sr. and his descendants in the 1930s in the Trenčín area and surrounding districts: Of 38 localisation points I managed to find from the 1930s, 28 come from today's Trenčín district, of which 14 are from Trenčianska Teplá itself, while seven further points include today's Ilava district, Prievidza, Bytča, Martin and Žilina.[227] An exception are three records from Northern Moravia (Místek 1931, Kunčice 1931, Český Těšín 1934), of which one concerns Štefan[228] and two his eldest son Ján.[229] This indicates that this branch of the family was also mobile in parts of Moravia not too distant from Slovakia.

Another unique source that contains much information about the life of Štefan Stojka, Sr. is a chapter from Slovak journalist Slavo Kalný's book *Cigánsky plač a smich* [Gypsy Tears and Laughter] entitled *"Ukrivdený koniar"* [The wronged horse trader]. In it the author describes the main events in the life of "Štefan Stojka from Trenčianska Teplá", described as a famous horse trader whom the author repeatedly used to meet and who was growing old at the start of the 1960s in a small cottage in Trenčianska Teplá.[230] The chapter starts with an outline of the areas in which Štefan Stojka carried out his trading activities. Given the context of what comes next, the description clearly concerns the interwar period:

> Even today, when you ask older farmers in the villages, the meadows and the hills from Trnava to Liptovský Mikuláš, from Bánovce to Nové Zámky,

---

227 I base this on archival material in ŠA Trenčín, f. ObNÚ Trenč. Teplá, ev. č. 77, k. 19 – Evidencia trestaných občianov obce Trenčinska Teplá 1933–1949.

228 A report from the local authority in Místek dated 15 May 1931 states that Štefan Stojka, Sr. had arrived there and was asking to renew the itinerancy document issued to him in April 1929 in Žilina and renewed there in April 1930. Štefan was accompanied by his partner Karolína and daughter Iboja. SOkA Frýdek Místek, f. OÚ Místek, I. č. 868, Signatura: III/1.

229 In 1931, Ján's daughter Papuša was born in Kunčice, see ŠA Trenčín, f. ObNÚ Trenč. Teplá, ev. č. 77, k. 19 – Evidencia trestaných občianov obce Trenčinska Teplá 1933–1949.

230 Kalný, *Cigánsky plač*, 60.

and even on the Moravian side around Uherský Brod, Hodonín and Vsetín whether they know the old gypsy Stojka, they will cast their minds back, think hard, suddenly come to life, a fan of wrinkles will spread over their faces and they will say: "The trader?... Of course we knew him. He outsmarted every other dealer he traded so cleverly.[231]

At the time of the chapter cited (1960), Štefan Stojka was almost 70 and had been trading horses for over 50 years in a highly unique way. The author of the book spends several paragraphs describing how Stojka was said to carry out his trade, no doubt drawing on various stereotypical anecdotes circulating about Romani horse traders at that time. I shall give two examples which, according to Kalný, showed Stojka, Sr.'s brilliant professional astuteness combined with his use of various ruses and sharp dealing practices:

Stojka knew how to transform horses! With his expert touch, secret dressage and strange fodder, he would change even a carcass into a galloping horse."[232]
"...few could outwit him, few could knock him out in a slippery trading duel. His omnipresence and gypsy originality had made him popular. With his dealings and methods he was famous as a trade partner, a broker, a salesman, feared, hated, three hundred times cursed.[233]

Štefan Stojka, Sr., who according to Kalný was present as a trader literally everywhere, appearing at the right time at every significant horse market, was said to have amassed not just prestige, but also a relatively large amount of money. Kalný expresses horror at Stojka's exploitative practices and alleges they were behind the amount of money he made. We have to take into account the fact that Kalný was starting from the contemporary principles of socialist doctrine, which rejected "exploitative self-enrichment" as a sign of capitalism. This was certainly reflected in the generally mocking tone used to describe Štefan Stojka, Sr. and his trading methods, combined with a markedly racist disdain for his "gypsy origin". This was clearly the way in which Kalný came to terms with the fact that Štefan Stojka, Sr., as a "gypsy", a member of a group that at that time was assumed to be on the fringes of society, had managed to amass so much property and social recognition at that time.

---

231 Ibid., 59.
232 Ibid., 60.
233 Ibid., 61.

Kalný states that Štefan Stojka, Sr. used to travel with the aid of a ladder wagon, to which he harnessed "the thoroughbred brindled horses, the others he attached with ropes behind the wagon, put his family inside and off they went."[234] These descriptions may, however, correspond more to the postwar period, from which I have found photographs of Štefan Stojka, Sr.'s family with a horse harnessed to a ladder wagon. What type of wagon he owned in the 1930s is not known precisely.

In the municipal register of horses that was kept between 1936 and 1939, there are three records of horses that Štefan Stojka, Sr. declared to the authorities. In 1936, he was listed as the owner of a bay horse with a blaze, estimated value 2,400 Czechoslovak crowns, which died in 1937 in the municipality of Velká Udiča, Povážská Bystrice district. In July 1937, Štefan Stojka, Sr. bought from Juraj Kotlárik of Orechové a nine-year-old gelding draught horse, chestnut with a star, estimated value 3,500 crowns. He sold it to someone in Kunčice on 2 December 1937. He bought another registered horse from his neighbour Ladislav Lehota of Teplá, apparently in 1937, and sold it in June 1938 to someone from Bolešov, Ilava district, but neither the price nor a description of that horse are given.[235]

I also have discovered a relatively large amount of information on Štefan Stojka Sr.'s eldest son Ján, born in 1905. In his case, too, it is possible to reconstruct his territorial shifts during the period in question, above all in the area of the neighbouring districts and in the surroundings of Trenčianska Teplá, where he was domiciled. In 1935, the notary's office in Trenčianska Teplá issued him a certificate of domicile at his request.[236] While in the records from 1933 to 1935 there is a note next to his name saying "residence unstable", in the records from the second half of the 1930s, Trenčianska Teplá is listed as his place of residence.[237]

As can be seen from the records of his profession in the local notary office's register, Ján earned his living as a horse trader too, and it may be assumed that he set out independently to buy and sell horses, without Štefan Stojka, Sr. I have found just sporadic evidence of Ján's activity. For example, there is an announcement of livestock passes lost, published in the periodical *Krajinský vestník pre Slovensko* in 1935,[238] mentioning the

---

234 Ibid., 59.

235 ŠA Trenčín, f. ObNÚ Trenč. Teplá, Administratívne spisy 1939, složka Klasifikácia koní, ev. č. 5542.

236 Ibid., ev. č. 77, k. 19, Evidencia vydaných domovských listov k obci Trenčinska Teplá 1933–1939.

237 Ibid.

238 "Ločaj Juraj z Hája oznámil sratu dvoch dobitčích pasov", Rubrika Straty, *Krajinský vestník pre Slovensko* 8, April 10, 1935, p. 187.

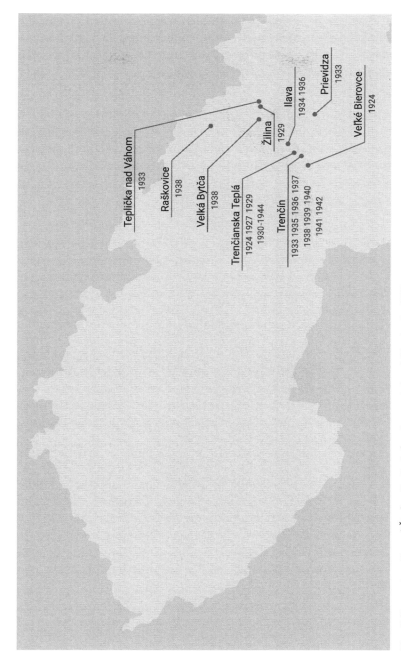

Map 1: Reconstruction of Štefan Stojka's family spatial mobility in the 1930s.

sale of a horse – an eight-year-old dark brown gelding with a small white star – for which a livestock pass was issued in Trenčianska Teplá to Ján Stojka, domiciled there. Ján subsequently sold that horse to Juraj Ločaj of Háj near Turčianske Teplice. In February 1939, Ján Stojka bought another officially-registered horse from Ján Mandinec of Vyškovec (Uherské Hradiště district).[239]

It is clear that the mobility of Štefan Stojka Sr.'s family branch in the 1930s was chiefly connected with the territory of Western Slovakia, to which were added occasional journeys to North Moravia[240] at the start of the decade. From countless records noting the residence of Štefan Stojka, Sr. and his family in the municipality of Trenčianska Teplá for various reasons, I infer that they either returned to the municipality frequently or had a permanent base there. Once again the question arises of to what extent Štefan's family may be presumed to have resided in Trenčianska Teplá on a more permanent basis. Although their itinerant activities were carried out most frequently in the immediate geographical surroundings of the municipality in which various members of the Stojka family were registered as both resident and domiciled, and while this might suggest that they were at least partly settled there, I have not managed to find any proof that they had a reasonably permanent presence in the community before the second half of the 1930s.

Štefan Stojka, Sr. applied to the notary's office in Trenčianska Teplá a total of four times (in the years 1935 to 1939) for a domicile document (the reasons are mostly unspecified, and just once is a reason listed, that of marriage). In all cases, domicile and residency in Trenčianska Teplá is listed next to his name on the basis of his "right to domicile on the basis of Section 6, Art. XXII/1886."[241]

On the other hand, there are notes in the official records regarding the unstable residence of Štefan Stojka, Sr. and his family members. For example, in the cases of his daughters, partner, and niece (the daughter of Štefan's sister Mária), the register sometimes lists their residence and domicile as in Trenčianska Teplá, although the note: "domicile unstable/

---

239 ŠA Trenčín, f. ObNÚ Trenč. Teplá, Administratívne spisy 1939, složka Klasifikácia koní, ev. č. 5542.

240 The journalist Kalný also remembered the area around Uherský Brod, clearly on the basis of details given to him by Štefan Stojka, Sr. himself (Kalný, *Cigánsky plač*).

241 ŠA Trenčín, f. ObNÚ Trenč. Teplá, ev. č. 77, k. 19 – Evidencia vydaných domovských listov k obci Trenčinska Teplá 1933–1939. and Evidencia vydaných domovských listov k obci Trenčinska Teplá 1939–1945.

unascertained" or "residence unstable" sometimes appears next to their names. The repeated notes added next to their names, such as "gypsy vagabond", "gypsy – vagabond", "travelling gypsy" and "gypsy without employment", do not, however, mean that these people did not live in the municipality, since the term "gypsy vagabond" was used at that time as a synonym for the term "gypsy". The disproportion between the lack of detail about Štefan Stojka Sr.'s children and the women in the family and the figure of Štefan himself shows that he was the one who had dealings with the authorities as head of the family. In some cases his son Ján might have been involved, but the other members of the family were little known to the non-Romani surroundings and to the authorities in particular. The authorities at that time operated via the official heads of such groups, for whom the majority population used the word *vajda* (later, during the war, this became a compulsory, elected function). It was these "heads of families" or *vajdas* who dealt with officials on behalf of their family members. This allowed the *vajdas* to keep the other members of the local community in a certain limbo.

A turning point came in the second half of the 1930s, when Štefan managed to buy a house and land in the municipality. This detail first appears on an official list of domicile certificates issued with the date 22 January 1938, when his residential address is given as "no. 273 Trenčianska Teplá". This is the first time that a residence linked to a particular address, a specific house, appears in the municipal records in connection with the Stojka, Sr. family. According to Kalný, the land was bought and the house built in 1936 or 1937.

In 1936 or 1937, when his wallet was so full it was bursting at the seams and the leather bag he kept under the seat of the wagon was stuffed round and fat with money, Stojka threw a wedding party for his daughter that is still remembered to this day. It lasted three days and three nights and not only did the wedding guests and the innkeeper come to the feast, but villagers who were not shy or who wanted to have a free drink and to congratulate the newlyweds and father Stojka came too. After the wedding he counted his money and found he still had a huge amount, not much had disappeared either from his wallet or his leather bag.

All I'm lacking is a house, he thought to himself. – Even if I never sleep in it, I need a house. A house is a house, a house counts for something. People will say: That Stojka's different, he has a house.

One day he set out with a brickmaker friend along the road that leads from Trenčianska Teplá to Trenčianske Teplice and chose a suitable piece of land.

Stojka most liked a place close to the quarry. Maybe because he'd get some stone for free. Which is what happened.[242]

The book *Gypsy Tears and Laughter* goes on to describe how Stojka's house was built by a bricklayer who cheated him and did not do a good job. However, the author writes, in buying a house Štefan Stojka was not looking for a place to live. He wanted to *have a house* in the sense of a status symbol (although Kalný does not use this term). The author suggests that even after the house was built, Stojka continued to sleep outside under blankets and tarpaulins, using the house just to stable his horses. He appeared in the house "most often when there were fairs in the Trenčín region and it was not far from the house to anywhere else, to Púchov or to Žilina."[243] Stojka reportedly said the following to the author when the latter was writing the book (the extract is enclosed in quotation marks in the original source, evoking direct speech or a direct citation):

> Believe me, young man, we slept better outside, under a tarpaulin, by the fire and in the fresh air, than in the house in a feather bed. We couldn't breathe in the house, we found it stifling. A horse can't cover himself up and hide from the rain. A farmer's horse was more used to a roof than we were.[244]

Since this is literature and not an academic text, the direct speech may just be an artistic stylisation the author has invented in order to create a more exotic picture of Štefan Stojka, Sr. The reliability of Slavo Kalný's commentaries is therefore unclear.

Nevertheless, according to the 1930 census[245], Štefan Stojka, Sr. was already the owner of the house in Teplická street No. 273 in Trenčianska Teplá in 1930 (see Fig. 2b). The census lists him as the owner of the house, although the house was at the time inhabited by other tenants. These were a three-member local, non-Romani family, whose two adult members, a mother and daughter, worked as ancillary staff and cleaners for the Czechoslovak railways. Štefan is clearly listed on the census document as the owner of the house.[246] It is not clear how he came to own it, and it is possible that he himself did not live in it until the late 1930s, but rented it out. During the time about which Kalný is writing,

---

242 Kalný, *Cigánsky plač,* 60
243 Ibid., 61.
244 Ibid., 61.
245 ŠA Trenčín, f. ObNÚ Trenčianska Teplá, Sčítanie ľudu z roku 1930, ev. č. 6009/30.
246 Ibid.

Štefan may have been rebuilding or adding to it in some way; at any rate, it seems that it was at this time that he started to use it regularly. The Stojkas lived in it or had a base there in subsequent years, and after the ban on itinerancy during the Second World War, he must have resided there permanently.

In the ensuing wartime years, that address was given as the residence of Štefan Stojka, Sr. and other Roms from the Stojka family in Trenčianska Teplá. In the documents from which I will cite further, the property is described as being in Štefan's ownership (living in "his own house",[247] "the dwelling place of Štefan Stojka",[248] etc.). In the list entitled *Evidencia cigáňov 1942* (Register of gypsies 1942), Štefan Stojka, Sr.'s property status is given as: "own dwelling".[249] In the archive in Trenčín I managed to find confirmation of the payment of property tax from the postwar years (1947 and 1948),[250] where Štefan is listed as the owner of a house that by that time had already been destroyed with the arrival of the front.

The fact that Štefan Stojka, Sr., as a Rom and a horse trader, became the owner of a centrally-located property in the municipality, in the close vicinity of non-Roms, must have been something very unusual at that time. Indeed, 80 years later the staff of the registry office in Trenčianska Teplá also considered it unlikely. "A gypsy owning a house? Not likely! And at that time!", was their comment on my original question as to whether the house at the address stated could have been his own. However, the archival documents clearly show his ownership of that house at an address on the main street of the municipality.

The migration trajectory of Zaga and her children in the 1930s

During the 1930s, there was a considerable change in the mobility of Zaga Stojková's branch of the family. While all the records I could find from the 1920s showed the movements of her family as being limited to Trenčín and the surrounding districts of Western Slovakia, from the early 1930s their migration trajectories broadened to include journeys to

---

247 ŠA Trenčín, f. ObNÚ Trenč. Teplá, i. č. – Cigánské pomery 2523, Report from OÚ in Trenčín (15. 5. 1940), čj. 8867/40, *Trenč. Teplá, umístenie cigáňov.*
248 ŠA Trenčín, f. ObNÚ Trenč. Teplá, Cigáni – neprístojné chovanie a nariadení na ich vystehovanie č. 944 from the year 1947. Report by police commander to the MNV in Trenč. Teplá (10. 4. 1947).
249 ŠA Trenčín, f. ObNÚ Trenč. Teplá, i. č. 99, k. 23 – Evidencia cigáňov 1942.
250 ŠA Trenčín, f. Domovská Daň Trenčín, daňová obec Trenč. Teplá. *Vyrubovací list daně činžovej* for the address Teplická č. p. 273 for the years 1947 and 1948.

Moravia and Bohemia. While Štefan Stojka, Sr. and his eldest son had also travelled to such destinations, their trips were marginal compared to those of his sister Zaga's family. As I shall show, Zaga's family travels were not so much single-destination trips to sell horses, as seems to have been the case with Štefan, but geographically-complex movements around Bohemian territory and mainly around Moravian territory which were year-round in nature.

On the basis of the fragmentary information on record it is not possible to state with certainty when this change in their spatial mobility took place. However, I can try to establish the stop-offs or sections of their spatial trajectories through the spatiotemporal points where I know the family was present on a certain territory and when.

The oldest records I have found of the family's presence in the Czech lands come from 1931. I have managed to find a total of five records from that year. The first and second were made on the same day and in the same place, 2 July 1931 in Moravská Ostrava, and were clearly connected to each other: They concern the arrest of Anna Lakatošová (*1902)[251] and her sister-in-law Barbora Stojková, Zaga Stojková's daughter (*1914),[252] for vagrancy. Barbora was just 15 at the time of arrest and very probably was travelling with the family of her brother Filo and his partner Anna. Another two records concern Zaga Stojková, whose identity was checked on 8 October 1931 in Odry in North Moravia and subsequently on 22 November of the same year in Brandýs nad Labem, a municipality north of Prague. The final record was made just four days later on 26 November 1931 in Mnichovice,[253] a municipality southwest of Prague belonging to what was the Říčany district at the time. For an idea of what distance the Lovara were capable of covering in horse-drawn wagons, it is interesting to mention that those two municipalities are approximately 40 kilometres apart. According to the Mnichovice municipal police station's register of residency applications by "gypsies" (*Hlášení cikánů k pobytu*) police there checked a 16-member group of Roms with the surnames Stojka and Lakatoš. Of the names listed, it is possible to identify Zaga Stojková (age 43) and her four minor children (Barbora, Josef, Kuluša and Grofojka), her son Filo Stojka (age 24), his wife Anna Lakatošová (age 29) and their three

---

251 NA Praha, f. Policejní ředitelství II – všeobecná spisovna – 1931–1940, k. 8259, sign. L119/1, f. 1, zpráva četnické stanic v Moravské Ostravě (2 July 1931).

252 NA Praha, f. Policejní ředitelství II – všeobecná spisovna – 1941–1950, k. 11057, sign. S6254/47, f. 1, zpráva četnické stanic v Moravské Ostravě (2 July 1931).

253 SOkA Přemyšlení, f. OU Říčany, i. č. 427, ev. č. 246 – Výkaz cikánů potulných přistižených v roce 1931 četnickou stanicí v Mnichovicích.

children. The 10-member family of Zaga Stojková's children and grand-children was accompanied by the six-member family of Pavel Lakatoš, at which I will look in more detail later. From the records it can be seen that the group had itinerancy documents and "gypsy" identity cards and that they were subsequently ejected from the municipality. The last two checks took place at the end of November, so on the threshold of the winter period.

Records from subsequent years find the family on the territory of Bohemia and Moravia not just in the summer, but all year round, including the winter months. Of a total of 58 different records of stays by Roms from the family of Zaga Stojková and their children (including their partners and grandchildren) during the 1930s on the territory of Bohemia and Moravia I know the precise date of a stay in a certain place for just 43 records. Of these, 26 were in the winter and 17 in the summer. For these purposes, I do not define winter astronomically or meteorologically, but from the emic perspective. From the Lovara point of view, winter (*jivend*) was defined by cold, inclement weather, typically with freezing temperatures and probably with snow. Such weather must have seriously complicated movement with carts and horses along the roads of the time. Winter defined in this way could, in these latitudes, be expected at least from mid-November to the end of March, which are the months I include in the winter or cold period. I found records from these winter months showing that the family was present in the Czech lands in all such winter seasons of the 1930s.

It therefore has to be asked whether this part of the Stojka family ever returned to Slovakia at all during those years. Although such journeys are probable, none of the archival records confirms that they took place. If they did happen, it was clearly not for the reason of a regular return to a wintering place, because these families spent the winter in their wagons, probably on the road or in designated standing places on the edges of Moravian and Czech towns. I believe they had no wintering place during this period and lived all year round in their wagons, with the possible use of tarpaulin tents when camping.

Given the large number of official records on the family's presence in the Czech lands, I shall look at only some of them. In December 1933, the family was moving around the border between Bohemia and Moravia. On 5 December 1933 in Domamil, Anna Lakatošová declared the loss of her gypsy identity card and itinerancy document, alleged to have taken place on 3 December on the road between Martínkov and Domamil. On

11 December she received a duplicate issued by the Moravské Budějovice district authorities.[254]

The name of Anna Lakatošová's partner, Filo Stojka, features on the official document *Přihlášky cikánů* (Registrations of gypsies)[255] maintained by the municipality of Lhota Rapotina, Blansko district, dated 13 January 1934, where the authorities used to record Roms who camped in the municipality. Only "heads of the family" were listed in the records, in other words, the people in whose name the itinerancy document was issued for the family under Act no. 117/1927. The size of the family travelling with Filo is thus unknown. The date of the check once again shows that the family was in the Czech lands during the winter months.

The family of Filo Stojka and his wife Anna Lakatošová, together with the family of Filo's mother Zaga, were apprehended on 31 July 1934 by policemen in Horní Cerekev, Pelhřimov district, in a small municipality close to the historical border between Bohemia and Moravia. The report to the police headquarters in Prague says that "hordes of gypsies were ejected and accompanied by a guard from the police station here back to Moravia, from whence they had come, and they were handed over to the police in Batelov,"[256] a municipality several kilometres away in Moravian territory. In addition to the three nuclear families of Stojkas, the report to police headquarters from the Horní Cerekev police also records eight other adult Lovara with the surnames Rafael or Bihari, probably accompanied by their own nuclear families. The whole group must thus have numbered several dozen people. They travelled in four wagons.[257]

On the very next day, 1 August 1934, the family of Filo Stojka was arrested in Třešť, Jihlava district, 13 kilometres from Horní Cerekev. That Filo Stojka was not put off by being ejected from the historical Czech lands is confirmed by the fact that three weeks later, on 20 August 1934, he was found by police with other Lovara (with the surnames Rafael, Bihari and Stojka) in Strakonice in South Bohemia. All the men were taken into custody, although the reason for doing so is not mentioned

---

254 NA Praha, f. Policejní ředitelství II – všeobecná spisovna – 1931–1940, k. 8259, sign. L119/10, f. 1, zpráva četnické stanice Domamil čís. 30, odd. Jihlava, pátrací čís. G/14. Pátrací oběžník, subject: Lakatošová Anna, ztráta cikánské legitimace a kočovnického listu (30. 12. 1933).

255 SOkA Blansko, f. AO Lhota Rapotina, kn. i. č. 8 – Evidence cikánů 1927–1935.

256 SOkA Pelhřimov, f. OU Kamenice nad Lipou, inv. č. 1008, k. 505, fol. 1–4 – Příkaz okresního úřadu v Kamenici n/L. č. j. 21.423/1933 ze dne 23. 7. 1933, č. j. 897/3, Horní Cerekvice (1. 8. 1934).

257 Ibid.

in the report. The district authorities in Strakonice then issued a resolution through which, under Section 2 of Act 88 of 27 July 1871, in order to police in the interests of public order and safety, they banned the six named people, including Filo Stojka, from "all further stays on the territory of Bohemia for all time, and you shall be escorted out by the police". Failure to observe the ban was subject to the punishment indicated in Section 324 of the Criminal Code.[258]

This decision to ban Filo Stojka from the territory of Bohemia clearly carried considerable weight and may be considered the reason why the further spatial mobility of his family, as well as the mobility of Zaga Stojková's other descendants, was from then on limited to the territory of Moravia. Their residence was not dealt with under Act no. 117/1927, which ought to have related to them *de iure*, but was dealt with under the law on public order.

Zaga Stojková's children form new branches of the family in the 1930s

From approximately the first half of the 1930s, Zaga Stojková's offspring need to be tracked separately in terms of their spatial mobility. At the beginning of the decade, her eldest son Filo's nuclear family with his partner Anna Lakatošová and their children became independent, which (partly) makes itself seen in their independent mobility. In subsequent years I also see not only these separate spatial trajectories among other parts of the family, but also concurrent stays by several family units at the same time in one place (attendance at a horse fair, or a camping place checked by police). Here it should be remembered that the size of groups who were allowed to "travel" or "camp" together was limited by Act no. 117/1927, concretely Section 7, which stated that "wandering gypsies are not permitted to travel and camp in hordes exceeding the [nuclear] family." As can be seen from the records cited above and also from other evidence, Romani families in practice violated this rule. This resulted in their expulsion or ejection, as happened in the above-mentioned police checks in Mnichovice in 1931 and in Kamenice nad Lipou in 1934. These experiences of being expelled from a certain territory could lead to the strengthening of a strategy whereby the individual branches of the fami-

---

258 NA Praha, f. Policejní ředitelství II – všeobecná spisovna 1931–1940, k. 11157, sign. S 6417/17. Hlášení OÚ ve Strakonicích, č. j. 32567/34–8-ST/40 (20. 8. 1934), fol. 4.

ly, broadly corresponding to nuclear families, moved around the territory independently and then met up again at arranged places.

The family of Zaga's daughter Barbora (*1914) and her partner and later husband, Juraj Horváth (*1912) split off from Zaga's family in the early 1930s. Their first child was born in February 1933. A few years later, Barbora's sister Kuluš (*1920) also peeled away from the family. She married Antonín Horvát, whose Romani nickname was Vido (*1914) and who was the brother of her brother-in-law, Barbora's partner Juraj.

I shall spend a little time on the Horvát brothers now. They came from a Lovara family domiciled in Bohdanovce, Trnava district. Their father, Pavol Lakatoš, was born in Bohdanovce in 1871 to parents named Joannes Lakatoš and Mária Stojka. In the register of births he is entered as Paulus Lakatos (the Latin form of his first name), and the note *Zingari vagi* [Gypsy vagabonds], *hic dicti* [here called = so-called] *Valachici* [Wallachians] *RCath* [Roman Catholic].[259]

Pavol Lakatoš took a wife, Mária, whose surname was Horvát and who was born in 1885 in Trnava to parents named Pavol Horvát and Mária Stojková. According to the records, Pavol Lakatoš and Mária Horvátová had four sons – in addition to Antonín and Juraj there was the eldest, Martin (*around 1910, probably Mária's illegitimate son from her previous relationship) and the youngest, Ludvík (*1918). As was the custom with unmarried couples, all the sons took their mother's surname, Horvát. Pavol and Mária did get married in the end, but only after all their sons were born, in July 1918.[260] With the marriage their mother gained the surname Lakatošová, but her sons remained Horvát. With this family, as with the Stojka family and Trenčianska Teplá, it is possible to observe territorial ties with a municipality, in this case Bohdanovce nad Trnavou. The father of the family, Pavol, was born there in 1871, as was Juraj in 1912, Antonín in 1914 and the youngest, Ludvík, in 1918. The family was last recorded in 1931 in the official "register of gypsies"[261] living on territory falling in the administrative area of the then-notary's office in Boleráz, belonging to the municipality of Bohdanovce. This was also the only Romani family living in Bohdanovce. The head of the family, Pavol Lakatoš, is listed as a "horse trader" by livelihood. A note at the end of the census entry for the whole family reads: "Wandering in an

---

259 Slovakia Church and Synagogue Books, 1592–1935, *FamilySearch* (https://familysearch.org /ark:/61903/1:1:V1CR-8Y2),), [cit. 1. 6. 2023]; FHL microfilm 2,386,075.
260 Štátny archív Trnava. ObNÚ Boleráz k. 48, kn. Evidencia cigáňov 1931–1935.
261 Ibid.

unknown place", and the record is dated 2 December 1931.[262] Thanks to archival finds in the state district archive for Praha-východ in Přemyšlení, however, I am able to state with certainty the name of the place where the family was present at about that time. It was this family who, together with the family of Zaga, Filip and Anna, had been checked by policemen in the Central Bohemian municipality of Mnichovice on 26 November 1931 just a couple of days before this official record was made.[263] On the list made during the police control in Mnichovice, all the members of the families checked were mentioned by name. The family headed by Zaga included her daughters Barbora (age 17) and Kuluš (age 11). Right behind them are the names of Pavol Lakatoš, his wife Mária, who by then was already using the surname Lakatošová, and their four sons. It is interesting that the surnames of the sons are not listed precisely, but recorded as being the same as their parents, Lakatoš. Their real surname was Horvát, which they had used in previous years and would also use after the war. It is likely that by then Juraj, at 21 officially an adult, was already living with the 17-year-old Barbora. Their parents (the seemingly widowed Zaga and the couple of Pavol and Mária) may have seen each other already as *chanamikura*, a term that establishes a relationship between the parents of a young couple. Among the Lovara, this was a relationship traditionally connected with mutual respect. It is likely that the family of Pavol Lakatoš and his children, like that of Zaga Stojková, moved around the Czech lands a large part of the time in subsequent years, probably mostly in Moravia.[264]

Nevertheless, Barbora and Juraj moved around independently from February 1933, when their son was born in the Slovak municipality of Teplička nad Váhom. This is also, for a number of years, the last official record that I have found regarding a stay by someone from Zaga Stojková's branch of the family on Slovak territory; all the other records find the family in the Czech lands. I managed to localise the family of Barbora and Juraj Horvát in September 1933 in Brno, in December 1933 in Kunštát,[265] and for the last time in 1936 in Moravská Ostrava, where

---

262 Ibid. The data is confirmed as still valid as of 3 March 1933. No other record of them was made in this book for the municipality of Bohdanovce.

263 SOkA Přemyšlení, f. OU Říčany, i. č. 427, ev. č. 246. Výkaz cikánů potulných přistižených v roce 1931 četnickou stanicí v Mnichovicích.

264 I am not able to identify the precise movements of Pavol Lakatoš and Mária Lakatošová during the subsequent years because their names are too common, making it impossible to identify any points on their migration trajectories uniquely with certainty.

265 ŠA Trenčín, f. ObNÚ Trenč. Teplá, ev. č. 77, k. 19 – Evidencia vydaných domovských listov k obci Trenčinska Teplá 1933–1939.

another son was born to them in March. His birth certificate contains the following note (fairly unusual for this type of document) next to the name of his mother Barbora: "a gypsy vagabond trader, domicile not ascertained, resident in Trenč. Teplá. Unmarried concubine of Jiří Horvát".[266]

When exactly her younger sister Kuluš separated from Zaga's family is not known. Antonín, together with his father Pavol Lakatoš and his father-in-law Filo Stojka, was falsely accused of stealing horses in Frenštát pod Radhoštěm in 1935,[267] so their families were at that point both in the same place at the same time. Kuluš and Antonín's son was born in May 1937 not far from Opava. In 1937 and 1938 Antonín is found repeatedly registered with the authorities in the district of Místek[268] and in July 1938 he was checked by the authorities in Opava.[269]

Localisation of Zaga Stojková's mobility points on the map

The scattered records relating to the Stojka family in various Czech and Slovak archives cry out to be mapped spatiotemporally. By analysing the different points localised in time and space it is possible to portray this family branch's mobility.

In order to localise members of the Stojka family during this period, I use all the data on the birthdates and birthplaces of their children[270] and also police reports (the "gypsy registrations") and other official records on "vagabond hordes" arriving. An occasional archival source that is complicated from an ethical point of view is the record book from the district notary's office in Trenčianska Teplá entitled *Evidencia trestaných občianov obce Trenčianska Teplá 1933–1949* (Register of the convicted citizens of the municipality of Trenčianska Teplá 1933–1949), in which all the offences committed by persons domiciled in Trenčianska Teplá that

---

266 The birth certificate is part of the personal file on the above-mentioned son, Silvester Stojka, in his application for a certificate under Act no. 255/1946, Coll. of applicant S. S. (*1936). Jiří was in fact named Juraj, q.v. the trend described above for registrars in the Czech lands to use the Czech equivalents of Slovak names.

267 *Lidové noviny*. Brno: Vydavatelské družstvo Lidové strany v Brně, 31 March 1935, 43 (165, morning edition), p. 8.

268 Černý, "Lovárové", 22–23.

269 ŠA Trenčín, f. ObNÚ Trenč. Teplá, ev. č. 77, k. 19 – Evidencia trestaných občianov obce Trenčinska Teplá 1933–1949.

270 It follows from these sources that children from this part of the family were born in 1931 in Kunčice, in 1936 in Moravská Ostrava, in 1937 in Opava and in 1938 in Paskov, Místek district.

took place on Czechoslovak territory were listed. I discussed the problematic nature of using this source in the introductory chapter.

When I was putting together an outline of Zaga's branch of the family and its members' spatial mobility, this source helped me to localise individuals precisely while at the same time saying something about the permanence of their relationship with the municipality to which they administratively belonged. In January 1933, Zaga's family was in Místek, two months later they were in Frýdek, in September 1933 they were in Brno, in December 1933 they were in Kunštát, then in August 1937 they returned to Frýdek, in March 1939 they were in Chomutov (northwest Bohemia, in the Sudetenland) and in July 1938 they were in the Silesian capital, Opava.[271]

The presence of these family members in Moravia is also shown by historian Rostislav Černý in his study of the Lovara community in the Místek district during the First Czechoslovak Republic. He cites archival police records according to which, in March 1933, "Anna Lakatošová came to the office with a request for the issue of a duplicate itinerancy document for herself, Zaga Stojková and Filo Stojka".[272] He goes on to say that Anna had an original itinerancy document issued in 1930 in Žilina that was damaged. The district office in Místek in March 1933 then extended her itinerancy document for a year. In May, according to the Šumperk police records, the said Anna declared the loss of her itinerancy document in the municipality of Frankštát (Nový Malín), Šumperk district, and the lost document was to be sent to her in Ústí nad Orlicí, where she was said to be.[273] Černý also provides evidence of these family members being present in the Místek area in 1931 (Anna Lakatošová and Zaga's daughter Grófa) and in 1936 (Zaga Stojková and other persons), and adds that groups of Lovara were to be found in the district when the horse and livestock fairs were being held.[274] Černý also cites the chief of the Paskov police station, who describes regular "movements of a large group of Romani horse traders who pass through the municipality on their way to the livestock fairs on the route Opava-Moravská

---

271 ŠA Trenčín, f. f. ObNÚ Trenč. Teplá, ev. č. 77, k. 19 – Evidencia trestaných občianov obce Trenčinska Teplá 1933–1949.

272 Černý, "Lovárové," 13–14.

273 SOkAFrýdek-Místek, f. OÚ Místek, k. 723, i. č. 824 – Opis úředního záznamu Policejního komisařství v Šumperku z 26. 5. 1934.

274 Černý states that horse dealing was the main reason why the Lovara regularly, month after month, visited the district town of Místek, where livestock fairs were held during a certain period. (Černý, "Lovárové", 24).

Ostrava-Český Těšín-Frýdek/Místek."[275] As we can see on the map, in the second half of the 1930s in particular, the Opava area became the region around which the family repeatedly moved, passing through various municipalities. If we take into account the fact that the reason for their presence in the Frýdek and Místek areas was the livestock and horse fairs, there remains the interesting question of why their family and other Lovara families also moved around in other districts. Did the Lovara also attend horse fairs in other places? Was their increased movement in the Opava and Litovel districts connected with the sale and purchase of horses traded on the market in Místek? In this regard the archival reports are fragmentary, and there is no explanation of the reasons for their presence in other villages or towns. The police reports from Místek and Frýdek are, in this respect, unusually detailed. The report from the Krásná police station, for example, contains this detailed description:

> "At each horse fair in Frýdek taking place annually in the markets, several male members of the gypsy hordes appeared in order to trade horses. Their women and children usually camped in one of the villages surrounding Frýdek, and after the fair the gypsies would leave our ward."[276]

Although this description does not identify a specific Romani group, it corresponds to Lovara testimonies describing the horse fairs as involving Romani men who then took their earnings back to their women and children.

Information on the places where the group stayed is also provided by the press of the time. Despite the undoubted difficulties[277] of working with such sources, I managed with the help of the media of the period to localise members of the family in March 1935 near Frenštát pod Radhoštěm,[278] and in 1936 and 1937 several times in the Opava district in Silesia.[279]

---

275 Ibid.

276 SOkA Frýdek Místek, f. OÚ Frýdek, i. č. 780, k. 641, Oddělení Český Těšín, stanice Krásná č. 27 – Cikáni – podání zprávy (30. 1. 1935).

277 As I stated in the introductory chapter on methodology, this source needs to be treated with caution, since information on "gypsy vagabonds" most often appeared in sections reporting on the criminal activities of these groups, with the tendentious aim of fuelling anti-Romani feeling and exoticising these people.

278 [author] -in. "Cikán jako vyděrač a tajný." *Lidové noviny*, vol. 43, no. 165 (31. 5, 1935), 8

279 [author n.a.] "Ausgeforichte heudiebe." *Neues Tagblatt für Schlesien und Nordmähren*, vol. 4, no. 260 (5. 11. 1937), 4; [author n.a.] "Diebische Zigeuner." *Neues Tagblatt für Schlesien und Nordmähren*, vol. 3, no. 51 (29. 2. 1936), 9; [author n.a.] "Berhastete Zigeunerin." *Neues Tagblatt für Schlesien und Nordmähren*, vol. 4, no. 289 (9. 12. 1937), 6.

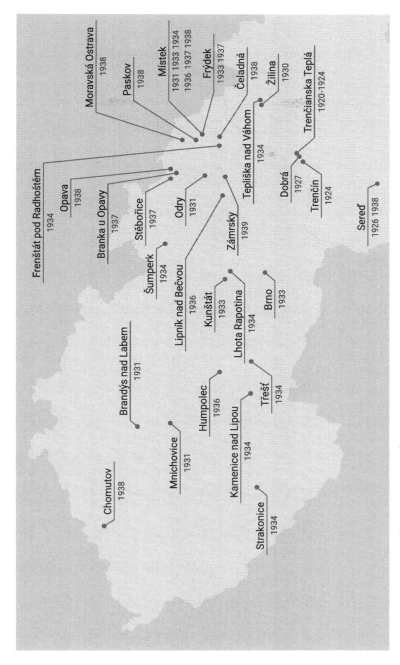

Map 2 Reconstruction of Zaga Stojková's family spatial mobility in the 1930s.

From the data available, I created a list of the transit points where the members of this group appeared at a certain time. This map of Zaga Stojková's family branch and its spatial mobility, including her sons and daughters' nuclear families, who moved around independently, needs of course to be seen as just a very much reduced cross-section of the group's real movements, which cannot be fully reconstructed today.

The trajectories of Zaga Stojková's family (including her son Filo Stojka's family and those of her daughters Barbora and Kuluš) led not just through Western Slovakia to northeastern Moravia and Silesia, but also into the Bohemian interior. This is shown by the above-mentioned records of their camping near Mnichovice and Kamenice nad Lipou, as well as by the birthdates and birthplaces of the family's children in Lhota u Chroustovic, Chrudim district (1934) and Humpolec (1936) on the border of Bohemia and Moravia, although only in Moravia after the family of Filo Stojka was banned from Bohemia in 1934.[280]

The group managed to get around fairly quickly, considering that they travelled in horse-drawn wagons. Over the course of a year they moved around to various places in the country (e.g. in 1931: 8 October Odry, North Moravia; 22 November Brandýs nad Labem, Central Bohemia – places almost 300 km apart; or in 1934: 1 August Třešť, Jihlava district, west Moravia; then 20 August Strakonice, southwest Bohemia, places about 140 km apart). Their journeys may have been connected with the profession of horse dealing, i.e., heading to horse fairs for the purpose of buying and selling horses, but they may also have been attempts to find new territories for their other economic strategies. It is likely that the reason they left Slovakia was an attempt to find a new territory for their professional activities from which it was hard to earn a living in their original territory in the Trenčín area, given the high degree of competition between people engaging in the same economic activity (horse trading).

Štefan Stojka, Sr. earned his living as a horse trader and was clearly fairly well-known in the wider vicinity of Trenčianska Teplá. His eldest son Ján was also a horse trader. For Filo Stojka, Zaga's eldest son, who also became a horse dealer, it must have been fairly problematic to find clients in his original district without competing with his uncle and cousin. Moreover, there were also other Romani horse traders in the region. Leaving this area and trying to do business in a new territory must have been an attractive proposition, indeed a necessity. After the creation of

---

280 ŠA Trenčín, f. ObNÚ Trenč. Teplá, ev. č. 77, k. 19 – Evidencia trestaných občianov obce Trenčinska Teplá 1933–1949.

Czechoslovakia, the logical solution was to move to the territory of Bohemia and above all Moravia, which was just over the nearest mountain ridge from Trenčín.

However, we should not forget that in North Moravia in particular there were other active horse-trading families, above all from the Sinti group, while other Bohemian and Moravian Roms also earned their living through horse trading, and so there was competition from other Romani families providing the same services and clearly also using similar practices on the other side of the mountain ridge, too. We may assume that over the course of the 1930s, when there was a rapid increase in the number of towns and villages in the Czech lands from which "gypsy vagabonds" were banned, along with a general rise of anti-gypsy sentiment in society, it was harder and harder to find new markets and to cultivate a permanent circle of clients and territories where it would be possible to do business.

2.2 The transformation of the spatial mobility of the Lovara in the Czech lands after the creation of Czechoslovakia

The paths of Zaga Stojková's family branch, and to a lesser degree the paths of Štefan Stojka, Sr.'s family branch toward Moravia and Bohemia from the early 1930s correspond to the movements of other Lovara families from Slovakia in the period in question. As I indicated in the previous chapter, after the breakup of the Habsburg monarchy and Czechoslovak independence in 1918 there was an overall transformation in many Lovara families' mobility. Above all, there was a gradual change in the overall composition of the Lovara families in the Czech lands, with a gradual reduction in the number of Lovara coming over the new, southern border with Austria and an increase in the number of Lovara families coming into the Czech lands from the Slovak part of the republic. However, this transformation also noticeably affected Lovara living in Slovakia, above all in the belt along the newly-created Slovak-Hungarian border. Before the break-up of Austro-Hungary, the Lovara who lived there would also move around in Hungary south of the Danube river, areas which at that time were not yet separated by a border from the future Slovak territory to the north. After the creation of Czechoslovakia, their trajectories no longer included journeys into Hungary. This pushed individual Lovara families to search for new territory on which to do business. It was in reaction to this fact that the Lovara gradually moved from Western Slovakia to Moravia and Bohemia.[281] Another hypothesis for their departure from Slovakia was the above-mentioned growing competition between providers of very similar services in the larger Lovara (but also wider Romani) community in Slovakia, which required the territorial dispersion of this activity. Some Lovara families seem to have come to the Czech lands mainly for business, chiefly horse fairs, or in order to perform crafts (mostly kettle-makers looking to sell, clean or tin kettles, blade sharpeners and so on), but regularly returned to Slovakia. However, some families aimed to move wholesale into this new territory.

Lovara in the Czech lands in the 1920s

The Lovara presence in the Czech lands has so far been of only marginal interest to Czech historians. Ctibor Nečas and Jana Horváthová have agreed that it was a group that did not dwell permanently in the Czech lands, but merely transited through them.[282] However, my research shows that although the Lovara did not form a large proportion of Roms, historical research should pay attention to them because of their continuous presence in the pre-war and postwar periods. In the 1930s in particular, the Lovara spent long periods in the Czech lands, some staying there continuously year round.

Let us return, however, to the start of the period, in other words, the period immediately following the birth of Czechoslovakia. Lovara from Austria continued to travel to Bohemia and Moravia even after the breakup of Austro-Hungary, as is shown by the 1920s news reports cited above,[283] as well as by genealogical data from various Vlax Romani witnesses currently living in the Czech Republic who have spoken about

---

281 Andrš, "Our God", 71–72.
282 E.g., Jana Horváthová, "Meziválečné zastavení mezi Romy v českých zemích (aneb tušení souvislostí)." *Romano džaniben*, vol. 12, no. 1 (Summer 2005): 65; Nečas, *Romové na Moravě*. Nečas describes the example of Vlax Roms arriving en masse in Central Bohemia in the summer of 1933, which I will discuss below. However, he describes the event as more or less episodic, with no further repercussions (Ctibor Nečas, *Historický kalendář: Dějiny českých Romů v datech*. Olomouc: Palackého univerzita, 1997: 60–61).
283 For example, reports describing the sale and/or theft of horses by a certain Josef Stojka from Fischamend in Austria not far from Vienna in the Znojmo area in the early 1920s, published in the same form in the periodical *Venkov*, [Countryside the organ of the Czech Agrarian Party] ([author n.a.] "Krádeže koní." *Venkov, orgán České strany agrární*, vol. 19, no 245 (17. 2. 1924), 4.) and in The Czech, a Catholic political weekly [author n.a.] "Krádež koní." *Čech: politický týdeník katolický*, vol. 49, no. 53 (23. 2. 1924), 6.

their ancestors and other relatives who came from Austria. As my research shows, however, from the end of the 1920s and above all in the 1930s, the Lovara who came from Slovakia gradually started to numerically predominate. The Lovara had already been coming to the Czech lands from Slovakia to a lesser extent earlier in the 1920s,[284] but during this period they cannot, for the most part, be clearly identified in official records under the general reports of "gypsy hordes" or "gypsy vagabonds". An exception are the police reports in which there are individual names of Roms whom my research indicates may be included among the Lovara. An example is a report from the Frýdek station of the Český Těšín police division dated 3 January 1928 stating that "on 10.2.1927 Pavol Stojka and Štefan Kotlář from Topoľčany, horse dealers" arrived in the town.[285] Another example is a report from a police check of Antonín Stojka, also of Topoľčany, on whom a repeating pistol was found in Místek in the summer of 1927.[286]

The movements of Roms in the Czech lands during the First Republic

The Lovara formed just a small proportion of the Roms who lived in the Czech lands during the interwar period. There were also families of Bohemian and Moravian Roms and Sinti who earned their living like the Lovara, through activities that required travelling – trading, services (mending umbrellas, wire work, making and selling slippers and so on) or entertainment (artists, fairground people and so on).[287] In Moravia,

---

284 Černý, "Lovárové", 14 and 19–20; Andrš, "Our God", 72.
285 SOkA Frýdek Místek, f. OÚ Frýdek i. č. 780, k. 641, odd. Český Těšín, stanice Frýdek č. 19 – Cikáni – výroční zpráva (3. 1. 1928). Once again I draw attention to the habit among Czech policemen and officials of recording the Czech forms of Slovak names: Kotlář is the Czech form of the original Slovak name Kotlár, still relatively widespread among Vlax Roms, but also found among Slovak (non-Vlax) Roms.
286 SOkA Frýdek Místek, f. OÚ Místek, i. č. 876, k. 997, – *Report from district police command in Místek*, c. j. 594, Zákon o potulných cikánech, opatření. This is the well-known figure of Anton Stojka, alias Báno, who in 1951 was murdered in Komárno and sewn up inside his horse's skin. This is still a living legend told among the Lovara in the Czech lands and Slovakia. According to archival records, Anton Stojka had a gun licence, and so he was allowed to keep his gun, partly for the reason that when he was arrested, "the police stations did not yet know the new law on wandering gypsies of 14 July 1927, which explicitly states in Section 6 that wandering gypsies are utterly banned from holding weapons, munitions, etc." (Ibid.)
287 Jana Horváthová looks in detail at Bohemian and Moravian Roms in her recent publication (Jana Horváthová, *...to jsou těžké vzpomínky*. Vol. 1. Brno: Větrné mlýny, 2021).

specifically in the strip along the Slovak border, Slovak Roms from nearby northwest Slovakia or musicians mostly from central Slovakia sought a living, but the way in which they travelled around was different.[288] It may also be assumed that Sinti domiciled in Slovakia moved around the same area, although I have not found any data on them in the archives. Others who lived on the road included families who were not Roms but fell into the category of travelling showmen (in Czech, *světští*), most frequently those with amusements such as puppet theatres, shooting ranges, swings and roundabouts, circuses and other attractions.[289] These families often came into contact and gradually there were interethnic and intergroup marriages across the groups, which Jana Horváthová calls "mingling", above all between Bohemian Roms and Sinti, but also between Sinti and Moravian Roms or between Bohemian and Moravian Roms.[290] It should, however, be added that from an emic perspective, in other words from the perspective of the Roms themselves, the boundaries between the groups were perceived as clear. The Lovara seem to have remained outside this process and maintained a high level of endogamic marriages.[291]

However, the Lovara were not the only Vlax Roms who moved about the territory of Bohemia and Moravia. Kalderash Roms from Poland did so as well. An example of an extended family who made the Czech lands their home, so to speak, is a family of kettle-makers with the surname of Běla who were present therefrom the late 19th century. A linguistic sample collected from Josef Běla (*1886) "probably near Pardubice" is cited in a publication devoted to the Romani language by linguist Jiří Lípa,[292] who labelled this subgroup "kettle-makers". Going by the excerpt of the language sample as transcribed, it is undoubtedly a Kalderash dialect of Romani. There are plentiful occurrences of the name Josef Běla, as

---

288 Černý states that Slovak Roms mostly moved around the territory in the immediate vicinity of Slovakia, often travelling just on foot and in much smaller groups. (Černý, "Lovárové", 11).

289 Horváthová, "Meziválečné zastavení", 65; Tlamsová, *Lexikon*.

290 Horváthová, "Meziválečné zastavení", 68–69.

291 On the territory of the Czech lands I managed to find just one example in archival reports from this period where the surnames might suggest an interethnic relationship. This was a request for the renewal of an itinerancy document issued on 11 April 1929 to a Štefan Stojka (this is not the same Štefan Stojka, Sr. I am following in this book, but a coincidence of names) and his concubine Maria Kováčová. The surname Kováč did not appear among the Lovara, so this must have been a *Rumungro* woman, judging by her surname. Official municipal record of Místek, 14 March 1933. In SOkA Frýdek Místek, f. OÚ Místek, k. 723, i. č. 824 – OÚ v Místku, sign. 12 III/6 Cikánské legitimace.

292 Jiří Lípa, *Cikánština v jazykovém prostředí slovenském a českém. K otázkám starých a novějších složek v její gramatice a lexiku* (Praha: Nakladatelství Československé akademie věd, 1965).

well as other people with the surname Běla, throughout the interwar period in all kinds of Czech archives, although not in files listing "gypsy vagabonds", but in registers of trade licence holders. In the trade licence register for the district of Mladá Boleslav, for example, Josef Běla, born in 1880 in Blonice, Poland, was listed in 1922 as the owner of a kettle-maker's licence, and in 1923 a Michal Běla, born in 1875, also in Blonice, is also listed as owning such a licence.[293] We find records of trade licences for kettle-making issued to men with the surname Běla in subsequent years until the end of the 1930s, in registers kept in several Czech archives.[294] In all the cases, everybody with the surname Běla has "kettle-making or mending" listed as their trade. According to a record from the town hall in Pardubice from 1935, "Polish citizens" Josef Běla (born in Hradec Králové, no date listed), Marie Běla (*1897, Chotěboř) and Bohumil Běla (*1919, Radonice), who were on the register of "gypsy vagabonds", decided to return their gypsy identity cards to the land authority and asked for this return to be duly noted. All of the above-named individuals had previously had their residency permitted by the Interior Ministry for an unlimited length of time. After their cards were returned, however, the authority proposed that they be deported from Czechoslovakia.[295] Still, my research shows that at least part of the Běla family remained in the Czech lands until the postwar period – indeed, their descendants are still here – probably because they gradually managed to conceal their Romani origin from the authorities. In fact, they managed to do this for the whole of the 1930s, since they were listed only in the register of tradesmen and not in the register of "gypsy vagabonds."[296]

Another example of Roms from Poland, also Kalderash Roms,[297] was a group of families with the surname Kwiek that in the first half

---

293 SOkA Mladá Boleslav, f. OÚ Mladá Boleslav, kn. 137.
294 For example: SOkA Mladá Boleslav, f. OÚ Mladá Boleslav, kn. 138; SOkA Mělník, f. OÚ Kralupy nad Vltavou, ev. č. 228 – Záznam vydaných vidovaných licencí k provozování živností obcházením (pro živnosti kočovné); SOkA Benešov, f. OÚ Benešov, i. č. 74 Seznam vydaných cikánských legitimací; SOkA Opava, f. OÚ Opava, i. č. 21 – Jmenný rejstřík o vydaných podomních knížkách (1926–1937); SOkA Přemyšlení, f. OkÚ Říčany, i. č. 25 – Vidovací kniha pro kočovné živnosti (1923–1942). These registration books list birthplaces of persons with the surname Běla as alternately Blovice and Blonice, Tarnów district, Poland while other records give the birthplaces of these and other people as in the Czech lands, for example in Hradec Králové, Albrechtice in the Pardubice district, Předletice in the Brandýs nad Labem district and Malá Bělá in the Mnichovo Hradiště district.
295 NA Praha, f. Zemský úřad Praha, k. 853, č. j. 46580, 31. 7. 1935.
296 Proving these facts will, however, require more detailed research.
297 Alicja Gontarek, "Matejasz Kwiek (ca. 1887–1937). A 'Baron' and 'Leader of the Gypsy Nation' in Interbellum Poland". In *Roma Portraits in History: Roma civic emancipation elite in Central,*

of the 1930s attracted much Czechoslovak media attention. The group was said to be accompanying the supposed "gypsy king" Michał Kwiek and to have settled for a short time in the Prague suburb of Strašnice, although the police then announced an extensive search for them all over Czechoslovakia.[298]

Despite the diversity outlined above and their sub-ethnic variety, all these groups of Roms were perceived by the police and local authorities as a single mass of "gypsy vagabonds" whose movements were to be constrained through decrees and restrictive approaches.

The basic legislation regarding the "gypsy question" in Czechoslovakia became Act no. 117/1927, which defined "gypsies"[299] on the basis of their lifeways as people "living a gypsy lifestyle" (in the sense of a travelling, "vagabond" lifeway). This vague definition resulted in considerable discrimination against the Romani population as a whole.[300] Although the law was originally aimed at "gypsy vagabonds", it served the authorities as a means of going after all ethnic Roms, including those permanently settled and those long-term settled, who did not fall under the letter of the law.

Act no. 117/1927 "on wandering gypsies" laid down what sort of movements, settling or camping were permissible for the "gypsies" defined in it, enabled police to check them more strictly, and required them to be listed in special police registers with their fingerprints to be taken and compulsory "gypsy" identity cards to be issued to them. Itinerancy was permissible solely on the basis of itinerancy documents[301] in which,

---

South-Eastern and Eastern Europe from the 19th century until World War II, ed. Elena Marushiakova and Veselin Popov, 327–344 (Brill, Schöningh. Paderborn, 2022).

298 The situation of the Polish gypsies who came to Czechoslovakia in 1933 onvisas for "trade and spa treatment" with Michał Kwiek (*1886) who, according to the cited report, was considered the "gypsy king" and who subsequently settled in August 1933 in the Prague suburb of Strašnice, is reported on by a circular to police stations nos. 401 and 402 issued by the Provincial Authority on 6 April 1934 entitled "Polští cikáni neoprávněný pobyt v Československé republice", archived, for example, in SOkA Mělník, f. OÚ Mělník, k. 892, sign. III/9/2. Compare Baloun, *"Metla našeho venkova",* 136–137. More on this can be found in Ctibor Nečas, "'Cikánský král' Michał Kwiek a jeho působení v Československu", in: *Vlastivědné listy – dějiny, umění, příroda, dnešek,* vol. 34, no. 2 (2008): 19–22.

299 I look at the definition of "gypsies" in this law in the introduction to the chapter "Roms, gypsies and gypsy vagabonds".

300 Schuster, "Jinak bychom", 21; Baloun, *"Cikáni, metla venkova",* 51–83 and 121–52.

301 This permission to travel around in the form of a passbook became compulsory for "gypsies" travelling either in groups or individually with wagons and draught animals. It was issued in the name of the family head but was valid for the entire group, listing their names and authorised vehicles/animals. These permits were issued by the political offices of the regional courts for no more than one year (Nečas, *Romové v České republice*: 32–33).

under Section 5 of the law, the direction and type of travel had to be stated. The document could also designate the territory (the whole country, or only certain districts) in which itinerancy was allowed.[302] For the context of this study, Section 9 of the law is also important, stating that "foreign gypsy vagabonds are banned from staying in the Czechoslovak Republic unless they can show special permission from the Interior Ministry." Act no. 117/1927, on which a number of decrees and measures were also based during the war, remained in place until 1950. On the basis of that law, a new expert Czechoslovak police body, the Central Police Patrol Division, was created in order to keep a register of "gypsy vagabonds". This central register replaced all the previous locally-kept, internal police registers of "gypsies" from the beginnings of Czechoslovakia, which had never been based on any law. The division also functioned as a central point for the registration of "gypsy vagabonds". With its scientific methods (fingerprinting, a card index, and cooperation with the criminal police), its organisation and its ability to provide information through continuous updates from the police patrol stations, the division was quite advanced compared to the previous record-keeping by police headquarters.[303] The fact that the register of "gypsy vagabonds" was physically located next to the register of "professional criminal groups" indicates the way in which the state bodies were used to thinking about "gypsies". The division had several stations under it. In Bohemia these were in Vysoké Mýto and Březnice, in Moravia the station was in Kuřim, and in Subcarpathian Ruthenia it was in Berehov.[304] These stations were meant to perform "detailed recording of the gypsy movements based on brief notifications sent by police stations about their checks on hordes of nomads."[305] The result of these notifications, according to a report on the Central Police Patrol Division's work from January 1932, was "an endless stream of names and personal data" corresponding to about three dozen surnames listed in the report in alphabetical order. Among them we find typical Lovara surnames such as Banda, Bihari, Rafael and Stojka, or names that were also found among the Lovara, such as Horváth, Daniš, Kolompár, Kotlár and Lakatoš.[306]

---

302 Nečas, *Českoslovenští Romové,* 190.
303 Zdeněk Šípek, "Cikánské legitimace v Čechách v meziválečném období", *Český lid,* vol. 76, no. 3 (1989): 137.
304 NA Praha, f. Zemské četnické velitelství, k. 1076 – *Zpráva Přehled o činnosti ústř. četn. pátr. Oddělení,* č. j. 9, int. 1922–1931, Prague, 8. 1. 1932.
305 Ibid.
306 Ibid.

The state view of Lovara movements around the Czech lands in the early 1930s

The Lovara can be identified in official documents to a greater extent from the start of the 1930s when, in various parts of the Czech lands, police reports started to appear regarding the movements of "gypsy hordes from Slovakia." Some reports were then dealt with at the central level or became the object of media interest. As well as using labels which are, from today's point of view, heavily pejorative and dehumanising ("gypsy vagabonds/travelling hordes from Slovakia"), these notifications and reports often featured surnames of the persons described which clearly identify them as Lovara.

An example of a media report that ended up having numerous repercussions in the police bulletins and was also dealt with at the central level is an article entitled "Flood of gypsies from Slovakia into central Bohemia" published in the periodical *A-Zet* no. 117 in June 1933. Subtitled "Police are helpless against the travellers, gypsies are allowed to travel all over the country", the article tried to describe the powerlessness of police officers to combat the "travelling Slovak gypsies" who had allegedly received permission to travel all over Czechoslovakia. It also tried to describe how permission to travel was issued to "gypsy groups".

> For several weeks, Central Bohemia has been living with a flood of gypsies from Slovakia. In the Czech lands, hordes of gypsies are able to travel just in the districts for which they are given permission. The practice is that they are given permission for three neighbouring districts at the most. This is so there are not too many gypsies in any one district and so the movement of each horde, and above all its activities, may be followed. This practice has suddenly been violated by the Slovak authorities, who have given hordes of gypsies from the Lakatoš and Stojka families permission to travel all over the country. Hordes of these families immediately invaded the Czech lands and are doing what they will here.[307]

According to the article, the Lakatoš and Stojkas are more dangerous in that they travel in large crowds with lightweight, spring wagons and a lot of horses, which allows them to move around at speed. They are

---

307 NA Praha, f. MV – stará registratura, 5/98/3, k. 2431, A-Zet no. 117 (17. 6. 1933) entitled "Záplava cikánů ze Slovenska ve středních Čechách", fol. 45.

able to divide themselves quickly into smaller groups and then to meet up again, travelling mainly at night, which allegedly allows them to avoid the police".[308]

According to the report, one such group had most recently appeared on 15 June 1933 in Obříství near Mělník. The article ends by stating that "there are now several of these large hordes roving around Central Bohemia."[309]

The article prompted an announcement to be issued by the police department in Prague, addressed to the command of the provincial police on 21 June 1933.[310] In it, the head of the department says:

> With respect to the article in *A-Zet* no. 117 of 17.6.1933, I confirm that its content corresponds to a verbal report from the commander in Obříství made to me on 18 June. Police Chief Jozef Šebl announced that some of the Lakatoš families have gypsy identity cards, but others have trade licences as horse dealers; they all live in the same way and travel together. This fact was also discovered by the police station at Vinoř. The Lakatoš and Stojkas who have gypsy identity cards have it stated in them that they are permitted to travel all over the territory of Czechoslovakia. It will be possible under Decree no. 243.238/33–22–179/117–32 of the Prague Provincial authorities of 13 May 1933 to limit entrance to certain territories in the surroundings of Prague just to those families who have gypsy identity cards, not to those who have trade licences. [...] On Friday 23 June 1933 the Lakatoš and Stojkas will be checked at the market next to the city abattoir in Prague–Holešovice.[311]

From the archival documents both of the police station itself and from the central provincial authorities it seems that there were efforts to prevent these groups in various ways from travelling all over Bohemia.

An announcement to the police patrol station entitled "Gypsy hordes of Lakatoš and Stojka – troubles", was sent two days later directly from Obříství, a municipality to the north of Prague. It more or less repeats the information published in the newspaper *A-Zet*:

> In the last two years, several hordes of gypsies from Slovakia have been roving around Bohemia. These hordes have smaller, lighter wagons and fast horses

---

308 Ibid.
309 Ibid.
310 Ibid. Zpráva zemského četnického velitelství, č. j. 837, *Cikánské tlupy Lakatošů a Stojků – závady*, fol. 43.
311 Ibid.

harnessed to them. They travel very quickly and are capable of covering several dozen kilometres in a day. They assemble in smaller or larger hordes. They also trade in horses, and individuals appear to have trade licences to that effect.[312]

The report also contains numbers, although we cannot consider these to be precise, followed by a warning of the security threat that these groups represent, in keeping with the contemporary pejorative idea of "gypsy vagabonds":

> It is thus impossible for the police to make a list of these gypsies, of which there are found to be more than 100–150 persons and sometimes more than 60 wagons together, and so these hordes pass through with no guarantee that there are not among them elements highly dangerous to the state (spying, intelligence during the war?).[313]

In closing, the author returns to the subject of itinerancy documents: "From a random check of these hordes it was ascertained that they have itinerancy documents which, according to what is written in them, permit them to travel over the territory of the entire state."[314] The report also states that every Friday these "gypsies" attend the horse fairs in Prague near the city abattoir in Holešovice.

Two days later, a bulletin from a Prague police station reacted to the report from Obříství, stating that:

> In the department here, 15 male and 14 female gypsies from the Lakatoš family and 31 men and 25 women from the Stojka family have been registered. According to information from the police station in Obříství, there are sometimes up to 140 such family members roaming in the vicinity of Mělník, with some of them having trade certificates as horse dealers, which makes it difficult for the police on duty to check them as gypsies.[315]

The above-mentioned mobility of the Stojka and Lakatoš families in Prague is an interesting fact, given that over a month before these events,

---

312 Ibid. Zpráva zemského četnického velitelství, č. j. 1048/33 *Cikánské tlupy Lakatošů a Stojků – závady* (19. 6. 1933), fol. 44.

313 Ibid.

314 Ibid.

315 NA Praha, f. MV – stará registratura, 5/98/3, k. 2431, č. j. 172 – Hlášení četnické stanice Praha Velitelskému četnickému oddělení v Praze (21. 6. 1933).

on 13 May 1933, the provincial authority in Prague issued a decision entitled "Designation of the territory in the vicinity of Greater Prague that gypsy vagabonds are forbidden to enter". This decision, issued under Section 10 of Act no. 117/1927, designated land that, from the day the report was issued, was out of bounds to "gypsy vagabonds". As well as the city of Prague itself, this included the surrounding districts: Praha-Venkov, Říčany, Jílové, and part of the Brandýs nad Labem district.[316] This decree would have necessarily included the Prague district of Holešovice, which the Lakatoš and Stojka families were permitted to enter because they owned trade certificates, as the documents cited indicate.

The fact that members of the above-named families were allowed to travel all over the territory of Czechoslovakia made it difficult to control them from the police perspective. The fact that some Slovak districts issued itinerancy documents without any sort of territorial limitation, valid for the whole country, is also confirmed by a critical report from the Regional Authority in Bratislava produced in July 1931.[317] This said that Act no. 17/1927 was interpreted differently in each district of Slovakia. The itinerancy documents issued by some authorities were drawn up in a cursory manner without the necessary investigations being undertaken, the report said. It also admitted that itinerancy documents were being issued with no limitations, valid for the whole of Slovakia and often for the whole of Czechoslovakia, although such documents were meant to be issued only to "gypsy vagabonds who meet all the regulations concerning the trade they seek to ply".[318]

The practice of issuing itinerancy documents in some Slovak districts which were valid for the whole country was also confirmed by my archival findings. The district authorities in Topoľčany listed people in the "Register of gypsy itinerancy certificates" who had been issued itinerancy documents. Next to their names were listed the territories where the document would be valid. Of seven people with the surname of Stojka (the father, Michal, and his adult sons Ladislav, Pavol, Ondrej, Josef and Antonín) and the surname of Kotlár (Štefan; one case) who were all labelled "horse traders", five were issued itinerancy documents valid for Slovakia and Moravia in 1929–30, and the rest were issued documents

---

316 Ibid. A list of the territories and municipalities covered by this measure was drawn up in detail for Moravia and Silesia by the historian Ctibor Nečas (Nečas, *Romové na Moravě*: 201–209). No such list has as yet been drawn up for Bohemia.

317 NA Praha, f. MV – stará registratura, k. 2431, i .č. 6501, sign. 5/98/3. Krajinsky úrad Bratislava, Cigáni potulní, prevádzanie zákona č. 117/1927 Sb. z. a n. vl. nariad. č. 68/1928 Sb.z. a n.

318 Ibid.

valid for Slovakia, Moravia and Silesia. Another three people from other Lovara families in the same district, labelled "travelling gypsies" (so not "horse traders", who clearly had a higher status) had documents in which the territorial validity was limited, for example, to the districts of Topoľčany, Bánovce, Prievizda and Nitra, or in which a certain area was defined (such as between Bratislava, Žilina, Galanta and Komárno). All these permits were periodically renewed, but their territorial validity did not change.[319]

Still, the principle that an itinerancy document with wide-ranging territorial validity could be issued to a "gypsy vagabond" just on the condition that such a person already had a trade licence, as is indicated above in the report from the Bratislava Regional Authority, was only partially fulfilled for the seven men mentioned above. My further archival findings show that of the seven Roms from Topoľčany who had itinerancy documents valid for the territory of Slovakia and Moravia (or also Silesia), just four had a trade licence for livestock dealing. This is recorded for 1932 in the republic-wide *Gazetteer of the Czechoslovak Republic for industry, trade, business and agriculture*. This listed Michal Stojka, Ondřej Stojka and Ladislav Stojka from Topoľčany and Štefan Kotlár from Soľčany as livestock traders with their own trade certificates.[320] All three Stojkas were also listed as carrying on such a trade in the same gazetteer for 1935,[321] with the name of Štefan Kotlár no longer appearing. Nevertheless, in the case of three other men from the Stojka family in Topoľčany, namely Ondrej, Antonín and Josef, trade licences were not shown to the authorities, yet they still gained official permission to travel over the territory of Slovakia and Moravia, and in Antonín's case also Silesia.[322] Not one of them had a valid itinerancy document for the territory of Bohemia.

In July 1933, the Provincial Authority in Prague issued a circular entitled "Incursion of gypsy hordes from Slovakia into Bohemia", once again stating, in line with the above-mentioned newspaper article (*A-Zet*), that the districts of central Bohemia "have been flooded with hordes of gypsies, above all the Lakatoš and Stojkas of Slovakia, to whom the

---

319 ŠA Nitra – pobočka Topoľčany, f. OÚ Topoľčany, i. č. 25A – Evidencia cigánskych kočovníckych legitimácií.

320 Adresář Republiky československé pro průmysl, živnosti, obchod a zemědělství, 1932. Praha: Rudolf Mosse, p. 3119. NA ČR, Knihovní fondy a služby, Sign. 54 D 003848/1932. Sv. 1.

321 Adresář Republiky československé pro průmysl, živnosti, obchod a zemědělství, 1935 (Praha: Rudolf Mosse, p. 3063) and 1936 (Praha: Rudolf Mosse, p. 3079), NA ČR, Knihovní fondy a služby, sign. 4–0092.312.

322 ŠA Nitra – pobočka Topoľčany, f. OÚ Topoľčany, i. č. 25A – Evidencia cigánskych kočovníckych legitimácií.

Slovak authorities have issued itinerancy documents allowing them to travel all over Slovakia." The circular called on state bodies to proceed according to Act no. 117/1927 with the aim of ejecting these "hordes" from Bohemia and preventing them from returning. If it was not possible to proceed according to Section 13 of Act 117/1927, district and other relevant authorities were called upon to take the necessary measures leading to the ejection of "gypsy vagabonds" from Bohemia in the interest of maintaining public order and securing private property. [323]

Another circular from the Provincial Authority in Prague, no. 456.831 of September 1933, dealt with the "incursion of gypsy hordes from Slovakia into Bohemia" by requiring the authorities to amend the extent of the permission granted to the "gypsy hordes" to travel so that they were no longer allowed to travel in Bohemia. It ordered changes to be made to their itinerancy documents and subsequently that these groups "be ejected from Bohemia in the direction of Slovakia".[324] The proposed approach may be considered a gross breach of their personal freedoms. Clearly, however, it was this approach that was taken in the above-mentioned deportation from Bohemia of Filo Stojka and other Lovara in the summer of 1934 by the Strakonice district authorities.

The routes of the Lovara from Slovakia to Bohemia are traced in detail in a 2018 article by Rastislav Pivoň, who mapped the trajectories of several specific people domiciled in the Trnava district. Pivoň's study confirms my findings regarding the movements of Lovara from Slovakia not just on Moravian territory, but also in Bohemia before the summer of 1933, when police tightened their approach to "gypsy vagabonds" who did not "belong" to the region. A policy was adopted to strictly remove "gypsy vagabond" families, and clearly not just Lovara ones, from Bohemian territory.

Let us now look at the above-mentioned cases from another angle. The question presents itself as to whether the families with the surnames of Stojka and Lakatoš who were subjected to frequent checks in Central Bohemia in the summer of 1933 may have included members of the Stojka family from Trenčianska Teplá which I am researching. Unfortunately, this can be neither proven nor disproven, since I have not managed to

---

323 NA Praha, f. MV – stará registratura, k. 2431, i. č. 6501, fol. 42, sign. 5/98/3. Oběžník ZÚ Praha 334.782 ai 1933 *Vpád cikánských tlup ze Slovenska* (14 July 1933) addressed to all local authorities in the land of Bohemia.

324 Ibid. Oběžník ZÚ Praha 456.831 ai 1933 *Potulní cikáni závadné vystavování cikánských legitimací, nesprávný postup OU, vpád cikánských tlup ze Slovenska do Čech* (29 September 1933) – to all local authorities in the land of Bohemia.

find, in any archives, the lists of the named persons who were checked during the above-mentioned controls in the summer of 1933. However, given that the family was moving around the Czech lands at that time,[325] it would not be surprising if it formed part of this group of "gypsy vagabonds from Slovakia", as the group numbered up to 150 people.

Here it is necessary to perceive the family I am studying as forming part of a larger Lovara community whose individual parts would break off from the family with varying frequency and then join back up with it again. On their travels they would meet other Lovara who were not necessarily always their relatives. They then underwent police checks together with them, or together found their way into official reports for various other reasons. I thus believe that the boundary between the family in question and other Lovara families needs to be perceived as fluid and permeable. The Lovara moving around Czechoslovakia in various directions during this period should be considered a community of people who met each other not just at horse fairs and designated camping places, but also in various other places, and who spoke their own dialect of Romani not always comprehensible to other non-Vlax Roms. As is clear from the witness narratives and from the fact that the authorities often used the word "relatives" to label groups between whom there was no actual familial relationship, it was possible to find highly functional relationships of solidarity and various interconnected solidary and reciprocal networks among the Lovara. It is also important to note that *krísi* (Romani courts) were already being held during the interwar period, that respected Roms from far-off destinations would come to them, and that there existed sophisticated methods through which the Lovara let each other know that these courts were being held.

Lovara movements around the Czech lands in the second half of the 1930s

Attempts to deal with the presence of "travelling gypsies" from Slovakia can also be found in the state archives in the Czech lands in subsequent years, although to a lesser degree. In January 1935, for example, the Provincial Authority in Brno issued a circular dealing with the situation

---

325 In March 1933, Zaga's family branch was in the districts of Frýdek and Místek, but for the other months we lack information. It is not until July 1933 that a record of Filo Stojka appears in Olomouc, while a record of his sister Barbora appears in Brno in September 1933.

in the town of Polička and ordering the police "not to eject the Slovak gypsy hordes found there back over the border into Bohemia in general, and especially not into the Polička district".[326] The circulars gradually started to deal with "gypsy vagabonds" coming from Germany, Austria, and later from the Sudetenland. Groups of "Slovak gypsies" gradually stopped being mentioned in official reports and records, save for comments on the police checks of such families. Reports on the mobility of individual Lovara families and their arrivals in Moravian and Silesian municipalities in particular continued to appear until the early spring of 1939. We may also assume that the mobility of families from Slovakia on Bohemian territory was made considerably more difficult by the approaches and policies formulated in the above-mentioned circulars promoting a restrictive approach towards the "gypsy hordes" and above all the possibility of amending such persons' itinerancy documents with regard to their territorial validity and legally deporting entire groups from the territory in question.

No historian has yet looked at the question of how many Lovara there were in the Czech lands in the interwar period, so it is difficult to give any sort of estimate. Černý has estimated the size of the Lovara community moving around the district of Místek at about 100 people.[327] I also managed to find records for most of the persons named in his study in neighbouring districts such as Frýdek, Litovel and Prostějov. I also found many named in records for other areas of Moravia, Silesia and Bohemia. The police records from Prague and its surrounding areas from the summer of 1933, cited herein several times, mention 100–150 individuals. To state the total number of Lovara, however, we would have to look through the complete records of the Central Police Patrol Division, the central depository for records of "gypsy vagabonds" made on the basis of the 1927 law. Despite considerable efforts, I have not managed to find any such collections in the archives, just files containing statistics in the form of numbers where, once again, all the "gypsy (vagabonds)" are lumped together without their surnames being listed, providing no opportunity to carefully distinguish between them, therefore.

An interesting regional contribution to the question of how many Lovara were in the Czech lands in the 1930s is a newspaper article entitled "Gypsies and travellers – children of nature",[328] published in the

---

326 NA Praha, f. MV – stará registratura 5/98/3, k. 2431, ZÚ Brno č. j. 2913/III-7 Polička, určení území, do něhož jest potulným cikánům vstup zakázán.

327 Černý, "Lovárové", 24.

328 E. Peřina, "Cikání a kočovníci – děti přírody", *Polední list*, no. 75 (15 March 1936), p. 7.

periodical *Polední list* in March 1936. The article states the names "that are most often found among gypsies", and its author allegedly took them "from the statistics for eastern Bohemia over the last three years", in other words, probably from the period 1933–1936. Against each surname the number of people with that surname is listed, clearly once again from eastern Bohemia, and in some cases the supposed geographical origin of the Roms with that surname is also given. Among the dozens of names are surnames that occur among the Lovara, such as: Banda (4), Biháry (25), Danyš (12), Horváth (12), Lakatoš (51), Rafael (14), Stojka (70). Overall, therefore, 188 people are listed who are very likely to have been Lovara. This is an interesting fact, given that as I stated earlier, after 1933 or 1934, such families came from Moravia to the Czech lands just occasionally, so we may expect that the Lovara community moving around Moravia and Silesia was much larger than the Lovara in eastern Bohemia at the time. For two names, the author made a note regarding the origin of the Roms with that surname. Next to the name Lakatoš he wrote in brackets "Hungarian gypsies", and by the surname Stojka, "Moravian gypsies". Above all, the note on the Moravian origin of people with the surname Stojka indicates that from the perspective of officials in eastern Bohemia, these Roms in Moravia now seemed to have "put down roots" there after several years, which was maybe the result of Lovara repeatedly stating, when checked, that they were coming from Moravia, or showing itinerancy documents which said they were allowed to move around Moravia. Last but not least, it is important to mention that the list also includes two surnames of the Kalderash Roms whom I mentioned above: Běla, of whom there were 45 persons listed with the note "kettle-makers", and Kwiek (22 persons) with the note "Polish gypsies".[329]

Using my own database of Lovara families, described in detail in the chapter on methodology, I added 196 records from the 1930s from the Bohemian and the Moravian archives showing police checks or applications relating to people who, on the basis of several indices, were Lovara. These 196 people were accompanied by a further 580 people, according to the official records.[330] However, this figure is not particularly helpful, for two reasons. First, the number is underestimated, mostly because police reports often did not quantify the size of the group accompanying the "head of the family", but gave just his name. Of these 196 records, the number of additional persons accompanying the leader is not reported

---

329 Ibid.

330 I found these records in the following archives: SOkA Blansko, SOkA Frýdek Místek, SOkA Jindřichův Hradec, SOkA Olomouc, SOkA Pelhřimov, SOkA Přemyšlení, SOkA Zámrsk.

for 130 of them, which is a considerable number. In some cases, therefore, I included in the overall number just the "head of the family", although it is very likely that these people did not travel alone, but were accompanied by their families, of whose size we have no details. I am also aware that the numbers could be overinflated, because these notifications and lists repeat the names of some individuals, sometimes several times. As far as the "heads of families" are concerned, (in other words, the people who were recorded by state bodies), there were at least 92 in my database. However, I do not possess the necessary data for some, such as "gypsy" identity cards or other information to compare with other records, so it is not possible to determine whether a person named, for example, Ján Rafael, who is listed three times, actually appeared in various places with his family three times, or whether there were three different Ján Rafaels, each with his own family. In other cases, some names appear in various places at various times and it turns out that, according to other data, these are in fact multiple appearances of one and the same person. For example, František Lakatoš, born in 1896 in Sereď, Galanta district, is found a total of 11 times during the 1930s on the territory of Moravia: twice in December 1931 in the district of Prostějov, eight times in 1934 (Prostějov, Litovel and Svitavy districts) and twice in 1938 (Místek and Frýdek districts).

Regarding the extent to which the Lovara moved about Bohemia compared to Moravia, it can be seen from the database that of these 196 records, just 48 are from Bohemia, while 148 are from Moravia. With the exception of six records made by (the same) police station in the Hradec Králové district in 1938, all the other records from Bohemian districts end in the summer of 1934. This once again confirms my hypothesis regarding the tightening of restrictions on "gypsy vagabonds" from Slovakia by the Bohemian authorities. Of the 196 records, in only 140 cases do we know the precise date on which they were made. In 50 cases, just the year was recorded, without the day or month of the police check in the territory in question. To return to my thoughts regarding the seasonal presence of the Lovara in the Czech lands, where I investigated the likely year-round presence of Zaga Stojková's family in the Czech lands, my survey suggests that of the 140 cases where we know the precise date of an official check in the Czech lands, 76 were made in the winter period (from mid-November until the end of March, so less than half the year). This confirms my previous conclusions that many Lovara from Slovakia during this time spent the whole year in the Czech lands, rather than being there just seasonally.

Another question concerns the size, at that time, of the family groups which were labelled, using the highly pejorative terminology of the period, as "hordes" and which travelled together around the Czech lands. The size of the accompanying group was given only for some "heads of family". We see that some families had four members (three families) or five members (four families). However, it was much more common for there to be more than five family members (for example, 12 families had six members, while nine families had eight members). An exception was the group led by Ján Kudrik, stopped by police from Hvozd in the Litovel district in 1934. This family had 24 members and for that reason was taken to the police station for the offence of camping in "hordes exceeding the framework of the [nuclear] family".[331] This went against Act no. 177/1927, where Section 7 stated that: "wandering gypsies are not allowed to travel and camp in hordes exceeding the framework of the [nuclear] family". Nor in the other cases was it exceptional for groups to exceed 10 members (six of the 92 "heads of family" were travelling with 10 people, one with 11 people, one with 14 and three others with 16 people when they were checked by police). To make a qualified estimate of Lovara numbers in the Czech lands during the First Czechoslovak Republic is something I dare not do, therefore, not even on the basis of thorough study. Nevertheless, I estimate that the overall number of Lovara who, according to my database, might have undergone state checks in the 1930s was around several hundred persons.

Conclusions: The situation of the Lovara in the Czech lands in the interwar period

Several important conclusions may be drawn from the information above. While on the territory of Slovakia the Lovara were territorially anchored in some locations during the interwar period, I know of no instances, from the area of the historical Czech lands, of Roms from this group buying or renting a property to which they might regularly return. Nevertheless, it cannot be completely ruled out that some wealthy Romani families rented short-term accommodation or stayed in hotels, although I have found no record of such stays. An approximately 50-member Kalderash family, relatives of the Polish "gypsy king" Michał

---

331 SOkA Olomouc, f. OÚ Litovel, i. č. 797, k. 667, Dohled nad cikánským obyvatelstvem 1896–1961, Četnická stanice Hvozd: Úprava Stíhání cikánů – (20. 12. 1934), č. j. 2204.

Kwiek, briefly lived in the Czech lands in the first half of the 1930s this way, according to Nečas, successively renting apartments in the Prague suburb of Strašnice (for nine months), Hradec Králové, Chrudim, Kutná Hora, Karviná and Ostrava.[332] This once again shows that a sufficiently large sum of money was able to break down the otherwise impenetrable social boundaries whereby "travelling gypsies" were perceived as marginalized people. According to Nečas, the Kwiek family owned wagons (*maringotky*), but had them transported by rail for long distances (for example, from Pardubice to Bohumín),[333] which shows that the more affluent Roms were able to move greater distances by alternative means to that of horse-drawn transport.

The Lovara who remembered life in the Czech lands during the interwar period said they almost always travelled only with horses and wagons in which they spent the night and lived all year round. Their way of life and how they spent the night were described by J. B., whose family earned a living making and cleaning kettles:

> We had huge wagons, carriages pulled by horses. We children would travel all warm under the feather quilts and outside it would be cold. We'd travel like that for maybe 20 kilometres. Then we'd stop near a wood, they'd make a fire and then they'd make a big tent out of tarpaulins. That's what we'd sleep under.[334]

The way of life described by such witnesses indicates that Lovara spatial mobility was relatively intensive in the interwar Czech lands. There was clearly no territorial anchoring of Lovara families at all, with the exception of their repeated return to horse fairs or to see customers. The type of territorial bond common among the Lovara families in Slovakia during that same time was never created by Lovara in the Czech lands. Records of their fairly irregular, territorially extensive movements across the Czech lands in the first half of the 1930s show that Lovara families tried to find territory where they might do business, but we have no evidence that any of them managed to find such an area. Although Roms from the Stojka family and other Lovara families moved around several northern Moravian districts in the second half of the 1930s, we have no

---

332 Nečas, "Cikánský král", 19–22.
333 Ibid.
334 Witness J. B. (*1934), recorded on 5 February 2002 in České Budějovice, Czech Republic by Markéta Hajská. Archive of Člověk v tísni, o.p.s.

reason to believe that they considered those places to be their *home* in some sort of closer way.

It has to be asked why the situation in the Czech lands differed so much from that in Slovakia. We may assume that the generally more restrictive environment in the Czech lands, less tolerant towards "wandering gypsies", above all those who were clearly still not perceived as "local", caused the forced, permanent mobility of those Lovara families who lived here (or spent long periods of time here). After all, it was an area where historically it had not been possible for the families of Czech oreven Moravian Roms and Sinti to settle, despite their having lived there for centuries.

◀ Young people from Trenčianska Teplá in traditional local costumes in the late 1930s. In the background of the photo is the quarry, on the far right in the centre (in the background) is Štefan Stojka's house.

Part 3: The eve of war

3.1 The increased frequency of Romani mobility in the Protectorate[335]

In the previous chapter I reviewed the mobility of Lovara from Slovakia in the Czech lands during the interwar period. Mobility of a similar intensity continued to occur in 1938. As I shall show below, the breakup of Czechoslovakia in the spring of the following year had an impact on the ability of such Roms to move around and spend time in the Czech lands.

To better understand the situation at the end of the 1930s, it needs to be stressed that in the context of Roma movements, from the point of view of the police stations and the central provincial authorities, the arrivals of "travelling gypsy groups", first from Germany and later from Austria, were much more disturbing and also much more frequent – and more problematic from a police point of view. From the time of Hitler's rise to power in 1933, and after the race laws took effect, there was a tightening of policy towards "gypsies" in Nazi Germany. As a result, some Roms and (above all) Sinti from the German Reich attempted to cross the border into Czechoslovak territory, where they tried to stay and to secure local "gypsy" identity cards and itinerancy documents.[336] The provincial authorities in both Prague and Brno tried to prevent these practices, issuing various circulars warning the subordinate authorities not to issue such documents and in general banning "foreign gypsies"

---

335 I looked in detail at the subject of the Lovara leaving the Czech lands in an article (Hajská, "'We had to run away'"). In this chapter I have used some of the main findings and important facts published in that study in 2022. These are extended here and combined with further facts and circumstances from my new archival findings.

336 Baloun, "*Cikáni, metla venkova*", 308–310.

from staying on Czechoslovak territory.[337] The result was that in subsequent years there was an increase in the frequency of movement by Romani groups originally from German territory in the western, northern and southern border regions of the Czech lands.[338] The frequency with which such Romani families arrived increased after the Anschluss of Austria in March 1938 and after the Sudetenland, the extensive border area of the Czech lands, was annexed by the German Reich in September 1938.

In November 1938 the Central Police Patrol Division informed the commands of the individual police divisions that:

> following the occupation of the annexed territory, large numbers of gypsy and other travelling, workshy hordes are appearing, coming from the annexed territory and having never previously appeared on the territory of the current state, or not for many years. Under Section 9 of the law of 14 July 1927, no. 117, 'on wandering gypsies', foreign gypsies are banned from staying in Czechoslovakia. Under Section 4 clause 3 of the government Decree of 26 April 1928, no. 69, the gypsy identity card will be taken away from any gypsy vagabond found not to be a citizen of Czechoslovakia. These provisions require all gypsies who clearly belong to the annexed territory to be deprived of their gypsy identity card and the gypsies in question to be handed over to the relevant foreign authorities.[339]

The circular refers to the situation where at least some of the German Roms and Sinti had clearly managed to become Czechoslovak citizens by making use of gaps in the system of issuing identity cards to "gypsy vagabonds". They secured Czechoslovak "gypsy" identity cards or itinerancy documents purely on the basis of certain documents (such as christening or domicile certificates) which then served as official proof of their Czechoslovak citizenship.[340]

In practice, all travelling groups on the borders were prevented from entering Bohemian or Moravian territory if their members were not domiciled there, and in the other direction, Roms with Czech domiciles were not allowed to enter the territory of neighbouring states.[341] In

---

337 Above all the circular cited above, ZÚ Praha číslo 456831 ai 1933 of 29 September 1933. NA Praha, MV stará registratura 5/98/3, k. 2432.

338 Nečas, *Českoslovenští Romové*, Nečas, *Romové na Moravě*.

339 NA Praha, f. ZÚ Praha, k. 853, ÚČPO č. j. 28.798/1938 –Postup proti cikánům z odstoupených území pro velitelství četn. oddělení (5. 11. 1938).

340 Baloun, "*Metla našeho venkova*", 292–294.

341 Nečas, *Českoslovenští Romové*, 29–31.

reaction to this situation, on 13 March 1939 the provincial authority in Prague issued circular 36/128, entitled "Measures against gypsies and other vagabond persons: Orders", which called for Act no. 117/1927 to be properly upheld and stressed that "itinerancy on the part of gypsies with foreign citizenship will not be suffered any longer and their immediate deportation over the border is ordered".[342] The circular was the last comprehensive measure regarding "gypsies" to be issued by the Czechoslovak authorities before the division of Czechoslovakia, which occurred literally during the next few days.

After the Protectorate of Bohemia and Moravia was created, its new executive organs continued to proceed in line with this circular,[343] with the difference that "gypsies with foreign citizenship" now included "gypsies" with the citizenship of the independent Slovak State. This had serious consequences for their ability to remain on Protectorate territory.[344]

During the division of Czechoslovakia there was also increased movement of Roms at the Protectorate's newly-created eastern border.[345] Roms and other travelling groups from Slovakia found themselves forced to return to the newly-created Slovak State. It should be mentioned that in the official records, the mobility of Roms from Slovakia is paid only marginal attention. There are sporadic mentions in local police reports of the departures or transfers of Slovak "gypsies" being organised and registered by the police. The movement of "gypsy groups" around the new borders with Germany featured far more frequently in the police reports, above all in the months between the Sudetenland seceding and the division of Czechoslovakia.

Nevertheless, I managed to find, at both the central and local levels, several records relating to the departures or deportation of Romani groups to the Slovak State. The sudden departure of Roms after 15 March for the newly-created Slovak State understandably concerned not just the Lovara who had been moving about the Czech Republic, but also other Roms and Sinti with Slovak citizenship. This increase in mobility naturally also concerned Roms and Sinti who did not have

---

342 NA Praha, f. ZÚ v Praze – Policejní a bezpečnostní záležitosti, k. 853 – Opatření proti cikánům a jiným potulným osobám, pokyny, fol. 193, č. 36/128 for the year 1938 (13. 10. 1939).

343 Zdeněk Šípek. "Tzv. Cikanská otázka od Mnichova do konce roku 1939." *Český lid*, vol. 79, no. 2 (1992): 163.

344 Here it ought to be mentioned that during the breakup of Czechoslovakia, these circulars were only a collection of orders designed for the executive authorities. None was aimed in particular at Roms from Slovakia and their return to their place of domicile.

345 Ibid., 163.

citizenship of the former Czechoslovakia, but who were just fleeing registration by the state authorities and who became the main target of the police patrols, which subjected them to thorough identity and citizenship checks. In this study, however, I shall exclusively focus on the archival materials in which Lovara domiciled in Slovakia can be identified in some way, although the group I am following was in a marked minority in the existing reports compared to other Roms and Sinti.

Unsurprisingly, we most often find information concerning Lovara in the reports from police stations in the Moravian regions close to the Slovak border. The police station at Frýdek, for example, issued a report for 1939 stating that:

> during the year 1939, gypsy hordes appeared in this district some 43 times, being checked by individual police stations. They came mostly from Moravia, to a lesser extent from Bohemia, but earlier had also come from Slovakia. During the checks it was found that they were gypsy vagabonds from the ranks of horse dealers, umbrella menders, knife sharpeners, wandering musicians, etc. The gypsy hordes were not permanently settled in this district.[346]

For the same period, 1939, the police station at Unčovice, Prostějov division announced:

> The movement of gypsy hordes was greater this year, given the exceptional conditions, than in previous years. In all a total of 117 gypsy hordes were detained by police. [...] One foreign horde was transferred over the border. Gypsies of Slovak nationality returned back to Slovakia.[347]

In this document we see that Slovak Roms were not yet seen as belonging to the category of "foreign gypsies", although in practice they were already being deported from the Protectorate to the Slovak State. Similar news came from the Vilémov police station in its report from the end of December 1939:

---

346 SOkA Frýdek-Místek, f. Četnická stanice Frýdek, i. č. 22, Hlášení An den Der Oberlandrat Mahr. Ostrau, Frýdek (31. 1. 1940), no č. j.

347 SOkA Olomouc, f. OÚ Litovel, zn. fondu L 1–5, k. 667, i. č. 797, Dohled nad cikánským obyvatelstvem1896 až 1944 – Zpráva oddělení Prostějov, stanice Unčovice: Stíhání cikánů, (16. 1. 1940), č. j. 29035/1/III. Handwritten report, the word "back" in the last sentence was subsequently crossed out.

The gypsies with Slovak citizenship whom we checked after 15.3.1939 we returned mostly to the Slovak border. In the fourth quarter of 1939 we no longer found gypsies with foreign citizenship during the checks of gypsies travelling through the district.[348]

The Bouzov police station stated that in 1939 they checked "gypsy hordes" headed by Ján Stojka (a three-member family), Karolina Danišová (10 members), Maria Lakatošová (10 members) and other (non-Vlax) Roms and Sinti with the surnames Růžička (twice), Paffner and Kotas. According to the report, these "hordes" were controlled in January and February 1939 and from then on were not found in the district.[349] The report does not state whether the Stojka, Lakatoš and Daniš families were considered Slovak or foreign "gypsies", but merely represents confirmation of the fact that after March 1939, there was a transformation in the spatial mobility of these families. This fact was also confirmed by other reports. Most clearly describe their absence as the result of the restrictive measures, above all the limits on entering the country and the deportations over the border. Likewise, the report from the Trojanovice police station in the Místek district contains the following: "After the events of 15 March 1939, gypsy travelling almost stopped because gypsies from Slovakia were prevented from crossing the border."[350]

Concrete examples of transferring "gypsy hordes" to Slovakia are documented by a report from the Frýdlant nad Ostravicí police station from 13 December 1939, which states that in 1939 the station carried out, on the orders of the police directorate in Moravská Ostrava, the transfer of a "gypsy horde" to the Slovak border, the reason being that they were Slovak citizens. In another two cases, also concerning "Slovak gypsy hordes", the station checked them and called on them to return to Slovakia, which they apparently then did.[351]

Reports of Romani groups departing for Slovakia also appear sporadically at the nationwide level. In a report from the Interior Ministry to the Land Authority in Prague dated 11 April 1939 and entitled *Gypsies – foreign citizens*, it was announced that "according to a report from the Central Police Patrol Division in Prague, wandering gypsies have been

---

348 Ibid., Četnická stanice Vilémov, subject: Evidence cikánů, 23. 12. 1939, č. j. 1691/1939.
349 Ibid., f. Četnická stanice Bouzov, okr. Litovel, subject: Evidence cikánů, č. j. 29601/1/III/39 (15. 12. 1939).
350 SOkA Frýdek Místek, f. OU Místek, k. 997, i. č. 876, Úprava stíhání cikánů, zpráva.
351 SOkA Frýdek Místek, f. OU Místek, k. 997, i. č. 876, Úprava stíhání cikánů.

changing their stopping places rapidly and it is possible to observe their movement towards Slovakia."[352] This report indicates that the departures of "wandering gypsies" from the Protectorate in the direction of Slovakia were spontaneous – which, as we shall see below, was one of the ways in which this process was characterised by witnesses from Lovara families themselves. As we can see, however, the previous announcements from police stations had frequently mentioned the forcible ejection of Romani groups over the Slovak border and the prevention of their entrance into the Protectorate, which is what other Romani witnesses also describe.

3.2 Change of citizenship as a reason for leaving the Protectorate

The reason Slovak Roms left the Protectorate of Bohemia and Moravia or were deported from it after the breakup of Czechoslovakia was the change in their civil status. The legal frameworks and founding documents of the newly-created states (the Protectorate of Bohemia and Moravia and the Slovak State) redefined who would now be their citizens. After the end of the Second Czechoslovak Republic, around 300,000 Slovaks found themselves without citizenship in the Protectorate (which covered the territory of the Czech lands), suddenly becoming foreigners unless they were already domiciled in a municipality there. As historian Jan Rychlík has described, however, anti-Slovak feeling appeared only occasionally in the Protectorate, and there was no political interest in deporting the Slovaks who lived there. The German authorities approved residency in the Protectorate for non-Jewish, non-Romani Slovaks more or less without any difficulty and they were hardly ever deported. Deportation, Rychlík says, was used by the Protectorate only in the case of criminals such as beggars, thieves and prostitutes, in collaboration with the Czech police.[353] From his description it can be seen that the category of citizenship allowed the authorities a fairly free hand when it came to granting residence on Protectorate territory. Lawful deportation on the basis of citizenship, in other words, could be used to get rid of persons in the categories listed above who were unwanted by local authorities and the

---

352 NA Praha, f. ZÚ Praha, k. 853, č. j. 18.676/1939–5.
353 Jan Rychlík, *Češi a Slováci ve 20. století. Spolupráce a konflikty 1914–1992* (Praha: Vyšehrad, 2015), 12.

state.[354] Although Rychlík does not explicitly mention this category, on the basis of my research I can add that these unwanted persons included people labelled "gypsies" or "gypsy vagabonds" as the authorities had no political interest in their remaining in the Protectorate (on the contrary).

Roms from Slovakia were therefore moved *de iure*, literally overnight, from the category of *native* "gypsies" to the category of *foreign* "gypsies", whose deportation was enabled by Section 9 of Act no. 117/1927, which was still in effect. As the announcements from police stations show, however, on a local level police continued to distinguish between Slovak "gypsies" and other foreign "gypsies", even though both groups were deported. The authorities' approaches to these groups differed, and as we shall see below, in the case of "gypsies from Slovakia", a considerable role in the whole process was played by their spontaneous departures from the Protectorate, however much those might have been provoked to various extents. The change in citizenship resulted in Slovak Roms being prevented from entering the territory of the Protectorate and being expelled back to Slovakia should they try to enter. Police stations in the Protectorate managed to react very quickly to the new situation, and in the space of a few months at the most, Roms with Slovak domiciles or citizenship had been ejected from Protectorate territory.

Domicile became key to the question of who was able to remain in the Protectorate and who had to leave. Roms with a newly-acquired foreign citizenship had no chance of remaining, as can be deduced from the numerous records of intensive police searches for "gypsy hordes", above all for Roms with German citizenship, over the entire territory and the subsequent deportation of these "hordes". The need to return to Slovakia affected all Slovak Roms living on Protectorate territory. In the case of the Lovara, who as "wandering gypsies" were highly visible, departure from the Protectorate affected all the families living on the road on Czech territory across the board. The only ones who managed to stay in the Protectorate were individuals who were able to hide their membership of such travelling groups. In the case of entire families it has to be assumed that they did not stay in the Protectorate.

---

354 Slovak Jews were also deported, however, and found themselves in a difficult situation, since Bratislava was not interested in their immigration (Ibid., 224–226).

3.3 Returning to Slovakia from the point of view of Lovara witnesses

After the creation of the Slovak State, the Lovara had to return to the municipality in which they were domiciled, although they often no longer had functional ties to that locality. This situation occurred among those Lovara who had been moving about the Czech lands in the 1930s. Some of them had probably not returned at all in the previous decade to the Slovak municipality in which they were registered, and so their domicile there had become purely formal. Such families had no social ties there. They were understandably viewed as *foreign* and as *not belonging* to the municipality by both the local authorities and the autochthonous inhabitants. The authorities often had an interest in getting rid of these new arrivals, who were viewed as a security risk, and they prevented them from settling in the municipality. An example of such forced return to the place of domicile is the Lovara families who, at the behest of the authorities, had to return to Pastuchov, not far from Hlohovec,[355] where an extended family of Roms had been domiciled since the period before the creation of Czechoslovakia. During the First Republic, their trajectories changed in keeping with their livelihood, the manufacture and cleaning of kettles, which took them to the Czech lands. Witness J. B. remembers that in Pastuchov "some of my relatives had been born before then, some of my uncles, when we used to travel about there."[356] According to my archival findings, however, their ties to the municipality had been more intensive and permanent in the past, and all that remained of them was a formal bond – that of domicile. After the creation of an independent Slovakia in March 1939, several Romani families were forced on the basis of this domicile to return to the municipality to which they belonged. However, none had lived in the small village in recent years, and none of them had created any ties to the locality. According to the witness cited, 10 or 15 related families were forced to return to Pastuchov at the beginning of the war, headed by his grandfather. They were sent to a plot of land about a kilometre from the municipality. According to a report from the

---

355 I looked at this case briefly in my article (Hajská, "We had to..."), and here I will look at it in more detail and from another perspective.

356 J. B., male (*1934), recorded 5 February 2002 in České Budějovice, Czech Republic by Markéta Hajská. Archive of Člověk v tísni, o.p.s. To reconstruct the situation in Pastuchov I will also use the testimonies of other witnesses from this family such as O. B. (*1932) recorded on 15 April 2002 in Ústí nad Labem, Czech Republic by Milada Závodská, Archiv spol. Člověk v tísni, o.p.s.; and O. K. (*1932) and R. R. (*1935), both stored in the VÚA VHA Praha, f. Sbírka osobních spisů žadatelů o vydání osvědčení podle zákona č. 255/1946 Sb., os.

Rišňovce police station in 1941, in the municipality of Pastuchov there were "25 gypsy vagabonds, all with domiciles in Pastuchov. These vagabond gypsies have neither horses nor wagons and now they are all living in Pastuchov."[357] On the basis of this report, we may presume that the Roms had either sold their horses and wagons or that they had been confiscated. The number of persons in this report does not correspond to the number given above by the witness J. B. (10–15 families), but the report may have just counted the adults. At first it seems they built improvised accommodation for themselves on the plot outside the village, as witness O.B. describes: "In the meantime we had a shed, which is where we slept. We didn't have a stove back then, just a campfire. So that's where we lived before my father built our house. It wasn't until 1944 that he built the house."[358] Those houses seem to have been destroyed at the end of the war by German troops.

Arriving in a municipality where such Roms had never owned any houses, despite the whole family or at least one of the parents being domiciled there, often meant that they were officially allotted a specific place that had clearly been their camping place or wintering place previously. This experience was described by Lovara witnesses from three municipalities in the district of Trnava (Križovany, Bohdanovce and Hrnčiarovce). They said that several Romani families "returned" at the same time to these municipalities during the period in question and that sometimes they were extended families with many branches.

Witnesses of this transfer from the Protectorate frequently described their departure to Slovakia as forced, in reaction to the newly-approved "law"[359] ordering them to return to the municipalities where they were domiciled.[360] Other witnesses interpreted this event as an "escape", motivated by the attempt to "save their lives", thus indicating their role as actors in this process who had decided to choose where they would live.[361] The same motivation can be observed with Bohemian and Moravian Roms and Sinti who emigrated to Slovakia during the same period, thereby avoiding the mass deportations to concentration camps and oth-

---

357 ŠA Nitra/ Trnava, f. OÚ Hlohovec 1923–1944, k. 213 – Kočovní cigáni, bezpečnostné opatrenie, č. j. 509/4, subject: Úprava niektorých pomerov cigánov, šetrenie z 16. 5. 1941.

358 O. B. (*1932) recorded on 15 April 2002 in Ústí nad Labem, Czech Republic by Milada Závodská. Archive of Člověk v tísni, o.p.s.

359 This was not a new law, as some of the witnesses describe it, but the institution of domicile and the legal frameworks governing it were transformed after the creation of the Protectorate and an independent Slovakia.

360 Hajská, "We had to run away", 70–71.

361 Ibid., 78.

er drastic "solutions to the gypsy question" underway in the Protectorate of Bohemia and Moravia.[362]

The Lovara who had moved around the Czech lands in the interwar period and who were ejected from the Protectorate in 1939 also survived as a group the genocide of the Romani population on their territory. Their names did not appear on the lists of those interned in the concentration camps designated for Roms on Protectorate territory (Lety u Písku, Hodonín u Kunštátu), nor were they transported to Auschwitz.[363]

---

362 Ibid.
363 Ibid., 52.

◄ Old photograph of Trenčianska Teplá from 1945, when part of the local infrastructure was destroyed by the advancing front.

Part 4: The Second World War

4.1 Roms during the Second World War on the territory of the Slovak State (1939–1945)

Several historians have described the situation of Roms in Slovakia during the Second World War.[364] Researchers agree that although Roms in Slovakia were not subjected to genocide as a group, as happened on the territory of the Protectorate or in other countries, many discriminatory, persecutory measures targeted them. There was a significant slump in their socioeconomic situation and an increase in their overall pauperisation. Roms in Slovakia were subjected to harsh bullying from the Hlinka Guard, the paramilitary arm of the ruling Slovak People's Party, and were also often subjected to violent, unpredictable behaviour by German soldiers and SS members. They faced various persecutory decrees issued by the Slovak Government.[365] The survival of the Roms was aided by the formal independence of Slovakia, which meant that anti-gypsy persecution was delayed and the planned liquidation of Roms there was never undertaken. A further important factor was that a large proportion of Roms were well-integrated into Slovakia's stratified agricultural society

---

364 For example, Ctibor Nečas, *Nad osudem českých a slovenských cikánů v letech 1939–1945* (Brno, 1981); Nečas, *Českoslovenští Romové*; Nečas, "Slovenští Romové"; Hübschmannová, *"Po židoch cigáni"*; Milena Hübschmannová, "Roma in the so-called Slovak State (1939–45)", *Gypsies during the Second World War, vol 3: The Final Chapter,* ed. Donald Kenrick (Hatfield: University of Hertforshire Press, 2006); Arne Mann and Zuzana Kumanová (eds.), *Ma bisteren: pripomínanie rómskeho holokaustu*. Bratislava: Občianske združenie In minorita, 2014; Helena Sadílková, "Holocaust of the Roma and Sinti on the territory of Czechoslovakia", *Factsheets on Romani culture, history, language, literature and Roma related groups*, University of Graz, 2020, 5, http://romafacts.uni-graz.at.

365 Sadílková, "Holocaust".

and formed an important part of the economic structure of the Slovak countryside in particular.[366] Roms who had been settled for centuries in Slovak municipalities formed part of their local populations and there was therefore no eminent political interest in their liquidation. However, the approach of local authorities to Romani communities was not uniform, but varied from region to region and locality to locality and was based on their previous personal and socioeconomic relationships with Romani community members. In many municipalities in the Slovak State, Roms were thus protected, at least for a while, or were spared the application of some anti-gypsy measures. This is where "travelling gypsies", forced to return to the municipalities where they were domiciled formally but had no local ties, were in a disadvantageous position.

Soon after the declaration of the Slovak State, the first measures limiting the Romani population started to be published. The central authorities distinguished between "gypsies" and "that part of the race that has acclimatised to such a degree that they consider themselves Slovaks, and Slovaks do not see them as gypsies in the true sense".[367] In June 1940, the Slovak Defence Ministry issued a decree that defined "gypsy" on the basis of "belonging to the gypsy race, being descended from it through both parents, living a travelling life or a settled life with the avoidance of work".[368] The decree provided room for local authorities to decide subjectively who would be considered a "gypsy" and who not, as well as how the "anti-gypsy directives" would be implemented against them.[369] In January 1940, a law on military service was passed on the basis of which Jews and Roms were released from military service. In February they were dismissed from fighting service by the Ministry of National Defence. Instead they had to perform compulsory labour designed for Jewish and gypsy conscripts.[370] It was when decisions were being made on who was to be sent to perform labour and who would be considered a "Slovak" and conscripted into the classic army to be ready to take up arms that the subjective judgement of the situation of individual Roms came visibly into play as mentioned above. On the basis of her many years of experience with Romani witnesses, Milena Hübschmannová stated that the number of Roms in Slovakia who were sent by the

---

366 Hübschmannová, *"Po židoch cigáni"*, 52–53.

367 Nečas, *Nad osudem*, 70.

368 Ibid., 70.

369 Hübschmannová, *"Po židoch cigáni"*, 87

370 Nečas, *Nad osudem*, 73–74.

conscription committees to bear arms was surprisingly large,[371] which clearly correlates with the extent to which Roms had created good local relationships in Slovakia.

As a result of this decree, some Roms who were judged by the committees to be "gypsies" served in the labour battalions, while others, considered "Slovaks", fought in the Slovak army on the side of the Axis powers in Russia and Italy. [372] Later, Romani soldiers who were deserters or prisoners of war were reintegrated into the Allied armies, and after joining the 1st Czechoslovak Army Corps in the USSR, they became involved in the fight against the Nazis. They took part in the liberation battles of the Red Army on the territory of today's Ukraine, Poland, Slovakia and the Czech Republic.[373]

Roms in Slovakia were hit very hard by the Interior Ministry decree of April 1941 entitled "Adjustments to some conditions of the gypsies". The decree affected most of the Romani population in Slovakia, above all its Section 2, which ordered that in municipalities where"gypsies" lived close to state and local roads, their dwelling-places should be removed and located separately from the municipality, in a designated remote place.[374] The ensuing eviction of the Roms represented a terrible blow for their socioeconomic integration into local communities because it isolated them from the everyday exchange of communication, goods and services.[375] In a number of municipalities this decree was implemented soon after it was published, although in others it was implemented later or not until part of the decree was reiterated by the ministry in July 1943. The places to which Roms were moved were frequently unsuitable for living. A number of municipalities nevertheless managed to save their Romani inhabitants and spare them from having to move out of the municipality. The decree further required (in Section 3) a *"gypsy vajda"* (chief) to be created in any municipality where there were more than three Romani families, while Section 5 ordered "workshy" persons to be sent to labour units.

The Romani situation in Slovakia worsened in the closing phase of the war after August 1944, when repressive operations were led by units

---

371 Hübschmannová, *"Po židoch cigáni"*, 203.
372 Sadílková, "Holocaust", 6.
373 Ibid., 6.
374 ŠA Nitra/ Trnava, f. OÚ Hlohovec 1923–1944, k. 213 – Kočovní cigáni, bezpečnostné opatrenie, Vyhláška ministerstva vnitra z 20. 4. 1941, čís. 42.615 o úprave niektorých pomerov cikánů, č. j. 42.615/II.4–1941.
375 Sadílková, "Holocaust", 6.

of the German army, the SS and other divisions to crush the Slovak National Uprising and suppress the partisan movement. People involved in the uprising were brutally prosecuted and the partisan movement was put down. This also targeted Roms who had either been actively involved in partisan struggles or had supported partisan groups,[376] or who were suspected of such activity by German troops.

During this time, dozens of Romani houses or settlements were burned down and an unknown number of murders were planned and implemented either of individuals or en masse. In the closing months of the war, immediately after German units arrived in Slovakia, violence was unleashed against a huge number of Roms, forcing them to abandon their houses; the same happened prior to the arrival of the front in Slovakia. The Roms hid in the woods, often in desperate conditions with no food orequipment of any kind. They often remained there until the liberation.

The impact of the anti-gypsy decrees during the Second World War in Slovakia on the situation of the Lovara

The information that exists on how the political and social developments in Slovakia between 1939 and 1945 specifically impacted Lovara families is fragmentary. Once again, this is mainly because the sources available do not essentially distinguish between various groups of Roms as defined on the basis of subethnicity. Oral history research has so far focused mostly on witnesses from non-Vlax Romani families. One of the few exceptions is a study by Arne Mann looking among other things at the massacre of Roms in the municipality of Čierny Balog during the Second World War. Mann reaches the conclusion that the victims of this mass murder, committed not far from the municipality of Čierny Balog by German soldiers and partially documented in the literature, were probably Vlax Roms. Their number is thought to have been around 60.[377] That some wartime measures had an impact on the Vlax Roms in Slovakia is also mentioned in several places in the works of Nečas[378] and Hübschmannová, who says, for example, that the ban on horse trading in a circular issued by the Bratislava Provincial Office in June 1939

---

376 Hübschmannová, *"Po židoch cigáni",* 745–747.
377 Arne Mann, "Význam spomienkového rozprávania pre výskum dejín rómskeho holocaustu". *Romano džaniben,* vol. 20, no. 2 (Winter 2013): 37–51.
378 Nečas, *Českoslovenští Romové* and Nečas, "Slovenští Romové".

chiefly concerned Vlax Roms.[379] They are rarely specifically mentioned, though.

I shall try to recapitulate the most important measures taken by the Slovak wartime authorities explicitly directed against "travelling gypsies". These necessarily impacted the Lovara, who were perceived by those around them as "travelling". This group was fundamentally affected by the bans on horse trading and itinerancy in particular, as these were connected with their forced returns to their places of permanent residence. The ban on horse trading and on dealing in general was reissued repeatedly, with the result that the authorities organised raids on travelling traders and sent them to work camps.[380] However, this repeated reissuing also shows that the previous bans on horse trading were not being thoroughly implemented and upheld.

According to Nečas, from the beginning of the Second World War a number of repressive measures targeted travelling Roms.[381] Horse dealers were targeted through a directive issued by the Bratislava Provincial Authority on the eve of the Second World War on 23 June 1939, whereby all "gypsies" were banned from trading in horses. On the basis of this, all horse dealers were meant to return to their home municipalities where their travelling trade licences were to be confiscated.[382] The directive also ordered district authorities and notaries to undertake a revision of domiciles [383] and submit a proposal to deport all persons with no domicile in the municipality.[384] An example of the application of this decree is a report from Topoľčany district where, in reaction to the above-mentioned measure, district authorities revised the domiciles of all "gypsies".[385] The police arrested three Roms on that basis, two (non-Vlax) travelling blade-sharpeners from the Skalica and Čadca districts and one "gypsy labourer" named Stojka from nearby Chynorany. All three then had to leave for the places where they were domiciled.[386]

---

379 Hübschmannová, *"Po Židoch cigáni"*, 87.
380 Nina Pavelčíková, "Příprava a provádění zákona o násilném usazování Romů na Ostravsku", in: *Ostrava 19, sborník k dějinám a současnosti města* (Šenov u Ostravy: Tilia, 1999): 21.
381 Nečas, *Českoslovenští Romové*, 100.
382 Ibid., 169.
383 Citizenship review was also ordered. Foreign "gypsy vagabonds" were banned on the territory of the republic with reference to Section 9, Act no. 127/1927.
384 Nečas, *Českoslovenští Romové*, 99.
385 Report from OÚ Topoľčany no. 10859/39 of 11 July 1939: *Vykázanie všetkých cigáňov do domovských obcí a zákaz obchodovania koňmi týmto*.
386 Ibid.

However, the Provincial Authority decree created disagreement among various government authorities which saw it as problematic and as violating the traditional livelihood and job opportunities for a number of Roms. Pressure was brought to bear by the Slovak Ministry of the Economy, and on 12 October 1940 a decree was issued amending the Provincial Authority decree so that the ban on issuing trade licences and concessions now related to "gypsy vagabonds" but allowed horse trading in the case of Roms with a declared permanent residence.[387]

The situation worsened again in 1941 when the above-mentioned decree entitled "Adjustments to some conditions of the gypsies" had a very harsh impact on Roms in Slovakia, including Lovara. As I have already mentioned, it affected long-term settled Roms, in that it ordered their dwellings to be moved away from public roads to more distant places. Lovara families who until then had mostly earned their living through economic activities requiring movement along certain routes were affected above all by Section 1 of this decree banning the movement of "travelling gypsies" outside the territory of their permanent residence. The main impact on Lovara was that the decree cancelled their itinerancy documents and ordered the holders of such permits to return within eight days to the municipalities where they were domiciled. According to Nečas, the families of Vlax Roms were then put under police supervision in the municipalities and were only allowed to leave their allotted dwelling-places with the permission of the local security forces. They had to sell their wagons and draught horses or such property was confiscated and auctioned.[388] Since in many places these measures were not actually implemented, the Interior Ministry emphatically warned the heads of local and state police authorities in a circular of 21 July 1943 that they had to fulfil all the orders relating to the itinerancy, residency and work duties of Roms.[389] The repeated bans on horse trading led to Romani economic activities being limited to those that could be carried out from a fixed base, which meant either the end (or a major curtailment) of their itinerancy.[390] Vlax Roms were thereby deprived of their livelihoods, often without access to other sources of earning a living.

Roms in Slovakia were therefore left at the mercy of local authorities who were waiting for the first opportunity to get rid of them. Such an

---

387 Janas, "Pokusy vlády slovenského štátu o likvidáciu obchodu s koňmi v rokoch 1939–1941 (mikroštúdia)", *Romano džaniben*, vol. 10, no. 2 (Winter 2003): 90–91.
388 Nečas, "Slovenští Romové", 170.
389 Ibid., 170.
390 Ibid., 157.

opportunity came at the beginning of 1942, when the first labour camps started to be set up in Slovakia. Roms with no employment were sent there and labelled asocial.[391] The first camps were opened in Most na Ostrove and Očová in 1941, and then in 1942–1944 a further nine forced labour camps were created all over Slovakia (Hanušovce nad Topľou, Bystré, Nižný Hrabovec, Petič u Chmeľova, Revúca, Jarabá, Ústí nad Oravou, Ilava and Dubnica nad Váhom) in which Roms formed a significant part or a majority of the inmates.[392]

The forced returns of the Lovara to their domiciles and limited ties to local populations

From the spring of 1939, Roms coming to Slovakia from the Protectorate of Bohemia and Moravia, including Lovara, were sent to the municipalities where they were domiciled. Under the influence of the repeatedly-issued decrees banning itinerancy or even movement outside their domiciles, families of "gypsy vagabonds" were sent back straight away to their domiciles if they were caught travelling on the territory of Slovakia, in other words, anywhere outside their municipality of domicile.

For Lovara who had territorial ties to a specific municipality and who also lived there, these decrees limited their ability to move around and engage in traditional professions which required territorial mobility. However, the nationwide decrees understandably had a much greater impact on families who had no base in any municipality and whose places of residence had been allotted to them only formally. As I have already described, in the case of some Lovara families, their domicile was a purely formal matter. It was recorded in their documents, but frequently without any actual tie to the municipality or its inhabitants. Under the influence of the stricter measures introduced on the eve of the war and at its start, this fact suddenly became of fundamental importance. For such Roms, their return to these domiciles was complicated, since the authorities in these municipalities often refused them and did not want to issue confirmation of their residency.[393] A number of Lovara thus returned "home" to the place where they had been domiciled for many years, but had no house or base, a place where they were viewed by local

---

391 Janas, "Pokusy vlády", 91.
392 Nečas, "Slovenští Romové", 165–166.
393 Janas, "Pokusy vlády", 90.

inhabitants as people who did not belong there, as foreigners. Another problem was that sometimes only part of the family was domiciled in a certain municipality, while their partners and other relatives living with them had never had any sort of formal residence there. This forced residence of persons perceived as unwanted and foreign necessarily resulted in pressure from local non-Romani populations for a way to be found of ejecting the Roms from the municipality.

Let us now look at some concrete examples of situations in the villages where the Lovara arrived on the basis of their official domiciles and owned no houses or shelter of any kind. According to witness testimonies, they were often allotted a piece of land on which they were meant to stay permanently. Some became "settled" in shacks made out of the wagons in which they had formerly lived, against which lean-tos were made with tarpaulins, as was the case of some of the Stojka family in Trenčianska Teplá. In other cases, their wagons were confiscated and they had to improvise dwellings out of other materials. This was the case, for example, in Bohdanovice in the Trnava district, where the families of the Horvát brothers who were forced to return there made improvised "houses out of planks on the land beyond the playing field."[394]

Witness S. L., whose family was sent to the municipality of Križovany, Trnava district, described their situation in these words: "It was completely empty, we had nothing there. My parents and 10 children, there was nowhere to sleep. My mother had to sell our quilts so we could buy a stove."[395] Many Lovara families thus found themselves in an extreme situation where any sort of mobility was denied them. After their horses and sometimes their wagons were confiscated, they were left without any property at all and without access to ways of earning a living. The families were then forced to remain in the same place for several years.

Some families initially tried to ignore the decrees banning movement outside their domiciles. For example, witness R. B. says that at the start of the war, her family continued to move around the environs of Bratislava:

---

394 VÚA-VHA Praha, f. Sbírka osobních spisů žadatelů o vydání osvědčení podle zákona č. 255/1946 Sb., personal file of applicant S. S. (*1936). This was a widespread family into which two daughters of Zaga Stojková married.

395 Personal recording of S. L. (*1930) made in October 2008, Nymburk, Czech Republic. The recording is owned by and cited with the kind permission of the Portail du Centre de Documentation du Mémorial de la Shoah.

We travelled around western Slovakia until we decided to hide from the Nazis in the woods. [...] In December 1943 [396] we went off to live in the forest. We left our horses and wagon at the end of the village and just took our clothing with us. We hid there until the end of the war.[397]

Travelling in the first years of the war was also described by witness P. S., born in 1936 in the district of Pelhřimov, whose family over the course of the war spent time with various relatives in Bernolákovo, Bzenec and Hrnčiarovce, later in the woods: "When we came to Slovakia we travelled around until they issued the law saying that travelling was no longer allowed."[398]

Lovara in labour camps in Slovakia

Decisions on who would be sent to a labour camp as an "asocial" person depended in large part on whether the local authorities decided to spare Roms. In some localities, the mayors refused to send "their" (in other words, local) Roms to the camps and also refused to carry out other anti-gypsy measures, while in other places they complied with orders to do so.[399] The Lovara who on the basis of the anti-gypsy decrees were settled in municipalities where they had previously had only formally-stated domicile, had no functional social contacts. This meant it was difficult for them to be perceived by the majority population or the local authorities as "our Roms",[400] as people who belonged to the municipality and with whom they had close relationships – far from it. This was necessarily felt in the unwillingness of the municipalities to protect them from the repression ordered from above. On the contrary, such municipal authorities could demand that the state help them deal with the situation. In some local records we can observe an attempt to use any means possible

---

396 The witness is very probably thinking of the year 1944, after the Germans arrived in reaction to the Slovak National Uprising, when large numbers of people – not just Roms – in that part of Slovakia hid in the woods and other places.

397 VÚA-VHA Praha, f. Sbírka osobních spisů žadatelů o vydání osvědčení podle zákona č. 255/1946 Sb., personal file of applicant R. B. (*1921).

398 Personal recording of P. S. (*1936) by the author, made in October 2008, Nymburk, Czech Republic. The recording is owned by and cited with the kind permission of the Portail du Centre de Documentation du Mémorial de la Shoah.

399 Sadílková, "Holocaust", 6.

400 For example Tomáš Kobes, "'Naši Romové' – difrakční vzorce odlišnosti východoslovenského venkova", *Romano džaniben*, vol. 19, no. 2 (Winter 2012): 9–34.

to get rid of these unwanted new arrivals. However, that threat also hung over those Lovara who had maintained regular wintering places in certain municipalities, or who had lived there for variously long periods and with varying intensities but were not perceived as being entirely local. On the basis of Romani testimony, it is possible to state that a relatively large number of Lovara were interned in labour camps. Although the precise numbers and names of interned persons are not known, from the witness narratives we can state that the Lovara were sent to these institutions from the following districts and municipalities: Hlohovec (town of Hlohovec, municipality of Pastuchov), Nitra (Štitáre), Piešťany (Ratnovce), Púchov (Beluša), Senec (Bernolákovo), Topoľčany (town of Topoľčany, municipalities of Chynorany and Solčany) and Trnava (Bohdanovce, Hrnčiarovce, Madunice, Šúrovce).[401] According to witness narratives, the Romani men from these municipalities were most often transported to the labour camps at Dubnica nad Váhom and Hanušovce nad Topľou, and this seems to have happened mostly in the years 1942–1943.

Tense local relations are not just described by Romani witnesses. We also find records of them in the archives. An example of the hostile approach of local inhabitants to non-autochthonous Roms is a letter written by residents of the municipality of Chynorany, addressed to the Interior Ministry of the Slovak Republic, in which the inhabitants ask for all the gypsies living in the municipality of Chynorany to be sent to a labour camp. According to that document, some of the Roms who lived in Chynorany had also lived there earlier (this may have included not just non-Vlax Roms, but also Lovara families who had lived there long-term), but others were described as "travelling gypsies", who sometimes "do not even have permanent domicile and are thus a burden to the municipality".[402] The letter claims there had been a transfer of Roms several weeks earlier (it is not clear which kind of Roms) from their original dwelling

---

401 I identified the names of these municipalities by analysing the applicants for compensation for genocide in the Second World War, archived by Člověk v tísni, o.p.s., and on the basis of selected personal applications for a certificate under Act no. 255/1946 stored in the VÚA-VHA Praha archives. The witnesses described either their own personal experiences or their closest relatives' experiences (fathers, brothers, grandfathers). This list of municipalities was based on witnesses who then moved from Slovakia to the Czech lands in the postwar period where they later, mostly after the year 2000, applied for compensation via the organisation Člověk v tísni, or from the Defence Ministry of the Czech Republic for a certificate under Act no. 255/1946.

402 ŠA Nitra/Topoľčany, f. OÚ Topoľčany, k. 530, D 2488/44 – Odvody asociálnych osôb do pracovných táborov. "Politická obec Chynorany, okres Topoľčany, župa Nitra prosí o umiestenie všetkých v obci Chynorany bývajúcich cigáňov do pracovného útvaru". No č. j., dated 19 August 1943.

place to the municipal mill, where the Roms had allegedly caused considerable damage in the local fields. Apparently it was impossible to guard the place sufficiently:

> The municipality of Chynorany has no other place, and so we are turning to the illustrious Interior Ministry with a respectful request that all of the Chynorany gypsies be sent to a labour camp where they would learn not to beg.[403]

At that time the labour camps in Slovakia used only able-bodied men, however much the residents' demand suggests a relatively radical attempt to move "all gypsies" there, clearly including old (and unfit) people, women and children.

The archival file entitled "Transfers of asocial persons to labour camps" in the Topoľčany branch of the Nitra state archive provides further testimony on the way in which people were suggested for the list of "asocial" persons.[404] The file includes lists of persons from various municipalities in the Topoľčany district whom it was suggested should be sent to the camp for "asocial" persons in Dubnica nad Váhom or in Hanušovce nad Topľou. The various municipal notaries' offices produced lists of those proposed for transfer and already transferred. On the "asocial elements" list of 3 August 1942, among those who were to be sent to the work camp at Hanušovice nad Topľou from Topoľčany there were 27 non-Romani and Romani men. From their names it is possible to identify 12 Lovara with the surname Stojka and one with the surname Kotlár, all resident at number 11 Práznovská Street in Topoľčany and all with their occupation given as "gypsy". They were men from the Stojka family to which I have devoted previous chapters. They include the "head of the family", Michal Stojka, who at that time was 80 years old. On an earlier list of 26 July 1942 regarding the planned handing over of "asocials" to the labour camp in Hanušovce nad Topľou, the 27 names included 15 Lovara from the same family. Among them were five young women aged 14–20.[405] This contradicts the claim that the labour units used only men, and it is not clear how to interpret the presence of women on this list.[406]

---

403 Ibid.
404 ŠA Nitra/ Topoľčany, f. OÚ Topoľčany, k. 530, D 2488/44 – Odvody asociálnych osôb do pracovných táborov.
405 Ibid., č. j. 3174/42, Report from Žandárska stanica Topoľčany, subject: Hanušovce nad Topľou – zriadenie pracovného útvaru (26. 7. 1942).
406 The finding that in Slovakia during the Second World War women's names appeared on the lists of people to be sent to labour camps is a unique discovery that has so far not been investigated by historians. A similar situation from the Protectorate of Bohemia and Moravia was

Another list of "asocial elements" from September 1942 submitted by Topoľčany contained 47 people, of whom 11 were from the Stojka family. Most of them ultimately were sent to the labour camp in Dubnica nad Váhom on 8 October 1942.[407] The following day, the district authority in Topoľčany proposed the transfer of another 24 people ("asocial elements and able-bodied gypsies") to the labour camp in Dubnica, proposing that they should be allotted to the firm of Ing. Lozovský and Štefanec for the construction of the hydroelectric power plant in Dubnica. The men in the first group sent to Dubnica from Topoľčany worked there too. On the list of 24 men were two more Lovara from Práznovská Street.[408] According to a report from the police station at the labour camp in Dubnica nad Váhom, four of the Topoľčany Lovara (Ján Stojka, Jozef Stojka, Ondrej Stojka, Jr. and Ondrej Stojka, Sr.) came to join the camp in Dubnica nad Váhom voluntarily on 12 October 1942. A week later, the local command learnt from the police patrol in Topoľčany that the above-named people were meant to be on a transport list to the labour camp, but had ignored that, coming to the camp in Dubnica on their own and reporting as volunteers. Not long afterward, the father of Ján Stojka submitted a request for his son's release, but it was refused.[409]

This was not the last transport of "asocial persons" from the Topoľčany district, however. On 28 April 1943, the Topoľčany authorities carried out another round of such transfers, this time to the labour camp in Bystré, Giraltovce district. Of the 11 "asocials" who were called up, three were from the Stojka family, although in the end just one was proposed for transport.[410] How long the men spent in these labour camps is not clear from the official records.[411]

---

described by Baloun. He interpreted the attempt by some district authorities to put not just adult men, but also whole families on the lists of persons to be sent to the camps as a conflict between demands from "below" for the camps to be created to serve their purposes and the interests of the central state administration. (Baloun, *"Cikáni, metla venkova"*, 338–342).

407 Ibid., č. j. 4945/42. Subject: Doprava osob z asociálního živlu pre pracovný útvar v Dubnici nad Váhom. There was not an exact list of names attached to the report, so we can only guess how many men from the Stojka family were transported to the labour unit.

408 Ibid., č. j. 15.607/1942 – report from OÚ Topoľčany, subject: Dodatočný odvod asociálního živlu pre pracovný útvar v Dubnici nad Váhom (8. 10. 1942).

409 Ibid., č. j. 351/42, subject: Stojka Ján z Topoľčan, žiadosť o prepustenie z prac. útvaru (24 November 1942).

410 Ibid. Zápisnica OU Topoľčany, při příležitosti odvodu asociálních osob, (28. 4. 1943), no č .j.

411 From the documents we learn just fragmentary information regarding what happened to them next, for example, that Ondrej Stojka (*1898) and Josef Stojka (*1924) of Topoľčany were still in the labour camp in Dubnica nad Váhom in mid-January 1943 (ibid., č. j. 293/1943, report: Kartotéky asocialných osob (13. 1. 1943).

On 2 November 1944, on the orders of the Slovak Minister of National Defence, an internment camp for Roms was opened on the site of the former labour camp at Dubnica nad Váhom. It was used for the forced concentration of Romani families, irrespective of their members' age or sex.[412] The overall number and names of the Roms imprisoned there, like the Romani victims' names, are unknown. According to witness testimonies, individuals and whole families of Lovara were concentrated there, but once again, we do not know the number of those imprisoned, the victims, or even their names.

4.2 The situation of the Lovara on territory occupied by Hungary

After the Vienna Award of 1938, southern Slovakia was occupied by Horthyist Hungary.[413] Especially in the closing phase of the war, the Roms living in that annexed territory were subjected to cruel and thorough anti-Romani measures in the form of mass transports to concentration camps. This also concerned a large number of Lovara, who for generations had been territorially connected to this geographical area inhabited predominantly by Hungarian speakers and which, after the creation of Czechoslovakia, was situated in the south of Slovakia along the border with Hungary, above all in the former districts of Levice, Komárno, Nové Zámky, Galanta, Šaľa, Vráble and Šurany. Communities of Lovara also lived and travelled in more eastern districts such as Lučenec and Košice, which also belonged to Hungary during the Second World War.

Like the other Roms in Hungary, all of the Roms living in occupied Slovakia from 1938 to 1944 had to face crude violence and the Hungarian state's increasingly discriminatory, persecutory measures. Mass persecution of Roms started to occur after Hungary was occupied by German troops in March 1944, and especially after the fall of Horthy and the seizure of power by Szálasi and his fascist Arrow Cross Party (also known as the Nyilasists) in October 1944.[414] In a relatively short time the German Nazis together with the Hungarian Nyilasists managed

---

412 Nečas, "Slovenští Romové", 173.
413 This territory was slightly extended in March 1939 to include areas lying in the southeast and east of Slovakia (Gurňák 2014: 27–28).
414 Nečas, *Českoslovenští Romové*, 96–97.

to unleash their persecution and extermination in an exceptionally cruel and effective manner.[415]

Even earlier, however, some voices there had been saying that the "gypsy question" needed to be dealt with on a racial basis and there had been attempts to forcibly sterilise Roms.[416]

The fates of the Roms who lived in the southern Slovak territory that was annexed to Hungary during the war have been relatively under-researched, although some reminiscences of witnesses who lived in that area have been published. Probably the most extensive treatment of the subject was by Nečas in his book *Czechoslovak Roms in 1938–1945*, in which there is a short chapter entitled "The situation of the Romani population on the territory occupied by Hungary".[417] The Roms in the annexed territory, as in other parts of Hungary, were banned in spring 1944 from moving freely. Romani men were sent to dig trenches and build fortifications.[418] They were also conscripted into the army, and many of them had to fight on the eastern front.[419] In autumn 1944, a register of Romani men and women aged from 16 to 60 was made, after which many went into hiding. Those who did not manage to escape, or who were caught as they fled, were sent to the regional collection camp.[420] During this period, Nečas writes, the Roms from the occupied territory of Slovakia, together with the other Roms from Hungary, were transported to the Star Fort and the Sandberg Fort in Komárno, where they were imprisoned before being sent to Dachau concentration camp in Germany, and from there to other concentration camps.[421] Roms from the fort in Komárno were sent to Dachau in December 1944. Only women with children under 14 were released from the Komárno camp and spared internment.[422]

A number of witnesses from the Lovara families living in municipalities on the territory occupied by Hungary have testified that members of their families were transported to concentration camps during the

---

415 Katz, "Story, history".

416 Hübschmannová, *"Po židoch cigáni"*, 43.

417 Nečas, *Českoslovenští Romové*, 95–98. Another important study about this topic, Milena Hübschmannová's editorial work on the second volume of "Po Židoch Cigáni" had not yet been published at the time of writing of my book. According to the content published in the first half, Chapter XI in the second half was to be entitled "Roms on Slovak territory occupied by Hungary" and was to contain a five-page introduction to the subject and 10 testimonies from witnesses.

418 Ibid., 95–96.

419 Hübschmannová, *"Po židoch cigáni"*, 43.

420 Nečas, *Českoslovenští Romové*, 96.

421 Ibid., 96–97.

422 Katz, "Story, history".

war. Witness Viktor Salinas (*1941) of Dolná Seč, Levice district, said in a biographical interview that his grandfather Karol Lakatoš and five other Roms from Dolná Seč were taken to Štúrovo, where together with Roms from nearby Železovce and other places they were put on a train to Hungary. From there they were sent to Dachau. According to his testimony, his grandfather and several other Roms from his family died there.

The deportation of Roms from their families to concentration camps was also mentioned by the Lovara who applied to be issued with certificates for participants in the Resistance on the basis of Act no. 255/1946, whose testimonies are stored in the Military Historical Archive in Prague. I undertook a small survey of these applications, covering 20 applicants, Lovara who lived during the war in the districts of Galanta (5), Komárno (2), Levice (10), Nové Zámky (2) and Šurany (1).[423] Most of these applications were not made until after the year 2000, and during the war the applicants had been young children who were not subjected to internment. Some were applying for their forebears and did not themselves experience the war. Most of the applicants did not know where their relatives had been sent to be interned. Among the applicants for war compensation who submitted their requests through the organisation Člověk v tísni, o.p.s. at the turn of the millenium, I managed to identify Lovara who during the war had lived on Slovak territory occupied by Hungary and who said that members of their families had been sent to concentration camps. For example, witness A. B. from the municipality of Pozba, Nové Zámky district, said that from his family, his father and grandfather had been taken, but his father escaped the transport to Dachau by jumping out of the train. His grandfather did not come back from the camp. Witness A. K., who lived in Trávnica, Nové Zámky district, also mentioned his father's transport to Dachau at the beginning of November 1944. His father was then imprisoned in the Buchenwald concentration camp, where he died. Lovara claimants who lived during the war in the village of Kolárovo, Komárno district and in Komárno municipality also said that their relatives had been sent to concentration camps.[424]

These witness statements may be considered a unique source testifying to anti-Romani measures, raids and the subsequent transport to concentration camps of Roms from particular municipalities which

---

423 List created by analysing documents in VÚA-VHA Praha, f. Sbírka osobních spisů žadatelů o vydání osvědčení podle zákona č. 255/1946 Sb.

424 Archive of applicants for compensation for genocide during the the Second World War kept by Člověk v tísni, o.p.s.

belonged to Hungary during the war. Such testimonies are all the more valuable in that no historian has yet published lists of Roms transported to concentration camps from the Slovak territory that was annexed. On the basis of my research using online sources such as the Arolsen Archives database,[425] the United States Holocaust Memorial Museum, and a web page dedicated to the Dachau concentration camp[426] which allow one to search for persons interned in Nazi concentration camps, I managed to find examples of the Nazi persecution of Lovara community members who, during the Second World War, lived on the Slovak territory that formed part of Hungary.[427] So far I have identified by name 34 cases of Lovara individuals from that area who were transported and subsequently imprisoned in the Dachau concentration camp.[428] Of these, 29 were male and five female. Seven were children aged 14 and under, of whom two were girls. The three youngest were only 12 at the time of their transport to Dachau.

On the basis of digitalised documentation of their internment records, we can ascertain that most of these Roms came to Dachau on

---

425 Bad Arolsen: This is a facility for the International Tracing Service, originally set up by the International Red Cross, with its headquarters in Bad Arolsen in Germany where there is an archive of almost all the Nazi documents testifying to persecution during the Second World War (Lada Viková and Milada Závodská. "Dokumentace genocidy Romů za 2. světové války v Československu – nálezová zpráva: diskontinuita a kontinuita odhalování historie Romů po roce 1946." *Romano džaniben*, vol. 23, no. 2 (Winter 2016): 113).

426 Online search engine for the Arolsen Archives (https://eguide.its-arolsen.org/), United States Holocaust Memorial Museum – Holocaust Survivors and Victims Database (United States Holocaust Memorial Museum – https://www.ushmm.org) and a search engine for the list of those interned in Dachau concentration camp (Dachau One-Step Search Results – https://stevemorse.org). These search engines allow the digitalised lists of prisoners and card records of persons interned in the concentration camps to be searched just by entering names and surnames.

427 I looked for people with typical Lovara surnames (Banda, Lakatoš, Rafael, Stojka), considering a relevant result to be records where, according to my research, Lovara had lived during the war. I managed to find a total of 34 people who can definitely be identified as Lovara.

428 Of these 34 people, 19 had the surname Banda, 10 Lakatoš (written Lakatos, in one case Lakatosz), three Rafael and two Stojka. They were all deported to the Dachau concentration camp and labelled by the Nazi administration as "gypsies" / "Hungarian Gypsies" (*Ungarn Zigeuner*)". During the war, these Roms lived in the following districts and municipalities: Komárno district (17 persons) – in the municipalities of Hurbanovo (7 persons), Dulovce (5 persons), Komárno (4 persons) and Svätý Peter (1 person); Levice district (9 persons) – in the municipalities of Tekovské Lužany (4 persons), Mýtne Ludany (2 persons), Dolná Pial (1 person), Dolná Seč (1 person) and Kálna nad Hronom (1 person); Nové Zámky district (2 persons) – in the municipalities of Nové Zámky (1 person) and Pozba (1 person); Dunajská Streda district (1 person) – in the municipality of Trhová Hradská; Žitavce district, which lies in the Nitra district of Slovakia today, but during the war was joined to Hungary (1 person).

transports in November 1944 (the dates 14 November, 19 November and 21 November 1944 are repeated) and were imprisoned in Dachau for varying lengths of time. Four were transported a few days later to the Natzweiler-Struthof camp on the territory of occupied France or to its auxiliary camp in Schömberg. Another four persons were sent after almost two weeks (on 1 December 1944) from Dachau to the concentration camp at Ravensbrück. Another eight Lovara were transported to Buchenwald, of which six were sent together on 5 December 1944. Other Lovara individuals were sent to German concentration camps such as Sachsenhausen and Flossenbürg. We do not have detailed information regarding the further fates of these Lovara imprisoned in Nazi concentration camps. All we know is that a few of them were liberated in Dachau or Buchenwald. From the incomplete records available we also learn that seven of these 34 persons did not survive internment in the camps. Two prisoners died in Dachau, one in Schömberg, and four in Buchenwald.

A unique case is that of Josef Rafael, born in 1901 in Tekovské Lužany (Nagysalló in Hungarian). He was the grandfather of the witness Josef Molnár (*1945) mentioned in the previous chapter, and his imprisonment in a concentration camp and subsequent escape was described to me by his grandson in an interview in 2018. According to the documents found, Josef Rafael was transported via the SIPO (*Sicherheits-polizei*) in Budapest to Dachau on 14 November 1944, from where he was transferred to the Natzweiler concentration camp on 24 November 1944 and allotted to its auxiliary camp of Dautmergen. From there he managed to escape on 11 December 1944. In his personal documents there is a confirmation issued by the Federal Committee of the Czechoslovak Union of Anti-Fascist Fighters in Prague from 1972 stating that he was then arrested by the Gestapo of Konstanz in southwest Germany, approximately 100 kilometres from Dautmergen, where he remained until he was finally liberated on 9 June 1945.[429] According to his grandson, Josef Molnár, dozens of other Roms from Tekovské Lužany had been deported to the concentration camp with him but did not return. However, I have not managed to find out their names.

Imprisonment in concentration camps was just one form of the genocide perpetrated against the Roms in the Slovak territory that was annexed to Hungary during the war. At the close of the war there were concentrated, extreme fascist terror episodes in some parts of Hungary,

---

429 Documents on internment, 1.1 Camps and ghettos, 1.1.6 Dachau Concentration Camp, 1.1.6.7 *Schreibstubenkarten Dachau*. Doc ID. 10732936. ITS Digital Archive, Bad Arolsen.

including occupied Slovak territory, which led to the extermination of the local Romani population.[430] Nečas closes his chapter on Roms in Hungarian-occupied territory with a description of an event that was said to have taken place in Hurbanovo, Komárno district:

> As they retreated to the west, the Nyilasists took with them a group of Roms from the area of Hurbanovo and stopped with them on 30 March 1945 at a farm in Trhové Mýto. From there they took all the Romani men, women and children to the Klátov branch of the Little Danube, drove them into the water and shot them. The river, in flood, swept away the bodies of 53 adults and seven children. Only Alžběta Lakatošová survived the massacre.[431]

That event was described to me by Júlie Bandová (*1946), the daughter of the Alžběta Lakatošová named by Nečas, during the filming of her own reminiscenses. She confirmed that those who were executed were Lovara and also stated that two people had survived:

> They killed my mother's whole family. The Germans took them to the water, her father, her mother, her son, her sisters. They shot all the Roms by the water not far from Komárno. The village was called Hurbanovo. The Nyilasists took them away and shot them. All the Roms died there. My mother and one of her brothers hid in a haystack when they saw them coming, and thanks to that they survived.[432]

4.3 The Second World War in Trenčianska Teplá

According to the records in the municipal chronicle, Trenčianska Teplá was very much in favour of the new regime of Slovak nationalist Jozef Tiso, who visited there in person on 15 October 1938. According to the chronicle, people cheered him enthusiastically. In the Slovak parliamentary elections of December 1938, the fascist candidate list, dominated by candidates from the Hlinka Slovak People's Party (HSĽS), won an alleged 99.16% of the vote in Trenčianska Teplá. From a chronicle entry in 1938, we learn that this was one of the first municipalities in Slovakia where the Hlinka Guard was formed. By the end of 1938, the Hlinka

---

430 Nečas, *Českoslovenští Romové*, 97.
431 Ibid., 97.
432 Personal recording of J. Bandová (*1946) by the author, recorded on 31 March 2018 in Šurany, Slovakia.

Guard already had 300 members in the municipality and had taken over the local hall of the Sokol physical education movement, hung a cross in it, and was organising parades of Hlinka Guard members in their "beautiful uniforms".[433]

In March 1939, Czech citizens in Trenčianska Teplá were immediately deported to the Moravian part of the Protectorate, according to the chronicle. A train then came from the Czech lands to Trenčianska Teplá with interned Slovaks guarded by Czech police. The chronicle comments on the event thus: "In a moment, throngs of people ran to the station and, despite being unarmed, women as well as men set about attacking the policemen, who were armed to the teeth, and freeing their brothers from the claws of the Czechs." The chronicle goes on to boast that after the new Slovak State was declared, Trenčianska Teplá was one of the first municipalities to hoist the flag of the newly-created state. After Tiso was elected it was the first municipality to congratulate the new president.[434] The chief notary and government commissar in the municipality was the nationalist Karol Dembovský, a supporter of and campaigner for Tiso's political line. An enthusiastic, pro-regime tone celebrating nationalist activities continues to fill further pages of the municipal chronicle. After 1944, the records by another chronicler, clearly a supporter of a different political group, try to rectify things. In a section entitled "Additions to previous years" he tried to correct the record created by the previous chronicler's celebratory, pro-fascist approach. The chronicler after 1944 describes the expulsion of the Czechs from the municipality as "a shameful rampage by members of the Hlinka Guard" which he says dragged Czech men and women into a prepared room, stripped them naked, and forced them to hand over all their valuables. The postwar chronicler also adds that the chronicle entries during the war had left out the "heart-rending scenes" which had occurred when Jewish families were sent to concentration camps, as well as the subsequent looting of Jewish property.[435] He closes the section by writing that his predecessor omitted to mention that members of the municipality had been forced to join the Hlinka Guard.[436] Not a word is written about the treatment of Romani people in the village during the war by either chronicler.

---

433 *Obecná kronika obce Trenčianska Teplá, Období třicátých let a druhé světové války.* Archived in the Municipal Library of Trenčianska Teplá, 74–75.

434 Ibid., 80.

435 At another place the postwar chronicler writes that 80 Jewish inhabitants of the municipality died in the war, either after being tortured or murdered in the gas chambers. Ibid., 99.

436 Ibid., 86–88.

The family of Štefan Stojka, Sr. in Trenčianska Teplá during the war

The events described in the local chronicle are important to the explanation of something else I found in the state archive in Trenčín, in the file on "The Hlinka Guard in Trenčianska Teplá" containing membership applications and lists of Hlinka Guard members. Among several hundred applications there are also applications from Štefan's son, Ján Stojka (*1905) and (probably) Štefan's son-in-law Alexander (*1910) to join the Hlinka Guard.[437] Although the available records on the final composition of the Hlinka Guard squads indicate that neither were accepted as a member of these paramilitary divisions, the very fact that they made applications opens up a number of questions that can no longer be answered today. Was it an attempt on their part to formally comply with the decree exhorting men to join the Hlinka Guard?[438] Can we understand it as an attempt to fit in, or to imitate the behaviour of their non-Romani peers? Or do these applications suggest their loyalty to local people in a position of power connected to the new regime? Without a deeper knowledge of the context, it is very difficult to clearly interpret this today.

Given that there were active backers of the ruling pro-fascist regime in the leadership of the municipality who had many supporters, it may be assumed that the Stojka family must have viewed the situation in the community as tense or acute. The family must in some way have reacted to the growing waves of nationalism which it probably perceived as a threat.

Similar questions concerning the form of the social ties and status of Štefan Stojka in the municipality are provoked by the fact that in the 1930s or even earlier he became the owner of a house there, in which he lived with his family at the outbreak of the Second World War and from which he set out to trade horses while this was still possible. Compared to other Lovara in the region Štefan had a higher initial status and clearly also stronger social ties with local non-Roms than were usual at that time. On the basis of all the information available, it seems that he

---

437 ŠA Trenčín, f. ObNÚ v Trenčianskej Teplej, e. č. 254b, k. 59 – Hlinkova garda v Trenčianskej Teplej, zoznamy členov, prihlášky členov, year 1938.

438 Ibid. Announcement from the district authorities in Trenčín č. j. 1116/39/prez. calling on all citizens of Slovak nationality of male sex except Jews, on the basis of Act no. 125/1927, Sb.z. a n. of 14 July 1927, Article 3, to compulsorily join the Hlinka Guard according to Government Decree no. 220/1939 Sl.z. The applications are undated. In the case of both men, their profession is given as "labourer", no school education is listed for them, and the language column lists "Slovak and gypsy".

might have been perceived by residents at that time as *local*. I believe it is this fact that helped Štefan and his extended family to survive the war in Trenčianska Teplá without significant harm.

No records have been preserved in the archives describing the specific implementation of measures preventing Štefan and his family members from travelling or dealing in horses. It is not clear until what date the Stojka family owned horses, whether they were confiscated from the family, and if so, under what circumstances.

The return of Zaga Stojková's family to Trenčianska Teplá

As I described in detail in the chapter devoted to the trajectories of Zaga's family in the interwar period, unlike her younger brother Štefan, she spent the 1930s moving about the territory of Bohemia and Moravia with her family. All her children had grown up by the end of the 1930s (except for her youngest son, Josef) and had their own partners and children. During that time Zaga appears to have lived together with the family of her eldest son, Filo, but there are also records of her having moved about with her other children's families. Zaga's branch of the family had around 30 members, although they travelled in smaller, independent units. In 1938 the family was in Moravia, as shown by the eight records I have found of the Stojka family's movements in that area.

The family's last record in the Czech lands was the record of the birth of a child in the Přerov district from 3 March 1939, eleven days before the declaration of the Slovak State. Subsequently the family faced the same fate as other Lovara families who were on the territory of the Czech lands during the interwar period. They had to leave Protectorate territory and return to the municipality where they were domiciled in Slovakia. However, we do not know whether they decided to leave Moravia voluntarily or whether they were forcibly escorted over the border by police. During their relocation from the Protectorate, Zaga's branch of the family segment became divided. On the basis of their domiciles, Zaga's daughters and their families had to return to the places where their partners were registered as living, Bohdanovce and Šúrovce in the district of Trnava. Zaga, her youngest son Jouško and her son Filo and his family had to return during 1939 to Trenčianska Teplá municipality,[439] where both she and some of her children had been born and where they were still do-

---

439 ŠA Trenčín, f. OÚ Trenčín, Admin 1939, Sčítanie ľudu Tr. Teplá, šk. 427.

miciled. Filo Stojka was registered in the Index of Military Registration book for the year 1939,[440] the only Rom living in Trenčianska Teplá whose name appears in it. It is not clear, however, what this registration means or whether Filo, at that time 32, ever had to start his military service. Zaga and her children settled at the address of house number 273, in other words the place of residence of her younger – albeit higher in status – brother Štefan Stojka, Sr. According to the archival material I shall review more closely below, Zaga and her children did not live in the house itself but in the front yard.[441]

In the extraordinary census of 1939, the census-takers recorded 31 people as living at house number 273.[442] They belonged to three households. The first of them was the 12-member family of Štefan Stojka, Sr., consisting of his current wife, his minor children, and his adult son Ján with his wife and children. The second, nine-member household consisted of Zaga Stojková, their elder sister Mária, Zaga's son Filo Stojka with his partner Anna Lakatošová and their children, and Zaga's youngest son Jozef, who at that time was 13. In addition, the 10-member Milo family, who earned their living as musicians in Trenčianska Teplá, was also registered there.[443] Going by their name and profession these were not Vlax Roms, but a family of what are known as "Slovak" Roms. It has to be asked how the whole group, made up of two related households and one entirely unrelated family, coexisted at the same address. As I have already mentioned, however, the other Roms did not live in the house itself (only's branch of the family lived there), but in the area around the house, where they seem to have made lean-tos from their wagons, tarpaulins and tents. What was essentially an improvised Romani settlement was thus created. We may assume that the authorities may have billeted the above-mentioned family of Slovak Roms named Milo there, which had appeared in the municipality in connection with the new decrees. Clearly, according to the logic of the local authorities, all "gypsies" belonged to a "gypsy camp" like this. The grandson of Štefan Stojka, Sr., also named Štefan Stojka and born in 1933, son of Ján Stojka (*1905),

---

440 ŠA Trenčín, f. ObNÚ Trenč. Teplá, i. č. 82, kn. 20 – Index k vojenskej evidencii, from 1938–1942, no precise dates given.
441 ŠA Trenčín, f. ObNÚ Trenč. Teplá. Cigánske pomery i. č. 2523/41 admin. Subject: Trenč. Teplá, umiestenie cigáňov, č. j. 8867/40 (15. 5. 1940).
442 None of the Roms on the list have their "gypsy" nationality recorded there. In the neighbouring municipality, the census-takers counted 21 people from the Facona family living in three households in the village of Dobrá. All had their nationality listed as "gypsy" there. ŠA Trenčín, F. OÚ Trenčín, Admin 1939, Sčítanie ľudu.
443 ŠA Trenčín, f. OÚ Trenčín, Admin 1939, Sčítanie ľudu.

described this improvised housing as a "Romani settlement" in his application for a certificate under Act no. 255/1946. From what he writes, it seems that he lived there during the war with his parents Ján (*1905) and Anna (*1900). From his description "the family was forced to settle down after the passing of a number of anti-gypsy measures during the the Slovak State".[444] It may be assumed that coexistence with non-Roma could have been tense, especially for Štefan Stojka, Sr. as the owner of the land where this "camp" developed.

Complaints against "gypsies" in Trenčianska Teplá in the first years of the war

The growing settlement with its tents and wagons and the increasing number of Roms in the municipality soon became the target of complaints from other residents. On 15 May 1940, the district authority in Trenčín sent the authorities in Trenčianska Teplá a letter stating:

> On the left-hand side of the road leading from Trenč. Teplá to Trenč. Teplice live two gypsy families, partly in tents. [...] one family is not domiciled in Tr. Teplá, so please expel it from the town. If the other family wants to live in its own house, it needs to be found another place to live, because it makes a very bad impression on visitors going to Trenč. Teplice when they see a gypsy caravan there and children begging at the roadside, often hindering traffic on the road. If the latter family does not heed your call to live in a house and not let children near the road, it needs to be found another place to live so that it does not bring shame on the area. This family needs to be shown what path to take to the road in a place where it cannot be seen by visitors.[445]

The district head proposed that everything should be implemented on the basis of health measures according to Section 11 of Act no. 117/1927. In a record from 31 May 1940, the head notary issued a decision with the subject: "Gypsies – banishment from the municipality of Trenč. Teplá" in which he states that he considers it necessary "to come with a doctor and with the aid of the police station to the place inhabited by the local

---

444 VÚA-VHA Praha, f. Sbírka osobních spisů žadatelů o vydání osvědčení podle zákona č. 255/1946 Sb., personal file of applicant Š. S. (*1933).

445 ŠA Trenčín, f. ObNÚ Trenč. Teplá, Cigánské pomery i. č. 2523/41. Zpráva okresného úradu v Trenčíně pánu notárovi v Trenčianskej Teplej, č. j. 8867/40 – Trenč. Teplá – umiestenie cigáňov.

gypsies, force the Stojka gypsy family inside its house, and banish the others without domicile from the municipality." Following this is a record by the head notary of 24 June 1940 regarding the plan to banish "gypsy families who are not domiciled there" from the municipalities of Trenčianska Teplá and Dobrá, asking the district authority to indicate when the local police would be able to take action in accordance with the orders of the district authority. The record also states that:

> With regard to gypsies who reside here and are domiciled here, measures have been taken to force them to live in their own house and to not let their children run freely on the road so that they do not hinder traffic and cause a disgrace through their begging and other indecent behaviour in the style of a gypsy caravan, which makes a very bad impression on visitors travelling to Teplice and on the whole area in general.[446]

Here it has to be asked whom the local head notary included under the heading of "locally domiciled gypsies" and whom he included in the category of "gypsies not domiciled here", in other words, *foreign* "gypsies". It may be assumed that the family of Štefan Stojka, Sr. and his descendants were included under "local gypsies". Among the "foreign" ones might have been the above-mentioned Milo family, which does not seem to have been domiciled in Trenčianska Teplá. I have been able to find almost nothing more about its further residence in the municipality. All I know is that at the end of the war, 70-year-old Jozef Milo, the head of the family, was shot during the bombing and features on a list of "our citizens" killed in the final battles.[447] We can find out nothing more about the Milo family in the municipality from the records until the spring of 1947. It should thus be asked whether the banishment of the Milo family was in fact arranged in the official action plan or whether the moving of the family (maybe within the municipality) did not take place. No documentation of further steps toward them has been preserved. Zaga's family might also have been included in the category of those who did not belong in the municipality and were "foreign", given that for the whole of the 1930s they had appeared there just sporadically, if at all, and did not live in their own house, unlike Štefan's family. Still, on the basis of

---

446 ŠA Trenčín, f. ObNÚ Trenč. Teplá, Cigánske pomery i. č. 2523/41, č .j. 2616/40 – umiestenie cigáňov, vykázanie cudzích cigáňov z obce.

447 *Obecná kronika* [Municipal Chronicle of] Trenčianska Teplá, 1930s and 1940s, 96–97. Municipal Library of Trenčianska Teplá.

other official records, it is clear that Zaga's family was not ejected from the municipality.

The reaction of the municipality to the decree of April 1941 on some conditions of "gypsies"

The differing social status of the two siblings – Štefan and his elder sister Zaga – is also documented by a report from the notary's office reacting to the decree of 20 April 1941 on adjusting some conditions of the "gypsies".[448] The decree was sent to municipalities in the district by the Trenčín District Authority with an appeal that they should propose a "gypsy *vajda*" (head) according to Section 3 of the decree. The *vajda* would report to the mayor and would be responsible for adherence to the law in the "gypsy quarter". Under Section 5, the municipality was also required to designate "workshy persons" who were to be supplied to labour camps. In a reply from the notary's office in Trenčianska Teplá to the District Authority in Trenčín, it was announced that their proposed *vajda* was Štefan Stojka, Sr., "born 10. 11.1891 in Trenč. Teplá, domiciled and resident there, employed as a labourer."

In another part of the report, Zaga Stojková, born 1887, resident in Trenčianska Teplá and at that time 54, was designated a "workshy person".[449] The listing of Zaga as an "asocial person" is interesting, at odds with the fact that the labour camps existed only for men, not for women. At the time, that fact was fairly well known, so it is not clear how this matter should be interpreted.

It should be noted that by applying this decree from April 1941, specifically its Section 2, the municipality had an opportunity to "get rid of" the Romani settlement that had grown up around the house of Štefan Stojka on the main street in the direction of Trenčianske Teplice. Section 2 was used by a large number of municipalities in Slovakia to move Roms away from the built-up areas of municipalities and beyond their limits. However, this solution was not applied in Trenčianska Teplá, and so we can only speculate whether the policy not to apply it resulted from good local relationships with the Roma or whether there were other reasons for it.

---

448 ŠA Trenčín, f. ObNÚ Trenč. Teplá, Cigánské pomery i. č. 2523/41, č. j. 42165/11, later labelled OÚ Trenčín č. j. 7544/41.

449 Ibid., č. j. 2523/1941. Subject: Vyhláška Ministerstva vnitra zo dňa 20. apríla 1941, č. 42165 o úprave niektorých pomerov cigánov. Okresnému úradu v Trenčíne (3. 7. 1941).

One more thing about the record from April 1941 is interesting: Štefan Stojka, Sr. was not described there as a "horse trader", as he was in all the previous official records, but as a "labourer". Other official records show the gradual decline in the status of Štefan Stojka, Sr. A record from February 1942 describes Štefan as a horse trader without employment who had applied to the notary's office for permission to perform a trade (which one is not stated).[450] Another record from May 1944 identifies Štefan's occupation as a "rag collector". According to that record, he had asked the municipality to provide confirmation that he owned his house so he could apply to carry on the trade of rubbish collector.[451] From this it can be inferred that Štefan tried to maintain a livelihood connected with territorial mobility or travelling with a wagon and that he wanted to do this legally as his trade. This opens the question of whether he still had a horse or he wanted to acquire one again in this way. Nevertheless, a gradual decline in his status took place, from horse trader, an occupation he was no longer permitted to perform, to rubbish collector. Whether he had a licence to trade as a rubbish collector is not clear from the records.

Information on further activity during the war in Trenčianska Teplá is sporadic. Just a limited number of records have been preserved in the municipal notary's archival files concerning the way in which these new decrees affected the life of the Stojka family. A general register titled "Register of gypsies 1942" lists 16 people from the Stojka family who were residing in Teplá on 31 December 1942. This was not just a list of names, but had the aim of providing further details about the Roms in question, such as their "gypsy names", places of residence and domicile, health status, marital and property status, and also their parents' names. We do not find the names here of the three youngest children (born in 1935, 1937 and 1938) from either branch of the family, although they were on the list of 1939. However, we may assume that they continued to live with their parents and that the number of Stojka family members living in the municipality was thus no smaller than in the previous census in 1939, if we do not take into account the already-mentioned probable absence of the Milo family. Still, it is difficult to compare the two lists, since the 1942 list contains a number of falsifications in the names and surnames of the Stojka family members. For example, Filo's son, whose name was Viliam Stojka, is entered on the list as "Josef Lakatoš", while

---

450 ŠA Trenčín, f. ObNÚ Trenč. Teplá I. Knihy evidenčné 1941–50, i. č. 91–98, kn. 22, Evidencia svedectev rôzneho druhu 1941–1945.

451 Ibid.

his brother Milan Stojka is down as "Berci Lakatoš". However, it is easy to identify them by their birthdates and the names of their parents, which are also supplied. The information on domicile is interesting: Of the 16 people who figure on the 1942 list, 13 have a question mark in the domicile column. Filo Stojka was domiciled in the neighbouring municipality of Dobrá (although he lived together with the others in Trenčianska Teplá). Only in the cases of Ján (*1905) and Štefan, Sr. was it explicitly noted that they were domiciled in Trenčianska Teplá. In all of these cases their property status was given as "none" save for with the exception of Štefan Stojka, Sr., who had the additional note: "own house".[452]

From the records we also learn that on 16 March 1942, the official wedding of Anna Lakatošová and Filo Stojka took place, although by then they had formed a couple for almost 20 years. From then on, Anna Lakatošová used the surname Stojková.[453]

Members of the Stojka family outside Trenčianska Teplá

Not all Roms from the family in question spent the war in Trenčianska Teplá. Zaga Stojková's daughter Grófa, for example, had to stay with her partner's family in the municipality of Šúrovce, in today's Trnava district, where her father-in-law and maybe also her partner were domiciled.[454] Her location is confirmed by the birth of Grófa's son Něguš in February 1941 in Šúrovce. He himself later added that the family lived during the war in a small wooden house in a Romani settlement at the end of the village together with non-Vlax Roms. As I have shown, however, during the interwar years the family moved around the Czech lands, above all in northern Moravia, and probably spent long amounts of time outside the municipality. The witness also stated that his father, Josef Lakatoš, had been sent to the labour camp in Hanušovce nad Topľou, from which he escaped. The family had to hide in the woods for a long time.[455] Grófa herself said in her application for a certificate under Act no. 255/1946 that their house had been destroyed by "Germans" and the family had had to hide in the woods and the marshes in conditions of great hardship:

---

452 ŠA Trenčín, f. ObNÚ Trenč. Teplá, kn. 99, šk. 23 – Evidencia cigáňov 1942 (31. 12. 1942).
453 According to the records of the registry office in Trenčianska Teplá. Source: Personal visit to the registry office (Matriční úřad) in Trenčianska Teplá.
454 VÚA-VHA Praha, f. Sbírka osobních spisů žadatelů o vydání osvědčení podle zákona č. 255/1946 Sb., personal file of applicant G. S. (*1924).
455 Ibid., personal file of applicant J. S. (*1941).

"We were terribly hungry, my children were crying with hunger because I had nothing to put in their mouths. I had to give them grass and leaves because there was nothing else."[456]

Recalling their poverty during the war, with an especial emphasis on the lack of food, was a frequent theme in the Romani witness narratives of wartime events.[457] In the case of Grófa, we also have to take into account the fact that she was on her own with young children, with no livelihood, in a place where she had no functional social ties with villagers who might be willing to help her.

The family of Zaga's daughter Kuluš and her partner Antonín Horvát lived during the war in Bohdanovce, Trnava district, the place where Antonín had been born in 1914 and where he was probably domiciled. We may assume that his brother Juraj and Juraj's partner Barbora Stojková also lived in Bohdanovce during the war. The two brothers and their partners and children had remained in northern Moravia until the beginning of 1939, and it is to Bohdanovce that they clearly had to "return" after arriving in Slovakia. However, it is interesting that at the end of 1942, both Stojková sisters were listed on the register of "gypsies" living in Trenčianska Teplá together with their mother and siblings, but without their partners and children. They do not feature on either earlier or later lists in Trenčianska Teplá, which may indicate their mobility, to a certain degree, during this phase of the Second World War, since the two municipalities are over 80 kilometres away from each other. At the close of the war, they were both definitely living in Bohdanovce again. In March 1944 a son was born to Kuluš and Antonín there.[458] The son of Barbora and Juraj, named S. and born in Moravská Ostrava in 1936, gave more details in his application for a certificate under Act no. 255/1946 on the reason for and circumstances of the forced residence of this family branch in Bohdanovce:

When I was born, we were travelling with my mother and father. [...] When the Germans came, a law came out saying that everyone had to go live where they came from.[459] My grandfather came from Bohdanovce, Trnava. I went

---

456 Ibid.

457 Helena Sadílková, *War Testimonies by Slovak Roma – A Close Analysis.* (Master Thesis, Central European University, 2003).

458 SOkA Louny, f. ONV Louny II, k.t. 331. Register sheet of Antonín Horvát dated 4 February 1959.

459 It is not clear whether the witness means the arrival of the Germans in the Protectorate in spring 1939 or in Slovakia after the Slovak National Uprising in September 1944.

to Bohdanovce with my parents and we lived in a house made of planks on the land behind the playing field. In autumn 1943 – it was plum time – the Germans and the [Hlinka] Guard took my father to the camp at Hanušovce nad Topľou, where he had to work in a quarry. I and my mother and my four brothers and sisters escaped into the woods. We hid in the forest near Senec and Krúpa and we didn't have anything to eat or wear. [...] When we made it back home, our colony had been flattened [...] after my father returned, the whole family settled on the the village outskirts, where we built a kind of camp with anything we could get from people.[460]

The grandfather whom the witness is remembering was the above-mentioned Pavol Lakatoš, born in Bohdanovce in 1871. Until the beginning of the 1930s, his family had been territorially anchored in the municipality to a certain extent. We can assume that they used to have a wintering place or maybe even a dwelling place in the village, but that they apparently lost it when they were moving around the Czech lands. They thus had to once more build simple dwelling places out of available materials. They later escaped and hid in the woods until the end of the war.

From this witness's testimony it also follows that his father, Juraj Horvát, was interned in the labour camp in Hanušovice nad Topľou, where he seems to have been proposed for internment as an "asocial person", like the Stojkas of Topoľčany mentioned above. It is not impossible that his father's brother Antonín had a similar experience. It is questionable to what extent we may rely on the time detail regarding the drafting of his father, Juraj, given that the witness was such a small child at the time. I am inclined to think that given his age and the limited possibilities for keeping track of time during the period in question, it is more probable that this happened when "it was plum time" than that it happened in 1943. It is possible that the internment in the labour camp took place in autumn 1942, which was the case for the above-mentioned transport of Roms from Topoľčany to that same camp. That the witness's father (and maybe his uncle Antonín) was taken to Hanušovce in autumn 1942 would account for why their partners (who were sisters) went to visit their mother and their other siblings in Trenčianska Teplá, where at the end of December 1942 the register of "gypsies" caught up with them.

---

460 VÚA-VHA Praha, f. Sbírka osobních spisů žadatelů o vydání osvědčení podle zákona č. 255/1946 Sb., personal file of applicant S. S. (*1936). Shortened by the author.

The closing phase of the war: The arrival of the Germans and hiding in the woods

Let us return to Trenčianska Teplá, though. Unfortunately, there are no more records to cast any light on the subsequent circumstances of the Stojka family in the municipality. All we have to work with are the witness statements of several family members.

Štefan Stojka (*1933), the son of Ján Stojka (*1905) says the following in his application for a certificate under Act no. 255/1946:

> When the Germans burst into our settlement, we escaped any way we could. My mother and I escaped into the forest. We didn't even know where my father and my siblings were. I hid with my mother in the forest, there wasn't even any water. Some people we knew told us that my father and siblings were in another forest. So my mother and I went to look for them. After a while we all met up, we were hungry, we didn't have anything to eat or any clothes. My father went to the village to bring back something from the people there. We didn't even have any shoes. My mother tied rags round our feet. Once my mother and I snuck into the village to beg for something. When we got to the village, though, the Germans fired at us and they shot me in the leg, so we had to go back to the forest. We hid there for about a year and then the Russians liberated us. So we went back to the settlement and there was nothing there. The Germans had destroyed everything.[461]

In this witness's description of his family's situation during the war, we may notice that, just like other Roms living in Slovakia, in Trenčianska Teplá the Roms were also forced to hide in the closing phase of the war. From his very brief description, however, it is clear that they were not just hiding from the arrival of the front, but also that the Roms were in hiding while their non-Rom neighbours were still at home in the village, that the Roms would visit the non-Roms secretly to obtain food and clothing, and once they were even shot at by the Germans. This means the Roms were being persecuted by the Germans. The witness does not mention details, but this may have included various forms of bullying. Similar experiences of hiding in the woods were also recounted by many other Romani witnesses who were "Slovak" (non-Vlax) Roms when describing their suffering in Slovakia during the Second World War.

---

461 VÚA-VHA Praha, f. Sbírka osobních spisů žadatelů o vydání osvědčení podle zákona č. 255/1946 Sb., personal file of applicant Š. S. (*1933).

From the archival records it seems that the situation in the municipality must have been very unfavourable for the Roms, since the German troops stationed themselves there as soon as the Slovak National Uprising erupted.[462] Immediately upon entering the municipality, the German troops commandeered the buildings of the school, the Sokol hall, the sugar refinery and also many private houses. Their task was meant to be to guard an important road and railway crossroads and to prevent any transfers of people from the Protectorate into Slovakia.[463] The German commando, including its unit commanders, had its headquarters in the municipality. At the close of the war, frontline battle operations took place there, accompanied, for example, by the destruction of the railway line and aerial attacks. While nearby Trenčianske Teplice was liberated on 2 September 1944 by the partisans, they did not get past the German troops to Trenčianska Teplá. As the chronicle describes, the local inhabitants were forced to dig trenches for the Germans in the winter of 1944.[464] German soldiers from the first frontline came to Trenčianska Teplá in February 1945.[465] Subsequently, according to the municipal chronicle, Hungarian units and the Vlasov troops of the Russian Liberation Army reached the area. The partisan units had been fighting a resistance campaign all the while from their hiding places in the surrounding forests. The liberation struggles escalated in April 1944, when during the battles several strategic buildings and bridges in the municipalities were destroyed and the local population had to hide. The municipality was liberated on 25 April 1944 by divisions of the Romanian army.[466]

We may therefore assume that the Roms hid in the surrounding forests, maybe also in places further off, the entire time German units were present in the municipality, in other words, from September 1944 to April 1945. As in other Slovak towns and villages, their lives were at risk during the presence of German units. From the experiences of other municipalities, we know that Roms were very often helped to survive by the partisans while they were hiding in the woods at this time. However, we do not have more details relating to the Stojkas' hiding in the woods or their contacts with the partisans. Only from the testimony of T. S.

---

462 ŠA Trenčín, f. ObNÚ Trenč. Teplá, Prez. 1944 1–241 – Výkaz vyplatených účtov pre veliteľstvo nemeckého vojska ubytovaného v Trenč. Teplej 1944: „Kováč Adam rolník Tr. Teplá 140 žiada polit. obec o náhradu škody zavinenej nemeckou branou mocou" (9. 11. 1944), no č. j.

463 Obecná kronika obce Trenčianska Teplá, Obdobie tridsiatych let a druhé světové války, p. 89. Archived in the Municipal Library in Trenčianska Teplá.

464 Ibid., 89–94.

465 Ján Krátký, *Kronika obce Dobrá* (Dobrá: self-published, 2000).

466 Ibid., 99.

(*1927) do we know that at the end of the war, her husband, Štefan Stojka (*1923), the son of Ján Stojka and the grandson of Štefan Stojka, Sr., joined the partisans, but we do not have any details of his cooperation with them.[467] His older brother, also named Štefan (*1919) was said by his grandson Báno to have fought on the eastern front, where he joined General Svoboda's troops and took part in battle operations at Dukla and in Italy. According to his grandson's recollection, Štefan (*1919) returned home from the war to Trenčianska Teplá only in July 1945. His mother (Anna Stojková, *1900) had apparently already "buried" him, having assumed he had fallen in battle.[468] His conscription into the army, not into the labour camps designed for "gypsy" draftees, indicates that the conscription committee had him down as a "Slovak", not as a "gypsy". No information is available as to whether more than one man from the family was conscripted into the army.

The destruction of Štefan Stojka's house

In the above-mentioned testimony, Štefan Stojka (*1933) stated that at the close of the war the "Germans" destroyed his family's property. He was clearly referring to the destruction of the house belonging to his grandfather, Štefan Stojka, Sr. (1891). The circumstances of the house's destruction and other activity regarding its remains are described in relative detail by the journalist Slavo Kalný. He says that during the final battle operations there were several strikes (both bullets and landmines) on the house of Štefan Stojka, Sr. at a time when the Roms were clearly still hiding in the woods:

> [The house] partly collapsed, then fell apart even more under the influence of the weather, and finally all that was left was a pile of bricks, clay and halfrotten wood. And still Stojka did not come back. People started to hack at it with pickaxes and to take away the bricks and wood, even the foundations. Then Stojka returned to the village. Goaded by some envious, malicious villagers, he took himself off to the local authority and called on the functionaries to give him a replacement for his house, because the village 'robbers' had destroyed it. He sued the policemen and took them to court. He lost at the

---

467 VÚA-VHA Praha, f. Sbírka osobních spisů žadatelů o vydání osvědčení podle zákona č. 255/1946 Sb., personal file of applicant T. S. (*1927).

468 Personal recording of "Báno" Bihary (*1958) made by Pavel Kubaník on 3 October 2008 in Roudnice nad Labem, Czech Republic.

first instance. He appealed to Bratislava. In Bratislava it was as in Trenčín: They did not find the guilty party owed forty thousand, as the owner of the house would have it, but owed damages of five, ten, twenty, at the most thirty crowns. They had not, the court said, stolen a house, but had gone through a rubbish heap. Even the chairman of the authority confirmed it. Stojka took offence, refused to accept the money ('Money?! A pittance for a dog!'), raged against the municipality and the state and was against everybody.[469]

Several facts can be gleaned from this excerpt which correlate entirely with my other conclusions. Above all, the return of Štefan Stojka, Sr., as well as the return of other Roms, clearly occurred after some time had passed, not in the first few days after the fighting ended. In the meantime, the villagers took apart his bombed house. The destruction of his house is also mentioned in a record kept in the State Archive in Trenčín confirming payment of house tax in the postwar years of 1947 and 1948, where Štefan Stojka, Sr. is listed as the owner of the house. The document includes the following note: "Since the arrival of the front, the house is uninhabitable."[470] I have not been able to find the court case records, but they would provide a good explanation for Štefan's sudden departure from Trenčianska Teplá, which I shall describe below. In the period immediately after the war, Štefan seems to have built an improvised dwelling on his own land on the site of the original house. In the official sources it is later labelled a "gypsy hut" and was recalled by non-Rom witnesses remembering the postwar period as a "shack". His family lived in it for several years after the war and it was during those years that the court cases over the dismantling of his house took place.

The end of the war brought notable losses for the family. At some time during that period, Zaga Stojková must have died, since her name does not appear in any post-war lists, registers or other records. Her name appears for the last time in official records in January 1943.[471] However, I have not been able to ascertain the circumstances of her death. According to the employees at the register of births, marriages and deaths in Trenčianska Teplá, her death was not recorded in the relevant official register in the municipality. Once again, we can only try to guess when and how she died. It is not impossible that she was sent somewhere by

---

469 Kalný, *Cigánsky plač*, 62.
470 ŠA Trenčín, f. Domovská Daň Trenčín, daňová obec Trenčianska Teplá, Vyrubovací list daně činžovej pro adresu Teplická č. p. 273 from the years 1947 and 1948.
471 ŠA Trenčín, f. ObNÚ Trenč. Teplá, ev. č. 77, k. 19 – Evidencia trestaných občianov obce Trenčinska Teplá 1933–1949.

the municipality as an "asocial" person (A forced labour facility? The concentration camp at Dubnica nad Váhom?), where she then died. It is also possible that she survived the war and died shortly afterward on the way to an unknown destination. Whatever the case may be, the postwar registers of Roms no longer include her name.

At the end of the war, Zaga's son Filo Stojka also passed away. According to the testimony of his grandson Berci Stojka (*1949), Filo died in a bombing at the end of the war when his wagon was hit by a bomb.[472] However, such an event is not recorded in the registry office in Trenčianska Teplá in the register of deaths. Nor is Filo Stojka's death described in the municipal chronicle, which contains a list of persons killed during the massive bombing and shooting in the final phase of the war in April 1944. The question is thus whether the death of Filo did indeed occur during the bombing even though this violent death is not recorded in his home municipality. It seems that during this time the Stojkas were hiding in the forest from German troops. His grandson Berci's statement that the family had a caravan at this point in the war sounds rather surprising. Still, it is not impossible that such people could have hidden in the woods with their wagons. This type of hiding is described by other Lovara witnesses, who mentioned that they had wagons which were hidden and sometimes covered and altered so that they provided the family with shelter.[473] The family may have hidden on the territory of another municipality, maybe even some distance from Trenčianska Teplá, and for that reason the event was not recorded in the Trenčianska Teplá municipal register. The name of Filo Stojka does not appear anywhere in the post-war records. He left behind the widowed Anna Stojková, née Lakatošová (*1902), with several of their adult children and several minor ones. Her youngest son was just over a year old.

It was clearly at this time that Zaga Stojková's branch of the family regrouped upon her death and the death of her son, Filo Stojka. After her husband's death, the widowed Anna became the "head of the family" (above all from the authorities' perspective) and immediately after the

---

472 Personal recording of Berci (*1949) by the author, made on 18 December 2018 in Louny, Czech Republic.

473 For example, a witness to such hiding, H. D., from Solčany near Topolčany, described the hiding as follows: "We fled into the forest on 5 September 1940 with our horses and a pony. My father and brother built a roof out of a tarpaulin, which they covered in branches." Hiding "in the forest under our caravans (travelling wagons)" is also confirmed by another witness from Solčany with the initials V. S. VÚA-VHA Praha, f. Sbírka osobních spisů žadatelů o vydání osvědčení podle zákona č. 255/1946 Sb., personal file of applicants H. D. (*1940) and V. S. (*1944).

end of the war she set out with their wagons for the Czech lands, accompanied by her grown sons Janino and Bobko with their families, her two minor sons and her two daughters, one a minor and one on the cusp of adulthood. In subsequent years, her brother-in-law, who was a generation younger, travelled with them, the youngest son of the deceased Zaga Stojková nicknamed Jouško (*1924) with his nuclear family.

4.4 The end of the wartime chapter

The Lovara, who were perceived by those around them as belonging to the category of "gypsy vagabonds", had been affected by various relatively harsh measures, the banning of their itinerancy and horse trading, from the start of the war. Since these Roms did not have longer-lasting social ties in towns and villages and were not perceived as local ("our gypsies") by their residents, from the moment the decree of June 1940 was published they were often looked upon as people belonging to the "gypsy race". In many municipalities where they had to reside after the decree limiting their territorial movement was promulgated they were labelled "asocial elements" and "workshy" persons to whom a number of anti-gypsy measures applied, above all the ban on issuing trade licences and concessions to "gypsy vagabonds", the ban on itinerancy, dismissal from the army and being sent to the labour units (the replacement labour camps for gypsy draftees). It can be seen that a number of men from the Lovara community were placed in labour units such as Hanušovice nad Topľou and Dubnica nad Váhom. After the passing of two ministerial decrees adjusting some circumstances of "gypsies", and influenced by other local events during the war, the Lovara were *de facto* stripped of their livelihoods. They were no longer allowed to engage in horse trading, various types of door-to-door trade, or even waste collection and were thus reliant on various types of casual labour and service provision for which they lacked the ability and experience.[474] These measures had the most marked effect on the horse traders, who until then had been the highest-status, best-off class among the Lovara. When their trading activities were brought to a halt, this class of Roms lost their traditional livelihood and fell into the category of "asocials".[475]

---

474 Nečas, "Slovenští Romové", 170.
475 Ibid., 157.

These general conclusions regarding the situation of the Lovara in Slovakia made themselves felt in an interesting way in the case of the Roms in Trenčianska Teplá. At the beginning of the war, Štefan Stojka, Sr. had good local relationships with local non-Romani inhabitants and maybe also among some leaders of the municipality, which was generally atypical for a Lovara. This is indicated above all by the fact that shortly before the war, he succeeded in having a house built on the main road in the municipality, or that in the first years of the war, his grandson was conscripted into the classic army, not into the labour units where men were sent who were considered "gypsies". His family's situation may have been threatened by the forced arrival in the municipality of his sister Zaga with her numerous offspring and their settlement in shacks created from their wagons in front of Štefan's house. It is all the more interesting that despite repeated complaints in 1940 regarding this group of dwellings, labelled as being "in the style of a gypsy caravan", they were never taken down and these Romani shacks in a built-up area on the main road were never moved to a more distant place. The municipality did not even make use of the lawful possibility of expelling Roms from the municipality in their case, as was allowed and recommended by Section 2 of the April 1941 decree. Nor did the municipality seemingly try to send the members of the local Lovara community from the Stojka family to labour camps, as was usual in other towns and villages in Slovakia. Although in political terms the municipal leaders were fervent supporters of Tiso's pro-fascist regime, they exploited the opportunities provided by the decree to just formally appoint a gypsy *vajda*, and the only person who made it onto the list of asocials was Zaga Stojková.

It is somewhat surprising that such a large family clearly managed to survive until the arrival of German troops after the Slovak National Uprising in September 1944, living partly in Štefan Stojka's house and partly on the land in front of it. This fact makes me ask what helped the Stojka family to remain in the municipality. It should be remembered that the Stojka family, who belonged to the category "travelling gypsies/ gypsy vagabonds", must have been very visible. Moreover, the place where they remained was a potentially dangerous location on the main road, just a few kilometres from the labour camp at Dubnica nad Váhom. I believe the fact that they remained in the municipality must have been based on the existence of their good local relationships, which Štefan Stojka, Sr. who had lived long-term in the municipality, was probably able to maintain.

An analysis of how the authorities proceeded with regard to this family in the first years of the war suggests that the municipality's political leaders clearly did not have it as their goal to eject the family from the municipality, although the district authorities did encourage a more vigorous approach to "gypsies". In this respect, it is interesting that the municipality started to act more intensively and take measures against the residency of "gypsy vagabonds" only after 1945, and I shall look at this in the following chapter. It could be explained by a change in the composition of the local leadership, as indicated in the local chronicle.

The situation of Štefan Stojka, Sr. entirely correlates to the above-described decline in the socioeconomic and social status of horse dealers. As has been indicated several times herein, during the interwar period Štefan was capable of amassing a sufficient amount of money to build a house, and the very fact that he was allowed to buy land in the centre of the municipality is testimony to his functional ties and accepted social status among the other residents. During the war, however, Štefan Stojka's professional status gradually declined from horse dealer to labourer, to rag collector, to rubbish collector. The culmination of this degradation, however, was definitely the destruction of his house, which was then taken apart by local residents. Although Štefan Stojka, Sr. subsequently asked repeatedly for compensation for his destroyed property, he did not succeed, even after several years of court cases. This formerly successful, well-off horse dealer had become a "gypsy", a rubbish collector who lived in a "gypsy shack" (which he built on the site of his former house), travelling around the area in an old wagon with a scrawny horse. As we shall see in the next chapter, he gradually became the target of derisory comments from the other local inhabitants. This change of attitude by the municipality was certainly not just caused by the change in its political leadership and governing ideology. It was also the result of the degeneration of previously relatively good relationships as the society-wide application of anti-gypsy decrees led to an increase in racialised anti-gypsy feeling. The consequence of these changes, also influenced by the overall course of events and measures during the Second World War and by the related rapid worsening of interethnic relations, was the overall pauperisation of the local Roms, and Štefan Stojka, Sr., perceived as the local community's leader, underwent a decline in social position and status that was closely correlated with that impoverishment.

Photographs of Vlax Roms taken for record-keeping by the local national committee (ONV) in Lovosice in 1952. The photos feature Vlax Roms who were camping in the "gypsy camp" by the Elbe river.

Part 5: The postwar period

5.1 The forced departure of Roms from Trenčianska Teplá in 1947

The Stojka family remained in Trenčianska Teplá for several more years, although they renewed their movement around the area relatively soon after the war ended. Men from the family tried to restart their earlier livelihoods and renew their profession of horse trading. Trying to earn a living in this way must have been rather complicated, given the still-active anti-gypsy feeling in society and the overall low level of demand for such a service. As soon as the war ended, each family started to travel around the immediate neighbourhood with their wagons. In 1945, some of them were already renewing their routes to Moravia and Bohemia, but they all periodically returned to Slovakia. The adult children of Zaga and Štefan, who had lived elsewhere during the war, also seem to have returned to Trenčianska Teplá. This aroused fears among the non-Romani inhabitants of this and the surrounding villages over the growing mobility of the local Lovara.

During the years 1945 to 1947 we can see a continuous attempt on the part of the local authorities to get rid of Romani residents. In November 1945, the newly-renamed Municipal People's Committee (MNV) of Trenčianska Teplá asked the district authorities to allow them to issue an order to the national security forces to "banish all Gypsies living in the municipality who are not domiciled there" due to a "flood of foreign Gypsies and an increase in thefts in the municipality".[476] The district

---

476 ŠA Trenčín, f. ObNÚ Trenč. Teplá, zn. 20600/47 – Složka na cigánov, 1947, report for the ONV in Trenčín of 15 November1945 entitled Cigáni, vykázanie z obce Tr. Teplej, č. j. 4441/1945.

authority reacted to the letter with a request that the Trenčianska Teplá MNV send a list of persons for the purposes of expulsion from the municipality. It was to include personal data stating who was "work-shy", who was a "vagabond", and who was a threat to public security.[477]

Banishing Roms from the municipality was a subject that continued to be dealt with in the following months. The date of their banishment was originally set for 10 February 1946, but this attempt was halted by the MNV in Trenčianska Teplá for the reason that the planned list was still awaited.[478] The District Office for the Protection of Labour in Trenčín asked the MNV in Trenčianska Teplá to call on all "able-bodied gypsies" to report to the local office so that they could be incorporated into the labour process.[479] On the basis of this appeal, the MNV created a "list of [all] gypsies in Trenč. Teplá municipality". On it we find six people from the Stojka family: Štefan Stojka, Sr. (*1891) and his son Ján Stojka (*1905) with the note "not working" by both names, Ján's wife Anna Stojková (*1900) and another Anna Stojková, née Lakatošová (*1902), the widow of Filo Stojka. The list also includes Ján's 16-year-old daughter Papuša (*1931) and, somewhat surprisingly given the nature of the list (people to be included in the labour process), Anna and Filo's daughter, who at that time was just nine (*1938). The younger children who must have been living with Anna at the time are not listed, and neither, surprisingly, is the wife of Štefan Stojka, Sr., who was also living with them at the time. As well as them, the list also includes the six-member Milo family, consisting of the nuclear families of the two brothers Pavol (*1917) and Josef (*1919). In both cases a note states that they earn their living as musicians in Trenčianske Teplice.[480] Once again, however, we do not find out where their family had been in the previous years or what happened to them during the Second World War.

In March 1947, the MNV in Trenčianska Teplá sent the commander of the National Security police station in Trenčianska Teplá a letter stating: "There are still complaints from residents that the local gypsies harass the local population by blocking spaces with gypsy wagons and so on."

---

477 Ibid., č. j. 21.676/1945-VII, Trenč. Teplá – vykázanie cigáňov, together with number 4441/1945 of 13 December 1945.

478 Ibid., č. j. 21.676/1945-VII – letter to the ONV in Trenčín (23. 1. 1946), subject: Trenč. Teplá – vykázanie cigáňov.

479 ŠA Trenčín, f. ObNÚ Trenč. Teplá, ev. č. 944/1947. Cigáni – neprístojné chovanie a nariadení na ich vystehovanie č. 944 from 1947, letter from the district labour office in Trenčín of 15 April 1947 – subject: Cigáni – začlenenie do práce, č. j. 2469-III/2–47.

480 Ibid., list of all "gypsies" in Trenč. Teplá (26. 4. 1947) made by the local committee chair, no č. j.

The letter asks for the police to intervene against the "local gypsies" and to take measures so that in future "the population is not bothered by gypsies".[481] As we can see, a notable shift had occurred. While originally the call had been to resolve the situation of gypsies "who are not domiciled" in the municipality, attention was now drawn to all "local gypsies". The police chief in his response said the main problem was that the "gypsies" were on the edge of a state highway and proposed to "designate a camping place in the gulley behind the house of Štefan Stojka in the valley leading to Vršek to prevent them from being before the eyes of the public". In his answer, he asked the MNV to ban begging on its territory, which would "once again give the local police station the possibility of reporting gypsies for begging and taking them to the authorities," and would stop them from "roving about the municipality".[482]

In reaction to this, on 8 May 1947 the MNV of Trenčianska Teplá issued a notice ordering all "local Gypsies" to move to the designated place within 15 days. Štefan Stojka, Sr. was called upon by name in the notice to obey it.[483] For Štefan himself this decision must have been a huge burden: the new situation would mean that people from his extended family would be continually moving around his land and he would face responsibility for their behaviour. This order for the entire Romani community to move behind Štefan's house may be understood as the culmination of a long-term attempt to eject the Roms from the village.

At the same time, a joint memorandum on this issue was produced by the inhabitants of eight municipalities in the Trenčín region,[484] although not including Trenčianska Teplá. The memorandum, signed on 13 June 1947, began with these words:

> Do you realise that ever-increasing hordes of dirty, workshy, drunken creatures in human form, living entirely from theft, threatening public order, the public safety of working people and their property, are travelling freely around our villages (and towns) – the so-called travelling gypsies? That they are more feared in the villages than locusts, that they are ever more ruthless and ever more numerous? That with the proceeds of their theft they have

---

481 Ibid., letter from the chief of the NB MNV Trenč Teplá dated 10 April 1947, č. j. 944/1947.
482 Reaction of the SNB to the above-mentioned letter addressed to the local committee, Trenčianska Teplá, č. j. 482/47 (10. 4. 1947).
483 Ibid., Order of 8. 5. 1947, č. j. 1581/1947. The order also banned begging in the municipality. Violating it would lead to the use of force against the perpetrator.
484 The municipalities of Trenčianske Biskupice, Trenčianska Turná, Hámry, Mnichova Lehota, Soblahov, Kubra, Kubrica and Opatová.

bought themselves horses and carts with which they permanently invade our villages, graze on precious fodder and destroy the harvest?[485]

The memorandum then explicitly states: "The family horde of the Stojkas from Trenčianska Teplá alone [...] is constantly on the move with 7–8 wagons."[486]

On 28 June 1947, the ONV in Trenčín sent the memorandum to the MNV in Trenčianska Teplá with a letter starting as follows: "Complaints have been received from the district that travelling gypsies from Tr. Teplá (the Stojka family) who are moving about the district are stealing fodder and harvests from the fields." The letter asks the local authority to summon "the heads of the travelling groups (families)" and inform them that action might be taken against them under Act no. 117/1927, which was still in effect.[487] The MNV immediately wrote back to the ONV with a clear answer: "Travelling gypsies from Trenčianska Teplá (the Stojka family) are not resident in Trenčianska Teplá and since April 1947 have not even had temporary residence here. Their location is unknown to us."[488]

From the quotations above it can be seen that following pressure from the surrounding villages, the local authority, and clearly also the police, by April[489] or May[490] 1947 the Stojka family had been ejected from Trenčianska Teplá. It is interesting that the official records differ on the question of the date when the Stojkas left Trenčianska Teplá.

Immediately after the war, Zaga's daughters Kuluš and Barbora, who had been forced to spend the war in Bohdanovce, Trnava district with their husbands Antonín and Juraj and their children, started to renew their movements along their previous routes to Moravia and then on to Bohemia. The makeshift houses that they had built in Bohdanovce

---

485 ŠA Trenčín, f. ObNV v Trenč. Teplej, ev. č. 20600/47. Složka na cigánov, 1947, zn. 20600/47 – Memorandum pro Předsednictvo Sboru Povereníkov v Bratislavě (13. 6. 1947). The municipal committee in Trenčín passed it on to the district committee in Trenčín on 28 July 1947 with the subject *Cigáni kočovní a domáci, sťažnost MNV na ích potulovanie sa po obciach a robenie výtržnosti* under č. j. 3824/1947.

486 Ibid.

487 ŠA Trenčín, f. ObNV v Trenč. Teplej, zn. 20600/47 – Složka na cigánov, 1947, subject: Cigáni kočovní – obmedzenie pobytu a pohybu (15. 7. 1947), delivered 19 July 1947.

488 Ibid., subject: Cigáni kočovní – obmedzenie pobytu, č. j. 3618/1947 k č. j. 20.600/1947 of 24 July 1947.

489 Data given in reaction to the memorandum in the ONV letter of 24 July 1947.

490 The time between when the order was issued (8. 5. 1947) and when it was supposed to be delivered to Štefan Stojka, Sr. and to other Roms.

during the war had been destroyed with the arrival of German troops. At the end of the war, according to a witness, they had "a kind of camp [made] out of anything we could get from people" for a while on the village outskirts.[491] Soon after the end of the war, their families returned to a life of spatial mobility. The same was done by Grofa Stojková and her partner Josef Lakatoš, who had spent the war in nearby Šurovce and who in November 1946 were recorded by the authorities in Mělník, Central Bohemia.[492]

Like the Stojkas who lived in Teplá, these related Lovara families left Slovakia because it was impossible to continue to live in an environment where there was no means of earning a living, no work was offered them, and where they encountered a huge degree of animosity from the local population. As can be seen from the following example, in the post-war years the public attitude to "gypsies" was even supported by the Roms from the neighbouring village of Dobrá, the family of Zaga Stojková's partner. In a public statement dated March 1949, recorded in a report entitled "Action against gypsies" (no. 257/00–1-VB/2) by the central headquarters of the Criminal Police in Prague, Ján Facona of Dobrá is quoted as saying about the "travelling gypsies" from Trenčianska Teplá that "they include gypsy vagabonds who do not work, but need to be forced to work." Headquarters reported that this opinion of the "gypsies" from Dobrá was then confirmed by police in Trenčianska Teplá, who said that "the settled gypsies are of the opinion that not only do the [travelling] gypsy men belong in disciplinary camps, but also the [travelling] gypsy women, who do not work, but force their partners or men to travel."[493]

Štefan Stojka, Sr., who had clearly been territorially connected to the municipality for most of his life, including when, as a horse trader, he undertook various long business trips, finally left Trenčianska Teplá with his family in the late 1940s. As we shall see below, Štefan's son Ján and his family also set out for Bohemia, as did the Štefan's other adult children with their own nuclear families.

---

491 VÚA-VHA Praha, f. Sbírka osobních spisů žadatelů o vydání osvědčení podle zákona č. 255/1946 Sb., personal file of applicant S. S. (*1936).

492 ŠA Trenčín, f. ObNÚ Trenč. Teplá, ev. č. 77, k. 19 – Evidencia trestaných občianov obce Trenčinska Teplá 1933–1949.

493 Anna Jurová, *Rómska menšina na Slovensku v dokumentoch 1945–1975* (Košice: Spoločenskovedný ústav SAV, 2008): 281.

The arrivals of Roms from Slovakia in the Czech lands

In general, Roms from Slovakia started to come to the Czech lands immediately after the end of the Second World War. The main reason for their migration within the reconstituted Czechoslovakia was the uncertain socioeconomic situation in which many Romani families found themselves in Slovakia after the war. The process was also supported by the violent expulsion of ethnic Germans in the immediate aftermath of the war from localities in the Czech lands, which subsequently had an impact on the migration of Roma from Slovakia, for example in the form of numerous job and housing opportunities. As a group, the native Bohemian and Moravian Roms and Sinti were the victims of genocide during the Second World War. Just a few hundred of them had returned to Czechoslovakia from the concentration camps, and sometimes just a few individuals were the only survivors from their whole extended families.[494] This drastic context of the Romani population's transformation was something of which society was not yet generally aware or was indifferent to, however. In the postwar Czech lands, Roms continued to be viewed as asocial, problematic individuals, in keeping with the previous Nazi doctrine based on the idea of "gypsies" as a different, inferior race.

The newly-arriving Roms were not welcomed by the local Czech authorities or by the inhabitants of the municipalities concerned. They were perceived as a security risk and the municipalities very often tried in various ways to limit what they called the "flood of Gypsies".[495] Local authorities and residents often looked on their migration with displeasure and called for it to be limited. It is not surprising that Roms from Slovakia, coming into this atmosphere, met with considerable hatred from the local population.[496] Their arrival from Slovakia was met with horror, hate and xenophobia all over the Czech lands, as most Romani witnesses agree in their descriptions.

The intensive search for places that offered acceptable working conditions, and suitable accommodation was often connected with the repeated movement of individuals or of whole Romani families into the

---

494 Nečas, *Českoslovenští Romové;* Ctibor Nečas, *Romové v České republice včera a dnes.* Olomouc: Palackého univerzita, 1995; Sadílková, "Holocaust".

495 Helena Sadílková, "(Ne)chtění spoluobčané. Romové v poválečném Československu", in: *„Nechtění" spoluobčané. Skupiny obyvatel perzekvovaných z politických, národnostních náboženských i jiných důvodů v letech 1945–1989,* ed. Jaroslav Pažout and Kateřina Kotrmann, (Praha, Liberec: Ústav pro studium totalitních režimů – Technická univerzita v Liberci, 2018): 101.

496 Pavelčíková, *Romové v českých zemích,* 23–24; Nečas, *Romové na Moravě,* 90.

Czech lands. It is important to realise that the Roms who migrated to Bohemia were predominantly (non-Vlax) Roms whose families had lived in Slovakia for centuries in one place, but whose dismal economic and social situation had forced them to leave their homes in search of a new life. To the non-Romani inhabitants of the Czech lands, however, who had an historical experience of Romani groups from the period before the Second World War, their arrival and frequent movement seemed to confirm the stereotype of "gypsy vagabonds". The nomadisation of these newly-arriving Roms, together with the assumed risk that they would again "run riot" and "invade" Czech towns and villages, followed from the general concept of "travelling gypsies" that had existed before the Second World War. The postwar media and public discourse on this issue was similar to the interwar period, including the way in which information on these Roms was reported in official records. Various sources refer to Romani vagrancy, avoidance of work, asocial behaviour and poor living conditions. The most threatening thing was not the Roms themselves, but what they represented: Their "nomadic" behaviour, which was seen as incompatible with the idea of a modern state, provoked fear and displeasure at their ability to cross social and geographical borders.[497] For example, a report by the ONV security department in Tábor from 1947 warned of an expected "flood of gypsies" from the border area to the interior and labelled the "gypsies" a public threat: "There is a need for their rampaging to be prevented and for they themselves to no longer be a terror to other, peaceful inhabitants, but to be forced to live an orderly way of life that benefits the whole."[498]

In a report from August 1946, the Louny MNV asks of the state police (the SNB) that:

> travelling hordes of gypsies, vagabond knife-sharpeners, etc., not be tolerated in the outskirts, since at this time of great labour shortage, these persons may be integrated into the labour process to prevent their posing a threat to the property of orderly citizens.

Circular no. 1274, issued by the Provincial National Committee (ZNV) in Prague in November 1946, notes the ever more frequent occurrence of "gypsy hordes", above all in the border regions, and crimes allegedly committed by them, calling on the subordinate authorities to

---

497 Sokolová, *Cultural Politics*, 77.
498 SOkA Benešov, f. ONV Vlašim, i. č. 228, sig. III_9, k. 48 – ONV Tábor, bezpečnostní referát, subject: Stíhání přestupku zákona o potulných cikánech (č. j. 1330/47).

take the necessary measures based on the still-valid Act no. 117/1927.[499] In August 1946, the Interior Ministry issued a regulation entitled "Foreigners on the territory of the Czechoslovak Republic – measures", of which part concerned how to deal with "gypsies". In this regulation, it was pointed out that Act no. 117/1927, "on wandering gypsies", was still in effect.[500] The ministry called on the subordinate authorities not to issue new itinerancy permits under Section 5 of the law and to revoke the permits issued earlier. The regulation also banned all travelling gypsies with wagons from driving through towns that were ONV seats and through larger towns in general. This was not meant to apply to "gypsies who demonstrably hold Czechoslovak citizenship and who have transitioned from a travelling life to being settled in one place where they are engaged in productive work".[501] Here we see a characteristic feature that would grow stronger in subsequent years, the perception of "travelling gypsies" as the most troublesome "gypsies" against whom it was necessary to introduce the strictest measures.

According to the available information from the state-wide "Register of all Gypsy vagabonds and other workshy vagabonds who live a gypsy lifestyle", which was undertaken from 18–23 August 1947, a total of 16,752 persons were identified as belonging on this register,[502] of whom the great majority were from Slovakia. They would have had to come to the Czech lands over the course of the previous two years (from summer 1945 to summer 1947). Many Roms periodically returned to Slovakia to see their families, coming to the Czech lands just for work, and their place of residence could change from job to job. Romani postwar migration can be viewed as the "continual movement of people (and goods) between the Czech lands and Slovakia and within the Czech lands".[503] Their migration, therefore, should be perceived as temporary. It is not within the scope of this book to look in great detail at the situation in Slovakia after 1947. It was somewhat different compared to the Czech lands, and the degree to which restrictions on "travelling gypsies" were

---

499 SOkA Mělník, f. ONV Kralupy nad Vltavou, k. 88 sign III_9 (1. 11. 1946, č. j. ZOB-III-C-39/15 ai 46).

500 SOkA Teplice, f. ONV Teplice, sign. 257, i. č. 984, k. 246 (19. 8. 1946, č. j. z/s-8000/149–22/8–46).

501 Ibid.

502 Pavelčíková, *Romové v českých zemích*, 29.

503 Helena Sadílková, "The Postwar Migration of Romani Families from Slovakia to the Bohemian Lands. A complex legacy of war and genocide in Czechoslovakia", *Jewish and Romani Families in the Holocaust and its Aftermath*. Eliyana R. Adler and Kateřina Čapková (Eds.) (Rutgers University Press: New Brunswick, Camden, Newark, New Jersey, London, 2020): 202.

implemented was often considerably smaller and depended on local conditions, relationships, and political power hierarchies in various regions and locations. Indeed, the degree of Lovara itinerancy during the same period in Slovakia was, according to my conclusions, considerably higher and often continued to a certain degree and on a local scale in subsequent years, even after the passage of Act no. 74/1958.[504]

Restrictions on "travelling gypsies"

Czechoslovak policy towards Roms changed after the coming of communism in February 1948. There were several significant legislative changes. At the start of the socialist dictatorship, not only was Act no. 117/1927 from the First Republic repealed, but fundamental changes were made to the whole related system of criminal law, social policy and police practice. Among the most important were that forced returns to one's domicile were no longer undertaken, coercive workhouses[505] were closed, new forced labour camps were instituted, and a new Criminal Code and amendments to legislative procedures targeting economic "parasites" were passed.

However, there were also changes in the attitude of the state toward Roms on the ideological level. At the level of the central state, Roms started to be perceived as citizens who were materially and socially disadvantaged, the poorest victims of the previous capitalist and fascist regimes.[506] It was stressed that while capitalist states dealt with the problems of gypsies through racism and the Nazis through genocide, the socialist states dealt with them through socialist humanism.[507] The sought-after integration of "gypsies" into socialist society was to primarily take place by involving them in the labour process, as far as possible on their own initiative. As demand for labour grew, working Roms gradually stopped

---

504 See also Rastislav Pivoň, "Zákon č.74/1958 Zb. a jeho výkon v niektorých obciach trnavského regiónu (aj s ohľadom na práce iných bádateľov)". *Studia Ethnologica Pragensia*, no. 1 (2021): 78–106 or Hajská, "'Polokočovníci'".

505 Coercive workhouses (*donucovací pracovny*), already used during the First Republic, were intended to provide additional punishment for those convicted of crimes considered to be manifestations of „shunning work", as well as for their correction through work. Roma were one of the groups routinely sent to these facilities.

506 Matěj Spurný, "Pokus o převýchovu: Romové v objetí stalinské péče o člověka v 50. letech." *Paměť a dějiny: revue pro studium totalitních režimů*, vol. 11, no. 3 (2017): 4; Sadílková, "(Ne)chtění", 105.

507 SOA Litoměřice, f. SKNV, odbor vnitřních věcí, zn. 608, V-10 Soupis kočujících Cikánů 1959–1965.

being labelled "problematic".[508] Indeed, various local reports praised the work achievements of "gypsy shock-workers" and listed their working successes. However, this concerned just the "settled gypsies". The attitudes of the authorities and security services toward the "travelling gypsies" and the ideological justification of the approach taken toward them hardly changed. Although in general policy towards "gypsies" gradually changed over the course of the 1950s,[509] policy towards "travelling gypsies" continued unbroken for practically the whole postwar period and in many ways carried on the approaches used at the start of the war (for example their attempted sedentarisation).

The main pillar of this policy was measures limiting travel or stopping it altogether, coming above all from the higher authorities. "Travelling gypsies" were still uniformly perceived as a security risk, the scourge of the countryside,[510] and a socially dangerous group. The arrivals of "travelling gypsies" in the Czech lands at the start of the 1950s were covered in the reports by state bodies in keeping with the same racist discourse as had been seen in the immediate postwar years, wartime, and the interwar years. A report from the South Bohemian Region for the Interior Ministry in 1951 described the situation regarding "travelling gypsies" thus:

> We have very bad experiences of travelling gypsies. According to reports from the districts, between June and August 1951 a large number of gypsy hordes travelled through the districts of our region, terrorizing their surroundings. They lived in large part off theft, and sometimes by begging. They caused great damage to meadows and fields by grazing their horses on clover and oats, trampling meadows, etc. They very frequently got drunk and started fights with each other, which often ended in gypsies being wounded.[511]

At the end of the report, "travelling gypsies" are described as subhuman, sexually and socially deviant individuals, as follows:

> The morality of the travelling gypsies is very low. Thefts, drinking, arguments and brawls are daily occurrences. Their sexual life, too, runs counter to the

---

508 Sadílková, "(Ne)chtění", 102.

509 See Spurný, *Nejsou jako my,* 237–285; Spurný, "Pokus o převýchovu"; Helena Sadílková, "Čí jsou to dějiny? Dosavadní přístupy k interpretaci poválečných dějin Romů v ČS(S)R". *Romano džaniben*, vol. 13, no. 2 (Winter 2013): 73–74.

510 NA Praha, f. MV II Praha, k. 1283 – Cikánská otázka v kraji Ústeckém. The report stated that: "Where travelling gypsies have appeared in this region, they have been a real scourge of the countryside." (18. 9. 1951, č. j. III/1–215–1951-Kč).

511 Ibid., Report from KNV České Budějovicefor MV (20. 9. 1951, č. j. 215–23/8–1951-III).

rules of community life. The children are precociously sexually mature and girls of school age become mothers. The ONV in Soběslav describes the case of a 14-year-old girl who is the mother of three children and a 17-year-old who is the mother of seven children. [...] It is probable that sexual intercourse takes place between blood relatives.[512]

Throughout the 1950s, the central state authorities and the security forces called for the possibility of implementing restrictive measures nationwide against such persons in order to give them control over the hitherto-uncontrollable movement of various Romani groups.[513] Many regions said in their reports that the situation regarding "travelling gypsies" was acute. The historian Tomáš Zapletal has carried out a thorough analysis of the security forces' archives from the period in question and has concluded that in the 1950s, police reports came from various places in the country describing the problems primarily caused for the majority population by non-settled Roms and their high crime rates. He says there are even alarming cases in these reports of armed clashes between travelling Roms and the settled majority population, as well as armed clashes with policemen.[514]

From the beginning of the 1950s, it is possible to observe various local attempts at preventing such "travelling", often at the request of higher administrative bodies who, in various ways, were trying to force the sedentarisation of "travelling gypsies". However, after Act no. 117/1927 "on wandering gypsies" was repealed in 1950, and before Act no. 74/1958 "on the permanent settlement of travelling persons" was passed, the implementation of such restrictions did not have the necessary basis in law, which hindered the security forces in taking a more vigorous approach. Still, from the beginning of the 1950s we find various tools being used to prevent not just Romani groups, but also non-Romani groups who earned a living from itinerant trades or attractions from moving about. On the one hand, local police used a tried and tested tool of the Austro-Hungarian era and the First Republic, the ejection of Roms from municipal territory, accompanied by an unwillingness to permit Roms official residency in the places to which they came. At the same time, measures were implemented which were planned at the central and regional level and attempted to halt "travelling gypsies" in the places where they

512 Ibid.
513 Spurný, *Nejsou jako my,* 14.
514 Zapletal, "Přístup totalitního státu", 30–31.

appeared or were checked, mostly connected with an attempt to integrate them into the labour process in the places where they stopped. These two tendencies thus frequently ran counter to each other in specific cases: from above came measures meant to compel the Roms to "settle", while at the local level, from below, the authorities – often at the request of local residents – tried to stop the Roms from staying on their territory and to find a legal way of preventing their settling in the municipality or to move them on somewhere else.

One of the ways in which the state bodies tried to prevent these groups from travelling was to confiscate or buy their horses from them and force their caravans to halt. In a July 1952 report to the Interior Ministry entitled "Adjustment of the conditions of persons of gypsy origin", an official from Prague's Central National Committee (ÚNV) proposed that

> the Interior Ministry should, through vigorous nationwide activity, prevent this undesirable fluctuation of gypsies and, by confiscating their wagons and carts, prevent travelling gypsies from travelling. This would make the work of the local administrations much easier.[515]

Horse seizures and the forcible halting of wagons was something that happened repeatedly from the beginning of the 1950s. It was the approach chosen in the Ústí Region where, during the night of 9–10 September 1951, various municipal authorities working together with the police took "radical measures in which they confiscated the travelling gypsies' means of transport in order to prevent them from travelling further. Their horses were confiscated and the wheels taken off their wagons."[516] During the same period, the ONV in Kadaň confiscated horses and wagons "to make it impossible for these gypsies to travel". In that case, the seizures were ordered on the basis that the "gypsies" would receive adequate compensation for them.[517] However, it was not usual for financial compensation to be paid for seized horses, as I shall show below. Similar measures were also taken in the Plzeň Region, where the KNV even tried in February 1952 to formulate "Guidelines for the solution of the gypsy question",[518] which were meant to serve as support for the security forc-

---

515 NA Praha, f. MV II Praha, k. 1283 (9. 7. 1952, č. j. III-1–959/12–1952/Ji).
516 Ibid., Report from KNV Ústí n. L.: Cikánská otázka v Ústeckém kraji – zpráva (18. 9. 1951, č. j. III/1–215–1951 – Nč).
517 Ibid. Report of KNV Karlovy Vary (18. 9. 1951, č. j. III-1a-215–1951–205/10).
518 Ibid., in Plzeň (28. 2. 1952, č. j. III/4–215–26/2–1952 – Nč).

es in settling "travelling gypsies". The district authorities of the Plzeň Region in whose districts gypsies appeared were required by the guidelines to immediately see to it that they were permanently settled in that district. The guidelines recommended that the gypsies' own wagons be used for their accommodation, "with the wheels taken off and the wagons placed on blocks in a suitable place, ideally close to the gypsies' future workplace".[519] As a report to the Interior Ministry in July 1952 indicates, these repressive measures were indeed taken in some districts, which the regional officials assessed positively: "A very good effect on them has been achieved by the sale of their horses, because in this way their travelling has been partially prevented and the gypsies have been limited in their free way of life."[520] The Interior Ministry subsequently labelled the guidelines too repressive, at odds with basic laws and the political line for policy on national minorities, and also at odds with the guidelines of the ministry itself for dealing with the "gypsy question", where an approach of this kind did not have the necessary legislative underpinning.[521]

Another option the state had at its disposal was to integrate the persons concerned into the labour process in a targeted manner. This approach was aided by the law establishing the "general duty to work", which allowed the criminalisation of people with no fixed employment. This was often combined with the above-described tools of seizing or purchasing horses and the forced halting of wagons. The state authorities' plan was that these wagons should serve as accommodation for the groups who were discovered in them in a certain locality; the wagons would then be transported to their place of work.

In September 1951, all regional police headquarters issued a telex calling on local authorities, in conjunction with the police, to ensure that "travelling gypsies" were integrated into the labour process. It stated that all gypsies should have their horses confiscated. The horses should be given veterinary exams, after which the healthy ones would be handed over to state and collective farms and the unhealthy ones sent to the slaughterhouse. At the same time, the wheels should be taken off all of the "gypsy" wagons and their able-bodied members set to work.[522] Fur-

---

519 Ibid.
520 Ibid., (14. 7. 1952, č. j. III-257–14.7.-1952).
521 Response of the MNV Department for Interior Affairs addressed to Gustav Rada, KNV chair in Plzeň (19. 5. 1952, č. j. II/K-20–19/3–1952).
522 Telex from the regional headquarters of the SNB no. 186.187 of 8 September 1951: Kočující cikáni – zařazení do pracovního poměru. SOkA Litoměřice/Lovosice, f. ONV Lovosice, NAD: 328, č. p. 104, i. č. 114, k. 100. Občané cikánské národnosti 1951–1959.

ther reports from the regional and district level to the Interior Ministry from the same period show that these measures were in fact realised in great number.

A report from Division III of the Ústí nad Labem regional administration (KNV), sent to all the ONVs in its jurisdiction with the title "Travelling gypsies. Measures" recommends that:

> if travelling gypsies are found in your area, they should immediately be set to useful work, for example in brickworks, quarries etc., their wagons halted near the designated workplace, and their wheels removed. It is recommended that their good horses be purchased by collective farms. The unneeded ones may be sold to the slaughterhouse.[523]

In a report from the South Bohemian KNV in České Budějovice it was recommended that the Interior Ministry find permanent jobs for "travelling gypsies". The document also recommended that such groups be permanently accommodated as smaller groups and "since they do not have their own fodder base, it will be necessary to persuade them to sell their horses to the socialist sector and for care to be taken that the horses are made proper use of in the coming harvest".[524]

As well as the two measures mentioned above, this document also contains a further instrument of repression that was not infrequently used: the dividing up of large families into smaller groups and their dispersal among several districts, where they would be employed.[525] Likewise, the Prague KNV, in a report addressed to the Interior Ministry of 22 August 1951, proposes that these groups should be dispersed so that they do not form wholes and that no more than one [nuclear] family should be placed in each municipality, where that family should receive suitable housing and employment. The purchase of their wagons and horses should be connected with this settlement so they would have no means of moving away.[526]

In practice, however, the decisions of the state authorities meant that in certain workplaces there was a large concentration of people categorized

---

523 SOkA Teplice, f. ONV Teplice, sign. 257, i. č. 984, k. 246 (23. 8. 1951, č. j. III-257–23/8–1951-Zzil).

524 NA Praha, f. MV II Praha, k. 1283: Potulní cikáni v Českých Budějovicích – závady, Report from JNV České Budějovice (15. 7. 1952, č. j. II-3-215–15/7–1953).

525 For example, a report from the Liberec Region to the Interior Ministry from 17 September 1952: Úprava poměrů osob cikánského původu – zpráva, č. j. III/1–215–5/9–1952-Sp.

526 Ibid., 22. 8. 1951, č. j. 215–20/8–1951-II/3.

as "travelling gypsies". The large groups formed in this way were often viewed by local residents as a security risk and a source of various problems. A good example of state-managed forced relocation was that undertaken by the Hradec Králové KNV in April 1953, which relocated a total of 180 "travelling persons" who had appeared on 6 and 7 April in the Hradec Králové Region in the village of Trčkov in Žamberk district, part of the Orlické Záhoří municipality. The village's German population had been evacuated after 1945 and it now had just 150 inhabitants. The Žamberk ONV's report of 8 May 1953 states that the original agreement had been for "50 gypsies" to be relocated to Orlické Záhoří, where they would start as forest workers. However, this number had been exceeded by 130 people. Their transfer to the destination comes across in the report as forced, without the agreement of the people concerned:

"These people were gathered together from their existing places of residence and sent together to Žamberk, from where they were transferred to Orlické Záhoří. When the established number of persons was exceeded, however, the whole operation got out of hand and become totally unmanageable."[527]

The inhabitants of Orlické Záhoří produced a petition asking for the number of gypsies in the village to be reduced. It contained about a hundred signatures, so clearly all the adult residents. The group of Roms was subsequently divided up and sent to several other districts, to which they were ordered to go in smaller groups.[528]

Another way to limit "travelling gypsy" mobility was the practice of managing the ejection of such people over the district boundary. This practice is admitted to in a 1958 report from the Ústí nad Labem KNV which states that "the difficulties with gypsies were dealt with by ejecting the gypsies to another district, which in the past year cost some 20 million crowns".[529] Another possibility was to return "travelling gypsies" to Slovakia. A report from the Kroměříž ONV in September 1951 describes the escorting of "gypsies" to Slovakia as a common practice.[530] Another

---

527 Ibid., Report from ONV Žamberk: Ubytování cikánů v Orlickém Záhoří, okres Žamberk – hlášení (8. 5. 1953, č. j. 257.-3/5–1953-III).

528 Ibid., Úprava poměrů osob cikánského původu, Report from KNV Hradec Králové: Ubytování cikánů v Orlickém Záhoří – stížnost (13. 5. 1953) and Report from ONV Žamberk, subject: Ubytování cikánů v Orlickém Záhoří, okres Žamberk – hlášení (24. 4. 1953, č. j. II/3–215–15/4–1953).

529 SOA Litoměřice, f. SKNV, odbor vnitřních věcí, zn. 608, V-10 Soupis kočujících Cikánů 1959–1965: Zpráva aktivu o převýchově cikánského obyvatelstva (18. 12. 1958, no č. j.).

530 Ibid., Report from KNV III. (10. 9. 1951, č. j. III/1–257).

report produced by the ONV in Přerov in January 1952 gives an example of discordance between two neighbouring districts, neither one of which wanted to let "travelling gypsies" remain on its territory. According to an official from the Přerov ONV, on the orders of an official from Prostějov a group of 65 persons had been sent from Prostějov, where their horses had been bought from them, to Přerov, where they were sent with their wagons pulled by borrowed tractors. The report admits that the persons in question had protested against the transfer to Přerov and warned that they were being ejected against their wishes. The ONV in Přerov also objected to the approach taken by the neighbouring district and started to arrange for the Roms to be escorted to Slovakia. The report ends with a warning that "the gypsies were not told by the employee of the Přerov ONV that they were being sent to Slovakia by order of the Interior Ministry. The ONV in Prostějov was said to have prepared wagons in which the gypsies were to be taken to Slovakia."[531] However, the report said, not enough attention was paid in Slovakia to the escorted group, and so they returned to the Czech lands.

The reeducation of children of "travelling gypsies" as a case of social engineering

Among the most repressive tools of assimilation to be generally applied to "gypsies" were undoubtedly the attempts to reeducate Romani children by putting them in various boarding schools or taking them away from their families altogether and putting them in children's group homes. On the one hand, the idea of boarding schools was part of the state's attempt to end "gypsy" child illiteracy, which was partly dealt with by setting up special classes for such children. Since the schools complained that Romani parents were not interested in their children's education, that such children had very poor attendance records, and that in general the "gypsy" families had a bad influence on the education of their children, in some places the schools and local administrations decided on more radical solutions intended to wipe out illiteracy and lead to the children becoming more integrated into society. The best-known "special school" for Romani children of its time and the one in operation the longest was the "School of Peace" in Květušín near České Budějovice, headed by

---

531 ZA Opava – pob. Olomouc, f. KNV Olomouc, Narodnostni politika, sign. 608, i. č. 1745, k. 1029, 1951–1958 Report from ONV Přerov, subject: Skupina cikánů, eskortování z Přerova (28. 1. 1952, č. j. III-215/28–12/1952).

teacher Miroslav Dědič and created in the summer of 1950.[532] Over the course of the 1950s it was attended by some 300 children. That school is in many ways a symbol of the period's belief that educators could lead the Roms to a better life and, at the same time, exemplifies the risks of such social engineering.[533]

Another case of social engineering that seems to have been hitherto undescribed but was aimed squarely at the children of "travelling gypsies" was the forcible sending of Lovara children from Litovel and Prostějov to go on "holiday" to Jeseník in July 1953. The approach is described in a newspaper article entitled "Children from the gypsy wagons" written by the regional physical education inspector, J. Látal. An evaluation and detailed description of the event is also contained in reports from the Litovel ONV for the KNV in Olomouc, in the KNV's archive. From these sources we learn that since 1952 around 50 people from a group of "travelling gypsies" had been camping in wagons in Litovel. According to their surnames and places of domicile in Slovakia, these were definitely Lovara who had been forced to remain in Litovel and Prostějov on the orders of the state authorities. In December 1952, a "gypsy school" was set up in Litovel, designed especially for the children of "wandering gypsies" and led by an enthusiastic local communist named B. Šmakalová. The school was equipped with a bathtub where, according to both sources, this comrade bathed the "gypsy" children with her own hands daily and deloused them so that they would be clean. The ONV's reports over the following months praise the high level of participation among the children in the class and the fact that they were bathed and had clean clothes. The only problem for the school were the children's parents, who from the perspective of state representatives hindered the school's enthusiastic work by not supporting their children's learning and by attempting to move elsewhere.[534] It was therefore decided to send the children on "holiday" for three weeks to Jeseník. The whole operation was carried out on an order of the Ministry of National Security of 2 July 1953, for which two related reasons were given: the arrest of certain named "gypsy persons", and the care of the children who would be left behind as a result.[535]

---

532 Pavelčíková, *Romové v českých zemích*, 49.

533 Spurný, "Pokus o převýchovu", 8.

534 ZA Opava – pob. Olomouc, f. KNV Olomouc, Národnostní politika, sign. 608, i. č. 1745, k. 1029, 1951–1958, Report from ONV Litovel, subject: Úprava poměrů osob cikánského původu – zpráva za 1. pololetí 1953 (1. 7. 1953, č. j. III-215–30/6–1953/Kr).

535 Ibid., Report from ONV Litovel: Osoby cikánského původu – zatčení rodičů a zajištění dětí (3. 7. 1953, č. j. III-215-3/7–1953).

It is notable that the newspaper article does not mention the arrest of the parents at all, but describes the idea of sending the children on "holiday" as the school's decision:

"It was clear that the home environments had been hindering the good work of the educators. But in this case, too, the people of Litovel had a good idea. They put the children in a children's home and during the holidays sent them to a spa in Jeseník."[536]

The parents' arrests and detention in custody gives the impression of a deliberate plan with a simple aim, preventing the parents from complicating the smooth course of sending the children on a reeducation course and to a children's home.

During the planning of the operation, the state authorities exploited the fact that the Roms themselves had asked to be moved to Olomouc. Their agreement to the move now became part of an assimilation strategy and, it could be said, was the bait with which to draw the families into the trap of the planned operation. It was decided that after they had moved to Olomouc, a formal document check would take place and that at the same time the parents would be arrested and their children taken away. Subsequently, shelters were to be found for the children, and it was also planned to "send some of the children on a holiday, as has already been approved by the KNV".[537] The KNV agreed to the whole plan, adding only an order that the arrest should take place earlier, in Litovel.[538] In the end, the plan changed so that the Roms were told that they could leave Litovel and were invited to come to the MNV at a certain time in order to sign their mandatory residency cancellations.

There then follows a detailed description of the operation:

When they arrived, although there was some shouting, the action was carried out as follows: In one room they were registered, in another room they were each examined. The children were put into a special room and the men and women designated for arrest were taken to jail cells [...]. The police both held guard and carried out their tasks such as interrogation.[539]

---

536 SOkA Teplice, f. ONV Teplice, sign. 257, i. č. 984, k. 246 – "O dětech z cikánských vozů", unknown periodical (undated).

537 ZA Opava – pob. Olomouc, f. KNV Olomouc, Národnostní politika, sign. 608, i. č. 1745, k. 1029, 1951–1958 –Report from ONV Litovel, subject: Osoby cikánského původu: dotaz (9. 2. 1953, č. j. III-215–9/2–1953).

538 Ibid.

539 Ibid.

The adults were then escorted into custody in Pankrác prison in Prague. Subsequently the children were sorted by age. The whole proceedings were supervised by the police. The younger children, of whom the youngest was not even a year old, were taken to infants' shelters. Four children were sent to the infants' shelter in Plumlov, where they were "bathed and their gypsy rags returned" upon arrival. Two children went to a shelter in Štíty and two to a shelter in Jeseník. Most of the children were sent that same day on "holiday" to Jeseník on a chartered bus that arrived in the night. They were accompanied by their assiduous teacher, Šmakalová. The children were allowed to bring just "a few gypsy rags" with them. The report admits that during the bus ride the bigger children cried until Šumperk, and then the smaller children did too, and that the whole event "went off smoothly, except for the crying and sobbing of adults and children". The next day, relatives of the children arrived in Jeseník calling for them to be released. One woman even brandished an axe and one young man came in a horse-drawn wagon, but they had no luck. During the operation, 19 children aged five to 15 were sent to Jeseník, another eight aged one to three were taken to various shelters, and nine adults were taken into custody. The forced transportation thus concerned 36 people and just 16 Roms remained behind in Litovel. However, seven Lovara children from Litovel were not put on the administration's register, having hidden in an unknown place,[540] clearly with other relatives.

In the end, a total of 62 children from Litovel and Prostějov were sent to the holiday facility in Jeseník. A report by the KNV in Olomouc said in summary that the children had gotten used to their new environment and would not go back to the wagons, but that there was a fear their parents would want them back when they left prison. "It will now depend on the people's administration being able to reeducate, through increased care, the gypsy children at least, if not the old gypsies."[541] A handwritten note was added later as follows: "On their return from custody, the parents are asking for their children back. Although they are hindering their whole reeducation, we are able to give them the children, but they are being told that they ought to leave them in our care."[542] On their return from Jeseník, the children were accommodated in a children's home, where

---

540 Ibid., f. ONV in Litovel, Individuální seznam o rozmístění cikánů, při provedení dne 37. 1953, dle pokynů Min. nár. bezpečnosti (3. 7. 1953, č.j III-215–30).

541 ZA in Opava – pob. Olomouc, f. KNV Olomouc, Národnostní politika, sign. 608, i. č. 1745, k. 1029, 1951–1958 – KNV Olomouc, Úprava poměrů osob cikánského původu (3. 7. 1953, č. j. III/1–215–14/7–1953/SM).

542 Ibid.

Comrade Šmakalová continued to look after them. In September 1953, another 13 "gypsy" children from Prostějov joined them. Látal finishes his article enthusiastically, stating that the children are happy in school and enjoy learning:

> Most of all they like singing gypsy songs... they like drawing, but they don't like black, which is a sad colour, they like the bright colours they used to wear. Of all the animals they like the horse the best. If they see a picture of one, they stroke and kiss it.[543]

The author, no doubt an enthusiastic "builder of socialism", introduces a note of relative pathos to close the article, allowing us to consider that although the Lovara in Litovel had been targeted by a government-planned policy of assimilation and social engineering that turned their families and their way of life upside down, their children were still able to preserve their own cultural values in a new setting. From a July 1954 complaint by citizens of Litovel addressed to the President of the Republic, the Interior Ministry and the KNV in Olomouc regarding the behaviour of the "gypsies" who had been released from Pankrác prison and were calling for the release of their children from the children's home, we learn that the children remained in the facility for at least a year after they were taken away on "holiday".[544]

How long they stayed in the children's home altogether is not clear from any other reports. Another highly significant fact, however, emerges from the list of children placed there. Among the forcibly interned children were two sons of Grófa Stojková: Jaroslav (*1937) and Něguš (*1941), in other words, Zaga Stojková's grandchildren. Unfortunately, I have no further information regarding their stay there. It is therefore highly likely that Grófa was a victim of those police procedures and taken to Pankrác prison, where she was held without any clear evidence against her.

Lovara among "travelling gypsies"

Although during the immediate postwar period and the start of the 1950s there were thousands of Roms on the move in the former Czechoslovakia,

---

543 SOkA Teplice, f. ONV Teplice, sign. 257, i. č. 984, k. 246 – "O dětech z cikánských vozů", undated, unknown periodical.
544 SOkA Olomouc, f. MěNV Litovel, L 1–114, k. 108/11– č. j. 257/III.

most might be best described as labour migrants who were trying to improve their socioeconomic situations. Only a few of these were engaged in professions that required spatial mobility. Those few included a small number of families or individuals from the surviving Bohemian and Moravian Roms and Sinti who, after the war, returned to their interwar economic activities connected with moving around in wagons pulled by horses or tractors. Among those with professions requiring movement were the showmen (*světští*), who mainly operated various amusements, attractions and enterprises.[545] A significant proportion of the "travelling professionals" were Lovara from Slovakia.[546]

According to the Czech historian Nina Pavelčíková, it was Vlax Roms from south and southwestern Slovakia who formed one of the first Romani groups to come to the Czech lands and the depopulated Sudetenland. The arrival of Vlax Roms from Slovakia (above all from the surroundings of Nitra and Topolčany) continued in further years, she states, but estimates that their share in the total number of Romani migrants probably never exceeded 5–10%.[547] Among the Lovara families who arrived, a considerable proportion were returning to the Czech lands and thus renewing their trajectories from the First Republic which had been forcibly interrupted by the war.

The question of how many Roms in the Czech lands there might have been who had become, under the influence of previous events, mobile and unanchored is once again difficult to answer. In period reports we find only partial estimates of the total numbers of "travelling gypsies", and it is not easy to guess who should be imagined in this category.

Reading superficially through the reports of the ONVs throughout the Bohemian and Moravian regions from the beginning of the 1950s, it could seem that there were a considerable number of "travelling gypsy hordes". However, after comparing the data in the local archives and adding other genealogical data from several years of my research, I believe that these were often the same families or larger groups made up of several families which had moved previously through various regions and that their total number was actually much smaller. From the reports submitted to the regional and often to the district levels, such as the KNV reports for the Interior Ministry entitled "Adjustment of the conditions of persons of gypsy origin"[548] from the beginning of the 1950s, we do not,

---

545 Tlamsová, *Lexikon*.
546 Donert, *The Rights*, 115.
547 Pavelčíková, *Romové v českých zemích*, 36–37.
548 NA Praha, f. MV II Praha, k. 1283.

however, learn the names of those who were "travelling", so it is difficult to combine these reports with local records and genealogical data.

Zapletal cited in his study a "proposal of the HS VB [head of the police administration] for solving the question of homeless people and gypsies" from 1953 which puts the number of travelling Romani groups in Czechoslovakia as a whole at 93, each with a variable number of people (between 20 and 80) who moved about in 233 wagons of various types.[549] Given how the Lovara witnesses talk about their mobility, the size of the groups that is mentioned in this proposal is surprising. From what Lovara witnesses say, their families deliberately moved around in smaller groups so as not to attract too much attention from the police. However, we may notice that after the repeal of Act no. 177/1927, which had banned "travelling hordes" larger than families from moving about and camping, the size of the groups arrested on Czech territory increased. In various district reports from the 1950s it is not unusual to find descriptions of groups amounting to several dozen people, sometimes over a hundred. As I have shown, these families were sometimes artificially combined by the police and state bodies into larger wholes which were then settled together in places where they were to work.

An important question is the extent to which the period category of "travelling gypsies" overlapped with the sub-ethnic group of Lovara coming to the Czech lands from Slovakia. In other words, we may ask what percentage of those who were perceived by the state and police bodies of the time as "travelling" were Lovara, and also to what extent the Lovara were represented by the families who moved across Czechoslovakia in covered wagons and caravans. It is clear that these categories definitely do not relate to the same persons and families. Witness memories and the lists of persons registered subsequently under Act no. 74/1958 show that the category of "travelling gypsies" covered not just families with significant spatial mobility, but also very often families who, irrespective of how they moved, were only travelling to their workplace. The state authorities were not capable of precisely differentiating these two types of mobility, and in some areas it was difficult for them to distinguish between them. Some Slovak Roms were therefore perceived as "travelling" although they had never led a "travelling" lifestyle. At the same time, it may be assumed that a number of Lovara families were automatically included in this category who frequently fulfilled the stereotypes connected with it.

---

549 Zapletal, "Přístup totalitního státu", 31.

The nomadisation of the Lovara during this period took place in two ways: On the one hand, they were perceived by the administration of the day as "eternal" nomads, spatially unanchored and without any experience of sedentarised life. On the other hand, they were often referred to in this way by authors subsequently writing about this period of Romani history. An example is the following characterisation by the ethnographer Eva Davidová:

> Travelling and the tools which permitted this travelling way of life were characteristic of some of our [Czechoslovak] Roms – the *Vlachike Roma* – until the end of the 1950s. During the period in which they led a nomadic life, some of them at first used portable tents – *šátre*, primitive shelters, and then mainly covered wagons (*vurdona*) of various types. They lived either in simple wagons covered with a tarpaulin or mats, or in covered wagons, various types of caravans moving around for most of the year from place to place throughout Bohemia, Moravia and Slovakia until February 1959, when these groups were forcibly settled with the creation of a register based on Act no. 74/1958. The wheels were taken off their wagons, but the wagons themselves often served as their accommodation in the initial period after their forced settlement.[550]

This description involves considerable nomadisation of the Vlax Roms, who are described therein as a fairly uniform group that travelled until February 1959.

What emerges from my research, however, is that the situations of these individual Lovara families were far more varied and the degree of their spatial mobility substantially lower than Davidová suggests. No equivalency can be made between the categories of "travelling gypsies" and the ethnically-defined Lovara. A number of Lovara in Slovakia had a long-term, territorial connection with a certain location, and other Lovara were affected during the Second World War by the experience of their forced sedentarisation in the municipalities where they were domiciled. As I showed above using the example of the Stojkas from Trenčianska Teplá, the wartime and postwar developments in these localities led to the interruption of the social ties formed earlier by the Lovara, a sharp fall in the socioeconomic status of such Roms, and their subsequent departure from their domiciles. Therefore, while in previous decades it was possible to speak of these Roms as territorially-anchored,

---

550 Eva Davidová, *Romano drom. Cesty Romů 1945–1990* (Olomouc: Univerzita Palackého, 1995), 63.

those ties were then broken as a result of the wartime and postwar events. These formerly territorially-anchored families were forced to leave a certain location in Slovakia and to try and find more favourable living conditions in the Czech lands, as was also the case with other Roms from Slovakia. For example, the witness Helena Danišová of a Lovara family from Soľčany in the Topoľčany district said in her testimony that before the war her family did not travel at all and did not even have horses. Her father worked as a farmer's assistant. After their house was destroyed at the end of the war, however, the family had no choice but to acquire a horse and cart and set off to find a livelihood elsewhere. This brought them to northern Moravia.[551] A number of other Lovara families also did not return to a similar lifestyle after the war and, like other Roms from Slovakia, they came to Czech towns in search of work, with some remaining there permanently. Indeed, a number of these Lovara families did not come to the Czech lands in horse-drawn wagons, but travelled by train, like other migrants from Slovakia.[552]

Such families who were engaged in economic activities which required spatial mobility, therefore, accounted for just part of the Lovara community. The intensive, repeated attempts by the state administration, mainly in the Czech lands, to limit their mobility, connected with the use of the repressive tools leading to their sedentarisation and fixed employment, meant that the number of actual "travelling" families fell throughout the 1950s. Some such families voluntarily accepted official housing and offers of work, or found housing and jobs themselves. Other families had no such opportunity and were forced to stop "travelling" and "settle" in a place allotted to them, thus becoming the victims of measures undertaken by state bodies. The general duty to work, which required people to have fixed employment in a certain place, made the situation of families living on the road even more difficult and contributed to their criminalisation. Under this pressure, many Lovara families tried to find employment and housing, but this was often made difficult for them by the continuing anti-Romani prejudice in Czech society.

A change in Lovara professional strategies is also characteristic of this period, since earlier methods of earning a living could not be kept up after the war.[553] Modernisation and the introduction of a socialist economic system meant the demand for horses fell sharply. Horses were

---

551 Personal recording of Helena Danišová (*1940) by the author, made 29 March 2002 in Ostrava.
552 Personal recording of Josef Molnár (1945) by the author, made 19 January 2019 in Hořice district.
553 Pavelčíková, *Romové v českých zemích,* 22.

also confiscated or purchased from Roms by the state, so they stopped representing a viable form of financial investment. In reaction to this, the Lovara started to seek other livelihoods in the postwar period. Highly advantageous activities included dealing in food and clothing coupons and in sought-after goods, as well as engaging in supplementary livelihoods which verged on criminal behaviour.[554] Zapletal also says that these activities were widespread among travelling Roms. He states that cancellations of supplies were forged by them, and non-existent family members were signed up for short-term jobs which guaranteed confirmation from an employer entitling the non-existent person to the subsequent issue of food and clothing coupons. There would then be a search for new employment yielding another new confirmation to reap the benefits of the rationing system. By 1951, this activity by travelling Roms had reached such an extent that there was a nationwide police raid during which hundreds of Roms and several people of non-Romani origin were arrested.[555]

Understandably, the increase in such criminogenic behaviour was closely connected with the decline in Romani traditional livelihoods and the deterioration in such families' economic and social situations, meaning they were frequently pushed to the limits of their ability to ensure their own basic needs. This was also connected to insufficient offers of work by the state enterprises able to make use of their potential somehow, above all in the case of the former horse dealers. Their sophisticated experiences were not taken advantage of, and instead they were forced to perform manual labour that, given the existing traditional hierarchical system among Roms, they themselves considered inferior and demeaning and with which they had no experience. The dissatisfaction of their employers rose, therefore, and was often connected to an unwillingness to take on "travelling gypsies" as employees. Dissatisfaction and reluctance to perform such work also grew among the Lovara, who often tried to avoid this type of work experience.

5.2 The postwar trajectories of Štefan Stojka, Sr.

As I have shown above, Roms remained in Trenčianska Teplá until the spring of 1947, when they were driven out of the village by the MNV.[556]

554 Ibid., 22.
555 Zapletal, "Přístup totalitního státu", 27.
556 ŠA Trenčín, f. ObNV v Trenč. Teplej, i. č. 944/1947 – Cigáni – neprístojné chovanie a nariadenie na ich vysťahovanie.

The family symbolically represented by Anna Stojková (*1902) seems to have departed for the Czech lands straight away. The last such family to leave Trenčianska Teplá was the immediate family of Štefan Stojka, Sr., who had the closest relationship to the municipality. According to an official record from the spring (April or May) of 1947, all the other Roms left and Štefan Stojka remained with his wife and children in Trenčianska Teplá for a time, although the MNV had already declared in July 1947 that there were no more Roms living in the municipality and that they had all moved to an unknown location. However, the family of Štefan Stojka, Sr. was demonstrably still living there in June 1948 when, according to an MNV record, he declared himself to be the father of his youngest daughter (*1947) with his partner Kristina Horvátová, née Rafaelová. The record states his livelihood as "horse dealer", for which he had the necessary permission, and that he (still!) lived at house no. 273.[557]

According to a non-Romani witness from Trenčianska Teplá who was a former neighbour of the Stojka family, Štefan's family left the village several years after the war. Kalný gives the reason for Štefan's departure as his disagreement with the result of his court case, when he was refused compensation for the destruction and plundering of his house: "He still had a wagon. And horses. He carried on his 'trade', too." [558] We do not know much about his further trajectories, only that his paths led this time to Moravia. From a police registration form in the Brno City Archive we know that in March 1949, his son and namesake Štefan Stojka, Jr., born in 1929, registered for residency in Brno, where he lived first in a room in Komárovská Street sublet to him by another Lovara named J. Stojka who was renting it. Štefan Stojka, Jr. next resided in Pekařská Street with another Lovara, A. Pillo. On the applications, his profession was recorded as "worker", and his permanent residency as *Trenčianska Teplá, Vycházková ulice 273*. After less than a month Štefan Stojka, Jr. moved to Štramberk, Nový Jičín district.[559]

The eldest son of Štefan Stojka, Sr., Ján Stojka (*1905), already a widower and a pensioner, was proposed for permanent settlement and employment in Kralupy nad Vltavou on a list in December 1952 together with his own son Štefan (*1923) and his nuclear family, as well as the nuclear families of his cousins Barbora and Kuluš Horvátová, née

---

557 ŠA Trenčín, f. MNV Trenč. Teplá (9. 6. 1948, č. j. 2346/1948).
558 Kalný, *Cigánsky plač*, 62.
559 AM Brno, f. Z1.

Stojková. The whole group totalled 18 people.[560] Given that the archival documents from which I shall quote below indicate that the entire larger family unit moved around together before and after this stay in Kralupy and Vltavou, it is probable that Ján and his children moved around with them. Ján's son Štefan (*1923) and his nuclear family were also on the list of Roms who were camping in the summer of 1952 in Lovosice, who will be discussed below. It is not certain what the movements of Štefan Stojka, Sr. were at that time. It seems that during this period his adult sons were living independently, separate from Štefan Stojka, Sr.'s nuclear family, which included his new wife Kristína and their children as well as Kristína's two children from a previous relationship. It is possible to assume that they were moving around together with Roms from their aunt Zaga's branch of the family, at that time headed by Anna Lakatošová, with whom they had lived for several years in an improvised Romani settlement in Trenčianska Teplá during the war and with whom they had functioning, solidary relationships.

I have found evidence of Štefan Stojka, Sr.'s mobility from the early 1950s in northern Moravia and in Silesia. According to information published by Pavelčíková, Štefan Stojka, Sr. and his family were in a larger group of Vlax Roms who camped by the burned-out sugar refinery at Kateřinky, Opava, in 1950.[561] The Roms were said to have arrived in September 1950 in horse-drawn wagons (for the most part typical agricultural carts covered with tarpaulins, but clearly also at least one caravan) which they parked in the yard of a former sugar refinery that had burnt down during the war. Nine families were in the group, and officials estimated the total number of people at 64–73.[562] Although local police assumed the group was four generations of a broader family community, according to my genealogical records, Štefan Stojka, Sr. was not related to the other people in the group with the surnames Stojka, Kotlár and Lakatoš, most of whom came from Topoľčany and the surrounding area. In mid-September 1950, Štefan Stojka, Sr. (*1891) and his partner Kristína Horváthová, her adult son Milan, and another five children and youths[563] aged between three and 20 moved into the ground floor of

---

560 SOkA Mělník, f. ONV Kralupy nad Vltavou, k. 462. – Seznam osob cikánského původu předaných ONV v Kralupech n/Vlt. ONV v Mělníku za účelem jejich trvalého usídlení v tamním okrese a zařazení do trvalého pracovního poměru, sestavený OO-VB v Kralupech pro ONV – bezpečnostní referát Kralupy n/Vlt. (8. 12. 1952, no č. j.).

561 Pavelčíková, "Příprava a provádění", 49.

562 Pavelčíková, "Příchod olašských Romů", 41.

563 Some of them were Kristýna's children from a previous relationship, the father of the youngest was Štefan.

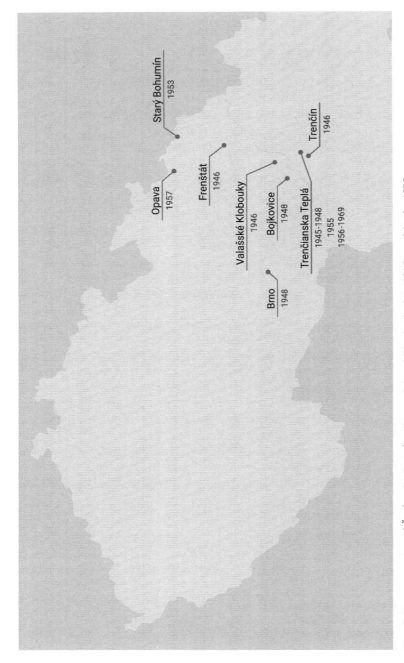

Map 3: Reconstruction of Štefan Stojka's family spatial mobility in the late 1940s and in the 1950s.

the burned-out sugar refinery.[564] The whole group then left in May 1951. However, it is not clear where Štefan's family went or planned to go. The next records of their stay in northern Moravia that I managed to find come from 1953, when Štefan's youngest son was born in Starý Bohumín. Štefan Stojka was 62 at the time. The family then spent time in Opava.[565]

According to a non-Romani respondent from Trenčianska Teplá, Štefan Stojka, Sr., his wife, and several of their youngest children returned to Trenčianska Teplá in 1955 or 1956. By then their house was no longer standing, however. She said that:

> The family lived immediately opposite us in their wagon, in some sort of tent, and they had a fire pit out front. Their daughter went to school with me. Then sometime in the early 1960s they moved them to the end of the village, to Hliník, which is a small road going in the direction of Nová Dubnica. They lived there next to the stream, because that's how they are, they always have to live next to a stream. They lived there in their wagon, with just the tarpaulins over them, and they cooked outside over a fire.[566]

Kalný gives a slightly different version:

> When [Štefan Stojka, Sr.] was banned from travelling, wandering, parasiting on society without working, when he had to sell his horses, he had nowhere to live. 'I won't live in a wagon without horses,' he said, and set out for the MNV, as well as the ONV in Trenčín, to ask for a house.[567]

Štefan Stojka, Sr.'s repeated requests were said to have ultimately been met and the MNV is said to have built him a cottage with a kitchen, a bedroom and woodshed at the end of the village on the path leading to Koľačín – Dubnica, on which the MNV spent 15,000 crowns.[568] According to his former neighbour, the building was made of wooden planks covered with fibreboard on each side and plastered.[569] Kalný visited him there before his book was published (it came out in 1960, so in about 1959) and found Štefan Stojka, Sr. lying on his bed, ill, disappointed

---

564 Pavelčíková, "Příchod olašských Romů", 41.
565 Data from an application for permanent residence from the mid-1950s archived in the registry office in Trenčianska Teplá. Verbal information from employees of the registry office.
566 Personal recording of A. L. (*1946) by the author, made on 30 October 2019 in Trenč. Teplá
567 Kalný, *Cigánsky plač*, 62.
568 Ibid.
569 Personal recording of Pavol Pytlík (*1950) by the author, made on 17 July 2024 in Trenč. Teplá.

and embittered by life, above all because the house he had built himself had been destroyed by the German front and then taken apart by his neighbours, and by the loss of his court case for compensation for those events, as well as from having had to get rid of his horses. The journalist's visit must have taken place not long after the register of travelling people that took place in February 1959.

A newspaper article entitled "The gypsy question" published in the Trenčín ONV newspaper in June 1961 confirms the information that the MNV had built Štefan Stojka, Sr. a cottage at the end of the village and added that the MNV had

> acceded to his request that he might be allowed to buy horses and collect rubbish. Štefan Stojka is thus employed. He also receives an old age pension and benefits for his three minor children, and all this ensures his livelihood. The question of Štefan Stojka is thus settled.[570]

However, another version of these events was given by a non-Romani witness, the former neighbour of the Stojka family. She said the fact that the family had returned in the mid-1950s and settled on their land caused discontent among the inhabitants and leadership of the municipality. After some time, there was pressure from his surroundings that Stojka, Sr. move to the area named Hliník at the very end of the village, where he is said to have bought a new piece of land.[571] This purchase is confirmed by a receipt from April 1957 showing that Štefan Stojka, Sr. bought a woodshed there for 4,000 crowns.[572] According to the non-Romani witness, Štefan parked his covered wagon on that land. This may have preceded the building of the above-mentioned cottage. It is not, however, clear whether the cottage described by Kalný and mentioned in the newspaper article was built on the land bought by Štefan or elsewhere. According to his death certificate, Štefan Stojka, Sr. died in January 1968 in his wagon at Hliník, a side road in Trenčianska Teplá. However, his then neighbour and amateur photographer Pavol Pytlík, who photographed Stojka's funeral, claims that Stojka did not die in the caravan, but in the house. He recalls that the family placed his body on the sofa under several piled-up blankets and heated the entire house to a high temperature.[573]

---

570 [author n.a.] "Cigánska otázka", *Trenčianske noviny: orgán OV KSS a ONV v Trenčíne*, vol. 2, no. 28 (28. 6. 1961), 3.

571 Personal recording with A. L. (*1946) by the author, made on 30 October 2019 in Trenč. Teplá

572 ŠA Trenčín, f. MNV Trenčianska Teplá, odbor výstavby, zn. Výst. 661–1957.

573 Personal recording of Pavol Pytlík (*1950) by the author, made on 17 July 2024 in Trenč. Teplá.

After Štefan's death, his partner Kristína and their children continued to live in the same place. According to his neighbour, Pavol Pytlík, after Stojka's death his widow Kristína and her children left Trenčianska Teplá for a while. As soon as they left, the people from Teplá dismantled the house, first the roof, then the rest, so that the house was uninhabitable (see Fig. 12). After their return, they had no choice but to live on the property again in the wagon. Towards the end of her life Kristína lived briefly in a rented house with a yard on Teplická Street, a few hundred metres from their original house[574].

After Kristína's death few years later, the children left Trenčianska Teplá, according to witnesses and employees of the local registry office, and went to an unknown place in Moravia. One of Štefan's youngest sons was still recorded as having permanent residence in Trenčianska Teplá in 2019, although (according to employees of the local town hall) he had not lived there for more than 30 years and was not even present.

Coda: The legend and legacy of Štefan Stojka

In February 2023, a photograph from 1955 was published on the Facebook page *Historia Trenčianskej Teplej vo foto*[575] (History of Trenčianska Teplá in photos) showing Štefan Stojka, Sr. with his horse and cart, in which his family is sitting[576]. Beneath the photo there soon appeared a number of commentaries, from which I select the following:

"Mr. Stojka and his horse were a legend." (P. B., 21 February 2023)

"Mr. Stojka was a *vajda*. [...] That horse lived for many years, I remember that if it hadn't had a harness, it would have fallen apart, it was so thin... I remember them very well..." (P. R., 21 February 2023).

"When I was little and I did something naughty, they'd frighten me by saying the Stojkas would take me away in their cart." (D. H., 21 February 2023).

"It was incredible, once I met him on the bridge in Hlohovec, all that way away." (M. K., 21 March 2023)

Pytlík dates Stojka's death to 1971, after Pytlík had returned from military service, but this statement contradicts Stojka's death certificate.

574 Ibid.

575 https://www.facebook.com/historiatrenciianskejteplejvofoto

576 See the cover photo of the book.

I remember them, when I used to walk to N. Dubnica with my sister-in-law A[.] We used to be afraid of them, because there were no gypsies in our village, but they told me I had no need to be afraid! And people used to say: 'You're like Stojka's horse, you only ever go to the same pub'. (E. K. 21 February 2023).

Our neighbours from over the road. They used to come to our garden for water. Old Mr. Stojka wanted to know once how many gypsies would come to his funeral if he died. So they spread the rumour that he'd died, and a huge number of gypsies came to Teplá. A lot of them slept on the ground in our garden, we almost had a heart attack in the morning. [...] Their daughter F. cooked, baked and was always sweeping their cottage. Then she went to Moravia somewhere, I didn't see her any more. (E. O., 21 February 2023).[577]

These commentaries by non-Romani natives of Trenčianska Teplá and former neighbours of the Stojka family are witness to the legacy left in the village by Štefan Stojka, Sr. in particular, who died almost 55 years before these commentaries. A number of legends are still being passed down locally about Štefan and his family, some of which involve stereotypes about Roms (for example, the threat that they would steal children, or fear of being hurt by "gypsies"). Other stories show Štefan in the light of somewhat incredible deeds, such as the memory of the rumour being spread that he had died when he was still alive, as well as his neighbour's surprise that Štefan had been capable of travelling with the (scrawny) horse and (rickety) wagon shown in the photo all the way to Hlohovec, 80 kilometres away. These memories provide ambivalent testimony about Štefan, reflecting his status and authority, above all among Roms, and also among non-Roms, somewhat. A newspaper article from 1962 describes Štefan in the same way: "Štefan Stojka, a resident of Trenčianska Teplá, is very well known in our whole region. Among citizens of gypsy nationality this 72-year-old man enjoys respect and authority."[578]

These commentaries portray Štefan Stojka, Sr. with amusement. They discuss and make fun of his family's pauperised position (for example,

---

577 This story is also confirmed by Stojka's neighbour at the time, Pavol Pytlík, who says that about 300 Roms came to Stojka's fake funeral. When he really died two years later, the Roms were angry and did not come to his funeral. His coffin was carried by non-Roma. According to Pytlík, not even Stojka's adult children and grandchildren came to the funeral. Personal recording of Pavol Pytlík (*1950) by the author, made on 17 July 2024 in Trenč. Teplá.

578 [author n.a.] *Trenčianske noviny: orgán OV KSS a ONV v Trenčíne*, vol. 2, no. 28 (28. 6. 1961), 3.

the mention of the horse so thin that only its harness stopped it from falling apart, the horse "only ever going to one pub", or his daughter continuously sweeping out the cottage). On the other hand, these commentaries cover up the fact that his neighbours played an active part in his bleak situation, having at various times helped to take apart his house, to drive the Roms out of the village, and to force Štefan off his own land in the centre of the village, not to mention the violent acts and racially-motivated behaviour of the local non-Roms, or Štefan's dogged attempts to do something about it.

If we connect these commentaries with the facts described above from the 1960s, it is interesting that the "hut" described by the former neighbours was clearly the "cottage" that the MNV built at the turn of the 1950s and 1960s and boasted about in the Trenčín newspaper. The commentator who writes that he remembers Stojka's horse in the photo from 1955 and that the horse lived for many more years is clearly mistaken, because we know that the horse was confiscated when the register of travelling and semi-travelling persons was made in 1959. We know that at the start of the 1960s Štefan acquired another horse with the permission of the MNV and that it could hardly have been the same one.

Nevertheless, these commentaries show that Štefan Stojka's legacy among the inhabitants of Trenčianska Teplá lives on until the present day. They portray him as a local resident, maybe as a rather eccentric one, and with a dose of amusement that reflects general stereotypes of "gypsies", but nevertheless also reflects his exceptional position as a *vajda* and horse trader whose life was connected not just with horses but with Trenčianska Teplá itself. This benevolent picture is, however, the result of long-term violence against him and his kind and efforts to forget that violence.

5.3 The trajectories of the late Zaga Stojková's descendants[579]

The branch of the Stojka family previously represented symbolically by its oldest member, Zaga Stojková, had changed significantly by the end of the Second World War. After Zaga Stojková died, her descendants'

---

579 This chapter is based to a certain extent on information that I have already published in my article for the periodical *Slovenský národopis* with the title "Forced settlement of Vlach Roma in Žatec and Louny in the late 1950s" (Hajská, "Forced settlement"). However, I have considerably reworked the article and added new material.

nuclear families started to become more distant from each other as the birth of new generations turned them into extended families. The families were divided into branches which moved around independently of each other to a large extent.

The first branch was represented by the widowed Anna Stojková, née Lakatošová (*1902), with the Romani nickname Čaja or Čajinka; her two adult sons, Bobko and Janino and their families; her one adult daughter and her daughter's child; and her three children who were still minors. They coexisted alongside the two adult children of the late Zaga Stojková: Grófa and Josef (Jouško), the late Filo's siblings. Anna Stojková was their sister-in-law. By that time, Grófa and Jouško both had their own partners and children who, by the end of the decade, were already grown and starting their own nuclear families. Grófa Stojková, who lived with Josef Lakatoš, originally from Šúrovce, often moved around the Czech lands separately with only her nuclear family. During the 1950s this branch of the family the oldest member of which was Anna Stojková, numbered around 30 people.

The other branch of the family consisted of Anna's two sisters-in-law, the sisters of the late Filo: Kuluš (*1920), who has already been mentioned above several times, and Barbora (*1914), the two brothers whom they married, Antonín Horvát (*1914) and Juraj Horvát (*1912), their children and grandchildren. This group, which in the mid-1950s took up residence in Žatec with their covered wagons, also numbered about 30 people. I will hereafter refer to this branch as the Stojka-Horvát family.

The dates and places where children were born in both parts of the family confirm that the extended family returned to the Czech lands soon after the war. A time-space localisation of the widowed Anna Stojková's branch goes as follows: In October 1949 they were present in Žatec (Anna's daughter, also named Anna, gave birth there to a son, Berci), two months later they were in Česká Lípa (where Anna's son Bobko was born), and in 1951 they were in the Choceň district (where Anna's brother-in-law Jouško's son was born). In January 1953, a son was born to Anna's son Janino in Nové Město nad Váhom in western Slovakia, some 30 kilometres from Trenčianska Teplá. This birth record is also the last record we have of Anna's family on Slovak territory. In 1953 another son was born to Bobko in Ostrava, and another son was then born to Bobko in 1955 in Most. Another child was born to Janino in 1956 in Žatec, and two more children were born in January and February of the following year in Roudnice nad Labem (Grófa's son Jaroslav's son and the son of Jouško). In November 1957 another son was born to

Bobko in Prague 14. This is also where, in July 1958, twins were born to Jouško, Anna's brother-in-law.

The presence of the family at various times in certain localities is also confirmed by documents issued to its members (identity cards and other documents). Anna's daughter-in-law R. Stojková was issued with a document by the MNV in Žatec in 1950, and their son Bobko received a citizenship document issued in 1954 by the ONV in Chomutov and an identity card in 1957 in Žatec. His wife V. Stojková then received an identity card in 1958 in Louny.

I have not been able to gather so much data on the other branch of the family. From the birthdates and birthplaces of their children, we know that the family of Antonín Horvát and his wife Kuluš was present in Chomutov in August 1949 and then again in August 1950, and in September 1952 they were in Radotín on the edge of Prague. Antonín Horvát was issued an identity card in 1949 in Karlovy Vary and another in 1950 in Žatec.

Overall, it is possible to observe that primarily in the first half of the 1950s, both branches of the extended Stojka family were intensively spatially mobile within the Czech lands. As we shall see below, in the second half of the 1950s their mobility gradually lessened to cover the area of North Bohemia (Most, Žatec, Louny, Roudnice nad Labem). The exception was their time spent in Prague in 1957 and 1958, where, however, just two of the nuclear families from Anna's branch seem to have been temporarily resident.

The early 1950s: Spatial mobility and attempts at sedentarisation

The fact that during the first half of the 1950s the Stojka family moved around the Czech lands in horse-drawn wagons is confirmed not just by archival records, but also by the memories of Anna's grandson, nicknamed Berci (*1949). He has described their property in detail:

> We had several types of wagons. There were covered wagons which were small wooden caravans, in which we had beds and a stove. We'd sleep in them when it was cold. We also had a big ladder cart with a tarpaulin, which is what we slept and travelled in during the summer.[580]

---

580 Personal recording of Berci (*1949) by the author, made on 18 December 2018 in Louny, Czech Republic.

It is also clear from the following description that a wagon was a status symbol for its owner:

> The Roms took care over the appearance of their wagons. When they were coming towards each other on the road, they would already be looking from a distance to see what other people's wagons were like. 'Look, he's got a lovely wagon! He must be successful,' they'd say. On the basis of the wagon they'd judge who was poor and who was rich, who was doing well and who wasn't.[581]

The Stojka and Horvát families who were related were in contact with each other. At least at the start of the decade, these families sometimes used to travel around or camp together. In the 1950s, Roms were still earning their livings from selling horses. The narrator Berci says of this:

> My uncles still tried to earn a living at that time through trading. I remember travelling to the big horse markets which took place in Žatec or Český Brod. Roms would buy and sell horses there. They'd buy one and resell it at a profit. Or they'd get food for it. Half a pig, or geese and hens. They'd also deal in food coupons. Both food and clothes were rationed back then. Roms made use of the fact that they would give them these coupons in various villages and then they'd sell them or exchange them with non-Roms. They caught my mother doing it and put her in prison for six years, so my granny raised me.[582]

The witness did not return to his mother after her release, but continued living with his grandmother, Anna Stojková, and the families of his uncles Janino and Bobko and his great-uncle Jouško (his late grandfather Filo's brother) until Anna's death in 1963.

When travelling around the Czech lands, the group divided up into smaller wholes. As Berci remembers, "a maximum of three or four families would always travel together,[583] each in their own wagon. We knew that if we all travelled together, we'd just annoy people." As I shall show on the basis of period records, however, in the early 1950s the extended family often moved around together, consisting of several nuclear families with minor children and other adult relatives. Often a very large group consisting of several dozen people plus other Lovara families with their horses and carts would arrive in various localities.

---

581 Ibid.
582 Ibid.
583 The narrator used the Lovara term *čalado* for his nuclear family, as compared to the extended family (*nipo*), the term which he used for the resultant whole when several nuclear families joined together.

Both newly-created branches of this extended family were mobile until at least the mid-1950s, having no permanent place to which they returned. The state undertook several attempts at settling them and employing them in the socialist economy, but those always ended in failure after a short time. In a few regional Czech archives I have managed to find records describing the family's residence on municipal territories in several central and northwestern regional districts. These records mostly contained detailed lists of names, often including personal details or even their Romani nicknames.

A report by the Ústí nad Labem KNV to the Interior Ministry described the presence of travelling Roms in Lovosice:

> Some 60 travelling gypsies were placed in this district in the spring. They lived in a camp together right in the town of Lovosice. Because they formed a single related unit (tribe), it was difficult to influence them in any way. In order to change their way of life, it was planned to disperse them so they would be placed in various municipalities as separate households. They were even offered detached houses.[584]

From the list of the "gypsies" in the archival records documenting the the "travelling gypsies'" stay in Lovosice, it transpires that some men, including five from the Stojka family, were employed there from 5 April 1952 on regulating the flow of the river Modla.[585] It is notable that the KNV, in the above-mentioned report, mentions "a single common tribe". As the report contains detailed lists of the Roms camping in Lovosice, we can see that in addition to the dozen or so people belonging to Anna Stojková's branch of the family,[586] over two dozen Roms belonging to other Lovara families from Topoľčany were temporarily resident there,[587] as was a 10-member Lovara family with roots in Pastuchov, Hlohovec district and other individuals with typical Vlax surnames from various

---

584 NA Praha, f. MV II Praha, k. 1283 – Report from KNV Ústí n.L., subject: Úprava poměrů osob cikánského původu (18. 2. 1953, č. j. II/3–215–28/1–1952).

585 SOkA Litoměřice/Lovosice, f. ONV Lovosice, NAD: 328, č. p. 104, i. č. 114, k. 100 – Občané cikánské národnosti 1951–1959 (no č. j.).

586 Above all Anna Stojková and her children, but also the two sons of Ján Stojka, in other words, the grandsons of Štefan Stojka, Sr., both with the first name Štefan (born 1923 and 1933).

587 In August 1952, the names of these Kotlár and Stojka families subsequently also appear in Říčany and Uhříněves, which means that these extended families appear to have lived together for a few months just on the basis of solidarity and a feeling of belonging to the Vlax Romani community. They may have also been related through marriage or through godfatherly relations and so forth.

places. On the basis of a comparison between the lists made during the war or during the First Republic and the genealogical details from all my data, we may infer that these were not close relatives, but probably Lovara from various family groups. Nevertheless, they were perceived by the authorities as a single, close-knit group.

Documents kept in the Lovosice branch of the state archives in Litoměřice provide a more detailed description of the time spent by the Roms in that "gypsy camp" by the Elbe. In addition to a description of all the "negative complications" that the report relates,[588] important facts emerge from it, such as that the Roms lived in a camp on the edge of the river Elbe in their covered wagons and let their horses graze on the adjacent meadows. The author of the report, a police commander, was trying to prevent such holding of horses, and he called on the MNV to prevent the Roms from being able to buy new ones.[589] This confirms that horse trading was still a source of sustenance for these Roms. There is also a unique find there, namely, portrait photos of these Roms taken in an office, probably the MNV or ONV building. At any rate, the photos were taken by officials for the purposes of issuing temporary "gypsy identity cards" to these Roms so that the ONV in Lovosice would have a better record of them. The identity cards were made from cardboard or were printed on the reverse side of the holder's dental records (see Fig. 16). They had a photograph stuck to them and the name and personal details of the "gypsy", his or her minor children's names, and a statement that the identity card served to prove identity in the Lovosice district. The cards had the ONV stamp and the signature of its chair. Of course, such cards did not have any legal validity and were clearly meant to serve as a tool not just to register, but also to intimidate the Roms.

Seemingly the first Romani person to be removed from Lovosice at the end of May 1952 was Anna's brother-in-law Josef (Jouško, born 1924) who at the decision of the ONV was taken to the Louny district where he was to be found employment. His wife and two children were meant to relocate there with him in a moving van.[590] The other Roms remained in the camp by the Elbe. At the beginning of July, the MNV in Lovosice

---

588 Above all the destruction of trees on the riverbank by cutting them down for firewood, a permanent water leak from a damaged pipe, and a problem with waste and toilets.

589 SOkA Litoměřice/Lovosice, f. ONV Lovosice, NAD: 328, č. p. 104, i. č. 114, k. 100 – Občané cikánské národnosti 1951–1959, Report from SNVB – velitelství stanice Lovosice, Subject: Cikánský tábor u Labe – závady (5. 7. 1952, č. j. 1666/195).

590 SOkA Litoměřice/Lovosice, f. ONV Lovosice, NAD: 328, č. p. 104, i. č. 114, k. 100 – Občané cikánské národnosti 1951–1959, report from ONV Louny (26. 5. 1952, č. j. III/3–463–26.5.1952-Za).

asked the ONV to disperse the remaining Roms among several municipalities.[591] The archives do not reveal why this plan was never undertaken. All of the archival records of Roms from the camp by the Labe bear just a handwritten note stating: "The gypsies left", and a report from the KNV states that in August [1952] they moved to Říčany.[592]

Light is thrown on their further trajectories by records in the archive for Přemyšlení, in the current district of Praha-východ (Prague-East). This contains a report to the KNV in Prague 16 describing the arrival of the above-mentioned group of "travelling "Roms in the (former) district of Říčany:

> During 1952, a large group of gypsies with their families and covered wagons came in August to this district from the districts of Lovosice and Teplice. Just four families (eight workers) were given permission by this district to enter, but the Lovosice district had given permission to 192 persons. Another group of gypsies from Teplice numbering 59 persons, also with covered wagons and families, came in search of this group from Lovosice. [...the ONV] did everything it could to place these families... either on state farms [or] in brickworks and factories.[593]

I have managed to collect a certain amount of information on the group that was transferred to the Říčany district from Teplice. Initially 16 "travelling gypsies" were sent to Teplice, where they were accommodated in their wagons on the BRAMSCH site which was the regular site of Circus Humberto, apart from anything else. Their number later grew with the arrival of their "large extended families" who, both with and without the permission of the ONV, had apparently settled at the same campsite, bringing the total number of people to 120. Later this apparently fell to 60 again. Because of the planned arrival of Circus Humberto in mid-July 1952, the authorities considered it necessary to "eject the travelling gypsies from the campsite",[594] solving the issue by moving them to Říčany. Another group that, judging by the surnames, consisted exclusively of

---

591 Ibid. Report from MNV Lovosice for ONV: občané cikánské národnosti: rozmístění (5. 7. 1952, č. j. 1565/1952).

592 NA Praha, f. MV II Praha, k. 1283 – report from KNV Ústí n. L.: Úprava poměrů osob cikánského původu (18. 2. 1953, č. j. II/3–215–28/1–1952).

593 SOkA Přemyšlení, f. ONV Říčany, i. č. 1440, sign. 257 – Zpráva referátu pro vnitřní věci pro KNV Praha XVI, Výnos min. vnitra –, Úprava poměrů cikánského původu (6. 1. 1953, zn. II/3–215).

594 SOkA Teplice, f. ONV Teplice, sign. 257, i. č. 984, k. 246 – Zpráva MNV v Teplicích pro ONV Teplice: Úprava poměrů osob cikánského původu (24. 6. 1952, č. j. III-215–52/P).

Lovara and numbered more than 200 people was also present there at the same time. According to the records, in the period from 11 to 31 August 1952 this group was divided between Uhříněves and Říčany. On the list of the 48 Roms accommodated in Uhříněves, we find the names of several families from the extended Stojka family: Anna Stojková, her two sons Bobko and Janino, and their families and minor children. In addition, those accommodated included the family of Juraj Horvát and Barbora, née Stojková, and their six (by that time mostly adult) children, with two of those children's partners, so in all a total of 10 people. All the men from the family who were capable of work started at the OCELANA state enterprise. However, this numerous group of Lovara did not stay long in Říčany and Uhříněves. As the report says, "...on their own decision and without the knowledge of the ONV they left on 31 August 1952 for, they stated, the district of Ústí nad Labem, where they apparently had work and accommodation arranged."

It is not clear where exactly these Lovara families lived over the next few years. The fragmentary information that we have relates just to the Stojka-Horvát family. In September 1952, Kuluš gave birth to a son in Radotín, which at that time was an independent municipality to the south of Prague. However, it is not clear how long the family spent there. A record in the archives in Mělník states that in early December 1952, the families of the sisters Barbora and Kuluš Horvát, together with their children, were in Kralupy nad Vltavou, where their husbands, the brothers Juraj and Antonín Horvát, were taken into custody. Their group numbered 18 people and the MNV first of all dealt with the necessity of finding employment for the able-bodied members. Besides the nuclear families of the two sisters, others there were Štefan Stojka, Sr.'s son Ján Stojka, born 1905, and Ján's son Štefan Stojka (*1923) with his wife and daughter.[595] After several days, however, the proposals of the authorities changed. In later documents there is talk of transferring the "gypsy" group to the neighbouring districts of Slaný and Mělník. This apparently took place with the aid of the police. The report ends with a decision to "receive unproblematic gypsy groups".[596]

---

595 SOkA Mělník, f. ONV Kralupy nad Vltavou, sign. 967, i. č. 215, k. 462 – Přemístění cikánské tlupy – report from 10. 12. 1952 and Seznam osob cikánského původu převedených z ONV v Kralupech n. Vlt. na ONV v Mělníku za účelem trvalého usídlení v tamním okrese a zařazení do trvalého pracovního poměru, sestavený OO-VB v Kralupech pro ONV – bezpečnostní referát Kralupy n. Vlt. (8. 12. 1952, no č. j).

596 Ibid.

Another unique trace of the Stojka family's presence is the appearance of siblings Jaroslav [597] (*1937) and Něguš Stojka[598] (*1941) on the list of the children forcibly taken from Litovel on "holiday" to Jeseník and then put in a children's home in July 1953 as part of the operation I described above. It seems that before the Litovel operation they had been with their mother, Grófa Stojková, and maybe also with their father, Josef Lakatoš, and with other siblings whom I did not manage to identify on that list.

The second half of the 1950s in the Louny and Žatec districts

Where the two extended families spent time before the first of them was registered as resident in Louny and in Žatec in the winter of 1957 to 1958 is something I have not been able to discover. According to the witness Berci Stojka, in the mid-1950s the Stojka family lived mostly in the districts of Žatec and Louny and in the nearby surroundings. He stated: "At that time we were still travelling with horses and wagons, mainly in the area around Žatec and Louny. I remember how at one market we camped by the river in Žatec, not far from the station, with our horses and wagons." His testimony is confirmed by the above-mentioned birthdates and birthplaces of his branch of the family.

Also present in these districts at the same time was the family of Štefan Stojka, Sr.'s grandson, also named Štefan (*1919), nicknamed Turko, whose own grandson, nicknamed Báno, said:

> In the 1950s we travelled. My family, at least my grandfather, spent most of the time in the Žatec region. Žatec, Louny, and around there. They travelled with horses and – I'll be honest – stole hens. They stole hens and tried to survive somehow. They were very good with kettles, though. They did the kettles in bakeries, or when butchers needed a tub, they'd tin it. My granddad was good with metal, he wasn't an actual kettle-maker, they were made by Roms from Poland, but he knew how to do it. In 1956 or 1955 they ended up in Roudnice, where they had to stop.[599]

---

597 ZA v Opavě – pob. Olomouc, f. KNV Olomouc. Národnostní politika sign. 608, i. č. 1745, k. 1029, 1951–1958. Zpráva ONV v Litovli, zn. III-215–3/7–1953 (3. 7. 1953). Osoby cikánského poměru – zatčení rodičů a zajištění dětí, fol. 646.

598 Ibid. ONV v Litovli – Individuální seznam o rozmístění cikánů, při provedení dne 3. 7. 1953, dle pokynů Min. nár. bezpečnosti (3. 7. 1953, č. j. III-215–30).

599 Personal recording of 'Báno' Bihary (1958) made by Pavel Kubaník on 3 October 2008 in Roudnice ad Labem, Czech Republic.

That the family of Štefan Stojka (Turko) lived in Roudnice nad Labem in the Slavín area at the end of the 1950s is also confirmed by archival reports and records for that area which were made when travelling and semi-travelling persons were being registered by the town of Roudnice.[600]

According to Berci's memories, that period at the start of the 1950s was very difficult for travelling Roms. They were forever encountering hostile reactions from the surrounding population and checks and pressure from the state authorities.

> The time after the war was bad. We travelled round the Czech lands and the non-Roms chased us out everywhere. When they saw us, they'd shout: 'Jews, gypsies, out! Go away! We'll send Hitler for you again!' They chased us out everywhere. They'd say to us: 'Gypsies, pack your bags and leave.' They wouldn't let us camp in one place even for a couple of weeks. The police would come and say: 'The locals are afraid you'll steal from them, that you'll kill their children and eat them. You have to leave.' But where we were supposed to go? We often had to sleep in the woods.

He also described repeated police raids and cases of being ejected from municipalities under police escort, which were said to happen in the mid-1950s in the Žatec and Louny districts:

> As I remember, the police checked us pretty often. Once, in the summer, it was very hot and we children were running around outside the wagon half-naked. Several police cars drove up and blocked our way. They said we'd beaten and robbed a non-Rom, but it wasn't true. 'Where is he? Let him say that it was us,' the Roms wanted to know. The police didn't answer. They'd just made it up as an excuse to bother us. They threw all our pots, clothes and other things in a ditch next to the road. They threw everything around and drove off. It was just bullying, nothing more. That sort of check was no exception. Other times the police would stop my Uncle Janino and take the gold that was our family inheritance, saying it was stolen. He couldn't do anything about it. That's how it was under the communists.[601]

We have to take into account that in the Louny and Žatec districts, where both parts of the Stojka (and Horvát) families were present during the 1950s, large groups of them must have been fairly noticeable, and so

---

600 SOkA Litoměřice/ Lovosice, f. ONV Roudnice n. L., k. 61.
601 Personal recording of Berci (*1949) by the author, made on 18 December 2018 in Louny, Czech Republic.

they must have soon found themselves in the sights of the security forces and the local and district authorities who started to take steps, first to limit their travelling, and later to settle them.

Roms from Slovakia started to arrive in both districts after the war,[602] and as in other parts of the Czech lands, predominantly labour migrants from the "Slovak Roms" sub-ethnic group went there from various regions of Slovakia. They headed there looking for work in factories, on building sites, or on state and cooperative farms. The above-mentioned "Register of all Gypsy vagabonds and other workshy vagabonds who live a gypsy lifestyle", carried out in August 1947, had recorded 1,166 persons in the Ústí Region. The precise number of Roms living in 1947 in the present-day district of Louny (in those days divided into two independent districts, Louny and Žatec) is not known. According to a police record I found, in October 1947 there were just two Romani families living in Louny.[603] In a report by the KNV of 18 September 1951, there were 82 people labelled as "gypsies" in the Louny district, 73 in the town of Louny and another 117 in the Žatec district.[604] The number of Roms there grew during the 1950s and by the decade's end was twice or three times as high.

The archival records indicate that the spatial mobility of Roms was gradually limited and rendered difficult over the course of the 1950s. Although there were several Lovara families moving about the two districts in the early 1950s, in the period that preceded their register under Act no. 74/1958 the two families, with a total number of approximately 60 members, were more or less the only "travelling gypsies". In the Louny district in particular, however, there were also several dozen people with "travelling livelihoods", who were not ethnic Roms but who might have been given the label of "travelling gypsies" by the authorities and were above all showmen. With the exception of these two families, the only other Lovara to appear in the district were individuals or nuclear families, for example, the Stojka and Bihary families who settled in Roudnice in

---

602 SOkA Louny, f. OÚ Louny, NAD 77, k. 509.

Before the Second World War, the Romani families present in Louny had the surnames Růžička, Vrba, Florián, Serynek or Kovář. They performed various itinerant professions, such as horse trading, repairing umbrellas, the manufacture and sale of slippers and wire work. (SOkA Louny, OÚ Louny I). Most seem to have been transported to what was called the "Gypsy Camp" in Lety u Písku and from there probably to Auschwitz. Their names are no longer found on postwar lists of the Romani population, so their history in this locality seems to have ended.

603 SOkA Louny, f. OÚ Louny I, NAD 77, k. 509 – Zpráva: Subject: Výsledek soupisu cikánů, Zvýšení zdravotního dozoru (4. 3. 1948).

604 NA Praha, f. MV II Praha – 850/0/ 3 MV II-D, kk 1283.

the second half of the 1950s but were only distant relatives of the family I am following.

The witness Berci Stojka (*1949) recalled that in the mid-1950s the family still had no fixed address:

> When I was five or six, I still used to run behind the wagon. My granny bought me a little colt, I called him Fricko. I still have a reminder of him, a big scar on my chin, because he hurt my face. He kicked me by mistake. He was grazing in a meadow and my granny said: 'Berci, go and get your horse.' I went to get him, I cracked the whip at him and said: 'Fricko, go home!' He just kicked his leg and split my face in half. They took me to the hospital in Louny. The police came for my family straight away and drove us off the meadow. We had to go somewhere into the woods where they couldn't see us.[605]

Forced settlement in the old brickworks in Louny and near the river in Žatec

By the second half of 1957 or early 1958 at the latest, the forced settlement of both family segments probably occurred. The families of the sisters Kuluš and Barbora Horvátová, née Stojková, and their husbands had to halt their wagons in Žatec on the banks of the Ohře river, in a place called Ostrov,[606] where Roms had camped repeatedly in the past. Unfortunately, we do not have the precise date of their possible settlement in Žatec.

As we know from the memories of witness Berci Stojka, the last place where the extended family of Anna Stojková lived before settling in Louny was also at the campsite by the river Ohře in Žatec. From there, it seems, the family set out on a journey during which the Roms were forced to head for the old brickworks in Louny and to park there permanently. When exactly Anna's maybe 30-member family reached Louny and was forcibly settled is something that the witness cannot remember. He just stated that: "Not long after I was kicked by my horse, they settled us in Louny." However, he describes the circumstances in detail:

> They put us with our wagons into a sort of gulley next to the barracks in Louny. Outside the town. There used to be a brickworks there. There were soldiers right next to us. They were always training and running about and

---

605 Personal recording of Berci (*1949) by the author, made on 18 December 2018 in Louny, Czech Republic.

606 *Ostrov* means "island" in Czech. It probably reflected the character of the place near the river.

firing guns. To begin with we were terrified that they'd shoot us too, throw a bomb at us. We stayed in that place several years. We were there for at least five or six years.[607]

According to this witness's memories, their settlement in the ruined brickworks clearly took place on the basis of an order from above, in other words, from the local or district authorities, probably also with the help of the security forces, and it was perceived by the Roms as something with which they complied involuntarily, to which they had to submit. I have not been able to find in the official records the precise date when the group was settled in the old brickworks, nor have I found any decision by the MNV to accommodate them there, a plan that was surely perceived initially as temporary.

Both branches of the family were from that moment on forced to remain in those two selected places, in Louny and Žatec. However, there was a fundamental difference between the localities on the bank of the Ohře and the old brickworks in Louny. While the area by the river Ohře in Žatec was a natural campsite, close to the water and in a place where Roms had been accustomed to park their wagons in previous years, the brickworks in Louny was an unused building in an abandoned industrial zone at the end of the town, one in which, as I shall show below, it was entirely unsuitable for these families to live. Apart from the extended Stojka family there was no one else living there except for the soldiers in the neighbouring barracks. Placing the Roms in their vicinity may be perceived as a tool of repression, aiming once again to control and intimidate the Roms, who were uniformly perceived by all as a security threat.

The Roms in Louny were far from being the only "travelling gypsies" during this time who were accommodated in a brickworks or similar building. Zapletal describes in his article attempts to put Roms in brickworks, gravel pits and stone quarries as part of the central state authorities' policy in the post-war period, the aim of which was partly to tie Roms down to permanent employment and partly to provide labour for these sites while limiting the Roms' travelling way of life.[608] In the case of Louny, however, the situation was different because the brickworks were no longer operational and therefore provided no employment which might have justified the Roms' being accommodated in a building otherwise not at all adapted for residency. The reports from the MNV or

---

607 Personal recording of Berci (*1949) by the author, made on 18 December 2018 in Louny, Czech Republic.
608 Zapletal, "Přístup totalitního státu", 23–24.

the "gypsy committees" in subsequent years confirm what Berci Stojka said: In the old brickworks there was no electricity to begin with and no accessible water or sanitary facilities the whole time they lived there. From the applications for permanent residency in the Louny archives[609] provided to me by the Louny municipal authority's department for the registration of residents, it is possible to partly reconstruct when persons with the surname Stojka were registered as resident at the address of the brickworks at 5. května Road, no. 449. The first to register at that address on 5 December 1957 was M. Stojka, Anna Stojková's son, followed on 18 December 1957 by Josef Stojka (Jouško), the son of Zaga Stojková, so Anna's brother-in-law a generation younger, who had already lived in Louny with the agreement of the ONV in 1952. Another seven adults from the extended Stojka family registered on various dates from 2 to 16 January 1958. They included Anna Stojková, her daughter-in-law R. and her daughter J. Stojková. More family members registered at the address of the brickworks during 1958: In February, Anna's son E. and in May her daughter A., while in December another Stojka family registered at the address whose relationship to the Stojka family in question I have not been able to identify. They were immediately sent, just before Christmas 1958, by the ONV to the district of Dobruška without any forewarning and to the considerable disgruntlement of the latter district.[610] They did not return to Louny.

If we ignore this last event, all the above-mentioned adult persons (a total of 12) were officially registered as living at the address of the old brickworks even before the register of travelling and semi-travelling persons was created, most for more than a year before that event. Given that only the adults were registered as resident, it may be assumed that they formed a group at least twice as large with their children. It is not clear for how long they had been living in the brickworks in their covered wagons before they were officially registered as resident, but we may assume that most of the family was moved there before December 1957. It is highly likely that the Roms were registered after they had been living there for some time. We may also observe such an approach in the case of the two adults from this family who officially registered as residents (again, probably with their nuclear families) later, in April and May 1959.

---

609 SOkA Louny, f. MěNV Louny, č. p. 338, i. č. 100, k. 10, subject: Evidence obyvatelstva cikánské národnosti v Lounech (1959–1969).

610 Zápis ze stálé schůze KNV Hradec Králové pro převýchovu cikánského obyvatelstva (7. 1. 1959). SOA Hradec Králové, AO Zámrsk, f. KNV Hradec Králové 1949–1960, k. 93 – Stálá komise pro převýchovu cikánů – zápisy ze šetření 1956–1960.

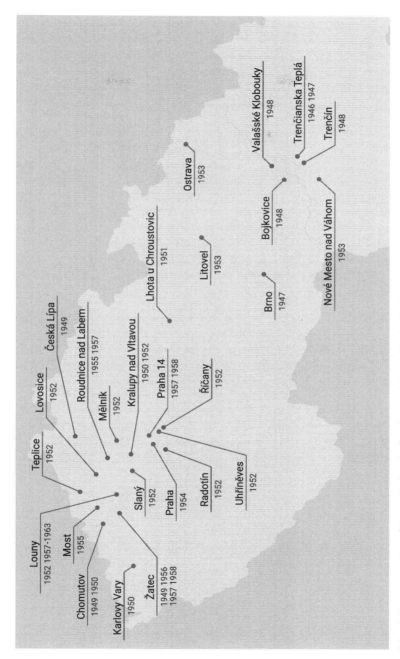

Map 4: Reconstruction of Anna Stojková's family spatial mobility in the late 1940s and in the 1950s.

According to the lists, both families had been living in covered wagons there in February 1959 when the register of travelling persons was made, and one had been demonstrably living there when the register was being prepared in January 1958. This suggests that their actual residency preceded their registering for residence with the MNV by several months. The witness Berci Stojka has described life in the brickworks:

> There were eight of our wagons, eight families, in the gulley by the barracks, but we were all related, one big family. To start with we had our horses there. There was no water there at all. They left us there like that without taking care of anything. They didn't give us anything, we didn't have anything. Luckily, one kind man who lived a little way away let us go to the well in his garden for water. We carried it from there for cooking and washing, there was no stream or any other water. I went to school in Louny, it was about five kilometres there and five back, on foot every day. My granny built a chicken coop next to the wagon and kept hens in it so that we'd have eggs. We were very poor. In time the soldiers started to talk to us, some came to visit us and they'd bring us food, tins. We were terribly hungry.[611]

I managed to find in an online publication some memories of the "travelling gypsies" who lived in the old brickworks in Louny as described by one of the soldiers who at that time was serving in the adjacent barracks. His testimony confirms the harsh living conditions and overall pauperisation of the Roms who lived in the brickworks:

> I served there from 1958 to 1960. Just beyond the fence of the barracks in the Chlum direction were the remains of an old brickworks, and some travelling gypsies wintered in it. The young gypsy women were hungry, and for bread and cheese they would perform for us an experience that was entirely new to us – striptease.[612]

It should be added that rather than a "striptease", this interaction involved the women unveiling their body parts while simultaneously cursing or scorning the person watching them, a traditional Lovara practice that the soldiers misinterpreted. Otherwise the memory entirely confirms the inhumane conditions and poverty the Roms were subjected to in the place of their enforced settlement.

---

611 Personal recording of Berci (*1949) by the author, made on 18 December 2018 in Louny, Czech Republic.

612 Memories of former soldier Jaroslav Gregor, "Mladé cikánky tančily, stromy se v zimě barvily na zeleno", 31 December 2020, online periodical Zblízka.cz.

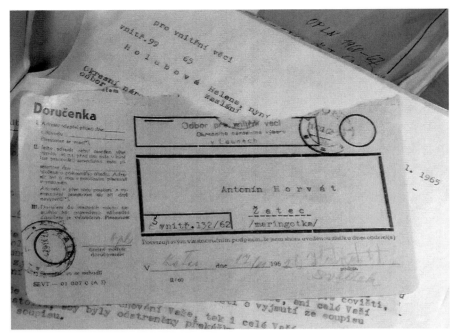

Postal delivery note – a rejection of a request for removal from the register of travelling and semi-travelling persons, autumn 1962. The address is given simply as: Caravan, Žatec.

Part 6: The implementation of the law on the permanent settlement of travelling persons and its impact

6.1 The drafting of Act no. 74/1958 at the central level

Anna Stojková's family was one of those for whom the state authorities planned and subsequently implemented their forced sedentarisation. Before I describe the implementation of this law on the local level, I should like to mention the procedures at the central level which preceded the drafting and execution of this legislation to permanently settle "travelling persons". Historical analyses show that throughout the 1950s, the central state authorities and security bodies called for nationwide restrictive measures to limit travelling by groups of Roms who were still not settled[613] and to enable the elimination of their mobility. In a study based on analysis of the security service archives, the historian Zapletal has looked in detail at the measures created by the Interior Ministry during the 1950s with the aim of ending the "travelling way of life".[614]

In spring 1958, the drafting of the law to permanently settle "travelling persons" was taken over from the Interior Ministry by the Central Committee of the Communist Party of Czechoslovakia. On 26 March that same year it distributed a draft of the new law for comments. According to Zapletal, the law represented a departure from the Interior Ministry's previous concept, which had taken into account the structure of Romani society, their customs, and Romani specifics as possible causes of their current state. In comparison, the proposal put forward by the Central Committee of the Communist Party explained the whole problem in terms of repression by the previous regimes' ruling classes and,

---

613 Spurný, "Pokus o převýchovu", 14.
614 Zapletal, "Přístup totalitního státu".

as the sole crucial distinction between Roms, divided them into three groups: "settled", "semi-travelling" and "travelling".[615] This division was also central to the final version of Act no. 74/1958, "on the permanent settlement of travelling persons", passed by the National Assembly on 17 October 1958 and published on 11 November 1958. The law made it compulsory for MNVs to provide help to travelling persons during their transition to a settled way of life and banned such persons from continuing to travel under the threat of criminal sanctions, according to Section 3. The date of 3–6 February 1959 was set to register "travelling and semi-travelling" persons.[616] Before the law was passed, an order at the central level had been issued for a preliminary list to be made of all "travelling and semi-travelling" persons. This was carried out mostly by the police and summarised by the regional security administration. In addition to the overall number of "travelling and semi-travelling" persons, it also recorded their ages and the means of transport they used, as well as recording the holders of trade licences separately (at that time mostly showmen). In her work, Pavelčíková looks how that preliminary list differed considerably from the final one of early February 1959, both with regard to the methodology used and the resulting numbers. The preliminary list found 46,016 "travelling and semi-travelling" persons in Czechoslovakia, of whom the vast majority (42,672) were included in the category of "semi-travelling" and just 1,686 were recorded as "travelling" (of whom 615 lived in Slovakia and 1,071 in the Czech lands). Those were exaggeratedly low figures, according to Pavelčíková.[617] The preliminary list also found, republic-wide, a total of 154 horses, 585 wagons and 296 towing vehicles or tractors designed to move wagons,[618] which suggests a much greater number of "travelling persons". Many families who lived in their covered wagons or caravans were no longer mobile, however, and had their wagons parked at their place of work, for example. They may thus have been understood by the state authorities as belonging to the category of "semi-travelling". This, indeed, was the case in Louny, where some people from the Stojka family were described on the list as "semi-travelling" and some as "travelling".[619] The larger num-

---

615 Ibid., 41–42.

616 Jurová, "Niektoré aspekty",14

617 Pavelčíková, *Romové v českých zemích,* 67–69. From my perspective, the number of "travelling persons" living in Slovakia especially is vastly underestimated.

618 Ibid., 68.

619 SOkA Louny, f. ONV Louny II, vnitř. 608, k. 332 – undated document from January 1959 entitled "Souhrnný arch – soupis cikánů", issued separately for each family (no č. j.)

ber of wagons than horses (and towing vehicles) indicates that for many families the seizure or purchase of their horses had happened before Act no. 74/1958 was implemented.

On the territory of the Ústí Region, the preliminary list recorded 340 "travelling" people who owned a total of 25 wagons, cars or tractors and 13 horses, as well as 6,657 "semi-travelling" persons.[620] The number of horses for the Ústí Region was clearly once again underestimated because it corresponded approximately to the number of horses which, according to witnesses, were owned just by the Lovara settled in Louny and Žatec. The number of wagons was clearly also underestimated. As we know, wagons and caravans were also owned and operated by more than two dozen showmen families from the Louny area alone, so here, too, the number would seem to correspond more to the figures for one or two districts, not to the whole of the Ústí Region.

The categories of "travelling", "semi-travelling" and "settled" in Act no. 74/1958

Act no. 74/1958 used only the category of "travelling persons", the permanent settlement of whom was aimed at in its very title. Section 2 then defined what was understood by this category: "A travelling way of life is led by one who, in groups or individually, wanders from place to place and avoids honest work or earns a living in a dishonest way, even if he is registered as permanently resident in a particular municipality."

The law was purposefully free of references to ethnicity, and "travelling" was defined in it as a "way of life". This was Communist Party official policy, which was to avoid a discriminatory focus just on ethnic Roms in the law. However, there was a different concept of the target categories in the secret instructions which were issued by the Interior Ministry and sent to the MNVs for the purpose of implementing the law. In those, three categories were used: "semi-travelling", "travelling" and "settled". Citizens of "gypsy origin" were to be classified into these three categories. The fact that these categories were defined in a controversial way, which allowed the MNVs a free hand in placing people on the register, has been looked at by several researchers.[621] Pavelčíková has pointed out that at the local level, officials tended to understand the categories

---

620 Pavelčíková, *Romové v českých zemích,* 68.
621 Pavelčíková, *Romové v českých zemích*; Jurová, "Niektoré aspekty"; Slačka, "Usazení kočovníků".

of "travelling" and "semi-travelling" in very different ways,[622] meaning that the practice of the local register committees varied greatly. In some municipalities, "local officials clearly did not understand the accompanying instructions at all and listed the entire Romani population that had been living there uninterruptedly since 1945", which in South Moravia had even older roots.[623] In many districts the authorities included among the "travelling persons" not just Roms who travelled across the regions in covered wagons, but also those who had set out from Slovakia in search of better housing and work in response to the calls from Czech recruiters, or sometimes just to visit their families.[624]

Donert, too, reached the conclusion that Act no. 74/1958 forcibly settled not just the not very large group of travelling Roms, but also affected the much greater number of Romani migrant labourers.[625] Personally, I believe that by far its greatest impact was on Slovak Roms who were migrant labourers. The percentage of Roms who really were moving around in the Czech lands when the register was made was very low. As is illustrated by the trajectories of the Stojka family and other families whom I described in the previous section, throughout the 1950s and above all in the period before the register, extreme pressure was put on non-territorially anchored, freely-moving persons to start living in just one place and to become integrated into the labour process. By now it was almost impossible to keep living on the road, and a number of Roms, including Lovara, voluntarily found work and accommodation. Some of them were then no longer even included in the lists either of "travelling" or "semi-travelling" persons,[626] and others were forcibly sedentarised during that time through the application of different measures by the state authorities. By the end of the 1950s, the sub-ethnic Lovara group's mobility is therefore fairly theoretical and is more likely to have concerned individuals and nuclear families who were not too large or visible. Compared to the received notions, therefore, the register brought to a halt only a minimum of Lovara or other Romani families.

---

622 According to Pavelčíková, this category – in line with the accompanying guidelines described above – was meant to include primarily those families and individuals who were still "commuting" between Slovakia and Czech regions or towns and who were unable to find a permanent home or employment anywhere (Pavelčíková, *Romové v českých zemích,* 73).

623 Ibid., 74–75.

624 Slačka, "Usazení kočovníků", 59.

625 Donert, *The Rights,* 141.

626 For example, Viktor Salinas, who at that time worked with other Roms from Dolná Seč in Karosa, Vysoké Mýto (Eastern Bohemia), said that because they were good workers they were not put on the register (Hajská, "O trajo", 155, 157).

In her monograph devoted to the history and current situation of the Roms, *Cesty Romů / Romano Drom 1945–1990* [The Paths of the Roms / *Romano Drom* 1945–1990] Davidová presents the register of "travelling and semi-travelling" persons vividly as a fundamental milestone that forced mainly Vlax Roms to settle overnight and abandon their traditional way of life:

> Until February 1959, therefore, the Romani travelling wagons – *vurdona* – and caravans, pulled by horses, cars or small tractors – travelled our [Czechoslovak] roads. On the cold night of 3–4 February 1959, Romani families were visited by census-takers who woke up adults and children and listed all those present. In whatever village or town the Roms happened to be present that night, that village then had to 'take care' of them as their 'home municipality' the next day. [...] The wheels were taken off carts using force, and the horses were usually taken away to be sold. The Vlax Roms understandably tried to prevent this the most, since the horse had always been their great friend and helper. It was a raid that violently changed a way of life that had gone on for centuries, and that interfered in the personal freedoms of these people.[627]

The description that Davidová gives, of course, took place just hypothetically in such a form. In reality, it rather summarises into one moment the measures against "travelling gypsies" which had been happening in practice throughout the 1950s. When recording memories of this period among Lovara, even after intensive searching I did not find a single witness who remembered being registered as Davidová describes it in this extract. I did not find anyone who had experienced the wheels being removed from the family's wagon by force on the day of the register, or who had experienced the police or MNV officials forcibly halting them at a random place in their journey and ordering them to settle in that same place.

This same excerpt of Davidová's work has also been criticised by the researcher Rastislav Pivoň, who points out that her description of the register as a night raid by census-takers on the dwellings of travelling Roms is invented, of course, and that it did not happen that way at all, at the campsites, but was done by summoning those who were to be registered to visit the MNV or another official place where they would turn up in person, with very few exceptions voluntarily, and often with

---

627 Davidová, *Romano drom*, 198.

optimistic expectations.[628] In February 1959, not even the Lovara settled in Pečky near Kolín were still travelling, but it is they who are depicted in Eva Davidová's impressive photographs in the above-mentioned publication accompanying her description of the register and its impact on Vlax Roms. According to archival sources, some five Romani families had already come to Pečky in April 1958 (according to their names they were Lovara, totalling 40 people). They were subsequently forced to park their two caravans and several open carts (described by local officials as "unbelievably rickety") on an area of land by the Izola factory. In June 1958, the MNV asked the ONV to provide railway cars that had been taken out of service, and the Roms were moved into those that year.[629] The register in February found them in Pečky, living in those railway wagons, which were raised off the ground on concrete blocks.

The low number of actually "travelling" people when the register began is also confirmed by a table stating the results of the register under Act no. 74/1958 for the Ústí nad Labem Region, created as an appendix of a report to the Interior Ministry in April 1959. According to this table, the register contained a total of 1,302 people over 15 and 1,611 children aged 15 and under in the Ústí nad Labem Region. In that region, covering 14 districts, just 22 families were listed as "living in wagons", of whom four families were in Louny, five in Žatec, five in Litoměřice, three in Roudnice nad Labem, one in Teplice, three in Most and four in the city of Ústí nad Labem. As we know, however, the Roms in Žatec and Louny had already been forcibly settled by the time the register was made. The families had to stay in one place, living in their wagons under a strict ban on travelling anywhere in them.

The situation was similar for another part of the Stojka family, descendants of Ján Stojka, who, before the register, had already been accommodated in Roudnice nad Labem at Slavín, where various Romani families were crowded into unsuitable spaces. In Litoměřice, in three cases those listed were showmen (non-Roms) who did not have a licence to operate their attractions or to do blade-sharpening.[630] For the other districts I have not managed to find out who was listed in the category of families living in wagons, but clearly they were not Lovara families, as such names are missing from the lists here. They may have been

---

628 Pivoň, "Zákon č. 74", 79.

629 SOkA Nymburk/ Lysá n. L., f. ONV Poděbrady, MH b15 – report from MNV, subject Zajištění ubytování cikánů v Pečkách (17. 6. 1958, č. j. 2297/58 vnitř.).

630 SOA Litoměřice, f. SKNV, odbor vnitřních věcí, zn. 608, V-10 Soupis kočujících Cikánů 1959–1965 – report from KNV Ústí n.L. for MV ČR (17. 4. 1959, č. j. vnitř. 587/59).

showmen. At any rate, in the Ústí Region it is probable that no case of wagons being forced to halt and have their wheels removed took place as described by Davidová.

As I have mentioned several times, in addition to ethnic Roms who were included by the state authorities in the category of "travelling and semi-travelling" people, Act no. 74/1958 also affected a significant number of showmen (*světští*) who at that time performed their professions itinerantly. Of 46,500 people who in February 1959 were entered in the register of "travelling and semi-travelling" persons in Czechoslovakia, 3,034 of them were listed as showmen. A significant proportion, 2,620 people, were listed in the Czech lands.[631] The showmen group in the Czech lands thus formed a relatively significant share (14%) of the 18,564 persons[632] whom the register found in the Czech lands. The remainder undoubtedly consisted of ethnic Roms. As I shall show further, in the Louny district in particular there was a very high proportion of showmen on the register. It was usual to include in this category during this period those who performed various categories of itinerant trades as well as the operators of merry-go-rounds, circuses, shooting ranges, swingboats and other amusements, some of whom had licenses for such activities, while others (by then already the majority) did not.

6.2 The preparation of the register in Louny

Preparatory work on the register in the Ústí nad Labem Region had been going on since mid-1958, and by mid-September 1958 the preliminary lists of people proposed for the register had to be made, although they continued to be made more precise until the register itself. However, the preparation of the lists was one way this republic-wide operation was readied.

On 4 December 1958, the KNV in Ústí nad Labem sent all the relevant departments in the MNVs subordinate to it the "Instructions for the implementation of Act no. 74/1958", calling on the MNVs to immediately contact the local police chiefs, who were supposed to already have the preliminary lists of "travelling and semi-travelling" persons drawn up in the summer of 1958. The MNVs were tasked with making those preliminary lists more precise so that they could serve as the basis for

---

631 Pavelčíková, *Romové v českých zemích*, 71–72.
632 Ibid.

the register.[633] The KNV's communiqué included a sample list and also proposed instructions for implementing Act no. 74/1958, pointing out that in previous materials, the concepts of "travelling" and "semi-travelling" had in most cases been interpreted too broadly and that these concepts had to be more clearly defined, therefore. The "most important question" in the proposed instructions was described as that of "how to assess showmen" versus "how to assess gypsy persons". The "gypsy persons" were divided into "permanently settled", "semi-travelling" and "travelling". Despite this attempt to clearly differentiate between the various categories, the instructions also underline the need to take an individual approach, based on local administrations' experiences.[634] A wide variety of implementations in practice and understandings ultimately accompanied the execution of the law as a whole due to this non-uniform interpretation. From the drafting phase of the law we have several varied and differently-conceived lists of the persons who were to be registered. The ONV in Louny issued its "District overview of the number of travelling and semi-travelling persons and list of names as of 10 July 1958", in which it stated that in the town of Louny there were 164 "travelling and semi-travelling" persons, of whom 88 were children. There were 20 "travelling" and 144 "semi-travelling" persons. In the Louny district in its entirety there were 296 persons designated for the register, 24 labelled as travelling (of these, 20 were in Louny town, while four travelling persons were recorded in the village of Vrbno nad Lesy). From these records, it appears that the authorities did not include in the category of "travelling persons" in this district the numerous showmen families who engaged in itinerant professions, but just those who were believed to be "travelling gypsies".[635] The 20 travelling people counted in Louny town broadly corresponds to the size of the Stojka family who at that time were settled in the old brickworks, and their family can very probably be recognised as represented by this number.

According to the instructions issued by the North Bohemian regional administration (SKNV) just before the register was undertaken in January 1959, the interior affairs departments of the local administrations and police bodies were to perform a final check of the persons designated

---

633 SOkA Louny, f. ONV Louny II, k. 332 – Report from ONV Louny: Provádění soupisu osob kočujících a polokočujících (10. 2. 1959).

634 Ibid. Report from KNV Ústí n. L. Provedení zákona č. 74/1958 Sb. o trvalém usídlení kočujících a polokočujících osob (4. 12. 1958).

635 SOkA Louny, f. ONV Louny II, vnitř. 608, k. 332 – Organizační opatření k provedení soupisu kočujících a polokočujících osob v okrese Louny (January 1959).

in the preliminary lists for register, with a number of functionaries and bodies taking part: members of the police, MNVs, street committees, women's committees, building administrations, local security committees, committees for the "reeducation of persons of gypsy origin" and others.[636] A report from the SKNV shows that these fact-finding missions differed in form, but that most frequently the officials of all the bodies involved visited the dwellings of "gypsy families and other citizens who come into consideration" during which, according to the report, they gained much experience regarding their way of life . The most active were the members of the police, who were said to have the best knowledge of these people.

The "List of semi-travelling persons in the district of Louny of January 1959"[637] has 444 persons proposed for register in the district of Louny (294 adults and 150 children) of whom 135 were included in the category "permanently settled" (62 adults and 71 children), 135 were labelled "semi-travelling" (69 adults and 66 children) and 24 were labelled "travelling" (11 adults and 13 children). All the people proposed for the category of "travelling" were counted in Louny and in all cases they were Lovara from the Stojka family I am following, who were settled in the old brickworks. The data for Louny indicate that in the record from January 1959, which served as a basis for the subsequent register, there was a category of "permanently settled gypsies" (135 people) who were not ultimately registered in February 1959.

The above-mentioned archival file from January 1959 contained sheets of paper with the title "Summary sheet – register of gypsies" drawn up by ONV employees which were designed for recording "gypsy families", as is directly stated on them. In the case of each family it was highlighted whether they were "travelling" or "semi-travelling". Part of the Stojka family was labelled as "travelling" and part "semi-travelling", although the whole family lived together in a similar way. The members who were labelled "semi-travelling" were the nuclear families of Anna's son Bobko (six people total) and her brother-in-law Jouško (four people total), clearly because they had been officially registered as living at the brickworks in Louny for the longest time. Anna and her children and grandson (five people total), her sister-in-law Grófa, and Grófa's son with

---

636 SOA Litoměřice, f. SKNV, odbor vnitřních věcí, zn. 608, V-10 Soupis kočujících Cikánů 1959–1965 – Zpráva o provedení soupisu kočujících a polokočujících osob podle zákona č. 74/58 Sb. (13. 2. 1959, č. j. vnitř. 304/59).

637 SOkA Louny, f. ONV Louny II, vnitř. 608, k. 332 – Organizační opatření k soupisu kočujících a polokočujících osob v okrese Louny.

his wife and daughter (five people total) were included in the category "travelling". To the right of the note saying "gypsy family", showmen were labelled with the adjective "showman" and were listed alternately as "travelling" or "semi-travelling" with no clear key as to why. On some sheets the itinerancy level was crossed out and corrected, which indicates that people were later moved between categories and that these categories were also not clear to ONV officials, who had been meant to include in them people planned for the register.

During the preparation of the register the category of "permanently-settled persons" was also used, and included all Roms living in dwellings in the town of Louny, with the exception of the Roms from the Stojka family. They were evidently listed on the basis of ethnic criteria, not the itinerancy level that was meant to be key for the register. Inclusion in this category was entirely at odds with the concept of Act no. 74/1958 as declared by the Communist Party, which was that it was non-racist and non-discriminatory. In the district of Louny, this category was not ultimately included in the actual register, although on a republic-wide scale this was rare. In the Louny district, the actual register included just the Lovara from the Stojka family (perceived as "travelling", although they had been sedentarised by that time) and also showmen (most of whom also engaged in travelling professions). In the town of Louny, no non-Vlax Roms were included in the register, i.e., no one from the earlier category of the "settled". The municipal administration (MNV) explains this as follows:

"Persons of gypsy origin are in part permanently housed in the district town and have adapted well. New arrivals, however, have only provisional accommodation, for example in the brickworks. In the district town they cannot count at all on gaining even the worst flats, given that there are 600 people on the waiting list for a flat."[638] Some smaller towns and villages in the Louny district chose another approach and proposed seasonal Romani workers for the register, in other words, migrant labourers who were Slovak Roms temporarily working on state farms or in other enterprises.

Things were different in Žatec, which in 1959 was still a separate district. Minutes from a meeting of the Communist Party cell in Žatec in August 1958 stated under the agenda item concerning work among the gypsy population that 54 "gypsy" families lived in the town, a total of 241 people. Of this number, five families were labelled as travelling

---

638 SOkA Louny, f. ONV Louny II, vnitř. 608, k. 332, – č. j. vnitř. 038/58, Přehled pracovních a ubytovacích možností u kočujících osob (10. 7. 1958).

(28 people).[639] This was the Stojka-Horvát family living by the river Ohře. In the Žatec district, the officials all ultimately proceeded on the ethnic principle, and the total number of 372 persons[640] included essentially all those labelled "gypsies" regardless of the extent to which they were "settled" or "travelling".

In the Louny district, a large number of showmen found their way into the register. Of 192 persons recorded, 113 were showmen, 58% of the total, while there were just 79 "gypsy persons" (42%). The Roms from the Stojka family formed 13% of all those registered. Whether someone was labelled by the authorities as a "gypsy" or a "showman" was carefully noted by hand in the upper corner of the sheets with the note "cik." (*cikán*) or "svět." (*světský*), respectively. The Communist Party's promise to implement Act no. 74/1958 in a non-discriminatory, non-racist way therefore turned out to be an empty declaration.

Concrete preparations for the register

The start of preparations for the actual register was marked by a region-wide organising meeting in December 1958 in Ústí nad Labem, attended by the chairs of the ONVs, the heads of the interior affairs departments, district police chiefs and other officials from the ONVs, police and other organisations to establish the political line and the organisational principles of the register. Tasks were distributed, working groups created, and rooms were prepared for the register everywhere. Each MNV had a daily and hourly plan for registering the designated people. It was expected that it would be possible to register about 25–30 adult people per workday, so the MNVs sent out summons in advance for certain times and places which were delivered to the designated registrees in person by the MNV employees, the members of the street committees and other activists.[641]

---

639 SOkA Louny, f. KSČ OV Žatec, č. p. 247, i.v. 270 – Usnesení ze schůze byra okresního výboru KSČ v Žatci, značka: Přísně tajné (27. 8. 1958, no č. j.).

640 SOkA Louny, f. ONV Žatec, kt. 66 – Zápis z 11. řádné schůze rady ONV v Žatci (3. 3. 1959). According to the minutes of the Communist Party cell meeting on 27 August 1958, there were five travelling families living in Žatec (28 persons), which represents around 8% of the persons registered in the entire Žatec district. SOkA Louny, f. KSČ – okresní výbor Žatec, č. p. 247, i. č. 270, k. 15.

641 SOA Litoměřice, f. SKNV, odbor vnitřních věcí, zn. 608, V-10 Soupis kočujících Cikánů 1959–1965 – Zpráva o provedení soupisu osob kočujících a polokočujících podle zák. č. 74/58 Sb. (18. 12. 1959).

The organisational measures for the register also contained lists of persons for the various places where the register was to be taken and their estimated numbers, divided into "gypsies" (adults and children separately) and "showmen" (again adults and children separately). In each MNV the necessary rooms were reserved for the register, and a working group was set up to perform the register consisting of officials from the ONV, the secretary of the MNV, clerks and a police officer to ensure order and escort people if necessary.[642]

Register of "travelling" and "semi-travelling" persons in Louny and Žatec

The register of "travelling" and "semi-travelling" persons took place nationwide on 3–6 February 1959. In Louny, all the members of the family being followed here were processed on 3 February 1959. On the preserved register sheets[643] there is a note next to the three families in Anna Stojková's branch of the family stating that they owned a "covered wagon – caravan", and that one also owned a "drop-sided wagon". In the January 1959 preliminary lists, two families had a note next to their names stating that they owned either a "drop-sided wagon" or "wagon with a tarpaulin", but those same families have a note next to their names in the February register reading "no means of transport." In the interim these families may have been moved inside the brickworks. The number of wagons does not correspond to the information that the ONV later provided in a report to the KNV on 10 February 1959 which states that "five gypsies, of which four are children, still live in a covered wagon".[644] It is interesting that just one family (Jouško, Anna's brother-in-law) is stated to own a horse: "one gelding, grey 12 years".[645] A horse (grey) was also noted in January 1959 in the case of another family, but not in the final register.

---

642 SOkA Louny, f. ONV Louny II, vnitř. 608, k. 332 – vnitř. Organizační opatření k provedení soupisu kočujících a polokočujících osob v okrese Louny v lednu 1959 (with no date, no č. j.).

643 The register documents have not been preserved for all the families. I have documents for seven nuclear families and two childless individuals over 15.

644 SOkA Louny, f. ONV Louny II, vnitř. 608, k. 332 – Report from ONV Louny: Provádění soupisu osob kočujících a polokočujících (10. 2. 1959).

645 Ibid.

In Žatec, the register took place on 4 February 1959. I have managed to find just two register sheets in the state archives in Louny[646] for the family of Antonín (Vido) Horvát, his wife Kuluš and their six minor children, and the family of Bakro, their adult son. We learn that they all lived together in a caravan at Ostrov in Žatec and did not have a driving licence or a trade licence. Horses are not mentioned for them and no other information is available. The course of the register is described in a report by the ONV dated 10 February 1959 that states:

> In the district of Louny the register took place [...] in accordance with the organisational plan. During the register no disturbances took place and all those who were summoned turned up for register at the various centres. No one was brought by the police.[647]

Another report for the KNV on 15 April 1959 stated that: "In our district there were no complaints that anyone had been wrongly registered."

An entirely different version of the register process was described by Berci Stojka, who witnessed this forced sedentarisation:

> When they brought us to the brickworks we had horses to start with, so my uncles could travel to horse markets and do other business, but then the ban on travelling came and they took our horses. Policemen and soldiers came for us, plus civilians, probably from social services or the local authority. About a hundred people. That was the worst thing that could have happened to us. We couldn't travel any more. I still remember how we all cried. Grown-ups, old Roms were crying, screaming. The children were sobbing. My grandmother was crying, wailing with pity. There was nothing we could do. They came to us armed, with guns. We were worried that if we defended the horses, they'd shoot us. The Roms ran into their wagons. We children hid under the wagons, we were afraid they'd take us. My grandmother called to me: 'Berci, run away, hide!' She was afraid they'd take us to a children's home, because my mother was in prison and she was looking after me by herself. I ran inside and hid under the bed. The police took our horses, eight horses in total, and put them on wagons. Then they said: 'Right, they're going to the knacker's.' They took away all our horses, even my little horse Fricko. He'd grown up with me, from a colt. And we stayed there in those wagons for several more years.[648]

---

646 Ibid., Register lists by names of persons.
647 Ibid., Report from ONV Louny: Provádění soupisu ... (10. 2. 1959).
648 Personal recording of Berci (*1949) by the author made on 18 December 2018 in Louny, Czech Republic.

This testimony, showing the register as a fundamentally violent event that took place in the presence of the armed forces, differs so much from the register's official description that I am inclined to think it must have taken place on a different day from the officially planned register at the MNV premises on 3 February 1959. This may have been an incident from the end of January 1959, when preliminary lists of "gypsy families" were drawn up on the spot by officials and functionaries in the presence of security forces. For the witness, at that time a child, this may have merged in his memory with the filling-in of forms at the MNV in February 1959. In any case, the above-cited instructions from the KNV called for the February preparations for the register to be attended by all sorts of security forces and organisations, which might account for the large number of people whom the witness remembers coming to the brickworks. Still, the description urgently conveys the Roms' powerlessness and fear of the state representatives, whom the Stojka family perceived as a fundamental threat against which they were afraid to protest in any way. Whether this event took place on 3 February or several days earlier at the end of January 1959, it is clear that for these Roms, the "register" represented an act of repression and violence against them by the state bodies.

An important question is how and when their horses were confiscated. Neither the report on the register nor any other reports in the archives contain any further information on whether, how or when the horses were confiscated from the Stojka family and transported elsewhere. As I said above, horse ownership at the time of the register is recorded in the case of just one family (one gelding, grey, 12 years old, belonging to Josef, Anna Stojková's brother-in-law) and one more horse (a grey) was on the preliminary list of January 1958 as belonging to Anna's son Michal. According to the witness, however, these Roms owned eight horses that were confiscated at that time, and 60 years later, Berci Stojka could remember their names and what they looked like. It has to be asked when the violent act he describes took place. For Berci, the confiscation of their horses was the crucial, most tragic event of the whole register process. Although the Interior Ministry's instructions for the register did contain orders on how to handle horses and wagons, the archival sources do not mention the question of how they were actually dealt with at all.

That horses were taken from the Roms living by the river Ohře is, however, admitted by a report from Žatec of April 1959 where, in a section evaluating successes in finding employment for the Roms, the report says:

It has to be remembered that in the case of persons from the gypsy camp, things were much helped by an operation in which the police seized their horses, which were then confiscated. This deprived them of their permanent, easy income source.[649]

Although we do not know when these horses were taken away, it is confirmed here that this was done by the police and that the Roms did not receive any compensation for their horses. In the brief reasons given for the operation, we see that the step was intended by the security bodies as an instrument of repression and assimilation, but its result was merely to increase the isolation and criminalisation of the persons in question. It has to be asked where these horses ended up after they had been seized without any proper official documentation of the whole process. It is clear that the Roms' property was fraudulently taken off them and devalued, and that the local representatives of the state bodies and security forces took advantage of the Roms' disoriented, marginalised position to steal their horses. Discrepancies in the number of horses are, indeed, remarkable in the February 1959 register on a nationwide scale. According to the official statistics of the register, a total of 61 horses were recorded in the Bohemian and Moravian regions and 11 of them were seized.[650] This number is clearly very understated and is entirely at odds with what Lovara witnesses say. In Louny alone, according to the witness Berci Stojka, eight horses were seized (and put down), but other Lovara from other localities also report that horses were seized (and put down),[651] although this understandably need not have happened on the exact date of register.

Horses were very highly prized by the Lovara, and not just in the sense of their financial value, or as a status symbol. They perceived the seizure and putting down of their horses as a fatal incursion into their lives, and the whole event had a huge emotional dimension for them. Some Lovara witnesses showed greater sorrow at the loss and death of

---

649 SOA Litoměřice, f. SKNV, odbor vnitřních věcí, zn. 608, V-10 Soupis kočujících Cikánů 1959–1965 – Report from KNV, subject: Cikánská otázka do schůze (7. 4. 1958, no č. j.).

650 ABS, 8. schódza kolégia MV – 23. 3. 1959. A 2/1, k. 306.

651 For example, Ludmila Lakatošová (*1943), recorded in Veltruby on 3 April 2009; personal recording of Štefan Stojka (*1940) by the author, made in Ostrava on 30 March 2017; personal recording of Štefania Stojková (*1936) by the author, made on 1 April 2023 in Ostrava; personal recording of S. L. (*1930) by the author, recorded in Kovanice in October 2008: and a personal recording of Mária Lakatošová (*1951) by the author, recorded in Pečky on 24 April 2018.

their horses than at their own forced sedentarisation, which leads us to realise the cultural error and insensitivity of the state administration.

6.3 The listing of persons in the register

The register undertaken under Act no. 74 of 17 October 1958 "on the permanent settlement of travelling persons" had a long-term impact on the people included in it. They were now on a special official register established in 1959 at all the ONVs and police commands. This register subsequently recorded all changes concerning the people in question. The persons in the register had strict limitations on their ability to move around, especially in the years immediately following their register. According to Section 3 of Act no. 74/1958, continuing to maintain a travelling way of life was punishable by six months to three years in prison. In practice, this meant a ban on leaving the municipality and the larger district where they were resident at the time of their register.

From Berci Stojka's perspective, the register meant his family's freedom of movement came to an end:

> When the Roms were registered in 1959, it meant they wrote us all down. The adults got a stamp on their identity cards that we lived in Louny. That meant we were banned from leaving the district. If we went out of the Louny district, it would be taken as if we'd tried to flee to the West, for example. Anyone who wanted to leave had to be able to show some sort of special permission. A special piece of paper, a discharge, but what was on it I don't remember. In time, however, we got used to Louny and we didn't even want to leave. Even if we'd wanted to, we couldn't have left. We had to stay there.[652]

In the spring of 1959, quite soon after the register was completed, critical reports began to appear regarding the way in which Act no. 74/1958 was being observed in the Ústí Region. At the district level, the register agenda was the responsibility of the ONV interior affairs departments, which sent regular reports to the regional level in Ústí nad Labem. The reports by the interior affairs department of the KNV council in Ústí nad Labem included regular reports on the supervision of those on the register. Critical comments about the register can be detected in the

---

652 Personal recording of Berci (*1949) by the author, made on 18 December 2018.

evalutions of the register process sent by the Louny ONV to the KNV in Ústí nad Labem, as well as warnings that the law was not being upheld. From the perspective of the state, the law was being insufficiently observed at the local level, especially by ONVs in Slovakia, but also by some Czech MNVs and ONVs which were arbitrarily de-registering people. The upkeep of the register was therefore assessed as inconsistent. In the Louny and Žatec districts, however, the people entered on the register were checked fairly strictly. These measures had an undeniable impact in the Louny district (which in the 1960s joined with what was previously the Žatec district), above all on the Stojka and Stojka-Horvát families. Because they were registered as "travelling", which in some official documents was shortened to "K persons" (for *kočující*, travelling), they were assessed by the state bodies as the "most backward" and "most problematic" among the "persons of gypsy origin", and as such they were paid greater attention. They found themselves under the scrutiny of "gypsy" commissions, police bodies, and the interior affairs department of the ONV, which devoted themselves in detail to these "gypsies" in various reports and announcements. The authorities looked carefully at the question of moving the families outside the district, but they also tried to prevent other Roms from being moved into the district, above all relatives of the two families. The MNVs were called on by the ONV not to deregister, without the agreement of the interior affairs department of the ONV in Louny, any of the people on the register if they were intending to move away.[653]

Dealing and not dealing with living in caravans

Although the register of "travelling" and "semi-travelling" persons was described in its immediate aftermath by local bodies as having been successfully carried out, one of the greatest problems in the Louny and Žatec districts was the fact that suitable housing had not been found for previously "travelling persons", which was meant to be one of the results of implementing Act no. 74/1958 at the local level. The thorn in the side of the authorities was the accommodation of the Stojka and Stojka–Horvát families, who continued to live in their caravans on the same sites, the old brickworks in Louny and at Ostrov in Žatec, for several years after being registered.

---

653 SOkA Louny, f. MNV Louny, i. č. 100 – Letter accompanying the register sheets (5. 5. 1959) from the Interior Affairs Department of the Louny ONV to the MNV.

An attempt to solve the question of the unsuitable accommodation in the Roms' own caravans was declared to be underway by the local and district authorities from the preliminary, preparatory phase of the register. Finding suitable housing for "travelling gypsies" had been a goal of the region-wide meeting "on the reeducation of the gypsy population" that took place in December 1958 in Ústí nad Labem.[654] On the other hand, in contradiction of these declared attempts to find suitable housing for these formerly "travelling gypsies", the local Economy and Transport Department of the KNV council in Ústí nad Labem issued a written order to all the subordinate departments of the MNV and ONV councils on 4 February 1959 as the register was taking place in which it stressed that for a temporary period, during the dispersal of such persons, it was still possible to make use of more substandard accommodation for them. The order expressly mentioned that such temporary, provisional accommodation could include the wagons used hitherto by "travelling" persons after the means of towing them had been removed.[655] As we can see, in the case of two extended families that decree was applied using a legalised exception. While this was meant to be just a temporary solution, no specific time limit for this approach was set by the order. The local and district committees continued to declare that they were trying to deal with the situation of Roms living in caravans, but in practice there was minimal action on this issue.

Immediately after the register, officials tried to move some of the Roms who lived in the yard of the old brickworks into the building itself, which was dilapidated. In a report to the Interior Affairs Department of the Regional National Committee Council in Ústí nad Labem in April 1959,[656] the ONV was able to announce that: "with the exception of three families who live together, the gypsy persons are already housed. The remaining three families will, according to the MNV, be given housing in the space of a month."[657] It also stated that the "housing standard of persons of gypsy origin, above all the Stojkas, is not good enough, be-

---

654 SOA Litoměřice, f. SKNV, odbor vnitřních věcí, i. č. 608, V-10 Soupis kočujících Cikánů 1959–1965 – Zpráva aktivu o převýchově cikánského obyvatelstva (18. 12. 1958, no č. j.).

655 Ibid. – Report entitled Ubytování občanů cikánského původu vypracovaná vedoucím oddělení MH (10. 8. 1959, no č. j.).

656 SOkA Louny, f. ONV Louny II, vnitř. 608, k. 332 – Zpráva pro odb. pro VV rady KNV Ústí n. L., Kočující a polokočující osoby: zpráva (15. 4. 1959, č. j. 726).

657 Ibid., Zpráva odb. pro VV rady KNV Ústí n. L., Kočující a polokočující osoby (15. 4. 1959, no č. j.). The report describes the moving of nuclear families from Anna Stojková's extended family into the brickworks building. As I shall show below, these families did not last long in these awful conditions and returned to their caravans.

cause it is difficult to break their habit of leading a travelling life and to adapt them to normal life.'[658]

Criticising the "travelling way of life" was somewhat absurd on the part of the authorities, given that the state itself had ended their mobility by putting the family in the brickworks, in entirely unsuitable conditions in a spatially-excluded and socially-segregated environment, entirely unsuitable for families with children. Although the authorities were responsible for deepening the social marginalisation of this family, they somewhat alibistically repeated their attacks on the family's "bad habits" left over from the period of their itinerancy which, from the authorities' perspective, were behind the failed integration of the Roms from this family into local society. This approach once again shows that official reports from the socialist period are untrustworthy, one-sided sources.

Finding suitable accommodation for "former travelling persons" became a key task of their planned reeducation and was discussed at a number of local committee meetings, including those of the "gypsy committees". The "Committee for dealing with the gypsy question" met on 19 May 1959 and its minutes reveal that no rapid solution to the housing situation of these families had been found. It was merely stated that the task of repairing the brickworks building had not been fulfilled, and so the Louny local committee was once again asked to resolve this question once and for all.[659] The same thing was repeated at the next meeting of the committee in September 1959,[660] when the MNV in Louny was once again called upon to "finally, rapidly and as a matter of priority deal with the rehousing question"[661] for the family of Anna's sister-in-law R. Stojková, who had cooperated with the authorities, and to relocate them from the brickworks to a proper flat. However, no such move took place either in the autumn of 1959 or in the subsequent year.

In January 1960, members of the "Committee for the gypsy question" checked and surveyed the accommodation of the "gypsies" in the brickworks behind the barracks. As was stated in a detailed report from that check on them, "it was found on site that all the families had moved from the former brickworks into caravans. The families who previously had no caravans had since bought older ones. There are now seven caravans

---

658 Ibid.
659 Ibid. – Zápis ze schůze komise pro řešení cikánské otázky (19. 5. 1959, no č. j.).
660 Ibid. – Zápis z porady cikánské komise (3. 9. 1959, no č. j.).
661 Ibid.

on the site and all are the property of the Stojka family." [662] The caravans stood in the courtyard a couple of metres from the temporarily-adapted interior of the old brickworks, in which the Roms had no interest in living.

The report also described the caravans' equipment and state of repair in detail:

> The first caravan... [where] [R.] Stojková lives, was in good order. The family had bought chrome beds and more recently leased a new, white stove.[663] Everything was tidy and there were white bedspreads. The floor was scrubbed and covered with worn but clean carpets... In the second caravan there was a mother with a three-day-old baby. The children from the whole camp were also concentrated there.[664]

As we learn from the report, "after much negotiation, electric light was arranged for these families, which considerably improved the situation of the accommodated persons of gypsy nationality."[665] However, access to drinking water had not yet been dealt with, nor had any lavatories been built. The committee also surveyed their neighbours, summing up its findings as follows:

> When citizens living nearby were asked what kind of difficulties they had with the citizens of gypsy nationality, there were no critical comments. They are generally satisfied with their presence in the neighbourhood. The main comment was that a lavatory should be built.[666]

In conclusion, the "Committee for the gypsy question" once again passed a resolution that with regard to R. Stojková, whom they assessed as cooperating with the authorities and the school, it was necessary as a matter of priority to find her "a decent flat and isolate her from the others".[667] The "others" here refers to the other members of the Stojka family, who could clearly have a "bad" influence on her. Another task was to arrange with the street committees neighbouring the old brickworks

---

662 SOkA Louny, f. Okresní prokuratura Louny r. 1960–1965, i. č. 26, Pd 460, k. 5 – Zápis ze schůze komise při radě ONV Louny (21. 1. 1960, no č. j.).

663 Author's note: This was a solid-fuel kitchen stove with a stovetop and oven, in the shape of a table.

664 Ibid.

665 Ibid.

666 Ibid.

667 Ibid.

that they would take on the responsibility of supervising the families' behaviour.[668]

The committee did not conclude that suitable accommodation needed to be found for all those living in caravans, but just for one family that was "cooperating well". The critical unavailability of drinking water was also not dealt with. In a report sent in February 1960 to the Internal Affairs Department at the KNV Council in Ústí nad Labem on the state of the records regarding those registered, the ONV once again points out that:

> There are still five families to be housed. These families are living in caravans for now. The Louny MNV is not devoting adequate care to finding housing for these families although the Committee for the Reeducation of Gypsy Persons is urging them to do so. The measures taken by the ONV Council have also not met with results. The attention of the district prosecutor has been drawn to the situation. Recently, gypsy persons have been committing theft and moral offences, which is caused by the fact that the MNV has not managed to house them properly.[669]

The repeated argument used by the Louny MNV as to why the Stojkas' housing had not yet been dealt with was that there were not enough flats free. From a report by the committee of the district prosecutor, however, we can see that during this same time other Romani families (non-Vlax, living outside the brickworks) had been given "four flats already [...] and yet not a single case from the Stojkas has been dealt with."[670]

The Roms were not moved out of the old brickworks during the following year, either. The urgency of dealing with their totally substandard housing and lack of basic amenities and equipment, as well as the attempts to deal with this, gradually stopped being mentioned in the reports of the ONVs and MNVs. From time to time the problem reappeared in the reports of the ONV and MNV in Louny and was repeatedly dealt with by the district prosecutor and the Regional National Committee, but nothing changed in subsequent years. A report from the Department for Interior Affairs of the Louny ONV for the KNV in February 1962 once again admitted that a main shortcoming of the situation in the district

---

668 Ibid.
669 SOkA Louny, f. ONV Louny II, vnitř. 608, k. 332, Pro odb. pro VV KNV Ústí n.L. – Zpráva o stavu evidence osob vzatých do soupisu podle zák. 74/1958 (24. 2. 1960, č. j. vnitř. 99/1960).
670 SOkA Louny, f. Okresní prokuratura Louny r. 1960–1965, i. č. 26, Pd 460, k. 5 – Zápis schůze komise pro občany cikánské národnosti na ONV Louny (24. 2. 1960, č. j. 4/60).

was that it had not yet proven possible to disperse the persons of "gypsy origin" who still lived all together in caravans in Žatec and Louny. The department blamed the situation on the MNVs which, it said, had not taken care of the housing issue. The report said the situation was such that "the life they live is not leading to the reeducation of these people, who then commit criminal acts of stealing socialist property."[671]

The minutes from a meeting of the Louny ONV committee responsible for issues concerning persons of "gypsy" origin held in January 1963 once again repeated that "the MNVs in Louny and Žatec have still not provided housing for the gypsies in caravans"[672] and these authorities were called upon to draw up a report on how they intended to move the "gypsies" out of the caravans. However, according to the records of further meetings, no such report was submitted in the coming months.

The local bodies' behaviour is entirely in keeping with the conclusion of the historian Anna Jurová that the committees' executive bodies were well prepared to register people, but not well prepared to create the conditions for the genuinely permanent settlement of "travelling" and "semi-travelling" persons, above all for the reason that there was a lack of housing and employment on the local level.[673] People with few qualifications and zero work experience in industry and agriculture had to stay in places where there were not enough jobs for such difficult-to-employ people, according to the logic of the law. While they were on the register, they were not allowed to move elsewhere or to travel to work. This fact is another reason why this assimilationist policy led to their criminalisation and social exclusion.

I also managed to discover fragmentary information on the situation of the Stojka–Horvát family who, for several years after their register, lived in caravans in the middle of Žatec near the river Ohře. In August 1959, a report from the KNV in Ústí nad Labem by the head of its local Economic Department states that the "gypsies" living in caravans in Žatec were apparently offered very substandard housing which they refused, preferring to continue living in caravans. The reason they gave for rejecting the housing was that they were looking for suitable accommodation outside Žatec, and after their family members returned from

---

671 SOA Litoměřice, f. SKNV, odbor vnitřních věcí, zn. 608, V-10, Soupis kočujících Cikánů 1959–1965 – V2c: Stav soupisu kočujících a polokočujících sob podle zák. č. 74/1958 Sb. v evidenci ONV (23. 2. 1962, č. j. vnitř. 36/32).

672 SOkA Louny, f. Okresní prokuratura Louny 1960–1965, k. 28 – Zpráva Aktivu pro řešení otázek osob cikánského původu při radě ONV v Lounech (28. 1. 1963, no č. j.).

673 Jurová, "Niektoré aspekty", 15–16.

prison, they were planning to settle in their caravans in a place where they would perform agricultural work.[674] The report said that these people need to be closely followed so they would not return to their travelling way of life under the pretext of looking for suitable employment.

In another report assessing the register of "travelling persons" on the regional level, the information appears that the "gypsies" in Žatec had not all been housed, but that five families were still living in wagons. The councils of the MNV and ONV were said to be dealing with the case and it was planned that "these persons also" were to receive a flat in July 1960.[675] A report by the Committee for the Protection of Public Order from April 1961 looked, in several points, at the situation of people living "in gypsy camps in Louny and Žatec". That report, which covered the whole Ústí nad Labem Region, mentioned the bad hygiene situation first and foremost, a result of the fact that "in the winter period the gypsies do not even wash", clearly declared the importance of eliminating places where "gypsies" were accommodated in large numbers, and set specific, regional-level goal, namely, "the urgent elimination of the two gypsy vehicle camps in the Louny district". Specifying the situation more closely, the report described the "camp" in Žatec as a "wagon park near the Lučany playground with seven families accommodated in seven wagons (33 persons total, of which 12 children)".[676]

An ONV report from July 1962[677] notes that four families comprising 24 people were living in caravans by the river. The MNV had reportedly repeatedly tried to move them elsewhere, but apparently there had been no available housing in Žatec at all. As a result, several attempts were made to transfer these Roms to the surrounding municipalities. One was a plan from June 1962 to move them to houses previously occupied by the German population in the small villages of Kryry and Blatno, where they would commit to working on a state farm. The plan, which has been preserved, contained a list of six families (33 persons named) from the Stojka–Horvát family and the villages to which they were to be moved.[678] However, this never happened. Although in 1963 one or

---

674 SOA Litoměřice, f. SKNV, odbor vnitřních věcí, zn. 608, V-10 Soupis kočujících Cikánů 1959–1965 – Report entitled Ubytování občanů cikánského původu, drawn up by the head of the local Economy Department (10. 8. 1959, no č. j.).

675 Ibid. – Zpráva odb. pro VV rady ONV v Žatci (8. 3. 1960, č. j. vnitř. 899/60).

676 Ibid. – Zpráva Odb. pro VV SKNV (18. 4. 1961, no č. j.).

677 SOkA Louny, f. ONV Louny II, vnitř. 608, k. 332 – Zpráva o současném stavu mezi občany cikánského původu od MěNV Žatec pro ONV Louny (date of receipt 9. 7. 1962, no č. j.).

678 Ibid. – Report from MNV Žatec, Aktiv pro řešení cikánské otázky, Subject: Dosídlenecké domky v Kryrech a Blatně obč. cik. původu (5. 6. 1962, č. j. Vl. škol./451–62.T).

two families seem to have managed to move into a house in the centre of Žatec, according to the available archival materials the others were still living in caravans in the summer of 1966.[679] In August 1966, the MNV in Žatec sent three families from the Stojka–Horvát settlement a "Decision on removal from the register" to the address "Žatec, Ostrov – caravan",[680] which once again confirms that these people remained in their caravans or covered wagons at the former campsite by the river Ohře for more than seven years after their register. How much longer the Roms stayed there in such conditions I have not been able to ascertain.

The dismal housing situation of the Louny and Žatec Roms living in their caravans was mentioned in reports dealing with the issue of the register or with work among "the gypsy population", not just at the regional level, but also at the highest level. For example, the "Report on the fulfilment of the resolution of the Central Committee of the Communist Party on work among the gypsy population" of December 1961 writes that: "Those gypsies who earlier used to rove around in wagons today no longer travel, but in many cases they still live in their caravans." The places mentioned as alarming examples are localities in the towns of Nový Jičín, Přerov, Opava, Karviná-město, Olomouc, Hořovice, Zdice, Žatec and Louny.[681]

After their register, some Roms registered in the category of "travelling persons" lived in caravans without wheels, unused railway carriages and various other unsuitable structures. On the territory of the Czech lands, and indeed all over Czechoslovakia, there were several such sites consisting of wagons and caravans. Some Roms continued to live in these improvised dwellings until the 1970s. The state bodies at various levels also repeatedly criticised different enterprises for not observing the law in their recruitment policies. They would try to acquire the workers they needed, but they did not intend to give the Roms from these localities suitable accommodation or conditions which would allow them to bring their families there to live.[682]

---

679 Ibid.

680 Ibid. – Three decisions on the approval process for removal from the register of "travelling" and "semi-travelling" persons sent to the MNV in Žatec (3. 8. 1966, č. j. vnitř./605.1–3131–1966-jnA).

681 NA Praha, f. KSČ Ústřední výbor 1945–1989 Praha, oddělení ideologické, zn. KSČ ÚV – 05/3, sv. 10, arch. j. 57 – Zpráva (23. 12. 1961).

682 Jurová, "Niektoré aspekty", 17.

Assimilatory efforts to rid "gypsies" of their old habits

In Louny, the ONV Committee for Citizens of Gypsy Nationality as well as other officials and functionaries had attempted to reeducate the Roms there on several fronts. With this aim in mind, bureaucrats would make repeated visits to check on the Roms, observing in detail and describing in reports the Roms' behaviour and the cleanliness of their dwellings. The committee's minutes describe attempts to find housing and employment for the Roms, to place their children in school, or to take control over their state of health.

Members of the committee for dealing with gypsy issues also aimed to change the way in which Romani women dressed. A committee report from May 1959 stated that a change in the attire "of gypsy women first and foremost would improve the relationship of our [i.e., non-Roma] people towards them".[683] The greatest problem was considered the length of Romani women's skirts. However, long skirts (*lungi cocha*) were considered in the Lovara community at that time to be the only acceptable dress for a Lovara woman and also an important symbol of group identity.[684] For the authorities, therefore, a change of behaviour in this area could represent a certain symbolic success in their assimilation efforts.

As an example of this tendency to change Romani feminine attire, in this case the dress of girls, related to the attempt to reeducate Romani children and to correct the supposedly detrimental influence of their parents, I shall again use a newspaper article, this time from the communist magazine *Průboj* of May 1959 entitled "Teacher". The article describes the approach of the zealous teacher Hladíková, who had a class of Romani children in her charge in Žatec. The piece is written somewhat untraditionally as an address to the teacher in the second person. It mentions that the teacher started her reeducation of the "gypsy" children by sprinkling delousing powder in their hair and sending them home so their parents could wash their hair with vinegar water. She then started to "enlighten" them on the question of dress:

> Then you started on altering their clothes, above all shortening the skirts that dragged around the girls' feet. It went well, only Máňa Stojková did not want to hear of a shorter skirt, not her. You said: 'Máňa, don't wear long skirts, it's not pretty, look at Margitka and Sarina, how nice they look.' Máňa just

---

683 Ibid. – Zápis ze schůze komise pro řešení cikánské otázky ONV (19 May 1959).
684 Hajská, "Hranice jazyka", 99; Lakatošová, "Některé zvyklosti", 6; Šusterová, *Život olašskych žien*, 89–90.

lowered her eyes and shook her head. And you said: 'Why don't you want to look like me? Look, I wear shorter skirts too.' Máňa turned her glittering eyes at you and answered: 'I, comrade teacher, do not want a skirt like that. You wear one, you brazen woman, but not me.' She didn't mean it badly. She probably thought a shorter skirt was a sign of shame. And today? Máňa has a nice, pleated skirt, and it's even shorter.[685]

Máňa Stojková, undoubtedly a girl from the Stojka–Horvát family settled in Žatec, is described as a person whose Czech language skills are very limited, with a high level of interference from Slovak and a considerable number of mistakes: she cannot decline words properly. Also underlined is her wild ("glittering" eyes) and haughty nature (she shakes her head, averts her eyes), symbolising the "travelling gypsies" who refused to adapt. The "gypsy children" are described as dirty and unhygienic. The article culminates in the victory of the teacher over traditional Romani dress. Convincing Máňa to shorten her skirt seems to symbolise the climax of the communist ideological assimilation attempts, or more widely the general demands made by Czech society that "travelling gypsies" adapt to conventional norms.

The Louny district MNVs made efforts to rid the "gypsies" of their "old habits", as they labelled all such displays of the alien, strange Romani culture: their traditional way of dressing, as we have already seen, their Romani language, their familial hierarchies and roles, or their observance of various customs. In the archival records on such work with the "gypsy population" after their register, their observance of "old customs" is perceived as causing the asocial nature and increasingly criminal behaviour of Romani family members: "Their old customs, traditions and morals are continuously strengthened and this group, by staying together, continuously seeks various ways to make an easy living."[686]

The idea of increasing crime is something that is often mentioned by the security bodies and various committees and representatives of the authorities in relation to these persons. It is symptomatic that when the Lovara came to Louny, their criminal activity was not mentioned or was assessed as minimal. For example, a report by the Department for Interior Affairs of the KNV in Ústí and Labem from April 1959 states under the heading of criminality that: "With a very few exceptions, we

---

685 SOkA Louny, f. Okresní prokuratura Žatec 1949–1960, k. 68 – A clipping of an article, "Učitelka", labelled by hand as coming from the periodical *Průboj* (23. 5. 1959, no č. j.).

686 SOkA Louny, f. Okresní prokuratura Louny r. 1960–1965, i. č. 26, k. 5 – Zápis schůze komise pro občany cikánské národnosti na ONV Louny (24. 2. 1960, no č. j.).

have managed to limit begging from house to house by travelling people in the towns and villages. No other cases of stealing occurred, save for the theft of one hen."[687]

In subsequent years, however, crime among this group started to rise sharply, it seems. A report from the Committee for the Protection of Public Order from April 1961 drew attention to the high rate of crime among the Roms from the "gypsy camps" in Louny and Žatec. According to the report, 22 offenders from these "camps" accounted for 178 of the 268 crimes committed (it seems) in the district,[688] which represents two-thirds of all crimes. Given that there were about 65 Lovara (from the Stojka and Stojka-Horvát families) in these localities, including children, the number of 22 people would include nearly all the adult individuals.

It is clear, however, that the cause of the increasing crime was the spatial and social exclusion of the group and above all their ensuing exclusion on the economic level. The families in question were not allowed to engage in their previous livelihoods, which had included trading in horses and other products. The "gypsy" committees set up by the state repeatedly declared they were trying to find employment for the Stojka family. However, the manual positions that they offered them in factories or on state farms did not at all reflect the competences, skills or preferences of these former horse traders. Berci Stojka pointed out this fact in his testimony:

> Our Roms used to live by trading horses, they didn't know how to do any other work, but my family never stole before. When the ban on travelling came, the Roms suffered terrible hunger. They didn't have any way of earning money. There was nothing to eat. The Romani woman were forced to go and steal food. They didn't know how to do the manual work that they gave the Roms, they threw the Roms out everywhere and didn't even want to hire them. All the Roms knew how to do was trade, they couldn't cope with such work, and for the work they wanted to do they needed a vocational certificate.[689]

Reports from various state bodies repeatedly stated the failure to integrate Roms from the families in question into the labour process which,

---

687 SOkA Louny, f. ONV Louny II, vnitř. 608, k. 332 – Kočující a polokočující osoby: zpráva (15. 4. 1959, no č. j.).

688 SOA Litoměřice, f. SKNV, odbor vnitřních věcí, zn. 608, V-10, Soupis kočujících Cikánů 1959–1965 – Zpráva odb. pro VV SKNV (18. 4. 1961, no č. j.).

689 Personal recording of Berci (*1949) by the author, made 18 December 2018 in Louny, Czech Republic.

according to the authorities, was not just because of the Roms' poor working habits, frequent job-hopping and avoidance of manual labour, but also because some enterprises refused to employ these persons.[690] Over the course of a few years, however, Roms from the Stojka family gradually found positions that suited them (for example, in a meat-packing factory) and so in reports from the early 1970s there is also praise for individuals' good working habits.

The ONV documents also allow us to detect the specific steps leading to the assimilation of these Roms. The way in which the local authorities treated the oldest woman in the Stojka family, Anna Stojková (*1902), is redolent of social engineering. A report from a meeting of the gypsy committee in September 1959 mentioned that: "All the members of the committee agree that as long as Anna Stojková has any influence on the family, the reeducation of the whole family will be difficult."[691] Anna Stojková was a figure of authority for her whole family, and for this reason was perceived by the employees of the committees as a brake on their assimilation efforts. A few months later, according to another document, "R. Stojková and old Anna Stojková were taken off to Bukov for treatment".[692] Given that Bukov was a psychiatric hospital, it is not clear whether Anna Stojková and her daughter-in-law were placed there voluntarily, on the basis of actual psychiatric problems, or whether they were put there at the instigation of the state authorities to remove Anna from her family or punish her for her behaviour. However unlikely this solution may seem from today's viewpoint, during the period in question this possibility was not infrequently used for dealing with people who posed a problem to the regime. At any rate, the committee exploited her hospitalisation to try and influence her son,

born in 1943, who had already once been taken to hospital but who had escaped with the aid of old Stojková. The committee passed a resolution that the current situation, when Anna Stojková was away being treated, should be used to ensure an operation on the boy's crippled leg in the hospital."[693]

The committee also intended to exploit the hospitalisation of Anna's daughter-in-law, R. Stojková, to take her children into children's homes.

---

690 SOkA Louny, f.ONV Louny II, vnitř. 608, k. 332 – Zápis ze schůze odboru pracovních sil, zdravotnictví a sociálního zabezpečení ONV Louny (20. 2. 1960, no č. j.).
691 Ibid. – Zápis z porady cikánské komise (3. 9. 1959, no č. j.)
692 Ibid.
693 Ibid.

The agenda of deregistration from the register
of "travelling" and "semi-travelling" persons

People put on the register in February 1959 and subsequently held in the records of the state authorities were allowed to apply for deregistration. After being successfully taken off the register, the measures of Act no. 74/1958 ceased to relate to the persons in question and they were able to move house without requesting permission. Many made use of this option, but their requests for deregistration were not always granted: the authorities took into account the opinion of the state enterprise where the person worked, the local committee, and sometimes of other bodies.[694] The Louny ONV, in its records of people on the register, continued to distinguish thoroughly between showmen and persons of "gypsy origin", continuing to label them in pencil, on the basis of their ethnicity, on their register document and other records as "svět." (*světský*) or "cik." (*cikán*). The study of this data from the relevant archives brings me to the conclusion that officials also treated the two groups differently when it came to taking people off the register.[695] From the spring of 1962, only people registered in Louny in the category "gypsies" were still registered. All the "showmen" from Louny had had their deregistration approved.

All the people still registered and remaining in the category of "gypsies" were from the Stojka family (as of 20 February 1963 there were 30 persons). Those registered could also be deregistered due to their having relocated to another district. For this, however, the Interior Affairs Department of the District Committee had to give its approval – and as the documentation shows, these departments always refused Romani families' requests to move, with the exception of a single case in which a son moved in order to be with his parents in another district. From the register archives it can be seen that in the case of families and individuals from the "showmen" category, moving to another district was allowed.

It was not until 1964 that the Louny ONV approved the removal of the first Lovara in Louny from the register. Of the 33 registered members of the Stojka family, 25 were taken off the register between April and August 1964 for the reason that they lived and worked permanently in Louny. At that time, however, the men of the Stojka family were already looking for work outside the district, which the authorities knew about, but this fact was not included in the argumentation put forward for

---

694 Zapletal, "Přístup totalitního státu", 58.
695 Hajská, "Forced settlement", 359.

their possible removal from the register. Four people were allowed to be taken off the register in 1968. The last nuclear family, that of Anna Stojková's youngest daughter, was still officially registered as living in the former brickworks in January 1969 when, as the last such family in the district, they were officially taken off the register of "travelling" and "semi-travelling" persons. [696]

Roms from Žatec were forced to remain on the register for a similarly long time. Of 25 Roms from the Stojka–Horvát families for whom we have the date on which they were removed from the register, three people were taken off in 1963, another eight people in 1964, and 14 people not until 1966.[697]

The family of Antonín Horvát, for example, had its request to be taken off the register rejected several times. The first application was refused by the ONV in Louny in November 1962, the reason given being that: "It has been found that the work habits and behaviour of you and your family are not such as to allow us to meet your request for deregistration."[698] Another rejection followed in October 1963, when the District Committee for the Protection of Public Order stated that: "The family has not yet been sufficiently reeducated to fulfil all the conditions for deregistration. There is even a danger that after being deregistered they might return to a travelling lifestyle."[699] At the time these deregistration requests were made, the family still lived in a caravan by the river Ohře in the place known as Ostrov. This may have been one of the reasons for their rejection, although it was not directly stated. The family was not deregistered until the following year, in April 1964, when they had already moved into a flat in the centre of town.[700]

These cases show that living in covered wagons or caravans was a significant factor that could prevent a family from being taken off the register of "travelling" and "semi-travelling" persons. Most Lovara, whether in Žatec or Louny, were taken off the register only after they had moved into normal housing. Here it is worth pointing out that almost all members of the families in question left their place of residence soon after they were deregistered and started to look for work and housing outside

---

696 SOkA Louny, f. ONV Louny II, vnitř. 608, k. 331 – Rozhodnutí (3. 1. 1969, č. j. 99/69). Sent to J. Lakatošová at the address "Louny – brickworks".

697 SOkA Louny, f. ONV Louny II, vnitř. 608, k. 331.

698 Ibid. – Vyjádření ONV k žádosti A. Horváta o vyjmutí ze soupisu podle zák. 74/1958 – zamítnutí (14. 11. 1962, č. j. 423/65–4).

699 Ibid. – Refusal (2. 10. 1963, č. j. 3511/63).

700 Ibid. – Approval (21. 4. 1964, no č. j.).

the district of Louny, which had been foisted on them as a location by bureaucrats at the time of their register. This, however, often brought a temporary return to their living in caravans until they found housing that appealed to them.

Leaving the caravans

It is not clear when the old brickworks in Louny was finally abandoned by the Roms. Berci remembers that a large part of the family moved into a detached house close to the Louny railway station, where some lived inside the house while two of his uncles brought their caravans into the spacious yard and carried on living in them with their families. According to the municipal committee's evidence,[701] the move must have taken place at the latest before June 1963, which is the date of Anna Stojková's death, and she lived in the house. Berci says the death of his grandmother Anna Stojková was the impetus for the entire family to leave Louny. The first family members clearly left after the three nuclear families of Berci Stojka's uncles were taken off the register in April 1964. The other families seem to have followed them. Berci Stojka has described how, after being taken off the register, his uncles worked in land improvement and ditch-digging, moving around according to their place of work to Odolená Voda, Valdice and other municipalities, until at the end of the 1960s they moved to Prague. Leaving Louny paradoxically meant a temporary return to spatial mobility, since the families doing land improvement work moved from one workplace to another by caravan, which they used tractors to tow to the destination where they were to work. They did so at a time when moving about in caravans was banned – but this type of work was a legal exception. Berci remembers that the Stojka family bought a house in Hostivař, on the outskirts of Prague, in the late 1960s for which they jointly took out and then repaid a loan. "We still had three caravans in Hostivař. When we moved into our house, however, we sold the caravans."[702]

---

701 SOkA Louny, f. MěNV Louny, i. č. 100 – Evidence obyvatelstva cikánské národnosti v Lounech. – This typewritten list of "citizens of gypsy nationality" in Louny as of 1 July 1961 still gives the address of the old brickworks for all the Lovara. In the case of two families this was later crossed out (with no date) and an address added that is close to Louny railway station, corresponding to Berci's localisation of their later residence.

702 Personal recording of Berci (*1949) by the author made on 18 December 2018 in Louny, Czech Republic.

In this new house the family then managed to create the sort of life they wanted, and their voluntary abandonment of spatial mobility and living in covered wagons was part of that.

The impact of the register under Act. No. 74/1958 on Roms in Louny and Žatec

The implementation of Act no. 74/1958 had an undoubted impact on both branches of the Stojka family living in Louny and Žatec. They were entered on the register of "travelling" and "semi-travelling" persons and, for periods raging from five to 10 years, were limited in their mobility and faced various assimilatory instruments and measures. There was also the confiscation of their property when their horses were taken from them without compensation, something that was perceived by the Roms as a painful interference with their lives. As I have shown above, the underestimated number of horses for which seizure was indicated on the register suggests that the Roms may have been defrauded, or their property may have been undervalued by the state authorities.

As we have seen, despite many years of declarations from authorities on several levels that they would try to find suitable housing for the Stojka family, in early 1963 the family had to deal with its inadequate housing in the old brickworks on its own by buying a house together. Several years later the family bought a house in the Hostivař suburb of Prague the same way, by taking out a loan. This says something about the agency of these Roms: while they had no choice but to stay in their caravans in designated places in the Louny district for the period that they were on the register, they still successfully managed to resist assimilation attempts. At the sites allotted to them, they preferred to keep living in their own wagons rather than in the dilapidated building into which officials tried to make them move. They managed to deal with the unavailability of water and food by creating functional relationships with their neighbours and even with the soldiers from the barracks, who brought them food. After they were deregistered, they then managed to find their own housing, to leave Louny and Žatec where they had lived unwillingly for years, and to find themselves legal livelihoods in Prague of their own choice.

The authorities who registered them in Louny and Žatec never managed to meet the requirements established by law, with the exception of its restrictions on the registered persons. They allowed the Roms (especially in Louny) to live in a totally unsuitable place. Instead of the basic sanitation and integration into society that the authorities were meant to provide, they instead concentrated on the Roms' "backward way of life" and how to change it.

Štefan Stojka, Sr. and his family with his horse and wagon in Trenčín, around 1955 or 1956.

Part 7: Conclusions

I have focused in this book on the life stories of the Stojka family which, towards the end of the 19th century, gained domicile in the municipality of Trenčianska Teplá. I pieced together the family history over several generations on the basis of various fragmentary records from all over Czechoslovakia, which I then tried to connect into a larger, interrelated whole. As far as possible, I tried to connect some of the events I came across in the records with historical facts and the policies of the time. Using a single family with many branches, piecing together their story from a large quantity of archival and ethnographic material, I have described the form of these inhabitants' mobility and territorial anchoring, identifying them as Vlax Roms from the Lovara group who were labelled by the state bodies of the time as "gypsies" or "gypsy vagabonds/travelling gypsies". The broad chronological sweep of this book, from the late 19th century to the late 1960s, means that it contributes a comprehensive view of their lives across highly diverse political regimes and changing socioeconomic conditions.

I shall try to divide my conclusions from the wealth of archival material and interviews presented in this book into several interconnected levels. The diachronically-ordered chapters have already contained partial conclusions for individual periods, and so I shall now try to briefly summarise them and to formulate conclusions that concern the main themes of the book. These are: the paths taken by the families in question; the historical circumstances and contexts connected with the Lovara community on the territory of the former Czechoslovakia; general thoughts about the debate on spatial mobility and territorial anchoring; and, last but not least, the effect of official state measures aimed at the individuals and families falling into the category of "travelling gypsies" which were connected with the paternalistic approach of the state and with the entrenched racial prejudices towards Roms in Czechoslovak society generally.

7.1 The interdisciplinary approach, combination of methods, broad spectrum of sources and other innovative aspects

My book offers a continual, dense portrayal of one Lovara family over several decades across Czechoslovak territory, created by combining various sources. It is in their combination and in the concurrent choice of an interdisciplinary approach that I see an enriching, innovative element here that could inspire future researchers. Previously, the historical studies focusing on the Czech or Slovak Vlax Roms and specifically on the Lovara[703] were based largely on archival material just from a single district. The authors did not place such microstudies in the larger biographical context of the individuals and did not combine sources from various localities and regions about them. Their authors did not have a particular family and its fate at the centre of their interest, but were focused more on the relationship between local governments or central bodies towards Roms living in a certain area and how they dealt with "problems resulting from coexistence". I tend to conclude that these historians may have been deterred from undertaking a more continuous tracing of Vlax families' trajectories by the very fact that the Lovara were identified as "travelling" families in "permanent motion", without particularly great ties to any one place. The archival sources regarding their lives were, therefore, perceived as scattered over a large number of regional archives, the assumption being that these Roms could have moved practically "anywhere". The challenge posed by such a broadly-conceived study lies not just in the logistics of the research, but also in the fact that it may seem difficult to continuously follow the spatial routes taken. As my study shows, however, it is possible to combine information from various regional archives to achieve such a result.

I arrived at various methodological innovations when writing this book. An important methodological enrichment of historical research is the integration of socioanthropological methods, above all entering

---

703 E.g. Černý, "Lovárové"; Pavelčíková, "Příchod olašských Romů"; Rastislav Pivoň, "K realizácii zákona č. 74/1958 Zb. o trvalom usídlení kočujúcich osôb na území Veľkej Bratislavy". *Studia Ethnologica Pragensia*, no. 1 (2018): 30–46; Pivoň, "Zákon č. 74".

data for individuals into a genealogical diagram and, during archival research, looking for records of individuals and families according to surname and for further personal data on these people. An example of partial innovation is my research into how Lovara territorial anchoring took place. Like other researchers, in determining this variable I focused mainly on where the members of the families in question were officially domiciled. This says something about the situation of a particular family or community in relation to the municipality and often played an important role in determining the (im)possibility of their staying more permanently or repeatedly in a particular place. The ties of Roms to the community may also be researched on the basis of other criteria such as their actual residence and its length as recorded by the authorities, a municipality given as the birthplace of more than one family member, and above all, the fact of owning property, which is best when it is repeatedly recorded officially. A continually-given precise address (including house number) may also indicate long-term residence or a base in a particular municipality – if not through actual ownership, then through renting. These ways of being territorially anchored then need to be researched in combination with the spatial mobility motivated by the performance of a profession or by social ties.

Another undoubted methodological enrichment that produces a fundamental shift in the picture of Lovara life in Czechoslovakia is the following of such actors' own perspectives, on the one hand, and the perspective of the state administration, on the other. These perspectives are essentially fairly opposed to each other, providing varied and, on a number of points, mutually antagonistic interpretations of various historical events. Many researchers writing about Roms on the territory of the former Czechoslovakia focus mostly on the perspective of the state. Although these authors try to objectively justify the motivation of the Roms' actions, they rarely present a comprehensive picture of the Romani perspective. Including the actors' perspective of the Roms themselves is something I consider to be a fundamental shift that has so far been entirely absent from the literature on this geographical territory and from the debate on "travelling" Roms. The fact that I have used not just data from archival research, but also analyses of ethnographic narratives, witness testimonies concerning the wartime genocide against the Roms and interviews made on the basis of oral history methods means that a dynamic, fluid picture of the subject in question has been created here.

My book also enriches research into the history of the Roms. During my gradual focus on the different historical events that involved the

Lovara, I came across various areas that had not been sufficiently researched by historians, or about which authors tended just to cite each other's somewhat oversimplified statements.[704] I also came across a number of "blank spots"[705] on which I had originally not intended to focus but which I nevertheless tried to fill in, at least in part, in my attempt to describe the historical contexts of the Lovara families' situations in Czechoslovakia. This required thorough study of various primary sources across the archival sources or various databases.

7.2 Conclusions for individual historical periods

Trajectories of the Stojka family from Trenčianska Teplá before the beginning of the Second World War

At the end of the 19th century, the Stojka family were granted domicile in the municipality of Trenčianska Teplá in Western Slovakia. This was also the birthplace of Zaga (*1887) and Štefan Stojka, Sr. (*1891), who became the main figures of the two largest family branches. Over the subsequent decades, various forms of their being both territorially anchored in the above-mentioned municipality and mobile were typical of these branches. According to the official records, from the end of the 19th century to the 1920s both branches of the family moved around the Trenčín district and occasionally also in the surrounding districts, while being territorially anchored in the municipality of Trenčianska Teplá. During that time, Štefan became a successful, fairly well-known horse trader with high social status and authority among the Roms, and seemingly also enjoyed a certain amount of recognition among non-Roms in his native Trenčianska Teplá, with whom he managed to build functioning social ties and contacts.

From the early 1930s in particular there was a diversification of the spatial mobility of both family branches. While Štefan Stojka, Sr.'s mobility and that of his branch focused mainly on western Slovakia, with

---

704 For example, the idea that the Lovara did not start to arrive on the territory of the former Czechoslovakia until the mid-19th century, or that until the ban on travelling in 1958, or rather 1959, they were itinerant and not territorially anchored, or that they started to arrive in the Czech lands just in connection with postwar migration.

705 For example, the presence of the Lovara in Bohemia before Czechoslovakia became an independent state, the postwar migrants arriving in the Czech lands viewing themselves as returning to the Czech lands after a forced stay in Slovakia during the war, or the fate of the Lovara during the Second World War on the territory annexed by Hungary.

just occasional journeys to Moravia to engage in horse trading in the 1930s, his sister Zaga and her descendants lived all year round in the Czech lands during that decade and did not return regularly to Slovakia. This did not change until the breakup of Czechoslovakia in 1939, when Zaga's branch were forced to return to Slovakia and Trenčianska Teplá.

Territorial anchoring and spatial mobility – the way of life of the Lovara in Slovakia before the Second World War

A number of Lovara families became territorially anchored in several regions of Slovakia even before the Second World War. This took various shapes and forms, which could change under the influence of various circumstances and with the passage of time. Some communities were connected with a certain municipality and others with a certain region around which the Lovara moved on regular routes leading through various municipalities, mostly in order to engage in a particular livelihood. These ties were often handed down from generation to generation. The territory in which the Lovara performed their professional activities could change, and there could be a reason for migration to a new region. This is also the way in which the shift of the Lovara away from Slovakia towards the historical Czech lands may be viewed, something that started to happen among some families to a greater extent from the early 1930s.

I consider the most marked display of such territorial anchoring in Slovakia during this time to be the fact that some Lovara families acquired their own houses in the municipalities with which they had created territorial and sometimes also social ties. They built themselves (or had built) houses of various types where they could live permanently (or at least some of their members did). This was how Štefan Stojka, Sr. proceeded, acquiring a house in Trenčianska Teplá a decade before the war. However, living in houses was just one way of being territorially connected to a municipality. Many Lovara engaged in professions which required geographical movement, including those who had acquired a house in a certain locality. There were thus various combinations of living in a village while performing a profession based on spatial mobility. The most typical example of such activity was the horse trading that was widespread among the Lovara. This could take the form of short journeys in the surrounding area or longer journeys to more distant places of a seasonal character. Other Lovara families during this time engaged in professions commonly described in the literature as being typical of "Slovak", non-Vlax Roms. These included the manufacture of unfired bricks or auxiliary work for non-Romani farmers. These professions required residency in one place, however. Other Lovara earned their living through professions that required spatial mobility and are connected in the Romani studies literature with other groups of Roms, such as metalwork, knife sharpening, the making and cleaning of kettles, or trough-making.

Spatial mobility and being territorially anchored could be realised in various ways and could also develop dynamically. As I mentioned at the start of the book, the Lovara are often depicted and described in the literature as "travelling people" who were not territorially anchored in any way. An important conclusion of my book is the diversification of this one-dimensional view by presenting the range of ways in which it was possible to combine active spatial mobility with being anchored in a certain municipality or region. When thinking about Lovara spatial mobility, we need to free ourselves of the entrenched categories of "travelling" versus "settled", seen as a binary opposition in which one state rules out the other. By analysing their "travelling" in detail, I reached the conclusion that the various types of spatial mobility and territorial anchoredness described by the Lovara witnesses were combined and were not mutually exclusive. It is important to abandon the idea that there was a simple historical development from "travelling" in the direction of a "settled way of life", since in reaction to various external measures and to various inter-group and intra-group events, lifestyle changes and dynamic transformations took place which were connected with a change in the degree and forms of their spatial mobility and territorial anchoredness.

The situation of the Lovara in the Czech lands in the interwar period

Although the Czech lands and Slovakia formed a single state in the interwar decades, the situation and position of Roms in society differed considerably in the two parts of the republic during that time, and the Lovara were no exception. While in Slovakia these Roms were territorially anchored in many municipalities, in the area of the historical Czech lands the creation of ties to concrete locations did not happen at all – at the most, there were ties to the local residents with whom the Lovara regularly traded (horse dealers) or to whom they offered their services (kettle-makers, knife sharpeners etc.) Despite a thorough search of the archives, I did not manage to find a single case of Roms belonging to this group buying or renting[706] a property to which they might have repeatedly returned in the Czech lands. On the basis of the information available, it is possible to assume that during the interwar decades, under the influence of restrictive measures and policies in the Czech lands, the Lovara were confined to time-limited camping in their own wagons that was often brought to an end by police who moved them on across the municipal boundary. The spatial trajectories of the Stojka family entirely confirm this trend. In the early 1930s, the family moved around the entire territory of the Czech lands, and according to the available information, they managed to cross this area relatively quickly.

The number of Lovara in the Czech lands increased from the early 1930s, according to media reports, until 1933 when circulars were issued at a central level recommending the approach that should be taken toward them by the security forces and district authorities. These orders also affected the family followed herein when, in the summer of 1934, Zaga's eldest son Filo Stojka and other Lovara were deported from the territory of Bohemia. From then on their movements can be traced in Moravia only, above all in the districts of Frýdek–Místek and Opava. The situation was the same, however, with other Lovara families whom the authorities and security forces prevented from moving around the Czech lands such that their spatial mobility in the second half of the 1930s had to be limited to Moravia. When Czechoslovakia broke apart in March 1939, the change in the legal framework of the successor states and their regulations regarding citizenship meant that all Lovara, like other Roms from Slovakia and various other "problematic" groups of people, were forced to return to Slovakia where they had domiciles and also citizenship. However, these Roms had no social ties in these municipalities, and this had a serious impact on their subsequent situation during the Second World War.

---

706 An exception was the case of the Kwieks, a Polish Kalderash family decribed by Nečas, "Cikánský král", 1922.

The impact of the absence of social relationships
on the situation of Lovara during the Second World War
in Slovakia

I have repeatedly used the category of "place" and belonging to a place in this book. From the perspective of socio-anthropological research, this category is connected to social status and also corresponds to the position of the Roms in local hierarchies of socioeconomic relationships. The observations of previous researchers regarding these categories as they relate to the situation of "Slovak" (non-Vlax) Roms[707] have also now been confirmed in the case of the Lovara. This could be seen markedly during the Second World War, when the quality and depth of those local relationships became decisive for the development of the Roms' situations in various municipalities. A number of Lovara who had been moving around the Czech lands in the 1930s, or who for other reasons were not significantly anchored in towns and villages, had not created social ties or functional relationships with local non-Roms. After their forced return to the places in Slovakia where they were domiciled, they were perceived by most of the autochthonous inhabitants as foreign and not belonging to the village. Not infrequently they were considered a security threat that the local authorities tried to get rid of and prevent from settling in the municipality. Not even the Lovara who were more permanently situated in certain municipalities were perceived as *local* if, for reasons of their professional activities, they were not permanently present there. This was shown through their insufficiently functional social ties to the local population, which could have cushioned them from the application of anti-gypsy measures in the years to come had such ties existed. For this reason, the Lovara found themselves in a highly disadvantageous position.

This was shown from the beginning of the war, when these Roms, perceived by their surroundings as "gypsy vagabonds", were relatively harshly affected by various measures banning itinerancy and horse trading. In many of the municipalities where they had been forced to remain after the decree limiting territorial movement took effect, they were labelled by the authorities as "asocial", "workshy" persons, and as such a number of anti-gypsy measures were applied to them. Many Lovara were put into work camps. They also found themselves under the control of local security forces and were deprived of their livelihoods

---

707 Ort, "Romové jako místní".

in practice, without any replacement livelihood being offered to them. This had the most marked and, in the long term, most fatal impact on horse traders, who until that point had enjoyed the highest status and were materially the best off within the Lovara community. As a result of these decrees their status plummeted until they found themselves in the category of "asocials". This was how their status also changed within the Romani community itself. This was noticeably felt in the situation of the Roms in Trenčianska Teplá. Štefan Stojka, Sr. as a successful, recognised horse trader who before the war had successfully created functional social ties with local residents, managed to acquire a house on the main street in the village where his family waited out the war until the arrival of German troops in 1944. Although after 1939 a settlement was created in Štefan's front yard using the wagons belonging to the family of his sister Zaga, the municipality did not opt to get rid of its Romani inhabitants on the basis of government decrees, above all the April 1941 decree on the "Adjustment of some conditions of the Gypsies". It was this decree that served as the legislative basis for moving and evicting Romani settlements in a number of other Slovak municipalities. The Stojka family was also not affected by any of the other measures, though – none of the men were interned in labour camps, for example, and Zaga Stojková, as an older woman, was the only family member on the list of "asocials".

The leadership of the municipality changed after the Second World War ended in Europe in 1945 and started to take measures against "gypsy vagabonds". During the war there had also been a sharp decline in Štefan's social status and socioeconomic position, which fell from that of a successful horse trader to a rag collector and then to a rubbish collector. He lost his house with the arrival of the front and it was subsequently plundered by local residents, which resulted in a further decline in his social status in the village. His postwar return to horse trading was complicated, since that profession had lost its earning potential and significance as a result of the overall society-wide transformation of the economic situation. The ejection of the Roms from the municipality was also aided by a petition from the inhabitants of surrounding municipalities – supported by the ONV – against the activities of the"gypsy vagabonds" from Trenčianska Teplá and by growing anti-gypsy feeling in society. All these pressures caused the Stojka family to be ejected from the municipality in the summer of 1947.

The post-war period: Facing attempts at forced sedentarisation by state bodies

After the death of Zaga Stojková, her successors were symbolically led by her daughter-in-law Anna Stojková, née Lakatošová. After the Roms were expelled from Trenčianska Teplá they returned with their horse-drawn wagons to the Czech lands. However, they did not come as inexperienced migrants, but were returning to the places around which they had travelled in the 1930s. After an initial phase of relatively extensive territorial mobility around the whole Bohemian part of the republic, their routes gradually narrowed to the northern Bohemian area, especially the districts of Louny, Žatec and the surrounding area. During the period in question, few Lovara led an "itinerant" way of life. In most cases, as with the Stojkas, this was the result of their wartime and postwar pauperisation and their attempt to find a better livelihood than the ones offered them by the wartorn Slovak countryside.

The last Lovara to leave Trenčianska Teplá was the nuclear family of Štefan Stojka, Sr. who, after losing lawsuits seeking compensation for the destruction of his property, set out at the end of the 1940s with his horse and cart to North Moravia, where he tried to find a livelihood and a place where he and his family might stay. In the mid-1950s, however, he returned for unknown reasons with his wife and children to Trenčianska Teplá. First, they camped in their wagon on the site of their former house, which by then had been completely razed to the ground. Štefan continued to try and earn a living as a collector of various things with his horse-drawn cart, but in 1959 his horse was confiscated. At approximately the same time after pressure was put on the local authorities by local non-Romani residents, his family was moved to a more distant place in the village, where the MNV built them a cottage. Nevertheless, Štefan managed to purchase another horse and to drive round the neighbourhood to a limited extent, collecting things. Štefan died in Trenčianska Teplá in January 1969 in his covered wagon and in a relatively impoverished social situation. After the death of both parents, his children left the village and it is not known where they went.

During the 1950s, Romani families moving around in horse-drawn wagons or in other ways became the target of attempts by state bodies to sedentarise and employ them. For the whole of the 1950s, such Roms, who were not particularly numerous, but were highly visible, travelled with horses and carts facing various police checks, attempts to seize their horses and, above all, attempts to employ them and other pressures to get them to leave their "travelling" way of life, which came to represent ever more clearly a possible escape from the paternalistic approach of the state. By moving to other regions in the first half of the 1950s, the Lovara tried to resist the forcible attempts to end their mobility, to re-educate them and the other forms of social engineering by state bodies which targeted them. From the early 1950s, there were repeated attempts at the forced settlement of these Roms, together with forced employment in various economic and agricultural projects. When "travelling" and "semi-travelling" persons were being registered in February 1959, the majority of Lovara living in the Czech lands had already been forcibly (or in some cases probably voluntarily) sedentarised in a certain place. The register led to the forced confirmation of such territorial ties and prohibited them from leaving their forced residences, a ban that for the individual families lasted for several years until the district committees allowed them to be taken off the register of "travelling" and "semi-travelling" persons.

The settling of the Stojka family in the late 1950s

In the second half of the 1950s, one Stojka family branch was forcibly settled by the river Ohře in Žatec, where they were allowed to stay in their covered wagons. The other branch of the family was forcibly placed, also in their covered wagons and caravans, in the former brickworks in Louny, in inhospitable conditions with no job opportunities or basic amenities for a dignified life, such as water, electricity, toilets and so on. In both localities the Roms were entered on the register under Act no. 74/1958 and for that reason were forced to stay there for years. During the register they were defrauded of their property when their horses were taken from them with no compensation, which was seen by the Roms themselves as a painful incursion into their lives.

The law on the permanent settlement of "travelling persons" had an undoubted impact on both branches of the Stojka family, whose members were in subsequent years kept on the register of "travelling" and "semi-travelling" persons. While they were registered they were limited in their mobility and had to face various assimilatory instruments and measures from the municipal, district and regional administrations without the issue of their housing being dealt with. Paradoxically, by limiting their movement and forcing them to settle in localities where it was not possible to gain dignified housing and employment, the administrations deepened the social marginalisation of these Roms and also contributed to a sharp rise in their criminal behaviour. The interventions and checks by representatives of the authorities and security forces are remembered by witnesses to this day with great bitterness, and it is clear that if the implementation of Act no. 74/1958 in these concrete cases had any impact, it chiefly contributed to the creation of barriers and distrust between the Lovara and representatives of the majority society.

7.3 The position of Roms in society: The paternalism of the state, anti-gypsy policies and the agency of Roms

I have tried to give space in the different parts of this book (with the exception of the chapter covering the earliest period) to two different perspectives: the description of events according to state records on the one hand, and the actors' perspective of the Roms on the other hand. As I have already mentioned, these two perspectives provide fairly contradictory explanations of the events described as they embody mutually antagonistic values. While from the outside point of view the Lovara, as "travelling gypsies", were perceived as a group situated on the very edge of society, the Lovara perceived themselves as the most prestigiously-situated group, followed by the non-Vlax Roms (*Rumungri*) and non-Roms (*Gadjos*) in much lower positions. The Lovara narrative describes the historical line of their movement around the former Czechoslovakia as an attempt to find their own space, despite the limitations and hurdles with which they were met on an almost daily basis. The witnesses generally did not think about the question of whether their parents and relatives, in various historical periods, had wanted to adapt to and fulfil the demands of the majority society, but rather thought about how they could defend their position in such a way as to main their own moral integrity and values, as far as possible while minimalising conflicts with their surroundings. From their point of view, the surrounding society was described as an environment that was none too accommodating and, at the same time, potentially threatening, dangerous to Roms in many ways, for which they tried to be permanently prepared. Reflecting on the Romani testimonies and their perception of the outside society's approach towards them, what emerges clearly are examples of various segregation mechanisms and displays of the anti-gypsy measures which Roms across time have had to face almost continuously. A number of these acts are evidenced by records in the archives, but their aim was differently interpreted there (for example, the attempts to reeducate Romani children by taking them into children's homes were described as an attempt to take the children on "holiday", and so on). This book presents the concretisation in detail of the partial but interconnected results of such "anti-gypsy" policies and the stereotypical approach to Roms that was entrenched in society in general (or in accordance with the concept of the time, the approach to "gypsies"), which can both be summarised under the heading of antigypsyism. I reveal herein its local-level repercussions for the daily life of the Lovara, more or less, in the Czech lands and Slovakia over a long period of time. However, it should be stressed that antigypsyism, as an umbrella concept describing prejudicial, racist and discriminatory attitudes toward Roms, cannot be perceived as a homogenous, uniform factor. On the contrary, in various periods of history it involved various forms of criminalisation and marginalisation, as well as various conceptions of "gypsies".

With regard to the state system, it is possible to observe the continuous view of "travelling gypsies" across various regimes, state formations and geographical areas. They were perceived throughout the period in question as the perpetrators of various offences and as a security risk to the autochthonous population. At various times they were also labelled using subhuman categories such as "packs" and "hordes", the "waves" and "floods" of which local populations had to face. Their itinerancy was perceived as innate and the tendency towards it as ceaseless, and so the state, during various historical periods, tried to limit it or confront it using various measures. After the coming of communism, the state took what might be described as a heavily paternalistic approach, aimed at the violent assimilation of "travelling" people that resulted in Roms having to face pressure from local functionaries and other politically-active people to get rid of their "old customs", in other words, to face their managed acculturation. It is this that the Lovara tried, mostly successfully, to defy. The researcher Eva Thurner has stated that as a result of their "host society" subjecting them to disdain and stigmatisation for many years, the Roms have ignored its rules, thereby giving up on trying to be accepted by the majority society and to integrate into it.[708] In the context of the material in this book, I conclude that their continuous experience of repression, segregation mechanisms and (above all in the 1950s) paternalistic attempts at social engineering which often included

---

708 Thurner, "Bez státní příslušnosti", 67–68.

direct displays of ethnic or racial discrimination as well as the curtailment of their basic human rights and freedoms mean the Lovaras' lack of trust when it comes to the world of non-Roms is entirely legitimate, whether we are discussing the state, local authorities, or individual non-Roms.

In the story of the Stojka family as described above, the Roms' active approach to trying to resolve their situations themselves is something that runs throughout the book as a powerful motif. A strong position as an actor can be seen in the case of Štefan Stojka, Sr., always searching for and choosing various ways of improving and dealing with his and his family's situation without having to wait for the local authorities to come up with something. The highly active approach of the Roms is also described at the very end of this story in the 1960s when, despite local administrations declaring that they would deal with the Roms' housing situation, the Roms finally took care of their own housing by buying a detached house in Louny. An active approach and an attempt to find a solution also helped them in the process of deregistration, leaving Louny, and subsequently buying their own house in Prague.

All these partial probes into and examples from the life of the Lovara also point to another important reality. There is a need to distinguish between the approaches and subsequent practices of the various state bodies, which differed very considerably in the case of the central, regional and local administrations, and indeed across the regions (above all between the Czech lands and Slovakia). For various periods of history, I gathered evidence on the highly inconsistent or notably diverse approaches to the implementation and enforcement of existing legislation and on the conflicting interests these components of the state had. In practice, primarily at the local level, state paternalism and social engineering could depend on the activity of a few individuals. This book reveals the cracks in the function of state policy in practice instead of just criticising it as a powerful actor, revealing how the Lovara managed to find those cracks and optimise their situation as a result.

Appendix

Fig. 1: The farm at Horní Stromka in the Prague suburb of Královské Vinohrady, where in 1913 the family of František Stojka was registered as living, and where during approximately the same period the Romani family of Jan Schubert also lived.

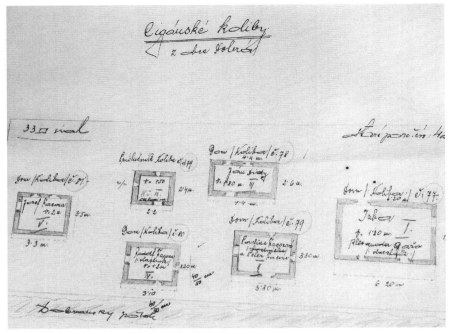

Fig. 2: Hand-drawn map of "gypsy shacks" in Dobrá near Trenčianska Teplá, 1936.

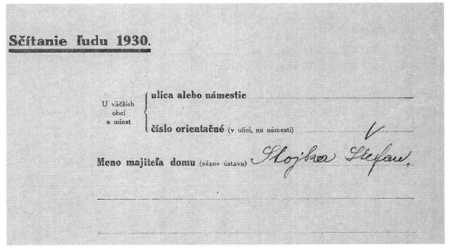

Fig: 3: Census form for the house at no. 273, Trenčianska Teplá, from the 1930 census.

Fig. 4: The regulation of the Teplička stream in Trenčianska Teplá, 1930s. In the background on the right-hand side the gable of Štefan Stojka's house is visible.

Fig. 5: Teplická street in Trenčianska Teplá in the interwar period. The photograph is taken from the quarry, on the hillside above the site of Štefan Stojka's house.

Fig. 6: Photograph of a young woman from Štefan Stojka's family, first name unrecorded, original description by the author: "Gypsy Stojková, 1950". The photo was taken in the surroundings of Trenčianska Teplá.

Fig. 7: Štefan Stojka's family in a meadow near Trenčianska Teplá. The photograph shows Štefan Stojka, Sr., his wife Kristína and their youngest children, and is dated by the author: 1955.

Fig. 8: Štefan Stojka, Sr. on his wagon in Trenčianska Teplá. In the background is the half-built house of another owner. Mid-1960s.

Fig. 9: Štefan Stojka, Sr. in the street in Trenčianska Teplá, in the foreground with a hat and a distinctive moustache, approximately mid-1950s.

Fig. 10: Štefan Stojka, Sr. with a goat.

Fig. 11: Kristína Stojková, née Rafaelová (*1913), Štefan Stojka, Sr.'s last wife and the mother of his youngest children, in front of the house at Hliník (now Žilinská street), mid-1960s.

Fig. 12: Kristína Stojková in the outdoor kitchen in front of the house at Hliník. The photograph was taken after the death of Štefan, approximately 1971.

Fig. 13: The abandoned house of Štefan Stojka at Hliník. When the family left the house temporarily following Štefan's death, it was immediately taken apart by local residents and became uninhabitable.

Fig. 14: Anna Stojková, neé Lakatošová (*1902) in a unique photograph taken in the office of the Lovosice local national committee in 1952 in an effort to record the "travelling gypsies" camping on the banks of the Elbe.

Fig. 15: Štefan Stojka (*1923), son of Ján Stojka and grandson of Štefan Stojka, Sr. in the records of the local national committee in Lovosice in 1952.

Fig. 16: Grofojka Stojková photographed by local national committee (ONV) officials in Lovosice who were making a list of "travelling gypsies". This was probably Zaga Stojková's daughter, who according to official records used various names and dates of birth (it was not until the register of travelling persons in 1959 that she was given an identity card). She seems to have been born in 1924, not 1926.

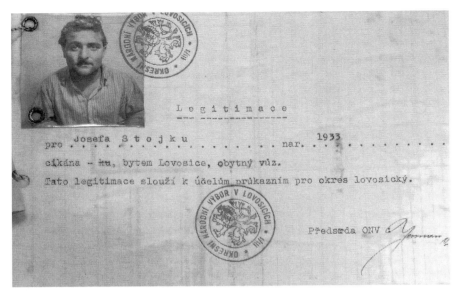

Fig. 17: A provisory "gypsy identity card" of the sort that were issued by the local national committee (ONV) in Lovosice in 1952 to all Roms camping on the banks of the river Elbe, in order to keep records of them. The photographs, which were taken without any legal basis, were stuck on the back of the documents from a dentistry card index.

Bibliography and sources

Literature

About, Ilsen and Abakunova, Anna. *The Genocide and Persecution of Roma and Sinti. Bibliography and Historiographical Review*. International Holocaust Remembrance Alliance, 2016.

Andrš, Zbyněk. "Our God is Gold: Vlashika Rom at a Crossroads?" *Ethnologia Actualis*, vol. 16, no. 2 (December 2016): 66–80. https://doi.org/10.1515/eas-2017–0005.

Asséo, Henriette. "La Gypsyness une culture de compromis entre l'Art et l'éclectisme savant." In *Bohémiens und Marginalität/Bohémiens et Marginalité*, edited by Sidonia Bauer and Pascale Auraix-Jonchière, Berlin: Franck & Timme, 2019, 111–130.

Baloun, Pavel. 'Cikáni, metla venkova!' Tvorba a uplatňování proticikánských opatření v meziválečném Československu, za druhé republiky a v počáteční fázi Protektorátu Čechy a Morava (1918–1941). (PhD diss., Charles University, 2020).

——. *"Metla našeho venkova!" Kriminalizace Romů od první republiky až po prvotní fázi protektorátu (1918–1941)*. Praha: FHS UK – Scriptorium, 2022.

Bodnárová, Zuzana. Gramatický náčrt romského dialektu maďarské obce Versend. Diplomová práce. Praha: FF UK, 2009.

Boretzky, Norbert. *Die Vlach-Dialekte des Romani. Strukturen, Sprachgeschichte, Verwandtschaftsverhältnisse, Dialektkarten*. Wiesbaden: Harrassowitz, 2003.

Brubaker, Rogers. "Ethnicity without groups." *European Journal of Sociology/Archives européennes de sociologie*, vol. 43, no. 2 (2002): 163–189. https://doi.org/10.1017/S0003975602001066.

——. "Neither Individualism nor 'Groupism' A Reply to Craig Calhoun." *Ethnicities*, vol. 3, no. 4 (2003): 553–557. https://doi.org/10.1177/1468796803003004006.

Clark, Colin and Taylor, Becky. "'Is Nomadism the Problem'? The Social Construction of Gypsies and Travellers as Perpetrators of Anti-Social Behaviour in Britain." In: *Anti-Social Behaviour in Britain: Victorian and Contemporary Perspectives*, ed. Sarah Pickard, 166–178. Basingstoke: Palgrave Macmillan, 2014.

Čajánková, Emília. "Život a kultura rožkovianských Cigánov." *Slovenský národopis*, vol. 2, no. 1–2 (1954): 149–175 and 285–306.

Černý, Rostislav. "Lovárové v době první republiky – na příkladu okresu Místek." *Romano Džaniben*, vol. 19, no. 1 (Summer 2012): 9–28.

Červenka, Jan. "'Cikán, Gypsy & Rom' – dynamika pojmenovávání Romů v různých diskurzech." In: *Čierno-biele svety. Rómovia v majoritnej spoločnosti na Slovensku*, ed. Tatiana Podolinská and Tomáš Hrustič, Bratislava: Veda, Ústav etnológie SAV, 2015, 324–345.

Davidová, Eva. *Bez kolíb a šiatrov*. Košice: Východoslovenské vydavateľstvo, 1965.

——. *Romano drom. Cesty Romů 1945–1990*. Olomouc: Univerzita Palackého, 1995.

——. "Poválečný život a osudy Romů v letech 1945–1989." In: *Černobílý život*, 67–78. Praha: Gallery, 2000.

Donert, Celia. *The Rights of the Roma: The Struggle for Citizenship in Postwar Czechoslovakia*. Cambridge: Cambridge University Press, 2017.

Dudeková, Gabriela. "Právo alebo milosrdenstvo? Domovská príslušnosť ako základný princip sociálnej starostlivosti v Uhorsku." In: *Sondy do slovenských dejín v dlhom 19. storočí*, ed. Dušan Kováč et al., Bratislava: Historický ústav SAV, 2013, 196–213.

Dzurko, Rudolf. "Sar man ile andro supisis / Jak mě vzali do soupisu." *Romano džaniben*, vol. 1, no. 4 (Spring 1994).

Džambazovič, Roman. "Rómovia v Uhorsku koncom 19. storočia (Výsledky Súpisu Rómov z roku 1893)." *Sociológia*, vol. 33, no. 5 (2001): 491–506.

Elšík, Viktor. "Interdialect contact of Czech (and Slovak) Romani varieties." *International Journal of the Sociology of Language*, 162 (January 2003): 41–62. https://doi.org/10.1515/ijsl.2003.037.

Elšík, Viktor, Wagner, Petr and Wagnerová, Margita. Olašská romština. Vlašské dialekty. (online). Praha 2005. Available at http://ulug.ff.cuni.cz/lingvistika/elsik/Elsik_2005_HO_Vlax.pdf.

Elšík, Viktor and Beníšek, Michal. "Romani dialectology." In: *The Palgrave handbook of Romani language and linguistics*, edited by Matras, Yaron and Tenser, Anton, 389–427. London: Palgrave Macmillan. 2020.

Fotta, Martin. "On ne peut plus parcourir le monde comme avant": au-delà de la dichotomie nomadisme/sédentarité. Brésil(s). *Sciences humaines et sociales*, no. 2 (2012): 11–36.

Fraser, Angus. "The Rom migrations." *Journal of the Gypsy Lore Society* 5, vol. 2, no. 2: 131–145.

——. *Cikáni*. Transl. Marta Miklušáková. Praha: NLN, 1998.

Glassheim, Eagle. *Cleansing the Czechoslovak Borderlands: Migration, Environment, and Health in the Former Sudetenland*. Pittsburgh: University of Pittsburgh Press, 2016.

Gontarek, Alicja. "Matejasz Kwiek (ca. 1887–1937). A "Baron" and "Leader of the Gypsy Nation" in Interbellum Poland." In *Roma portraits in history: Roma civic emancipation elite in Central, South-Eastern and Eastern Europe from the 19 th century until World War II*, ed. Elena Marushiakova and Veselin Popov, Brill, Schöningh: Paderborn, 2022, 327–344.

Gurňák, Daniel. "Špecifické črty vývoja územia Slovenska očami regionálneho geografa." In *Regionálne dimenzie Slovenska*, edited by Viliam Lauko, et al., 11–32. Bratislava: Comenius University, 2014.

Guy, Will. "Ways of looking at Roma: the case of Czechoslovakia." In: *Gypsies: A Book of Interdisciplinary Readings*. Edited by Diane Tong, 13–48, New York: Garland, 1998.

——. "The Czech lands and Slovakia: Another false dawn?" In: *Between past and future: The Roma of Central and Eastern Europe*, edited by Will Guy, 285–332. Hatfield: University of Hertfordshire Press, 2001.

Hajská, Markéta. "Ame sam vlašika haj vorbinas vlašika! (My jsme Olaši a mluvíme olašsky!) Nástin jazykové situace olašských Romů z východního Slovenska v etnicky smíšené komunitě." *Romano Džaniben*, vol. 19, no. 2 (Winter 2012): 35–53.

——. "Gažikanes vaj romanes? Jazykové postoje olašských Romů jedné východoslovenské komunity ke třem místně užívaným jazykům." In: *Čierno-biele svety. Rómovia v majoritnej spoločnosti na Slovensku*. Ed. Tatiana Podolinská and Tomáš Hrustič, 347–373. Bratislava: Veda, Ústav etnológie SAV, 2015.

——. "'Polokočovníci'. Migrační trajektorie olašských Romů na Prešovsku od poloviny 19. století do současnosti." *Romano džaniben*, vol. 23, no. 2 (Winter 2016): 7–37.

——. Gagarin. *Romano džaniben* 24, no. 2 (Winter 2017): 131–138.

——. "Hranice jazyka jakožto hranice etnické identity. Vztah užívaní jazyka a etnické kategorizace u olašských Romů na východním Slovensku." (PhD diss., Charles University, 2018).

——. "The presentation of social status on a social network: The role of Facebook among the Vlax Romani community of Eastern-Slovak origin in Leicester, UK." *Romani Studies*, vol. 29, no. 2 (2019): 123–158

——. "Forced settlement of Vlach Roma in Žatec and Louny in the late 1950's." *Slovenský národopis* 68, no. 4 (2020): 340–64. https://doi.org./10.2478/se-2020-20.

——. "O trajo si ťal pestrívo/ Život musí být pestrý. Vyprávění Viktora Salinase." *Romano džaniben*, vol. 27, no. 2 (Winter 2020): 141–164.

——. "'We had to run away': The Lovára's departure from the Protectorate of Bohemia and Moravia to Slovakia in 1939". *Romani Studies*, vol. 32, no. 1 (2022): 51–83.

Hancock, Ian. *The Pariah syndrome: an account of Gypsy slavery and persecution.* Ann Arbor, Mich.: Karoma, 1987.

——. *Země utrpení.* Transl. Karolína Ryvolová and Helena Sadílková. Praha: Signeta, 2001.

Horváth, Rudolf. *A magyarországi kóbor cigányok nyelvtana Czigány-Magyar Szótár.* Szeged: Primaware Kiadó, 2014.

Horváthová, Emília. *Cigáni na Slovensku. Historicko-etnografický náčrt.* Bratislava: Vydavateľstvo Slovenskej akademie vied, 1964.

Horváthová, Jana. 2000. "Kdo byli čeští Romové?" In: *Černobílý život.* Prague: Gallery: 47–66.

——. *Kapitoly z dějin Romů.* Praha: Člověk v tísni, 2002.

——. "Meziválečné zastaveni mezi Romy v českých zemích (aneb tušení souvislostí)." *Romano džaniben*, vol. 12, no. 1 (Summer 2005): 63–84.

——. "Rozhovor s Tony Lagrynem: Já už dneska se nedívám, kdo co jí, ale kdo jakej je, to mě život naučil. Životní příběh Tonyho Lagryna." *Romano džaniben*, vol. 20, no.1 (Summer 2012): 105–139.

——. ...*to jsou těžké vzpomínky.* I. Svazek. Brno: Větrné mlýny, 2021.

Hübschmannová, Milena. "Rozhovor s Terou Fabiánovou." *Romano džaniben*, vol. 7, no. 1–2 (Spring, summer 2000): 32–38.

Hübschmannová, Milena. "Vztahy mezi Romy a Židy na východním Slovensku před druhou světovou válkou." *Romano džaniben*, vol. 7, no. 1–2 (Spring, summer 2000): 17–23.

——. *Šaj pes dovakeras. Můžeme se domluvit.* Olomouc: Univerzita Palackého, 2002.

——. *Roma: Sub ethnic groups: Index of appellations.* In Rombase. Didactically edited information on Roma (online). Graz: Rombase, 2003. http://romani.uni-graz.at /rombase/index.html.

——. (ed). *"Po židoch cigáni." Svědectví Romů ze Slovenska 1939–1945. I. díl (1939–srpen 1944).* Prague: Triáda, 2005.

——. "Roma in the so-called Slovak State (1939–45)." In: *Gypsies during the Second World War, vol 3: The Final Chapter.* Ed. Donald Kenrick. Hatfield: University of Hertforshire Press, 2006, 3–44.

Janas, Karol. "Pokusy vlády slovenského štátu o likvidáciu obchodu s koňmi v rokoch 1939–1941 (mikroštúdia)." *Romano džaniben*, vol. 10, no. 2 (Winter 2003): 89–92.

Jurová, Anna. "Niektoré aspekty súpisu kočujúcich a polokočujúcich osôb v roku 1959." *Romano džaniben*, vol. 16, no. 1 (Summer 2009): 13–36.

——. "Domovské právo vo vzťahu k Rómom v predmníchovskej ČSR." In *Historický vývoj súkromého práva v Európe: zborník príspevkov z medzinárodnej vedeckej konferencie konanej v dňoch 27.-28. mája 2011 na Právnickej fakulte UPJŠ v Košiciach*, edited by Erik Štenpien, 121–144. Košice: Právnická fakulta UPJŠ, 2011.

——. *Rómska menšina na Slovensku v dokumentoch 1945–1975*. Košice: Spoločenskovedný ústav SAV, 2008.

Kára, Karel (ed.). *Ke společenské problematice Cikánů v ČSSR*. Praha: Ústav pro filosofii a sociologie ČSAV, 1975.

Karlík, Jozef. *Trenčianská Teplá*. Zvolen: Slovakiaprint, 1990.

Kabachnik, Peter and Ryder, Andrew. "Nomadism and New Labour: constraining Gypsy and Traveller mobilities in Britain." In: *Romani mobilities in Europe: Multidisciplinary perspectives*. International Conference, University of Oxford: Conference Proceedings, 2010, 110–125.

Kalný, Slavo. *Cigánsky plač a smiech*. Bratislava: Osveta, 1960.

Katz, Katalin. "Story, history and memory: a case study of the Roma at the Komarom camp in Hungary", in *The Roma, a Minority in Europe. Historical, Polical and Social Perspectives*, ed. Roni Stauber and Raphael Vago, Budapest, Central European University Press, 2007, 69–87.

Kobes, Tomáš. "'Naši Romové' – difrakční vzorce odlišnosti východoslovenského venkova." *Romano džaniben*, vol. 19, no. 2 (Winter 2012): 9–34.

Kochanovski, Jan. *Gypsy Studies, part 1*. New Delhi: International Academy of Gypsy Culture, 1963.

Kramářová, Jana (ed.) *(Ne)bolí: vzpomínky Romů na válku a život po válce*. Praha: Člověk v tísni, 2005.

Krátký, Ján. *Kronika obce Dobrá*. Dobrá: vlastní náklad, 2000.

Kutlík-Garudo, Igor. "Olaskí, valašskí alebo vlašickí Rómovia?" *Romano džaniben*, vol. 4, no. 1–2 (Summer 1997): 35–38.

——. "Lunga vi skurta lovárenge gila andal Vedréda / Lovárske piesne i popevky z Voderád." *Romano džaniben*, vol. 6, no. 1 (Summer 1999): 18–30.

Lakatošova, Margita. 1994. "Některé zvyklosti olašských Romů." *Romano džaniben*, vol. 1, no. 3 (Autumn 1994): 2–13.

Liegeois, Jean-Pierre. *Gypsies: an illustrated history*. London: Al Saqi, 1986.

——. *Roma in Europe*. Strasbourg: Council of Europe, 2007.

Lípa, Jiří. *Cikánština v jazykovém prostředí slovenském a českém. K otázkám starých a novějších složek v její gramatice a lexiku*. Praha: Nakladatelství Československé akademie věd, ed. Rozpravy Československé akademie věd, sešit 11, roč. 75, 1965.

Mann, Arne. 2013. "Význam spomienkového rozprávania pre výskum dejín rómskeho holocaustu." *Romano džaniben*, vol. 20, no. 2 (Winter 2013): 37–51.

——. "Historický proces formovania rómskych priezvísk na Slovensku." In: *Milý Bore... profesoru Ctiborovi Nečasovi k jeho sedmdesátým narozeninám věnují přátelé, kolegové a žáci*, Brno: HÚ AV ČR, HÚ FF MU, Matice moravská, 2003, 273–282.

Mann, Arne and Kumanová, Zuzana (eds.). *Ma bisteren! Pripomínanie rómskeho holokaustu*. Bratislava: Občianske združenie in minorita, 2014.

Marušiakova, Jelena. "Rodinný život valašských. Cigánov na Slovensku a jeho vývinové tendencie." *Slovenský národopis* 34, no. 4 (1986): 604- 634.

Marushiakova, Elena, and Popov, Veselin. "The Gypsy Court in Eastern Europe." *Romani Studies*, vol. 17, no. 1 (2007): 67–101.

——. "Segmentation vs. consolidation: The example of four Gypsy groups in CIS," *Romani Studies*, vol. 14, no. 2 (2004): 145–191.

——. *Gypsies in the Ottoman Empire: A Contribution to the History of the Balkans.* Hertfordshire: Univ of Hertfordshire Press, 2001.

Matras, Yaron. *Romani: A linguistic introduction.* Cambridge: Cambridge University Press, 2002.

——."Mapping the Romani dialects of Romania", *Romani Studies*, vol. 23, no. 2 (2013): 199–243. https://doi.org/10.3828/rs.2013.11.

Nečas, Ctibor. *Nad osudem českých a slovenských cikánů v letech 1939–1945.* Brno, 1981.

——. *Českoslovenští Romové v letech 1938–1945.* Brno: Masarykova univerzita, 1994.

——. *Romové v České republice včera a dnes.* Olomouc: Palackého univerzita, 1995.

——. *Historický kalendář: Dějiny českých Romů v datech.* Olomouc: Palackého univerzita, 1997.

——. "Materiál o Rómech na Slovensku z roku 1924." *Historická demografie*, 22, no. 1 (1998): 169–199. Praha: Komise pro historickou a sociální demografii, 1998.

——. "Slovenští Romové v letech 1938–1945." In: *Sborník prací Filosofické fakulty brněnské univerzity C 51*, Brno: Masarykova univerzita, 2004, 153–178,.

——. *Romové na Moravě a ve Slezsku (1740–1945).* Brno: Matice moravská, 2005.

Nováček, Josef. *Cikáni včera, dnes a zítra.* Praha: Socialistická akademie, 1968.

Ort, Jan. 2021. "Romové jako místní obyvatelé? Přináležení, cikánství a politika prostoru ve vesnici na východním Slovensku." *Sociologický časopis / Czech Sociological Review*, vol. 57, no. 5 (2021): 1–28. https://doi.org/10.13060/csr.2021.040.

Pavelčíková, Nina. 1999. "Příprava a provádění zákona o násilném usazování Romů na Ostravsku." *Ostrava 19, sborník k dějinám a současnosti města,* 34–48. Šenov u Ostravy: Tilia, 1999.

——. *Romové v českých zemích 1945–1989.* Praha: Úřad dokumentace a vyšetřování zločinů komunismu, 2004.

——. "Příchod olašských Romů na Ostravsko v padesátých letech 20. století (ve světle dobových zpráv)." *Romano džaniben*, vol. 16, no. 1 (Summer 2009): 37–66.

——. *Vztah Romů k práci – konfrontace stereotypů s historickými doklady. Český lid*, vol. 102, no. 3 (2015): 307–328.

Piasere, Leonardo. 1986. "Les slovensko roma: entre sédentarité et nomadisme." *Nomadic Peoples*, no. 21/22 (December 1986): 37–50.

Picker, Giovanni. "Nomads' land? Political cultures and nationalist stances vis-à-vis Roma in Italy." In *Multi-disciplinary perspectives on Romany Studies*, edited by Michael Stewart and Marton Rovid, 211–27. Budapest: Central European University Press, 2010.

Pivoň, Rastislav. "K realizácii zákona č. 74/1958 Zb. o trvalom usídlení kočujúcich osôb na území Veľkej Bratislavy." *Studia Ethnologica Pragensia* no. 1 (2018): 30–46.

——. "Zákon č. 74/1958 Zb. a jeho výkon v niektorých obciach trnavského regiónu (aj s ohľadom na práce iných bádateľov)." *Studia Ethnologica Pragensia* no. 1 (2021): 78–106.

Rychlik, Jan. *Češi a Slováci ve 20. století. Spoluprace a konflikty 1914–1992.* Praha: Vyšehrad, 2015.

Sadílková, Helena. "War Testimonies by Slovak Roma – A Close Analysis." Master Thesis, Central European University, 2003.

——. "Čí jsou to dějiny? Dosavadní přístupy k interpretaci poválečných dějin Romů v ČS(S)R." *Romano džaniben*, vol. 13, no. 2 (Winter 2013): 69–86.

——. "Resettling the settlement: recent history of a Romani settlement in south-east Slovakia". In *Das amen godi pala Lev Čerenkov: Romani historija, čhib taj kultura.* Ed. Kirill Kozhanov, Mikhail Oslon and Dieter W. Halwachs, Graz: Karl-Franzens-Universität Graz – trefpunkt sprachen, 2017, 339–351.

——. "(Ne)chtění spoluobčané. Romové v poválečném Československu." In: *„Nechtění" spoluobčané. Skupiny obyvatel perzekvovaných z politických, národnostních náboženských* *i jiných důvodů v letech 1945–1989*, edited by Jaroslav Pažout and Kateřina Kotrmann, 98–115. Praha, Liberec: Ústav pro studium totalitních režimů – Technická univerzita v Liberci, 2018.

——."Holocaust of the Roma and Sinti on the territory of Czechoslovakia." *Factsheets on Romani culture, history, language, literature and Roma related groups*, Univerzity of Graz, 2020. http://romafacts.uni-graz.at.

——. "The Postwar Migration of Romani Families from Slovakia to the Bohemian Lands. A complex legacy of war and genocide in Czechoslovakia." In: *Jewish and Romani Families in the Holocaust and its Aftermath*. Ed. Eliyana R. Adler and Kateřina Čapková, 190–217. Rutgers University Press: New Brunswick, Camden, Newark, New Jersey, London, 2020.

Sadílková, Helena, Slačka, Dušan and Závodská, Milada. *Aby bylo i s námi počítáno. Společensko-politická angažovanost Romů a snahy o založení romské organizace v poválečném Československu*. Brno: Muzeum romské kultury, 2018.

Serinek, Josef and Tesař, Jan. *Česká cikánská rapsodie*. I.–III. Svazek. Praha: Triáda, 2016.

Sidiropulu Janků, Kateřina. *Nikdy jsem nebyl podceňovanej. Ze slovenských osad do českých měst za prací. Poválečné vzpomínky*. Brno: Masarykova univerzita, 2015.

Shmidt, Victoria and Jaworsky, Bernadette Nadya. *Historicizing Roma in Central Europe: between critical whiteness and epistemic injustice*. London and New York: Routledge, Taylor & Francis Group, 2021.

Scheffel, David. "Belonging and domesticated ethnicity in Veľký Šariš, Slovakia." *Romani studies*, vol. 25, no. 2 (2015): 115–149. https://doi.org/10.1111/1467–8322.12483.

Schuster, Michal. "Jinak bychom tady nebyli." Příběh rodiny Dychovy z obce Hrušky (okr. Břeclav). *Romano džaniben*, vol, 27, no. 2 (Winter 2020): 7–53.

Slačka, Dušan. "Usazení kočovníků nebo řešení „cikánské otázky"? Kočovníci na Hodonínsku a provádění opatření podle zákona č. 74/1958 Sb." *Bulletin Muzea Romské kultury*, no. 23 (2014): 57–70.

Sokolová, Věra. *Cultural Politics of Ethnicity Discources on Roma in Communist Czechoslovakia*. Stuttgart: Ibidem-Verlag, 2020.

Spurný, Matěj. *Nejsou jako my. Česká společnost a menšiny v pohraničí (1945–1960)*. Praha: Antikomplex, 2011.

Spurný, Matěj. "Pokus o převýchovu: Romové v objeti stalinské péče o člověka v 50. letech." *Paměť a dějiny: revue pro studium totalitních režimů*, vol. 11, no. 3 (2017): 3–14.

Stojka, Peter and Pivoň, Rastislav. *Náš život. Amaro trajo*. Bratislava: Sd studio, 2003.

Sus, Jaroslav. *Cikánská otázka v ČSSR*. Praha: Státní nakladatelství politické literatury, 1961.

Sutre, Adèle. "'They give a history of wandering over the world'. A Romani clan's transnational movement in the early 20th century". *Quaderni Storici*, vol. 49, no. 2 (December 2014): 471–498.

Šípek, Zdeněk. "Tzv. Cikanská otázka od Mnichova do konce roku 1939." *Český lid*, vol. 79, no. 2 (1992): 161–9.

——. "Cikánské legitimace v Čechách v meziválečném období." *Český lid*, vol. 76, no. 3 (1989): 133–137.

Šusterova, Ivana. *Život olašskych žien*. Bratislava: Veda, 2015.

Theodosiou, Aspasia. "'Be-longing'in a'doubly occupied place': The Parakalamos Gypsy musicians case." *Romani studies*, vol. 14, no. 1 (December 2004), 25–58. https://doi.org /10.3828/rs.2004.2

Thurner, Eva. "Bez státní příslušnosti (téměř) až do konce života. Zvláštní úpravy práva na získání státního občanství pro „Romy" („Cikány")." *Romano džaniben*, vol. 16, no. 1 (Summer 2009): 67–93.

Tcherenkov, Lev and Laederich, Stéphane. *The Rroma. Otherwise known as Gypsies, Gitanos, Tsiganes, Tigani, Çingene, Zigeuner, Bohemiens, Travellers, Fahrende, etc.* Volume 1: History, language, and groups. Basel: Schwabe, 2004.

Tkáčová, Anna. "Rómovia v období od vlády Marie Terézie po vznik I. ČSR." In: *Čačipen pal o Roma. A Global Report on Roma in Slovakia,* edited by Michal Vašečka, 23–34, Bratislava: Inštitút pre veřejné otázky, 2003.

Tlamsová, Hanka. *Lexikon světem jdoucích.* Brno: Nakladatelství PhDr. Josef Sperát, 2020.

Trevisan, Paola. "Austrian "Gypsies" in the Italian archives. Historical ethnography on multiple border crossings at the beginning of the twentieth Century." *Focaal—Journal of Global and Historical Anthropology,* vol. 87 (2020): 61–74. https://doi.org/doi:10.3167/fcl.2020.012806

van Baar, Hugo. "Europe's Romaphobia: problematization, securitization, nomadization." *Environment and Planning D: Society and Space,* vol. 29, no. 2 (2011): 203–212. https://doi.org/10.1068/d2902ed1.

——."The Perpetual Mobile Machine of Forced Mobility: Europe's Roma and the Institutionalization of Rootlessness." In: *The Irregularization of Migration in Contemporary Europe: Deportation, Detention, Drowning.* Edited by Yolande Jansen, Joost de Bloois and Robin Celikates, 71–86 (London / New York: Rowman & Littlefield, 2015).

Vaněk, Miroslav and Mücke, Pavel. *Třetí strana trojúhelníku: teorie a praxe orální historie.* 2. ed., Praha: Karolinum, 2015.

Viková, Lada and Závodská, Milada. "Dokumentace genocidy Romů za 2. světové války v Československu – nálezová zpráva: diskontinuita a kontinuita odhalování historie Romů po roce 1946." *Romano džaniben,* vol. 23, no. 2 (Winter 2016): 107–124.

Viková, Lada. "Dlouhá cesta za důstojným postavením: Příspěvek aplikované etiky k výzkumu holokaustu Romů osmdesát let od událostí." (PhD diss., Charles University, 2020)

Vossen, Rüdiger. *Zigeuner.* Frankfurt: Ullstein, 1983.

Yıldız, Can, De Genova, Nicholas. "Un/Free mobility: Roma migrants in the European Union." *Social Identities,* vol. 24, no. 4 (2017): 425–441. https://doi.org/10.1080/1350463 0.2017.1335819.

Zahra, Tara."Condemned to Rootlessness and Unable to Budge": Roma, Migration Panics, and Internment in the Habsburg Empire." *American Historical Review,* vol. 122, no. 3 (2017): 702–726.

Zapletal, Tomáš. "Přístup totalitního státu a jeho bezpečnostních složek k Romské menšině v Československu (1945–1989)." *Sborník Archivu bezpečnostních složek,* no. 10 (2012): 13–83.

Zdařilová, Eva. "Faktory ovlivňující narativ na příkladu životních příběhů několika romských pamětníků války." *Romano džaniben,* vol . 20, no. 2 (Winter 2013): 13–36.

Archives

AM (Archiv města) Brno, f. Z1.

Archiv žadatelů o odškodnění za genocidu v době druhé světové války, uložený ve společnosti Člověk v tísni, o.p.s.

NA (Národní archiv) Praha, fondy KSČ Ústřední výbor 1945–1989 Praha, oddělení ideologické; MV (Ministerstvo vnitra) II Praha, MV – stará registratura, Policejní ředitelství II – všeobecná spisovna, Zemské četnické velitelství, ZÚ (Zemský úřad) Praha

SOkA Mladá Boleslav, fond OÚ (Okresní úřad) Mladá Boleslav
SOA Hradec Králová, AO Zámrsk, fond KNV Hradec Králové 1949–1960
SOA Litoměřice, fond SKNV,
SOA Olomouc, fond OÚ Litovel (L 1–2)
SOkA Benešov, fondy ONV Vlašim; OÚ Benešov
SOkA Blansko, fond AO Lhota Rapotina
SOkA Frýdek Místek, fondy OÚ Frýdek; OÚ Místek; Četnická stanice Frýdek
SOkA Litoměřice, pobočka Lovosice, fond ONV Roudnice n.l; ONV Lovosice
SOkA Louny, fondy KSČ OV Žatec; MěNV (Městský národní výbor) Louny;
Okresní prokuratura Louny r. 1960–1965; ONV (Okresní národní výbor) Louny II; ONV
Žatec; OÚ Louny I
SOkA Mělník, fondy ONV Kralupy nad Vltavou; OÚ Mělník
SOkA Nymburk, pobočka Lysá n.L., fond ONV Poděbrady
SOkA Olomouc, fond MěNV Litovel
SOkA Opava, fond OÚ Opava
SOkA Pelhřimov, fond OÚ Kamenice n. L.
SOkA Přemyšlení, fond OÚ Říčany
SOkA Teplice, fond ONV Teplice
SNA Bratislava, fond Sčítanie ľudu 1930
ŠA (Štátny archív) Nitra, pobočka Levice, fondy Hlavnoslúžnovský úrad v Levicích z let
1938–1944; ONÚ Dolná Seč
ŠA Nitra, pobořka Nové Zámky, fond ONV Nové Zámky
ŠA Nitra, pobočka Topoľčany, fond OÚ Topoľčany
ŠA Nitra, pobočka Trnava, fondy ObNÚ Voderady; OÚ Hlohovec; ObNÚ Boleráz
ŠA Trenčín, fondy Domovská Daň Trenčín; OÚ Trenčín; ObNÚ Trenč. Teplá; MNV
Trenčianska Teplá
VÚA-VHA Praha, f. Sbírka osobních spisů žadatelů o vydání osvědčení podle zákona
č. 255/1946 Sb.
ZA Opava – pob. Olomouc, fond KNV Olomouc

Journal articles

[author n.a.] "Ausgeforichte heudiebe." *Neues Tagblatt für Schlesien und Nordmähren*, vol. 4,
no. 260 (5. 11. 1937), 4.
[author n.a.] "Berhastete Zigeunerin." *Neues Tagblatt für Schlesien und Nordmähren*, vol. 4,
no. 289 (9. 12. 1937), 6.
[author n.a.] "Ciganska otázka." *Trenčianske noviny: orgán OV KSS a ONV v Trenčíne*, vol. 2,
no. 28 (28. 6. 1961), 3.
[author n.a.] "Cikánská krádež koní." *Večer, lidový denník,* vol. 11, no. 46 (25. 2. 1924), 3.
[author n.a.] "Diebische Zigeuner." *Neues Tagblatt für Schlesien und Nordmähren,*" vol. 3,
no. 51 (29. 2. 1936), 9.
[author n.a.] "K zatčení cikána Josefa Schuberta (Křivě nařčen.)." *Venkov: orgán České
strany agrární*, vol. 12, no. 67 (21. 3. 1917), 7.
[author n.a.] "Krádež koní." *Čech: politický týdeník katolický*, vol. 49, no. 53 (23. 2. 1924), 6.
[author n.a.] "Krádeže koní." *Venkov, orgán České strany agrární*, vol. 19, no 245 (17. 2.
1924), 4.
[author n.a.] "Ločaj Juraj z Haja oznamil sratu dvoch dobitčich pasov." Rubrika Straty,
Krajinský vestník pre Slovensko, vol. 8, no. 11 (10. 4. 1935), 187.

[author n.a.] "Mladé cikánky tančily, stromy se v zimě barvily na zeleno." *Zblízka.cz* (31. 12. 2020). https://noviny-zblizka.cz/louny/cikanky-predvadely-striptyz-na -doupove-25-pod-nulou-skvele-byly-silvestry-chlapi-vzpominaji-na-vojnu-v-lounech/.

[author n.a.] "Obviněn z vraždy." *Čech: politický týdeník katolický*, vol. 42, no. 73 (16. 3. 1917), 7.

[author n.a.] "Po devíti letech zatčen pro zločin zabití." *Večer*, vol. 4, no. 61 (15. 3. 1917), 6.

[author n.a.] "Pro loupežnou vraždu." *Moravská orlice*, vol. 36, no. 287 (18. 12. 1898), 5.

[author n.a.] "Tajemství cikánské rodiny Schubertů v Libni." *Národní listy*, vol. 57, no. 73 (16. 3. 1917), 4.

[author n.a.] "Ukradl dva páry koní." *Čech: politický týdeník katolický*, vol. 42, no. 190, (14. 7. 1917), 8.

[author] -el. "Cikáni Stojkové (Porota v Trenčíně)." *Lidové noviny*, vol. 32, no. 331 (3. 7. 1924), 6.

[author] -in. "Cikán jako vyděrač a tajný." *Lidové noviny*, vol. 43, no. 165 (31. 5, 1935), 8.

[autor] -fchil. „Mißglückte Zigeuner Königswahl in Troppau." *Neues Tagblatt für Schlesien und Nordmähren*, vol. 4, no. 128 (2. 6. 1937), 6.

Peřina, E. "Cikáni a kočovníci – děti přírody." *Polední list*, vol. 9, no. 75 (15. 3. 1936), 7.

Internet sources

Arolsen archives (https://eguide.its-arolsen.org/)

Atlas rómskych komunit na Slovensku (ARK) 2019 [online]. Úrad splnomocnenca vlády SR pre rómske komunity, 2019

Familysearch (www.familysearch.org)

História obce – Oficiálna stránky obce Kálna nad Hronom (www.kalna.eu).

http://www.government.gov.sk/romovia/list_faktov.php

https://mondonomo.ai/forename/Zaga

https://pamatky.praha.eu/jnp/cz/pamatkovy_fond/usedlosti_na_uzemi_hlavniho _mesta_prahy/vinohrady/index.html,)

United States Holocaust Memorial Museum – Holocaust Survivors and Victims Database (United States Holocaust Memorial Museum – https://www.ushmm.org)

Dachau One-Step Search Results – https://stevemorse.org.

List of abbreviations

Abbreviations of state organisational units

KNV	(Krajský národní výbor) Regional National Committee
MěNV	(Městský národní výbor) City National Committee
MNV	(Místní národní výbor) Municipal National Committee
ONV	(Okresní národní výbor) District National Committee
SKNV	(Severočeský krajský národní výbor) North Bohemian Regional National Committee
SNB	(Sbor národní bezpečnosti) National Security Corps
USSR	(Svaz sovětských socialistických republic) Union of Soviet Socialist Republics
VB	(Veřejná bezpečnost) Public Security [police corps]
HSĽS	(Hlinkova slovenská ľudová strana) Hlinka Slovak People's Party
HS VB	(Head of the Police administration)
ZNV	(Zemský národní výbor) Provincial National Committee

Abbreviations of institutions used in archive references

ABS	(Archiv bezpečnostních složek) Archive of Security Forces
AM	(Archiv města) City Archive
AO	(Archiv obce) Municipal Archive
AV ČR	(Akademie věd České republiky) Czech Academy of Science
ČSAV	(Československá akademie věd) Czechoslovak Academy of Sciences
KSČ	(Komunistická strana Československa) Communist Party of Czechoslovakia
MV	(Ministerstvo vnitra) Ministry of the Interior
NA	(Národní archiv) National Archives
NB	(Národní bezpečnost) National Security
NV	(Národní výbor) National Committee
ObNÚ	(Obvodný notársky úrad) District Notary Office
ObNV	(Obvodný národný výbor) District National Committee
OO	(Obvodní oddělení) District Department
OÚ	(Okresní úřad) District Office
OV	(Okresní výbor) District Committee
SAV	(Slovenská akadémia vied) Slovak Academy of Sciences

SNA	(Slovenský národný archív) Slovak National Archive
SOA	(Státní oblastní archiv) State Regional Archive
SOkA	(Státní okresní archiv) State District Archive
ŠA	(Štátny archív) State archive
ÚV	(Ústřední výbor) Central Committee
VHA	(Vojenský historický archiv) Military Historical Archive
VÚA	(Vojenský ústřední archiv) Military Central Archive
ZA	(Zemský archiv) Provincial Archive
ZÚ	(Zemský úřad) Provincial Office

List of archive abbreviations

č. j.	(číslo jednací) registration number
č. p.	(číslo popisné) description number
ev. č.	(evidenční číslo) item number
f.	(fond) record group
i. č.	(inventární číslo) inventory number
kart.	(karton) box
kn.	(kniha) book
NAD	(Národní archivní dědictví) National Archives Heritage
sign.	(signatura) shelf mark
zn.	(značka) note

Genealogical diagram

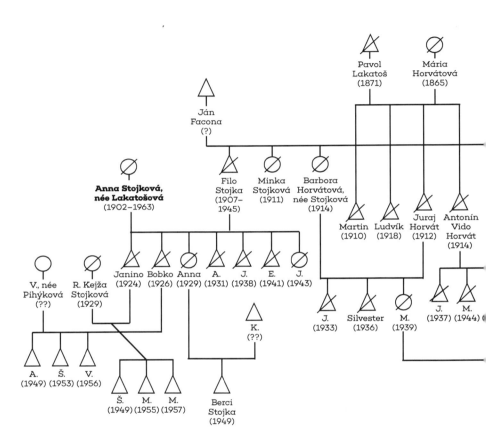

△ deceased male ⊘ deceased female
△ male ○ female

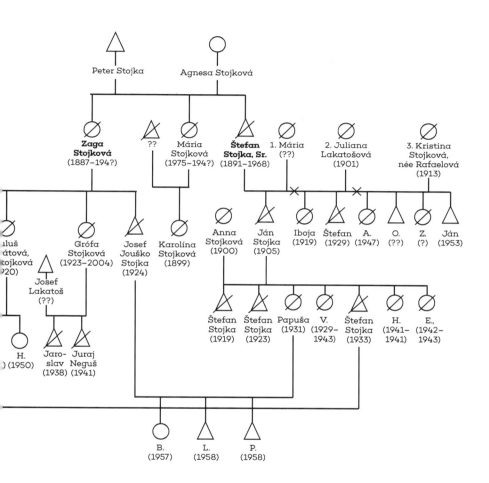

Index

Act no. 117/1927 on wandering gypsies 12, 23, 110–111, 121, 124–125, 129, 131, 136, 144–145, 149, 179, 198, 202–205

Act no. 255/1946 on Members of the Czechoslovak Army Abroad and on Certain Other Participants in the National Struggle for Liberation 42, 171, 179, 183–186

Act no. 74/1958 on the permanent settlement of travelling persons 12–13, 24–25, 39, 83, 203–205, 216–217, 237, 245–255, 260–261, 273, 276, 290

Act no. XVIII of 1871 on municipalities 73

Act no. XXII of 1886 on municipalities 73–74, 104

antigypsyism 30, 291

Arrow Cross Party (Nyilasists) 169, 174

asocial persons 165–168, 181, 190–192, 286

Asséo, Henriete 43

Auschwitz 152, 237

Baloun, Pavel 23, 30, 38, 168

Bánovce nad Bebravou 100, 130

Beash 94

Běla family 122–123, 134

Beluša, Púchov district 166

Biháry family from Pastuchov 91–94

Bihary, E. (Báno) 37–38, 188, 235, 237

Bihári, Tibor (Gagarin) 75, 93

Bohdanovce, Trnava district 112–113, 151, 166, 177, 184–185, 198

Brandýs nad Labem 108, 118, 129

Bratislava 16, 90, 129–130, 160–161, 189

Brno 113, 115, 132, 143, 220

Buchenwald 171, 173

Bystré, Giraltovce district 163, 168

Central Police Patrol Division 125, 133, 144, 147

Česká Lípa 228

Český Brod 230

Český Těšín 100, 116, 121

Chomutov 115, 229

Chynorany, Topoľčany district 86–87, 161, 166–167

Čierny Balog, Brezno district 160

concentration camps 151, 169, 170–175, 190, 200

Dachau concentration camp 170–173

Danišová, Helena 86, 147, 218

Davidová, Eva 19, 217, 249–251

decree on the abatement of the gypsy nuisance (from 1888) 56, 59–60

discrimination *see* racist discrimination

Ďivoj 77, 93–94

Dobrá, Trenčín district 61, 65–66, 96–97, 180, 183, 199

Dolná Seč, Levice district 14, 72, 79–81, 90, 171–172, 248

Dolný Hričov, Žilina district 88

domicile right 11–12, 26, 42, 47, 56, 60–66, 73–74, 78–81, 85–87, 91, 97, 104, 180, 183, 279, 281

Dubnica nad Váhom 163, 166–169, 190–192

Elšík, Viktor 15, 17, 20

Facona, Ján 65–66, 95–96, 304
fairground people *see* showmen
Flossenbürg 173
forced labour camps (*see* labour camps)
forced mobility 51, 89, 110–111, 131, 133,
145–152,162, 171, 175, 193, 195–199
forced sedentarisation (*see also*
sedentarisation) 11, 25, 217, 245, 257,
260, 288
Fotta, Martin 46–47
Frenštát pod Radhoštěm 114, 116
Frýdek 115–116, 121, 132–133, 146, 285
Frýdlant nad Ostravicí 147

Galanta district 16, 53, 130, 135, 169, 171
gypsy identity cards 109, 123–124, 127,
135, 143–144, 163, 166–167, 183

Hanušovce nad Topľou, Vranov nad
Topľou district 163, 166–167, 183, 185,
191
Hlinka Guard 157, 174–176, 185
Hlinka Slovak People's Party (HSĽS) 157,
174
Hodonín 101
Hodonín u Kunštátu 152
Horní Cerekev, Pelhřimov district 110
Horní Stromka, Prague 57–59
horse dealing *see* horse trade
horse trade 15–16, 57–64, 80, 82–91,
96–102, 107, 112, 115–118, 127–130,
161–162, 191, 193, 199, 220, 227, 257,
271, 282–284, 287
Horvát, Antonín (Vido) 36, 112, 114, 184–
185, 198, 228–229, 234, 257, 274, 304
Horvát, Juraj 36, 112–113, 185, 198, 228,
234, 304
Horváthová, Emília 45
Horváthová, Jana 120, 122
Horvátová Barbora, neé Stojková 36, 66,
108, 112–114, 118, 184, 198, 220, 228,
234, 238, 304
Horvátová Kuluš, neé Stojková 36, 66, 108,
112–114, 118, 184, 198, 220, 228–229,
234, 238, 257, 305
Hradec Králové 30, 123, 135, 137, 209
Hrnčiarovce, Trnava district 87, 91, 151,
165–166
Hübschmannová, Milena 16, 28, 94, 158,
160

Hungarian register of gypsies (from 1893)
45
Hurbanovo, Komárno district 77, 172, 174

Ilava district 26, 60–62, 100, 102, 163
Interior Ministry decree of April 1941 159,
181, 192, 287

Jeseník 211–213, 235

Kalderara/ Kalderash 15, 94, 122–123, 134,
136, 285
Kálna nad Hronom, Levice district 54, 172
Kalný, Slavo 63, 100–103, 105–106, 188,
220, 223–224
Kamenice nad Lipou, Pelhřimov district
111, 118
Karviná 137, 268
Komárno district 16, 53–54, 121, 130,
169–172, 174
Kralupy nad Vltavou 220–221, 234
kranga (a family group) 21, 77
Križovany, Trnava district 151, 164
Kunčice, Ostrava 100, 102
Kunštát, Blansko district 113, 115
Kwiek family 85, 123–124, 134, 137, 285

labour camps 163–169, 181–185, 188–192,
287
Lakatoš, Karoly 79–80, 171
Lety u Písku 152, 237
Levice district 16, 80, 82, 169, 171–172
Lhota Rapotina, Blansko district 110
Lhota u Chroustovic, Chrudim district 118
Liptovský Mikuláš 100
Litoměřice 30, 232, 250
Litovel 39, 116, 133, 135–136, 211–214, 235
Louny 11, 25, 39, 229, 232, 235–242, 246,
250–277, 288–292
Lovara dialect 15, 17, 94, 132
Lovara surnames 18, 31, 33–35, 55, 59, 78,
86, 108, 110, 125–126, 131, 134, 172,
211, 221, 231, 233
Lovosice 221, 231–233

Madunice, Trnava district 87, 91, 166
Mala 75, 93
Mann, Arne 18, 160
Martin district 100
Marushiakova, Elena 18–19

Marušová, Levice district 89
Mělník 31, 128, 199, 234
Milo family 178, 180, 182, 196
Místek 34, 100, 114–116, 121, 132–133, 135, 147, 285
Mnichovice, Říčany district 108, 111, 113, 118
Molnár, Josef 81–82, 173, 218
Moravská Ostrava 108, 113–115, 147
Most 229, 250
Mýtne Ludany, Levice district 88, 172

Natzweiler-Struthof 173
Nečas, Ctibor 28, 89–90, 94, 97, 120, 137, 170, 174
Nitra district 16, 75, 77, 130
nomadisation 23, 46, 50–51, 201, 217
Nové Město nad Váhom 228
Nové Zámky district 16, 31 53, 77, 100, 169–172

Obříství, Mělník district 127–128
Odry, Nový Jičín district 108, 118
Opava 114–116, 221, 223, 268, 285
Ostrava 137, 228

partisan movement 28, 160, 187–188
Paskov, Místek district 114–115
Pastuchov, Hlohovec district 14, 91–92, 150–151, 166, 231
Pavelčíková, Nina 16, 215, 221, 246–248
Pečky, Kolín district 250
Pezinok district 53, 77
Pivoň, Rastislav 19, 91, 131, 249
police check 23, 34, 51, 113, 121, 132–135, 149, 219, 236, 288
Popov, Veselin 18
Prague 57–58, 110, 124, 127–129, 133, 137, 208–213, 229, 233–234, 275–276, 292
Prievidza district 100
professions 33, 51, 75–77, 87–88, 91–94, 120, 137, 146, 150, 201, 235, 284–285
Prostějov 133, 135, 210–214
Pytlík, Pavol 224–226

racial discrimination 30, 32, 42, 101, 124, 157, 169, 170, 193, 203–204, 227, 280, 291–292
Ratnovce, Piešťany district 166
Ravensbrück 173

register of "gypsy vagabonds" 123, 125
register of travelling and semi-travelling persons (under Act no. 74/1958) 11, 14, 236, 240, 256, 261, 268, 274, 276, 289
Říčany 39, 108, 129, 231, 233–234
Roudnice nad Labem, Litoměřice district 228–229, 235–237, 250
Rumungro, Rumungri 21, 65–66, 86, 122, 290

Sachsenhausen 173
Šaľa 16, 169
Salinas, Victor 72, 79–80, 90, 93, 171, 248
Schömberg 173
Schuster, Michal 32
sedentarisation 11, 43, 45–47, 49–50, 75–76, 79, 83, 92, 104, 204–205, 217–218, 229, 254, 288–289
semi-travelling gypsies see semi-travelling persons
semi-travelling persons 14, 16, 46, 166, 185, 246–248
showmen 23, 121–122, 215, 237, 246–247, 250–256, 273
Slaný 234
Slovak National Uprising 165, 184, 187, 192
Slovak Roms 45, 65, 89, 99, 122, 178, 216, 237, 248, 254
social hierarchy 43, 47, 48, 203, 219, 270, 286
social status 14, 48–49, 64, 73, 85, 88, 93, 99, 181, 193, 282, 286–287
Solčany, Topoľčany district 86, 94, 130, 166, 190, 218
spatial mobility 11–12, 47–51, 53, 63, 71–74, 76–78, 84–85, 89–90, 95–96, 99–100, 103, 108, 111, 115–119, 147, 199, 215–218, 222, 237–241, 275–276, 279–285
Stojka family from Topoľčany 60, 79, 82–85, 90, 129–130, 167–168, 185, 221, 231
Stojka Ján 36–37, 61–62, 64, 97–98, 100, 102, 104–105, 147, 167–168, 176, 178–179, 183, 186, 196, 199, 220–221, 236, 250, 305
Stojka, (Berci) 25, 190, 228–230, 235–236, 238, 240, 242, 257–260, 271, 275, 304

Stojka, (Bobko) 25, 97, 191, 228–229, 234, 304
Stojka, (Janino) 25, 96, 191, 228, 230, 234, 236, 304
Stojka, Anton (Báno) 84–85, 121, 129–130
Stojka, Filo 36, 62, 66, 96, 97, 108, 110–111, 113–115, 118, 131–132, 177–178, 183, 190, 228, 285, 304
Stojka, Jaroslav 214, 228, 235, 305
Stojka, Juraj (Něguš) 183, 214, 235, 305
Stojka, Peter 61, 62, 305
Stojka, Štefan (Turko) (*1919) 37–38, 97, 188, 220, 235, 305
Stojka, Štefan (*1923) 37, 97, 188, 231, 234, 305
Stojka, Štefan (*1933) 37, 97, 186, 188, 231, 305
Stojka, Štefan, Sr. (*1891) 26, 36–37, 61–65, 95–108, 118, 121, 176–193, 196–199, 219–227, 282–283, 287–288, 292, 305
Stojka, Josef (Jouško) 25, 40, 66, 96–97, 108, 177, 191, 228–230, 232, 240, 256, 258, 305
Stojková, Agnesa 61–62, 305
Stojková, Anna (Čaja), neé Lakatošová (*1902) 25, 36, 95–96, 108–111, 115, 178, 183, 190, 196, 220–221, 228, 230–234, 238, 240, 245, 256, 258, 262, 272, 274–275, 288, 304
Stojková, Grófa 36, 38–39, 66, 96, 115, 183, 228, 235, 253, 305
Stojková, Mária 61–64, 107, 305
Stojková, Zaga 35–39, 61–66, 95–98, 108–113, 117–119, 132, 164, 177–178, 183, 189–192, 195, 198–199, 214, 221, 227, 283, 285, 287–288, 305
Strakonice 110–111, 118, 131
Šumperk district 115, 213
Šurany 88, 169, 171
Šúrovce, Trnava district 166, 177,183, 228
Sutre, Adéle 44
Svitavy district 135

Tekovské Lužany, Levice district 14, 54, 81–82, 172–173

Teplice 233, 250
Teplička nad Váhom, Žilina district 113
territorial anchoring 71–72, 78–89, 137, 279, 281, 283
territorial ties 12, 48, 72–73, 95, 112, 163, 289
Theodosiou, Aspasia 47
Topoľčany 14, 16, 31, 37, 39, 42, 79, 82, 84–87, 121, 129–130, 161, 167–168
travelling gypsies 11–12, 14, 22, 32–35, 45, 62, 126, 130, 132, 143, 147, 161–162, 166, 192, 197–219, 231, 233, 237, 239, 242, 249, 252, 270, 290–291
travelling professions *see* professions
Trenčianska Teplá, Trenčín district 11, 26–27, 36, 39, 42–43, 60–66, 85, 95–107, 112, 114, 118, 164, 174–193, 195–199, 217, 219–227, 279, 282–283, 287–288
Trenčianské Teplice, Trenčín district 187, 196
Třešť, Jihlava district 110, 118
Trevisan, Paola 29
Trnava district 312, 112, 131, 151
Tvrdošovce, Nové Zámky district 91, 93

Uherský Brod 101, 104
Uhříněves, Praha-východ district 231, 234
Ústí nad Labem Region 234, 250–251, 260, 267

vajda (chief) 64, 82, 105, 159, 181, 192, 225, 227
Veľké Lovce, Nové Zámky district 88, 91
Vienna 57–59
Villo 76–77
Voderady, Trnava district 88
Vráble, Nitra district 169
Vsetín 101

wintering place 82, 84–87, 98, 109, 151, 166, 185

Žatec 11, 25, 228–230, 235–239, 247, 250, 254–258, 261, 266–271, 274, 276, 288–289
Žilina district 100, 106, 130